# Pinter in Play

# PINTER IN PLAY

Critical Strategies and the Plays of Harold Pinter

**Susan Hollis Merritt**

Duke University Press   Durham and London 1990

To A. Jay Merritt and Bedonna Merritt

GOLDBERG. Play up, play up, and play the game.

. . . .

PETEY (*broken*). Stan, don't let them tell you what to do!
—*The Birthday Party*

# Contents

# Preface to the Paperback Edition

In the five years since *Pinter in Play* was first published, there has been much activity in Pinter studies and in the fields of literary criticism and theory and cultural studies. During this time Pinter has produced several new works. Smaller works include: *The New World Order,* a sketch which Pinter read and recorded on audiotape for the Pinter Festival held at Ohio State University in April 1991 and which subsequently served as a curtain raiser for Ariel Dorfman's *Death and the Maiden* at the Royal Court Theatre in July; "American Football" (August 1991), his controversial poem against the Gulf War, first read by Pinter at a meeting of an ad hoc International War Crimes Tribunal in London; and *Party Time,* a short play which Pinter directed (along with a revival of *Mountain Language*) at the Almeida Theatre in November 1991 and later expanded and adapted into a screenplay for Channel 4 television (17 November 1992). Larger works include: *Moonlight,* his first new full-length play in fifteen years, which premiered in London in September 1993, in a production first directed by David Leveaux at the Almeida Theatre, and then transferred to the Comedy Theatre in November, and *The Trial,* his screenplay of Kafka's novel, which was filmed under the direction of David Jones and opened in the winter of 1993. Pinter also directed the London premiere of David Mamet's controversial play *Oleanna* at the Royal Court Theatre in June 1993 (a production which moved to the Duke of York's Theatre in September 1993) and a revival of his own play *Landscape* (1968), with Ian Holm and Penelope Wilton, first at the Pinter Festival at the Gate Theatre in Dublin (2–21 May 1994) and, more recently, in November 1994, at the Cottesloe Theatre of the National Theatre in London.

A major literary event occurred when Harold Pinter placed his literary archive on deposit in the British Library. As of July 1994 it is contained in sixty-four boxes and includes many holograph first drafts and revised drafts. My essay "The Harold Pinter Archive in the British Library," currently in press, will appear in the seventh volume of *The Pinter Review* (an annual book publication since 1990). This volume will also include an early draft of *The Homecoming* from the British Library archive and "Evacuees," a previously unpublished interview, conducted in 1968, about Pinter's experience as a child evacuated from London during the early years of World War II.

In addition to the three volumes of *The Pinter Review* published since 1990, several other new books on Pinter's work have appeared, including *Pinter at Sixty* (edited by Katherine H. Burkman and John L. Kundert-Gibbs and published by Indiana University Press in 1993), a selection of papers presented at A Pinter Festival: An International Meeting, in honor of Pinter's 60th birthday. My annual *Pinter Review* bibliographies serve to update my list of works cited here. My related performance and book reviews, such as those published in *The Pinter Review* and *Modern Drama,* further augment this study.

Literary criticism and theory today strongly emphasize aspects of multiculturalism, moving issues of gender, including sexual orientation, class, and race from the wings to center stage. The marginal has thus become central—a process about which I raise questions in *Pinter in Play* (274)—at least for the foreseeable future. Yet debates about "political correctness" have become fraught with dangers, not only professional and personal but social, to the point where some argue, sometimes quite perversely and with destructive consequences, that to be politically correct is politically incorrect, or vice versa. When issues become too complex, they are frequently oversimplified.

Pinter's decision to direct *Oleanna,* exporting Mamet's take on both sexual harassment and political (in)correctness to the London stage, counterpointed the concurrent world premiere of *Moonlight,* Pinter's own moving, yet comic, drama about a dying "civil servant" named Andy and the forces generating the dysfunction of his family.

Pinter has continued his political activities through his involvement in campaigns on a wide range of issues: lobbying the government on behalf of Abbas Cheblak, a Palestinian writer and intellectual detained in Pentonville prison since January 1991; supporting his friend Salman Rushdie, still under an Islamic death threat; serving on the Mordechai Vanunu Trust, on behalf of Mr. Vanunu, considered illegally imprisoned in Israel; joining protests against reprisal murders of journalists in Turkey; calling for an inquiry into the British Museum's use of the bequest of George Bernard Shaw; and, most recently, participating in an effort by

British playwrights to persuade the subsidized theaters in Britain to stage at least three new plays a year.

Critical commentary about Pinter has concentrated lately on his politics. Last July, when he and I met in London, Pinter referred to the "just plain lies" promulgated about him in the press and said that he is most eager to set "the record" straight. He has already been "straightening out" the record through recent interviews with Mel Gussow, for *Conversations with Pinter,* published in 1994 by Nick Hern Books in London and Limelight Editions in New York, and with Michael Billington, for a critical study of his work, which I anticipate will present new information about Pinter's life, since Billington has his full cooperation. Pinter did not approve a biography proposed and planned by John Campbell, and, at Pinter's request, Campbell dropped the project.

As I observe in my essay on Pinter's archive in the British Library, the collection of manuscripts, drafts, and notes relating to most of his work through *Moonlight* and *The Trial* changes the direction of Pinter studies. Few scholars will be able to resist the attraction of the archive. It is a rich resource of potential new insights about Pinter's processes of composition and revision in every literary genre—plays, poetry, screenplays, prose— and perhaps even new strategies for critical (re)interpretation of his entire canon. Study of the archive, directed by the diverse currents in contemporary criticism, could lead to collaborative projects of important scope.

While preparing *Pinter in Play* for Duke University Press in the fall of 1989, amidst news of potentially cataclysmic changes in Eastern Europe—the coming down of the Berlin Wall, the breakup of the former Soviet Union, and the relatively peaceful democratization of Czechoslovakia—I became interested in the work of Václav Havel, the dissident playwright who is now president of the Czech Republic. This interest led to "The Outsider in Pinter and Havel," a paper that I presented, along with "Recent Critical Approaches to Pinter's Plays," at the 1991 Ohio State Pinter Festival, and its subsequent publication in *Pinter at Sixty.* My comparison of Pinter and Havel sparked my current study of the cultural politics of contemporary drama and criticism produced in and/or about Central Eastern Europe engaging issues of cultural identity, human rights, and social morality. My central concern with how the pre-1989 Czech and Slovak reception of plays by "Western" playwrights relates both to the post-1989 Czech reception of their work and to the reception of Czech plays formerly banned in the Czech and Slovak Socialist Republic has led me to study Czech and to investigate productions of Pinter's plays in Prague.

In November 1994 I attended the Czech premiere of *Moonlight* (*Měsíční svit*), translated into Czech by František Fröhlich and directed by Karel Kříž, with his wife, Vlasta Gallerová, as dramaturge, at Studio Labyrint in Prague, in conjunction with the 61st World Congress of International PEN, and another production of Pinter's *The Homecoming* (*Návrat domů*), directed by Ivo Krobot at Divadlo Pod Palmovkou, later performed on PEN Club Day (11 November) at the second annual International Theatre Festival (Divadlo '94) in Plzeň. There I also attended "Not Only about the Theatre" (Nejen o divadle), a roundtable discussion organized by President Havel ("Václav Havel Talks to His Friends, the Dramatists"), in which Havel spoke with Arthur Miller, Tom Stoppard, and Ronald Harwood, who served as moderator, at Great Theatre (Velké divadlo). Harold Pinter had planned to join them but was taken ill in London and could not come. (Edward Albee, though also invited, did not participate because he was in London for the first preview of *Three Tall Women*.) Of central concern to the playwrights during their discussion was the relationship between playwriting and politics and between politics and power, issues pertaining to criticism as considered in this volume.

Performances of Pinter's plays in other languages, especially those of so-called "small countries" (like the Czech Republic and Bulgaria, where productions of Pinter's plays are also popular), and his (at least intended) inclusion in such events as the playwrights' roundtable discussion in Plzeň demonstrate not simply Pinter's global critical reputation, but also the impact of global forces on criticism. As plays produced originally in one culture are subsequently translated into other languages and produced, performed, and received in other cultures, they undergo a process of interculturalization. Though *Pinter in Play* presents the development of mostly Anglo-American criticism of Pinter, this investigation widens, beginning with chapter 8 ("Cultural Politics"); part 3 points toward new directions for criticism of Pinter's work from intercultural and interdisciplinary perspectives.

The paperback edition of *Pinter in Play* enables university and college professors, and perhaps teachers at other levels, to include the book in reading lists for courses in drama dealing with Pinter's works; courses in criticism dealing with the development and deployment of critical strategies in literary, drama, and theater studies; courses in theater dealing with the history of dramatic criticism and theory; and courses in cultural studies. This book is also now more accessible to theater professionals and the general public.

I hope that this paperback edition of *Pinter in Play* will be enjoyed by all those who strive to understand how a living artist such as Harold Pinter develops and changes in contemporary culture(s), how artists such as Pinter affect and change contemporary cultures, and how the criticism of their work can also affect and change the cultures from which it emerges, including the cultures of criticism.

Bluff Point, New York
January 1995

# Preface

Charting developments in commentaries on literary works enables us to establish historically how critical attitudes appear and change. While analyzing the reception of any literature suggests valuable observations about cultural change, studying the reception of plays is particularly rewarding: as Arthur Holmberg says, "Drama is not only intellectual history, it is also the most social of literary genres, the one most immediately responsive to its audience and the temper of the times" (12). If we look at how critics and scholars—audience members with specialized interests—have responded to drama, we can observe important cultural trends.

The shifting attitudes toward dramatic works produced in the theater reveal how criticism participates in cultural change. As reading and writing are our foremost means of establishing and perpetuating our culture, and as criticism is the institution through which we organize such activities, to examine criticism, especially dramatic criticism, is to examine ourselves, as we produce and construe ourselves institutionally. Such institutional self-examination and introspection can stimulate salutary change in ways we produce and disseminate knowledge.

There is a literary kind of "dizziness of the depths" that George Steiner (borrowing the metaphor from Jacques Cousteau) has attributed to recent criticism and that I find an apt characterization of Pinter criticism. One of the dangers of literature, Steiner says, is that, to the reader, the imaginative world can seem more real than the real world, becoming, in this sense, "autistic." Both as performance-texts and as literary texts, Pinter's plays have generated so much controversy and paradox that the commentary threatens to overwhelm them (if it has not already done so). They have stimulated general critical consternation, resulting in energetic interpretive activity and paradoxical evaluations of the worth of the playwright and his plays. Critics have devised various strategies to understand and explain them. In examining some of these critical strategies, I make Pinter criticism a case study, a vehicle for a larger inquiry: an ethnography of criticism.

Charting the growth of a major contemporary literary figure like Pinter through criticism of his work traces the paths through which such authors are historically institutionalized in our culture. Developments in critical conflicts about Pinter and their resolutions suggest insights about Pinter criticism and other kinds of dramatic criticism (both academic and nonacademic), enabling us to understand better how such change occurs in the theater, criticism, and related cultural phenomena.

A Fellowship from the National Endowment for the Humanities supported a year of my research for this book. Clark University, Cornell University, and Oregon State University provided visiting research appointments, enabling me to complete it. I gratefully acknowledge these institutions for such support.

For their cooperation, encouragement, and comments, without implying their endorsement of my views, I thank those whom I interviewed: especially Katherine H. Burkman, Lucina Paquet Gabbard, Steven H. Gale, Lois Gordon, Ewald Mengel, Austin E. Quigley, and Elizabeth Sakellaridou; as well as Martin Esslin, John Finegan, Paul Goetsch, Adrian Hall, Sir Harold Hobson, Laurie Holland, Richard Kavanaugh, George Martin, Bill Moor, David Nowlan, Carey Perloff, Peter Riegert, Keith Scales, Hans Joachim Schaefer, Luisa Sermol, Jean Stapleton, Robin Stone, David Strathairn, Amy Van Nostrand, and Irving Wardle. Further thanks go to: Deirdre Bair, for her information and help; Gottfried Büttner, for his hospitality and advice in Germany; C. W. E. Bigsby, for permission to have a tape of Pinter's talk at the University of East Anglia; Elizabeth Sakellaridou, for this tape and a transcript; and Harold Pinter, for permission to photocopy transcripts of unpublished interviews and letters on file at the BBC Written Archives Centre and London Weekend Television; Marek Kedzierski and Sean Page, Rosemary Pountney, and Sean White, for help with my research in Germany and Ireland. For their collegiality, I also thank Lisa Ede, Robert J. Frank, Willard Potts, and Robert Schwartz (Oregon State University); Jonathan Culler, Bruce Levitt, and Dorothy Mermin (Cornell University); Angela Dorenkamp (Assumption College); and Charles S. Blinderman and the late James F. Beard (Clark University). To both David Bleich, for initiating my work in reader-oriented theory, criticism, and pedagogy, and Ralph Cohen, for guiding me toward a broader understanding of this work, I owe special thanks.

Other, now much revised versions of portions of this book also appear in scholarly publications: chapter 4 in the *Journal of Dramatic Theory and Criticism* (1 [Fall 1986]: 49–76); some pages from chapter 8 in *Modern Drama* (32 [1989]: 171–73); condensations both in the *Pinter Review* (1 [1987]: 68–76) and in *Critical Essays on Harold Pinter*, edited by Steven H. Gale (Boston: G. K. Hall and Company, 1990); and sections of chapter 8 in *Harold Pinter: A Casebook*, edited by Lois Gordon (New York: Garland Publishing, 1990). Quotations in several of my epigraphs are from Harold Pinter's *Complete Works*, in four volumes (New York: Grove Press, 1977–81), and *Mountain Language* (New York: Grove Press, 1989). "Partners," the epigraph for chapter 8, is from *Collected Poems and Prose* (London: Methuen London, 1986), by Harold Pinter; copyright 1986 by Harold Pinter. I thank the editors and publishers for permission to use this material.

My greatest personal gratitude is to A. Jay and Bedonna Merritt; Morris J. and Sherry Mishkin; and Thomas X. Carroll.

# Introduction

Critics put Pinter in play. As if his plays were objects of sport, critics keep them in play by producing commentary after commentary and commentary upon commentary. As Benedict Nightingale observes hyperbolically: "[Pinter's] reputation is so high and his dramatic writings are so few these days that he'd simply have to daub a word or two on his bathroom mirror for the world's scholars to jet in with fingerprint powder and glass-cutting equipment" (*Fifth Row Center*, 244). Whatever discipline or mixture of disciplines is mined for explanations of Pinter's "mysteries," scholars become sleuths.

In another sense too Pinter is in play: at stake. Critics' "play" with Pinter operates also as a very serious enterprise with important social implications and cultural consequences. What scholars, directors, and other critics do with Pinter's plays exemplifies what is for them at stake in their own work, as well as in the plays. While this study defines what is at stake for Pinter critics (as well as for Pinter), it goes beyond the mere trendiness of this aim. It explores psychological and cultural contexts of these stakes. It models an ethnography of criticism: instead of looking at cultural interactions of more primitive and illiterate peoples, this study scrutinizes a group representative of some of the most highly sophisticated and literate people in Western culture: those who write about the plays of Harold Pinter.

By focusing on some episodes in developing knowledge about Pinter, I mark them as more important than others; obviously, this importance must be based on some criteria. It is important to notice, in my view, writing on Pinter which aims to contribute something new to the field and which is generally recognized to have succeeded in doing so (the "seminal" and the "essential"), or, conversely, writing which, in my own view, contributes something new but has not been recognized as doing so or sufficiently noticed (the "not indispensable"). Whether what is new is *also* of value and of what *kind* of value it is are, as we will see, a matter of critical consensus. Among my subjects are evaluation of Pinter and evaluation of writing about Pinter.

We must be selective in what we choose to notice in any detail; otherwise, we could not ever finish writing our "critical works" (as Ruth and Teddy call them in *The Homecoming*). We must leave out a great deal that is worthy of inclusion. I would not like my omissions here to be understood as negative value judgments of exceptional work on Pinter or work produced in cultures that I do not know well enough to present authentically. I concentrate mainly on Anglo-American criticism of Pinter's plays. But my interviews with theater journalists in Dublin and directors and scholars in Kässel, Bamberg, and Freiburg, West Germany, and archival research in these cities and in Paris, revealed much fertile ground to investigate, as there may be elsewhere throughout the world as well. Such work necessitates an extraordinary collaborative effort of the kind I hope the Harold Pinter Society (founded in 1986) will both encourage and support (see chap. 10).

How the personal and social purposes of individual critics engage them in episodes of cultural change is a neglected matter in most critical accounts. In order to disclose these purposes, I have interviewed several scholars about their books on Pinter's work. The interviews function as an explanatory apparatus highlighting complexities of critical response. Thoughts not included in the critics' published work present important new perspectives on Pinter as a literary figure in our culture. The interviews show how critics' "play" with Pinter seriously enforces personal, professional, and political affiliations. Critics' class, gender, sexual-role orientation, and other social and psychological traits—the gamut of their identity and experience—affect their literary preferences, interpretations, and judgments: not only their discourse but the cultural influence of a living writer such as Pinter.

"It is sometimes the strategy of those who have been forced to acknowledge that all facts are contextual to posit context itself as a new fact or set of facts that can serve as a constraint," Stanley Fish observes, "but the perception of context is no less contextually determined than the facts that context determines in turn" (*Doing What Comes Naturally*, 565 n.12). Yet, as Gerald Graff points out, "the remedy for a poor contextualizing of literature is not no contextualizing but better contextualizing" (11; cf. 179, 256). Graff's "institutional history" uses contemporaneous published sources such as autobiographical memoirs, speeches and papers presented at professional conferences and other meetings, even the minutes of department meetings, articles and book reviews, letters, and recollections of his own and others' personal experiences. To such kinds of materials, I have added interviews and less formal conversations with scholars, critics, directors, and actors whose work is germane to the present book. Such accounts offer glimpses into how critical and performance strategies are formulated and practiced. Even more importantly, their stories suggest the strong influence of personal, professional, and social history and cultural identity in interpretations and evaluations of Pinter's plays.

A deplorable tradition of academic criticism is repression of these features in such work. We must do more than merely acknowledge that criticism is a product of personal and social experience. We must study how such experience figures in the cultural institutionalization of literature. To undo this institutional taboo, we must discuss our experiences with one another. Thus, a unique feature of this book is such dialogue between Pinter critics. I make use of both published criticism and published and unpublished interview remarks, using each kind of discourse to complement the other. Furthermore, cutting across traditional academic and nonacademic boundaries in criticism, I relate the viewpoints of journalists reviewing productions of Pinter's plays to those of scholars writing on the published plays. The aim is to revise customary conventions through which either author, reader, critic, or scholar (playwright, director, actor, or audience) is deemed most important so as to acknowledge the importance of each one.

As I try to describe Pinter's own rhetorical stance toward himself, his plays, and his intended or imagined audience, so I attempt to describe his critics' rhetorical attitudes. Such attitudes are not always *explicitly* defined by critics or scholars; to discover, uncover, or recover these attitudes in/from their published texts also involves some mediation or interpretation, interventions on my own part. As I use interviews in order to define developments in Pinter's attitudes toward selected topics (e.g., critical and audience reception, politics, and sex), so in order to complement my descriptions and analyses of critical attitudes, I use interviews with the critical writers to present a historical perspective on their work on Pinter.

One of my own main aims is to define the (changing) aims, purposes, and goals of these critical writers. Whereas Pinter himself has been quite direct at times about his aims as a writer, generally, he has not been willing to make his more personal motivations public. Like Pinter, while they were generally willing to make public more rhetorical concerns, most of the critics and scholars whom I have interviewed preferred their more personal motivations to remain "off the record." If they were willing to confide such things to me only privately, I have kept their confidences.

Another of my purposes in studying Pinter criticism and scholarship is to define some of its changing contexts in a way that respects critics' similarities and differences. Despite their idiosyncrasies, like all people, critics and scholars belong to a variety of communities of shared values. As the boundaries of these communities overlap or intersect, and these values coincide or conflict, accommodations occur and allegiances change. These writers belong not only to critical or academic communities but to a variety of others as well: families, religious sects, culture clubs, political parties, and so on. Even if they were "independent" (i.e., not affiliated with an academic institution or publishing organ), they would have some cultural identity, some social roles. Their various alliances and interests enter into their work in a variety of ways; such forces come "into play" in their criticism and scholarship.

While I reject notions of "absolute" value with regard to both Pinter's writing and writing about Pinter, concepts of value and evaluation themselves are among my subjects. The value judgments prevalent in criticism of Pinter (see chap. 9) are contingent on a great variety of sometimes inaccessible factors. As I try to suggest some reasons why some of them may have been made, I recognize that such judgments do not have entirely recoverable origins. They are often based on "tacit knowledge" and so far from their origins as to be virtually untraceable. As "traces," written value judgments (and, less often, verbal testimony) are all we have left of the complex human experiences on which they may have been based. Such value judgments, often merely reduced to sets of operational or disciplinary rules (variously termed "interpretive strategies" or "conventions"), are products of experiences involving changing personal and cultural contexts and rhetorical situations through which people learn such rules, including when to apply the rules and when not. The breaking of rules can be as important as the following of them. Writing about Pinter's plays is a case study in such change.

Providing some perspectives on Pinter's critical evolution, the first part of this book interrelates rather disparate notions of "progress" and "fashion" and shows how Harold Pinter's own statements have affected the study of his work. It also includes separate sections on the aims, kinds, and contexts of criticism; the metaphor *criticism as strategy*; and changing critical views of Pinter's "ambiguity." Delineating areas of conflict and competition among current critical theories builds a base for my argument for greater cooperation and collaboration among critics and for relating the strategies used by individual Pinter critics (as defined in the second part) to tendencies in recent literary and critical theory.

As Michel Foucault suggests in relating authorship and power, the metaphor *critical strategy* (or *interpretive strategy*) depends on continuing competition in this field of play. The social and personal reality of making a living further informs metaphors of *play* and *work* controlling Pinter's own description of himself as a "working man" and critics' descriptions of his "dramatic strategies." To counteract (or ameliorate) the dominant masculine mode of *strategic* criticism (competition, propriety), while still mindful that it is a context in which I work and play, I advocate the salutary effects that a certain kind of feminist critique (one that stresses the usefulness of cooperation and collaboration, as motivated by an "ethic of care") could have on the institution of criticism.

In order to manage the vast material written on Pinter, I have organized analyses of Pinter's plays into categories according to what appear to me to be writers' dominant topics or tropes reflecting their aims and modes: (1) themes and techniques, rituals and games, and fantasies and dreams (mostly psychological or psychoanalytic figures); (2) language, structure, and comedy; and (3) social and sexual relations.

I cover writing about the first series of topics in chapter 5, treating "thematic tactics" and "ritual ruses" as represented by the work of Steven H. Gale and Katherine H. Burkman, and chapter 6, dealing with "psychoanalytic maneuvers," including work by Lois G. Gordon, Martin Esslin, Lucina Paquet Gabbard, and Daniel Salem. "Some Other Language Games" (chap. 7) considers a variety of ways that writers have investigated Pinter's language, beginning with Esslin and Austin E. Quigley and moving toward more recent linguistic and semiotic approaches, including the use of discourse analysis and speech-act theory; here I also refer to Elin Diamond's work on Pinter's comic conventions and to relations between his acting and his playwriting discussed by David T. Thompson.

"Cultural Politics" (chap. 8) considers recent developments in Pinter's attitudes toward politics in view of his past remarks and some related critical controversies ("Pinter and Politics"); it also discusses Pinter's attitudes toward love and sex ("Pinter and Sex"). I analyze how both Ewald Mengel's interest in socioeconomic role-playing and Elizabeth

Sakellaridou's feminist orientation grow out of certain personal and social experiences and how these contexts affect their renderings of power relations between Pinter's characters.

The last part, on social relations of critical and cultural change, situates value judgments of Pinter as a playwright and some of his individual plays and concepts of Pinter's continuity and change vis-à-vis some current theories. My account of recent developments in Pinter's career and collaborative study of his work concludes with some guidelines for change.

The critical strategies applied to Pinter's plays and considered in detail in this book may seem engaging, even brilliant attempts "to understand" Pinter. Some of my readers might want me to determine which are "better" than others, which are "the best." I do not do this. Instead of adjudicating discrete interpretations, I define some of the contexts in which certain understandings of Pinter have been achieved delimiting the process of adjudication itself. I hope to suggest how various contexts may have both enabled and constrained these writers, leading to conclusions about change in criticism in general.

In citing interviews with Pinter scholars and critics, I hope to subvert any hierarchical relationship between critics' writings and their words spoken in interviews: to suggest no special "privilege" of one as opposed to the other, but rather to make use of them both, using each one to complement the other without assuming the "last word" character of either. As both modern textual criticism and editing demonstrate, interpretations intervene in formulating the so-called final intention of an author. As one who has arranged and conducted interviews with other writers, I am especially aware of the delicacy of my position as a writer interpreting their remarks about their work and presenting them here. I accept responsibility for any errors of transcription and for my own interpretations throughout this book.

Conventional aims of such a study as this would include providing guidance to those who are looking for new directions to take in Pinter criticism: those looking for what has not yet been done that they could do, for example, graduate students searching for dissertation topics or professors looking for topics of publishable articles and books. While this book could easily serve such needs, if it were to function only in that way for academics or be read by academics only, I would be disappointed. I hope that this book helps readers of nonacademic backgrounds to understand the vast industry that literary criticism and scholarship have become. I urge my academic readers to pause before contributing to it further, to become more vigilant regarding their reasons for doing so, and to contribute more carefully and more responsibly.

We write both for ourselves and for others. Amidst acknowledged forces encouraging competition, as we work from a variety of positions within our institutions to change them, we must cooperate and collaborate with one another. Cooperation and collaboration are alternatives to the "masculine discourse" dominant in most literary criticism and particularly noticeable in criticism of Pinter. They will help us move beyond mere self-perpetuation toward something worth perpetuating, so that critical strategies for self-survival can become ways to better both ourselves and others.

# 1

## Perspectives on Pinter's

## Critical Evolution

# "Progress" and "Fashion"

## in Pinter Studies

This really is an awful business, this fashion. I must tell you I feel that I've been unfashionable all my life. I was oldfashioned from the very beginning, and I'm unfashionable now, really.—Harold Pinter

Throughout Pinter's career critics have persistently found his plays puzzling. "Sitting through" the first production of *The Birthday Party*, in London in 1958, was, Milton Shulman complains, "like trying to solve a crossword puzzle where every vertical clue is designed to put you off the horizontal" ("Sorry"). Over a decade later, in 1969, many were finding Pinter's puzzles virtually insoluble: "Harold Pinter's plays still puzzle audiences and critics after almost a dozen years of acquaintance with his work. In spite of a growing body of criticism, there are perhaps more unanswered questions about Pinter than about any other major contemporary playwright" (Free, "Treatment," 1). "Nothing that has subsequently appeared in print has mounted a serious challenge to that statement," Quigley declares in his 1975 *Pinter Problem* (3). "It may well be that a *basic* cause of Free's 'unanswered questions,' and of the field's failure to progress, is a *persistent* attempt to find answers to the *wrong* kinds of questions" (5; emphasis added). Ignoring "distinctive functions" of Pinter's language is a particular "barrier to progress" (31, 34).

Nevertheless, in his 1978 annotated bibliography of over 2,000 items relating to Pinter, Steven H. Gale observes two trends: (1) "a growing sophistication among [Pinter] critics (or the human response of accepting the judgment of others, the 'jumping on the bandwagon' syndrome, sometimes with a corresponding blindness)," and (2) "a very real sense of development within [Pinter's] canon" (xi). Writing in 1982, Charles Carpenter describes "the kind of criticism that pervades Pinter studies today" as "sophisticated, ingenious, dispel-the-mystery analysis" ("Victims," 489). Since 1982, as we will be seeing later in this book, Pinter criticism has grown both in sophistication and ingenuity, though a common mode of "analysis" is to accept the "mystery" as that which cannot be dispelled.

Categorizing and explaining Pinter's "development" as a means of dealing with the mystery, critics like Gale place a greater premium on what and how Pinter's plays mean, on themes and techniques, and on the "evolution" of Pinter's ideas and strategies, than do some critics of linguistic, semiotic, deconstructive, or audience-response persuasions, who foreground instead the interactive and performative functions of Pinter's language and their effects on audiences, subordinating hermeneutics and/or stylistics to these other concerns. The "traditionalists" weaned on realistic and naturalistic drama are generally sympathetic to Freudian and existential psychology, existential and phenomenological philosophy; they tend to occupy various positions from essentialism and positivism to radical relativism. The "poststructuralists" seem to favor Artaudian, Brechtian, and new "political" theater; they are antagonistic to individual psychology and generally sympathize with Marxist philosophies underlying what they term "cultural politics"; they express Derridean skepticism. "Pluralists" like Quigley incorporate some values of both traditionalism and poststructuralism, advocating a "both/and" instead of a "dialectical" position. These apparently different directions in Pinter criticism reflect competing trends in the criticism and theory of literature and theater overall.[1] But if we value and recognize a need for cooperation in appreciating and understanding any author, we can see how approaches touted as being mutually exclusive are at least somewhat compatible and perhaps even collectively progressive.

## Progress

That progress in criticism (or perhaps any other field) is a "gradual process" (Quigley, *PP*, xvii–xviii) is debatable. To see change in general as occurring gradually, progressing from ignorance to knowledge in unified, coherent patterns or stages can blind us to some developments in criticism. As it limits our understanding of innovation and change, this notion of progress may actually hinder our progress. Yet such "gradualism" is still often taken for granted in literary studies.

Working in different disciplines, Ralph Cohen, the distinguished editor of *New Literary History*, director of the Commonwealth Center for Literary and Cultural Change, and a professor at the University of

Virginia, and Stephen Jay Gould, the renowned paleontologist and a professor of geology, biology, and the history of science at Harvard University, suggest some grounds for interrogating concepts of progress, for viewing critical change as a matter of both persistence and variation, and for recognizing that stability is an important aspect of change.

Gould alerts us to common notions, "biases" that need to be overcome in theories of biological evolution. Among these biases are "progress," "determinism," "gradualism" (the progression of change in "stately, logical stages"), and "adaptationism" (the perception of a just rationality in change).[2] In Gould's view stability is a greater aspect of change than variation, for systems and structures of phenomena form the stability against which we can perceive change. As seen from this viewpoint, comparable features of Pinter criticism (like some "dualistic distinctions" about Pinter's language criticized by Quigley) form the stability against which we can perceive change in this field.

Cohen emphasizes the importance of viewing literary (and critical) change in terms of both variation and persistence: "it is the nature of literary structures that change and persistence are present together. The kinds of relations between them account for the kinds of changes critics identify" ("Propaedeutic," 6).[3] Change consists in *both* continuities *and* discontinuities, similarity *and* difference, tradition *and* innovation. Moreover, if particular kinds of relations between change and persistence account for the kinds of changes that critics identify, these *kinds* of relations are *accounts* of the critics, Cohen also suggests, and the critics' own *interests* affect their accounts of change. On these grounds we must explore particular relations between change and persistence in the field of Pinter studies and investigate how particular interests have affected scholars' accounts of Pinter criticism.

Gould's idea of "punctuated equilibria" emphasizes Foucauldian *ruptures* in the status quo.[4] Extrapolating from his conception of the evolutionary transitions between species, we can construe such events in Pinter criticism as the reception of *The Birthday Party* since its initial debacle and the application of the phrase *comedy of menace* to Pinter's early work as episodes in a larger process of development; namely, the evolution of critical knowledge. Epistemological evolution, like geological and biological evolution, proceeds rarely in an orderly manner. Order is something we impose later. Rather, such evolutions occur through continuities and discontinuities, steps forward and backward (of varying size), some lateral leaps and bounds, and many hops in place. Visualizing it graphically, we might find it no more predictable perhaps than the cardiogram of a patient with arrhythmia or a chart of the stock market after the "crash" of 19 October 1987. These models of change, like any others, are metaphors, not predictive rules, and they themselves are contingent on a variety of unpredictable personal, social, and cultural contexts.[5]

The impact of particular pieces of writing on subsequent Pinter criticism and scholarship may be more unpredictable and abrupt than predictable and gradual. But however gradually or suddenly a particular piece of writing may seem to alter the course of knowledge is a matter of perspective, contingent on shifting temporal viewpoints. Perceptions of both suddenness and gradualness are relative to the period of time being studied, to the units of time marked within the larger period, to the distance of the time being studied from the present time of study, and to the aims and purposes of those doing the studies and the marking.

Obviously no two critical points of view are identical and even the most apparently traditional criticism aims to differ in some way from what has preceded it. Most published writers aim in some way to present something new and to avoid appearing so different as to be excluded; something conventional and something innovative characterize all writing. Cohen's view that both variation and persistence are empirical constituents of change cooperates with Gould's view that stability is the background against which we can perceive change. No matter which—sameness or difference—some critic's interest places in the foreground, for an event to be perceived as change, it must appear as different from something else, and that something else will be seen as the persisting convention. Change occurs both gradually and suddenly when innovations arise and overtake persisting conventions, altering them in the process. How a *new* convention *persists* (becoming an *old* one) is a complex transformation involving the interaction of literary, cultural, and social forces (Cohen, "History and Genre").

Given present vantage points, overall persistence/change may appear to occur "gradually"—over time (historically, diachronically)—while individual contributions may seem to appear "in spurts"—at particular "moments" in time (at once, suddenly, simultaneously, or synchronically)—even though they often take years to write and publish. Both kinds of changes—the diachronic and the synchronic—result in transforming knowledge. Though interrelations between these various kinds of change are complex and not readily fixed in categories, as Cohen demonstrates in "History and Genre" they can be *explained*. These *expla-*

*nations* of change, however, like any other critical productions, are empirical and temporal constructions: metaphors that serve the aims and purposes of the critics and theorists doing the explaining.

We can regard what has been written about Pinter's work and what is being written about it as a series of interrelated, but not necessarily coherent episodes in an ongoing "process" of change. There are both continuities and innovations in the evolution of Pinter studies. Whether or not critics perceive progress and what kinds of progress they find are functions of how they position themselves with respect to others.

### Relations between Progress and Fashion

To support his point that Pinter criticism is "proliferating but not progressing," Quigley cites Schroll's study of Pinter's critical reputation in the eleven years between 1958 and 1969: "for all of their work, few scholars of late offered new insights into Pinter's plays; the bulk of the writing over these recent years was merely a rewording of what had been said"; "basic questions about the playwright's talents, techniques, and significance were never resolved because his stature as a fashionable playwright intervened" (Schroll, 8, 34; see Quigley, *PP*, 4 n.4). But Quigley claims that "Schroll's attempt to account for this stagnation (by blaming it on the distorting effect of Pinter's growing reputation) seems less than convincing."

For Schroll, however, critical reactions to Pinter are "emblematic" of "the limiting tendencies of the modern theatrical environment": "Dramatic commentary, begun as an aid to an understanding of the plays, finally lost its effectiveness as resulting theatrical fashions prevented direct reaction to the plays and scholarly interpretations became so abstract that their categories hindered new ideas. [One can observe] a playwright's works being quite literally exhausted by overabundant critical enthusiasm compressed into too brief a time span" (8). A particularly striking factor in the creation of this phenomenon is "the massive influence that the playwright's television and radio plays had on his popularity and, in turn, on later reviewers" (9).[6] Unlike Schroll, Quigley seeks the causes of the Pinter problem in the limitations of modern literary critical inquiry. Yet even though they attribute the impasse to apparently different causes (Schroll to fashion; Quigley to outmoded theories of language), these explanations are more compatible than Quigley implies if we consider relations between fashion and progress.

Anticipating Quigley, in a review of Schroll, Warner detects some "methodological uncertainty" in the claim that Pinter is " 'trapped by fashion' ": Schroll fails "to define clearly what he means by fashion. At times he seems to suggest it is something created by the author and we are left with the image of an author trapped by himself; elsewhere fashion is said to be created by the critics or the public, and we are given the image of Pinter somehow bound by public taste" (748). In "New Waves on the British Stage"—a source for Schroll's thesis about fashion impeding Pinter criticism—Irving Wardle, the theater critic who first applied the description *comedy of menace* to Pinter's plays, does, however, define the insidiousness of "fashion":

> At close quarters fashion looks very much like progress; but even if you realize how ephemeral it is, your response will be nearer to nervous resistance than detached superiority.
>
> For there is something frightening about the way in which fashion operates. It has the effect of cancelling out individual judgment in a way that makes you doubt the validity of your reactions to any work, fashionable or not. At the moment when something new is being taken up there is a distinctly audible click, a slight earth tremor, and when you look again the object has been turned to gold. If you knew nothing of it before the transformation you cannot avoid seeing it in this new light; its public reputation intercedes between the spectator and the play—whatever his opinion, there is a danger that he will be reacting more to the reputation than responding to the work. (57–58; see Schroll, 6–7)[7]

Though acknowledging "a wearisome repetition of a few basic ideas in Pinter criticism" cited by Schroll, Warner attributes it "more to the failure of critical imagination than to 'stagnation brought about by fashion' " (748).

As Paul de Man has pointed out, however, "fashion, *la mode*, is itself a highly significant and, precisely, aesthetic and historical category that historians should not underestimate. When it becomes fashionable to dismiss fashion, clearly something interesting is going on, and what is being discarded as *mere* fashion must also be more insistent, and more threatening, than its frivolity and transcience [transience] would seem to indicate. What is being dismissed . . . is the play of the signifier" (introd. to Jauss, *Aesthetic*, xx). Imagination and fashion *interact* as the writings of an author like Pinter are put "in play."[8]

Though one way of warding off the appeal of fashion is to see it, as Warner does, as a sign of critical conformism—a "failure" to "imagine" or to construct one's own ideas—another way to account for the critical effects of fashion is to admit that it *engages* the popular imagination. Both public taste and their own repetitions catering to it have bound Pinter and his critics at various times in their careers. But fashion may also have stimulated as much as limited these writers' imaginations.

Harold Hobson's now famous review of the doomed first London production of *The Birthday Party*, "The Screw Turns Again," lauded Pinter as "equal" to Henry James and as "the most original, disturbing, and arresting talent in theatrical London," correctly predicting Pinter's future success and, it is generally regarded, helping to bring it about. Wardle's 1958 article "Comedy of Menace" labeling the play as such caused a similar "rupture" in Pinter criticism, altering the earliest notions of Pinter's work by "reforming" them. Yet in reviewing *The Caretaker*, only two years later (July 1960), Wardle retracted the label ("There's Music," 130). At first an innovative or "new way" of seeing Pinter, Wardle's "persistent" phrase was so quickly overused that it had already become a cliché, a "dead metaphor." Though Wardle apparently had second thoughts about the appropriateness of *comedy of menace* to Pinter's later work, Dukore observes, "its aptness made it stick" (*HP*, 25). People find *comedy of menace* useful in describing Pinter's plays because the phrase captures metonymically their own impressions of his dramas, but the term is used as well because it has become "fashionable."

As recently as 1986, Wardle's label resurged in publicity for John Malkovich's production of *The Caretaker* in an advertisement subtitling it "A Comedy of Menace." Wardle's *label* does not persist and limit the criticism so much as the critics' and directors' and publicists' *use* of it does. Yet in a way this persistent use of the phrase also *extends* criticism as critics question and move *beyond* comedy of menace and other familiar categories, developing other metaphors to serve as new ones; e.g., "plays of language" (Kennedy, *Six Dramatists*), "plays of impasse" (Rosen), "dramas of inquiry" (Quigley, *MSOW*), "drama of uncertainty" (Fuegi), and "theatre of discord" (Mayberry). The most extensive study of Pinter's comedy so far, Diamond's *Pinter's Comic Play*, revitalizes "comedy of manners." Though he echoes Wardle's concept, Gussow seems to avoid using *comedy of menace* when reviewing the CSC Repertory Theatre's 1988 production of *The Birthday Party*. While still emphasizing Pinter's "terrors" and the "shiver beneath the laughter," Gussow describes the play as "a play of intrigue, with an underlying motif of betrayal" ("Review/Theater"). Dukore calls the play "a comedy (of menace or otherwise)" (rev. of *Birthday Party*, 72).

Quigley argues that the same "seeming lack of explicitness" attacked by reviewers of the short-lived 1958 London production of *The Birthday Party* still "lingers" in the midseventies "in the less pejorative but equally ubiquitous remarks on the inexplicitness of many of the plays"; yet, "[r]ather than being rejected because of that irksome obscurity . . . the plays are now frequently held to be successful because of that very same element" (*PP*, 11). What was previously regarded as an unfashionable weakness—Pinter's "obscurity"—has become a fashionable strength—his "ambiguity" (see chap. 4 for further discussion). Pinter criticism *advanced* with Quigley's *Pinter Problem* partly because as it modifies Schroll's explanation, it enables us to *link* the cultural phenomena that Schroll labels "fashion"—trends in "theatre environments"—with trends in critical assumptions about language: the theatrical au courant with the critical au courant.

Progress is both relative and instrumental to the aims and purposes of critics. In order for there to *be* progress, writers need to perceive blockage, to feel frustration, to respond to incentives to break new ground, and to reach some consensus that such new ground has been found. Progress is *made* by critics and scholars, *instrumental* to their needs. For progress to be perceived as occurring, then, it must suit their purposes.[9]

Both Schroll and Quigley suggest that critics' interests in thematizing Pinter's plays might explain the impasse that they perceive in critical and scholarly writing about Pinter. "The theatrical climate of the late 1950s" was propelled by a search for hidden thematic meanings: "All of the reviewers looked for deeper meaning in the play; they demanded that a clear-cut, coherent, symbolic statement be made in a play. The majority of the reviewers, who found no deep symbolism clearly evident, became outraged at Pinter. Yet other early critics, perceiving a theme, immediately lauded his plays as major expressions of truth about modern man, and they hailed him as a sign of life in the British drama" (Schroll, 13). In order to advance understanding of Pinter's work, Quigley argues for "something more . . . than another survey of recurring thematic concerns" (*PP*, xviii).

As already cited, Gale begins his bibliography with a brief analysis of the developments that he perceives in this field, but the body of the bibliography says only that Schroll's book "includes a checklist" (178), neglecting entirely its first part (ninety pages), from which I have been quoting. The " 'jumping on the bandwagon' syndrome" that Gale sees in Pinter criticism recalls Schroll's thesis about the "distorting effect of Pinter's reputation" without taking account of Quigley's critique of its limitations. Gale neither uses Quigley's appraisal of the field of Pinter criticism as a point of departure for his own critical introduction nor takes account of the functions of Pinter's language that Quigley defines. Yet as Quigley expects *"theoretically adequate* linguistic generalizations" to "make possible a new perspective on the ways in which Pinter's dialogue functions" (book jacket and Princeton University Press catalog; emphasis added; cf. 20), Gale expects *interpretive adequacy* or *hermeneutic accuracy* to make a difference in Pinter criticism. Whatever judgment of previous explanations these critics suggest, their own syntheses reflect not ultimate truth-value but their own critical purposes and interests (see chaps. 5 and 7).

Gale stresses critics' perceptions of thematic and stylistic development in Pinter's canon: what his own critical analysis of Pinter's work attempts to demonstrate. Like Quigley, he accuses some critics of imposing their interpretations on Pinter's texts; and as Quigley suggests that language is "in" the texts (rather than "their subtexts"), Gale assumes that themes and techniques established by critics reflect the texts directly: "Tracing the subject matter which has been the concern of writers over the years leads to an appreciation of Pinter's stylistic development and thematic evolution because the extent of that development becomes clear as the subject matter of the criticism changes" (*B*, xii). In defining the changing "subject matter" of the plays, however, the changing "subject matter" of the criticism *also* reflects the changing perspectives of its writers. [10]

As Arthur Holmberg points out about the current perception of Shakespeare's plays, if in 1988 and 1989 *The Birthday Party* no longer looked or sounded or read the same as it did in 1958 or 1964 or 1967 or 1975—no longer raised the same "wrong kinds of questions" (Who are the two men? Where did Stanley come from? Were they all supposed to be normal? ["Pinter Unperturbed"])—this is partly because criticism and scholarship have changed the way we respond to and "interrogate" it, changed our "horizons of expectation," changed "the mode." Unlike those in Shakespeare studies, Pinter's critics and scholars have been able to use what the playwright himself has said and written about his works to aid them in their inquiries. Pinter himself has been a persistent influence on changing fashions in study of his work.

### Pinter on Pinter Criticism

Citing interview and other remarks made by Pinter for clues to solving his "puzzles" is an especially "fashionable" strategy of critics, both extending and limiting their perspectives. Despite arguments against doing so, in the 1980s Pinter critics still "exult in the challenge to plumb the depths of the subtext and expose the hidden secrets of motive, continuity, and intended meaning" (Carpenter, "Victims," 489). Most have read Pinter's remarks with the aim of using them to provide interpretive readings of his plays or explanations of his techniques. These critics assume a hidden thematology that clues from Pinter's own perspective could help them to discover. For these commentators his dramaturgy is one of subterfuge.[11]

Pinter provides us with another perspective on the impact of fashion on his own critical reputation: he calls into question whether he has ever been all that fashionable.[12] Nevertheless, along with Pinter's success with audiences and critics have come awards and honors and opportunities for him to speak directly about his plays and his attitudes toward what his critics and audiences have been saying about them. Although he is outwardly a reserved person who claims not to enjoy talking about his work, he does give interviews when the commercial aspect of his occupation requires him to do so, when he feels that he owes someone a debt, and/or when he is genuinely interested in the subject of inquiry; that is, in his own interest as an author/playwright, out of courtesy to others to whom he feels so inclined, or, more recently, as a platform for his political views. In February 1982, when I spoke with Pinter in Providence, Rhode Island, with regard to arranging an interview about the criticism of his plays, he said: "I can tell you right now. I'm not interested in critics." In correspondence later that year, he politely declined to be interviewed on this subject, in effect limiting production of more Pinter on Pinter criticism.

While Pinter's comments on his plays direct some critical attitudes, they are often reactions to statements already made by commentators. What Pinter has said in interviews, speeches, essays, correspondence, and on other occasions is so often cited and quoted that his attitudes toward his work do serve critics as "strategies" for understanding it. Yet, ironically, one point he generally makes quite emphatically is the danger of taking anything he says about his work as categorical; remarking on the fallibility of interview remarks, he has observed: "I don't see any good reason why whatever I say is going to be the least bit interesting. It's this whole problem again of assuming that because you're a writer you're some kind of prophet. Which I certainly am not" (Gussow, "Conversation," 134). Such rhetoric serves as Pinter's strategy to protect the textual integrity of his plays: to guard his (carefully revised) *writing* against his less carefully considered *verbal remarks* (which, when published, only *appear* as writing—they have not always been written in advance).

In a speech that Pinter gave when he accepted the Hamburg University Shakespeare Prize for his two plays *Landscape* and *Silence* in 1970, he stressed the difference between his aims as a writer and those of a critic: "In what way can one talk about one's work? I'm a writer, not a critic. When I use the word work I mean work. I regard myself as nothing more than a working man" ("Speech," 3). He explained that he dislikes talking publicly about his work, citing critics' misuse of a spontaneous remark made "with no thought at all and merely to frustrate this line of enquiry" that his work was about "[t]he weasel under the cocktail cabinet." Pinter goes on in this speech to qualify his previous remark about "the weasel under the cocktail cabinet": "What am I writing about? Not the weasel under the cocktail cabinet. I am not concerned with making general statements. . . . I can sum up none of my plays. I can describe none of them, except to say: That is what happened. That is what they said. That is what they did" (4).[13]

These remarks anticipate Pinter's brief 1981 introduction to a letter that he had written to Peter Wood, the director of the first production of *The Birthday Party*, in 1958, which he had just found and published: "It is not the kind of letter I could possibly write now and therefore I found it of interest. The debate between Peter Wood and me [about why Pinter did not want to write a program note] proved to be academic as the play closed in London after a run of one week" ("Letter to Peter Wood," 2). Here Pinter suggests a difference between the sort of interpretive comments he had felt able to make in writing to a director when he was first starting out and those he feels able to write in 1981 (perhaps none at all).

In his preface to this published letter, Martin Esslin says, "Pinter himself, at the time, steadfastly—and rightly—refused to be tempted into self-explanation and commentary on himself. It is not for an artist to provide a critical child's guide to his intentions. A work of art must speak for itself" (1). Esslin promotes the traditional assumption that authors should not comment on their own work and also its corollary that critics are dependent on literary artists. Yet Esslin also reflects comments that

Pinter has already made about his work. Such remarks, even those in which Pinter is explaining his refusal to explain, tend to serve critics and scholars as a means of explanation.

In the "Letter to Peter Wood" Pinter argues: "The play is itself. It is no other. It has its own life (whatever its merit in dramatic terms or accomplishment may be and despite the dissatisfaction others may experience with regard to it). I take it you would like me to insert a clarification or moral judgement or author's angle on it, straight from the horse's mouth. I appreciate your desire for this but I can't do it" (3). He elaborates this viewpoint in a 1959 interview, just after the failure of the play:

> I want to present living people to the audience, worthy of their interest basically because they *are*, they exist, not because of any moral the author may draw from them. In many recent British plays I find myself put off by the spectre of the author looming above his characters, telling the audience at every stage just what they are to think about them.
>
> I want as far as possible to leave comment to the audience; let them decide whether the characters and situations are funny or sad. . . . I think my job as a dramatist is simply to present the situation, shaped in dramatic terms, and let the audience decide for themselves. ("Mr. HP")

At first his audience's failure to understand did not seem to persuade him to change his mind. But, subsequently, perhaps in response to continuing complaints about the difficulty of understanding his plays, Pinter did succumb to public pressures. As a result Pinter himself has been one of the sources of the critical attitude toward his "ambiguity" of which he complained to William Gale in 1982 when they discussed the reception of *Betrayal* (1978): "There is a received idea that my work is supposed to be made up of some kind of ambiguity. And if I veer away a'tall, I am held to be culpable. Well, if people don't like it, hard luck. Go see something else. I'm my own man and I don't look at a piece of paper and say, 'Well now, how ambiguous can I be for my public?' I write only for myself" (16).

Throughout the 1960s, when reviewers and other commentators on his plays tended to despair of finding out what he "meant"—"the" meaning of his plays—Pinter responded to their concerns, allowing the validity of multiple individual interpretations. In 1962 he gave a speech at the Seventh National Union of Students Drama Festival at the University of Bristol, which had hosted the first production of his first play, *The Room*, in 1957. This speech was published in the London *Sunday Times* on 4 March 1962 and headlined "Between the Lines." The note to the published transcript says that Pinter "was persuaded by the National Union of Students and The Sunday Times to speak of his work and his ideas. The result provoked unprecedented discussion and was thought to contain much of value for a larger audience."

This speech has been a source of many critics' and scholars' understandings of Pinter's plays, yet in explaining his unwillingness to make critical and theoretical statements about his work, he warns his listeners not to use anything he says as "final and definitive." Nonetheless, critics have tended to interpret them as just that: for example, "Mr. Pinter's Bristol speech . . . offers, next to his plays, the most revealing insights into his purpose as a playwright" (Taubman). Critics seem to quote his Bristol comments on the "two silences" and "that tired, grimy phrase 'Failure of communication' " incessantly, often out of context, to correct the "misinterpretation" of Pinter's plays and to establish their so-called avoidance-of-communication theme, or theses about the function of their language. Cited over and over again, their critical utility widely recognized, these remarks have become embarrassingly overfamiliar. [14]

Critics' citation of such remarks generally disregard Pinter's sense of their unreliability: "If I am to talk at all I prefer to talk practically about practical matters, but that's no more than a pious hope, since one invariably slips into theorising, almost without noticing it. And I distrust theory" ("Speech," 3). His distrust of critics, like his distrust of words and theory, results from Pinter's sense that human discourse is unreliable and his awareness that critics lack theatrical know-how. Collaboration consisting of "a kind of stumbling erratic shorthand" and "an intelligence brought to bear on practical and relevant matters" is more likely to "get the curtain up at eight o'clock" than a "philosophical discourse or political treatise" (3). Having eventually become impatient with and less tolerant of the number of conflicting interpretations offered of his plays, Pinter seems less willing to accept the "manifold interpretations" as "valid," at least from a "practical" interest in staging the plays ("Harold Pinter Talks to Michael Dean"). If "people are going to start playing guessing games" with *Old Times* as they did with *The Homecoming*, Pinter told Gussow in 1971, "I think it's a waste of time" ("Conversation," 43; cf. D. Thompson, 3).

After what critics and scholars have done with Pinter's few speeches and essays, it is not surprising that, until recently, Pinter has generally been unwilling to analyze his own plays at all. With regard to his own artistic development, he has been even more explicitly reluctant to engage in discussion (Gussow, "Conversation," 43). In 1971 Pinter also told Gussow that he finds " 'theories of drama' and that kind of thing . . . quite unreadable" ("Conversation," 134). In 1979, in another interview with Gussow, Pinter said, "As you know, I don't proceed from any kind of system or theory" ("I Started," 5). Yet the 1964 essay "Writing for the Theatre" (a revised version of the Bristol University speech)—which begins with "I'm not a theorist" (80)—has been reprinted in Germany in a volume entitled *English Dramatic Theories*.

Given critics' plundering, it is also not surprising that for years Pinter has been reluctant to speak again in an academic setting. After receiving an honorary degree from the University of East Anglia in 1974, he was invited to talk there, but it took C. W. E. Bigsby several years of persistent entreaties to convince Pinter to accept the invitation in 1981 (Elliott, telephone conversation). Pinter began this talk by reading the 1958 "Letter to Peter Wood." Reiterating a "very strong distinction" between the man speaking and the man writing, Pinter insisted that he does not regard himself as an expert on his own work: "I feel that I haven't the vocabulary, the proper and accurate vocabulary . . . with which to describe . . . the act of writing itself, what happens. . . . There are other people very well endowed, I have noticed over the years, to tell me exactly what is in my work and what isn't. And I really do mean that. They are really much better endowed than I am. I feel in a way, sitting here, I am almost a stranger to my own work because the work took place in a territory in which . . . I lived while I was doing it but I now left. In other words, the work is now independent of me and I independent of it, not entirely perhaps." He had tried "to deflect [Bigsby] by various stratagems," as he put it, because of what he called "a deep-seated, even profound reluctance to engage in this sort of activity for one reason alone, and that is I really didn't see the point or value of such a thing."

Bigsby said that Pinter seemed very nervous during this appearance and that a videotape of the occasion shows his wife, Lady Antonia Fraser, "close to tears" at the beginning of the talk (Elliott, telephone conversation). The "deep-seated . . . reluctance," Pinter himself suggests in the talk, is a deep-seated "fear." The "reason" for this fear and refusing to accept the invitation "until now," he adds, was an "apprehension" that he was being invited to East Anglia year after year "to make a general comment or a serious and general observation."

Pinter expressed a similar attitude in his opening remarks in the Hamburg University speech twelve years earlier: "When I was informed that I was to be given this award my reaction was to be startled, even bewildered, while at the same time to feel deeply gratified by this honour. I remain honoured and slightly bewildered, but also frightened. What frightens me is that I have been asked to speak to you today. If I find writing difficult I find giving a public address doubly so" (3). At East Anglia, Pinter amplified this attitude: "I am not a public speaker and I've very very rarely done it. I am well aware, as you are, of this relationship which immediately assumes that I am [an] authority [on] the sources of one subject or another. I do not myself believe this to be the case. I am actually a working man and I always have been and I work quite hard but quietly and get on to it and I am not used to doing this sort of thing; however, so far, I am still alive." Though invited to speak at Brown University, when awarded an honorary doctorate in February 1982, Pinter declined to give a public address, simply thanking his hosts for the honor (see Elliott, "Stalking," 14). In contrast to these previous occasions, more recently, on 12 November 1987, when Pinter gave a reading of his dramatic sketch *Precisely* at Fairleigh Dickinson University, in Teaneck, New Jersey, he was relaxed and confident in his manner (Gordon, telephone conversation with author). Not only has Pinter visited Turkey, with Arthur Miller, and Nicaragua, where he met privately with President Daniel Ortega Saavedra, but "he has spoken frequently on politics and theater at universities and international conferences as well. On several occasions he has delivered one-man performances of his last two plays [*One for the Road* and *Mountain Language*)], playing all the roles, then responding to questions from the audience" (Gussow, "Pinter's Plays," 17). In his "enactment" of an excerpt from *The Hothouse* and of *One for the Road* at the Poetry Center of the 92d Street Y in New York City, on 3 October 1989, and during the ensuing question-and-answer period with *New York Times* drama critic Mel Gussow, Pinter exuded great theatrical poise and was indeed a triumphant success. Much has changed in Pinter's personal and public life since the early eighties to bring about this difference.

Pinter's stated inability to write such a letter in 1981 as he did to Wood in 1958 revealed concern that such "private" communications with his directors ultimately will appear in print and be mined for critical interpretations (see Gussow, "Conversation," 134). In various other modes, however, Pinter still provides a strong hand, ultimately guiding responses to his work. Objecting to the production of *Old Times* staged by Luchino Visconti at the Teatro di Roma in 1973, alluding to his "copyright," Pinter had considered suspending performances before consultation with his lawyers in London resulted in proposing "modifications" to Visconti and the managing director.[15] Since then Pinter has exerted significant control over major productions of his plays, demonstrating his view of what he calls the "proper collaboration" between himself as author and his directors. Like several of his contemporary counterparts (Beckett, Albee, Stoppard, Gray, Shepard), Pinter directs productions of his own plays. He directed, for example, the first production of *The Hothouse* in London in 1980, as well as the revival of *The Birthday Party* in London in 1964, and, more recently, the world premieres in London of both *One for the Road* and *Mountain Language* (giving a lengthy interview on the "politics" of *One for the Road* and writing a program note for *Mountain Language*). In October 1989 he traveled to New York to work in rehearsals with the director and cast of the American premiere of *Mountain Language*, spending even more time on their production of *The Birthday Party*.

Pinter's presence at rehearsals of the February 1982 American premiere of *The Hothouse* in Providence, Rhode Island, demonstrates his concern with what he would consider the *accurate* production of his plays, that is, with productions that he would consider faithful to the published texts and to his intentions. Adrian Hall directed this Trinity Square Repertory Company production and its subsequent run in New York. Pinter spent a week with the cast in Providence, functioning as author-consultant. I attended rehearsals of the production before Pinter arrived and after Pinter left, as well as opening night, and observed changes in the acting resulting from Pinter's help. According to several members of the cast, he was especially cooperative in answering their questions about the characters they played (interview with author). The result, I believe, was greater sharpness and clarity in their performances and other aspects of the production and, overall, a more emotionally concise style of portrayal. Although Pinter would not discuss "the meaning" of *The Hothouse* with the Trinity Square Repertory Company actors, they seemed to have greater confidence in their understanding of their roles after Pinter left than they had had before his arrival.[16] From this experience with Pinter,

Adrian Hall concluded: "He somehow wants us to think that he doesn't care. But he does. A lot" (interview with author; see Elliott, "Stalking Harold Pinter," 14).

Pinter spent a week in October 1989 in rehearsals of CSC Repertory's production of *Mountain Language* and *The Birthday Party* primarily to advise the former's American premiere, but he helped a great deal with the latter. When Artistic Director Carey Perloff asked Pinter "if he would like to direct his own work," he replied: "Not really, I'd rather other people do it. I did this one [at the National Theatre in 1988] just to make sure it was done right the first time" (Pittel, 5). Perloff and members of the CSC Repertory cast were "amazed" by "how much time [Pinter] actually spent in rehearsal" and impressed by Pinter's "commitment to the theater" (interview with author). He encouraged the actors, even inspired them. For David Strathairn, Pinter "was very forthcoming," his "presence" a "catalyst" for a more complex portrayal of Stanley than the actor had conveyed in the 1988 CSC Repertory production of *The Birthday Party*. For Bill Moor, Pinter clarified Petey's attitude toward life: " 'I want him to be very vital, very positive.' " For Jean Stapleton, Pinter was "very encouraging" and gave her "reassurance" that her Meg was "rich and on the right track." "Graciously," Pinter "did not encroach on Carey's turf. . . . He respected her position as director." Peter Riegert described "the relationship" with Pinter as "the way it is supposed to be. His sense of our contribution was no less than what he felt Carey's was or his was. . . . The stakes in his plays are enormous, absolutely enormous. . . . The most frivolous questions we could have had had a significance for him."

Noel King observes, "One very important aspect of *No Man's Land* [1975] lies in its indication of Pinter's attitude towards his public identity as Harold Pinter, playwright." Various exchanges offer a "game of cryptic challenge": "A character offers an anecdote to a listener as an act of subtle aggression, defying him to comprehend it, to locate a pattern in the maze. Pinter plays a parallel game of bafflement with his audience" (King, "Pinter's Progress," 252, 253; cf. Quigley, "Temporality," 19–20). But *No Man's Land* is "more than another instance of Pinter challenging the impulse towards categorizations and explanations; it is much more intensely about Pinter and the conditioned expectations of his audience" (King, "Pinter's Progress," 254). Milton Shulman was complaining that Pinter had grown into a "dedicated cult" as early as the first London revival of *The Birthday Party* in 1964 ("The Party"). Over fifteen years later, "[t]he cult-following Pinter has acquired is of such a settled kind that it inhibits his writing," and King sees *No Man's Land* as "intended to disperse this following" ("Pinter's Progress," 254).

However much Pinter may have succeeded or failed in this intention is still not clear. Wary of cultishness in his audiences and hyperactivity in his critics, Pinter is still polite to those who engage in critical inquiry about his work such as myself: "I appreciate the seriousness of your endeavours and wish you well" (letter to author). [17] Nevertheless, in 1982 Pinter was "not inclined to talk about the subject" of criticism and "that's that." Since then his inclination may have changed somewhat, making this pronouncement a bit less "final and definitive." In the 1985 interview "A Play and Its Politics," as we will see in chapter 8, Pinter offered some new comments on criticism of his early work, and after his October 1989 reading from *The Hothouse* and of *One for the Road* at the 92d Street Y, during the question-and-answer session with Gussow, he basically repeated these remarks. Quoting Simon Gray, Gussow wondered whether Pinter is "exasperated" by the " 'cathedral reverence with which [his plays are] sometimes received, thanks mainly to the industrious spadework of English departments and literary journals.' " Pinter quipped: "Well, in so far as I detect it, yes I am." After Pinter returned a question from the audience about the "job or responsibility of a theater critic" to Gussow (who declined to answer it), Gussow skipped my own question about how Pinter's attitude toward criticism has developed in recent years. Pinter was more inclined to discuss his political concerns and his "responsibility" as a "citizen of both my country and the world."

### On Aims of Criticism and Scholarship

Though modifying this position quite drastically through his political plays and his public remarks about his politics and his civic responsibility, throughout most of his career, Pinter has insisted that he has no responsibility to audiences, actors, directors, critics, or society at large. In contrast to this view of the writer, the responsibility of critics and scholars is generally thought to be to this larger community, to the author and his or her work, to audiences, and to one another. If only from this point of view, criticism, like the theater, is a *collaborative* endeavor. Though Pinter has at times claimed disinterest in audiences and critics and a desire to please only himself, he has discussed his collaborations with directors, actors, and other professionals in the theater and other media. He is quite aware of the objectification that takes place when a writer transforms personal knowledge about experience into what Arthur Holmberg describes as "the most social of literary genres—the drama."

*Betrayal* deals with an adulterous affair. Many critics, including one of Pinter's greatest champions, Sir Harold Hobson, have raised the issue of the autobiographical nature of this play, because it was written during a period in which Pinter left his first wife, the late actress Vivien Merchant, to live with Lady Antonia Fraser, who has since become his second wife. [18] In an interview, Pinter rejected "this notion," saying: "I don't regard [*Betrayal*] as 'personal.' I regard it as objective. I'm 'engaged' in anything I write. But I also distance myself" (Kissel, "HP").

However "personal" or "subjective" the nature of literary experiences, as many artists like Pinter do, critics and scholars still generally strive for a particular kind of "empirical objectivity": shareable knowledge— knowledge based on intersubjective negotiations of interests and ideas and feelings. [19] Critics and other writers may be "engaged" in what they read and write, but by making their own engagement an important part of their inquiry, they can achieve some understanding of that "distance" commonly described as "aesthetic" or "critical." The perspective tradi- tionally expected of critical reading and critical writing—the quality understood by *critical*, as in "critical thinking"—requires making a distinction between a reader's "subjective" engagement and a more ana- lytical mode of response, commonly believed to be "objective" and produced by "critical distance." But, as Stanley Fish argues about "crit- ical self-consciousness" (*DWCN*, 436–67), such dualistic distinctions, dichotomies, and binary oppositions as *right/wrong*, *accurate/inaccurate*, *proper/improper*, *appropriate/inappropriate*, *text/subtext*, *progress/stagnation*, *sudden/gradual*, *change/stasis*, *individual/social*, *subjective/objective*, and even such inclusive concepts as "intersubjectivity," "intertextuality," "inter- pretive angles," "perspectivism," and "stereoscopy" are perspectival and relational: contingent on changing contexts, assumptions, and purposes.

Though we may still attempt to discover or uncover "subtexts" (in Pinter's plays, in criticism), we must heed Ralph Cohen's caution in "The Statements Literary Texts Do Not Make": "we ought not forget that 'subtext' is a metaphor for an author's unstated, unwritten 'text.' The actual subtext is written by the critic, who, in writing it, becomes himself an author" (381). To define the "subtexts" of Pinter's dramas and writing about them is to rewrite other authors' texts in terms of our own purposes. To define their "contexts" is similarly to rewrite them in terms of our own more current interest in backgrounds.

Any criticism, including metacriticism, is a kind of rewriting. Whether critics aim to define larger issues raised by writers in their perceptions of Pinter's texts, as Austin Quigley has done, or to examine developments and alterations in views of Pinter's plays as instances of literary, critical, and cultural change, as I aim to do, at least in part, in the present study, such writing rewrites what has already been written.

This rewriting can be productive in more than one sense of the word. *Productive* can signify not simply results, but the proliferation of results as well. Pinter criticism proliferates as critics become authors. As I describe the *productions* of critics, I too am *producing* more Pinter criticism, even if I am writing in a metacritical mode. A great deal of Pinter criticism is about other Pinter criticism, and the industry seems self-perpetuating. One of my aims is to investigate *the modes of such production.*

My central metaphor for this inquiry—critical strategies—comes from Pinter's description of "speech" as "a constant stratagem to cover nakedness," in his notion of his audiences' and critics' behavior as "a pretty efficient smoke screen . . . against recognition, against an active and willing participation."[20] Lois Gordon borrowed Pinter's metaphor *stratagem* for her 1969 book, analogizing what his *characters* do and his playwriting techniques—"stratagems to *un*cover nakedness" (emphasis added). In a psychoanalytic sense, I used this metaphor to describe what *critics* (and other members of Pinter's audience) do rhetorically in response to Pinter's plays, their "strategic" defenses against "recognition" of their own emotional involvement in their versions of Pinter's "puzzling world" (see chap. 6).

The writing-as-strategy metaphor has become much more common lately, with images of criticism both as problem-solving and as a smoke screen implicit in much writing about it. These fashions owe much to the interests of critics in psychoanalysis and deconstruction. My continuing use of the metaphor *strategy* may bring to mind, for example, the concept of "textual strategies" presented by Josué V. Harari. *Strategy* has become current (fashionable) in discourse about literature and criticism (as *discourse* has too). Despite the pervasive self-consciousness of today's critical theorists, many seem to use the term *strategy* naively, caught up in the fashion. But for some even choosing a term *because* it *is* fashionable may be strategic. Just as any term borrowed from one field to use in another, this term conveys connotations with which many critics play, as I discuss in my third chapter. They use *strategy* strategically, just as I do here.

Some of the aims of criticism—the aims of critics and scholars—like the aims of Pinter's characters and of most people, are unstated. At times, however, writers do state their aims *in order to* achieve their desired goals. When this happens, their aims may be *strategic*. To search for hidden meanings, unconscious intentions, motivations, the "subjective"—*subtexts*—is to speculate about the unstated. To define *what strategy underlies or lies behind* a particular writer's aims as stated in his or her writing is likewise speculative. Perhaps all knowledge is speculative in some way.

As Kuhn has observed, "the particular conclusions" reached by a scientist working outside his (or her) field of study "are probably determined by his prior experience in other fields, by the accidents of his investigation, and by his own individual makeup" (4). Such variables would seem to affect anyone pursuing—that is, constructing—knowledge. If contexts of investigation are as far-reaching as these, determining *why* a particular investigator has reached particular conclusions seems impossible. The question is ultimately indeterminate. *How* the person did so may be a more feasible inquiry, but stating how requires similarly unverifiable description.

The impossibility of reaching definitive answers to such questions and their unverifiability need not deter us from raising them, from engaging in such speculation, from suggesting some possible answers. As writers, we are all engaged in depicting possibilities, "possible worlds." If we were not to raise such problems and to consider possible solutions, far less would be known, in the sense that we can understand knowledge today. Possibility becomes reality when theory is put into practice, especially if theory is just another "form of practice" (Fish, *DWCN*, 566 n.44).

As I expect the exchanges between Pinter and his critics illustrate, there are no certain answers to such "chicken-egg" puzzles as Which came first? Writerly attitudes or readerly ones?—"Chicken? Egg? Which came first?"[21] Given the Möbius strip of literature and criticism, text and subtext or context, reality and fantasy, truth and fiction, belief and feeling, defense and fantasy, work and play, theory and practice, such questions are so complex that there is no guarantee that verifiable answers can be ever reached, even with further empirical research.[22]

The "essential determinants" of critical "development," to borrow Kuhn's words about scientific inquiry, are as elusive as the essential determinants of any other phenomenon. Instead of trying to determine elusive "essentials" of critical development, it is both necessary and possible to acknowledge that we can only imagine and reconstruct *some* of the contexts in which critical developments have occurred. With these images and these reconstructions we can try to describe some of the sources of this process of change. But it is important to acknowledge that we are reconstructing events and that our descriptions are just that. They are not facts but rather heuristic fictions. They become facts only as we believe in their function as truths.[23]

# 2

## Aims, Kinds, and Contexts

## of Criticism

As far as critics go, I don't pay very much attention to these manifold interpretations. Occasionally, I've had amateur critics send me one or two things which do make a kind of sense, and they're gratifying, but I very rarely get that kind of pleasure from professional critics. —Harold Pinter

If we regard criticism as a genre of writing subject to processes of change like other genres, as Ralph Cohen does, we can understand how kinds or classifications of criticism change "through interrelation and competition." Seeing classifications of criticism as interrelational and competitive and thus "empirical, not logical" suggests connections between critical aims and kinds of criticism. Critical classifications are (in Cohen's words) "historical assumptions constructed by authors, audiences, and critics in order to serve communicative and aesthetic purposes"; we group them "in terms of distinctions and interrelations," and they too "form a system or community" with "social and aesthetic" purposes. Critical groupings, like other categories discussed by Cohen, "arise at particular historical moments," and changes in them occur as they increase in membership and are "subject to repeated redefinitions or abandonment" ("History and Genre," 210).

General statements about criticism or criticism of criticism constitute a genre of writing about writing classified as "metacriticism." Metacritical statements all written at about the same time for Paul Hernadi's collection *What Is Criticism?* make for a handy demonstration of interrelations between critical genres and critics' purposes. Goals defined by this group of metacritics and common to many practicing critics in a variety of contexts have motivated and continue to direct particular Pinter critics, guiding their choices of strategies, as we will see in later chapters.

## What Is Criticism?

Published in 1979, *What Is Criticism?* represents what René Wellek refers to as "a tug of war between the main trends—judicial, personal, scientific, historical" ("Appendix," 320)—a battle for dominance among contending critical goals. The resulting "tension" that Wellek thinks "was still continuing unabated in the 1970s" Hernadi predicts "will animate the pertinent debates of the 1980s as well" (xiv). By now many critics have begun to find this tension in criticism tiresome and yearn for some sort of reconciliation among its warring factions; however, there seems to be no truce in sight. Perhaps, if it is even possible for us to achieve any spirit of cooperation as critics, a starting point could be close examination of the *terms* of our battle. (1) What is at issue, in what language are the issues presented, and how could the conflicts among critical positions on the issues be resolved? (2) If they can be resolved, is it desirable to resolve them? Or, do certain goals of critical inquiry require the current tension in order that they be achieved? (3) If they do require this tension, do we really want to achieve them? Or, do we want to change them? (4) And if we want to change them, what do we want to do instead? Though I cannot address all of these questions at once, I do want to raise them now to direct my inquiry. Here I respond most directly to the first series of questions; yet, some implications relating to the others also arise. (Chap. 10 develops some of these implications further.)

The twenty-three contributions to *What Is Criticism?* exemplify "just about as many critical approaches" (x). In ordering these "polyphonic arguments," Hernadi describes criticism through three figures: "criticism as re-presentation"; "criticism as evaluation"; and "criticism as communication." Prior to three groups of essays highlighting these functions of criticism, several prominent critics ponder the question Why Define Criticism and How? arguing "for and against attempting to say what criticism is" (ix). As Hernadi observes, "the attempt can be made successfully," as "cogent arguments even against defining criticism will tell us a great deal about their not-to-be-defined subject matter." The aims of the critics writing these polemical essays are exposed in the senses of both *exposition* and *exposure*.

As Francis E. Sparshott, John M. Ellis, Stanley Fish, Morse Peckham, and Marie-Laure Ryan answer Hernadi's organizing question Why Define Criticism and How? they articulate strategically a variety of competing and conflicting critical objectives and purposes. An essay in Hernadi's

"Criticism as Communication" section by Mary Louise Pratt presents contextual distinctions that serve as more heuristic devices for exploring interrelations between academic and nonacademic criticism, two traditionally competing genres.

### Francis E. Sparshott:
### Strive for Critical Plurality

Sparshott maintains that it is not difficult to define criticism, but he concludes that reasons for doing so are mostly "bad" ones (13). Before reaching this conclusion, as Hernadi suggests, Sparshott follows the rhetorical strategy of defining what criticism is by looking at what it is not.[1] At first glance kinds of discourse we could confuse with criticism but are not criticism include biography, literary theory, and literary history (9). Since critics' aims are varied, Sparshott implies, no one *single* aim can be *the sole aim* of criticism. Criticism, like other forms of writing, has mixed aims and mixed modes.

A literary work is both "a verbal artefact" and "the utterance of a real person" (10). While critics "may choose to restrict" their "own interest . . . to some one aspect or set of aspects of a work," it is "merely silly" to attempt to *purify* criticism through such restrictions, and any attempts to exclude certain so-called improper interests from literary and critical domains are futile (10). Despite certain regulatory notions of critical propriety, "there can be no method of establishing all and only what has been done in a given work, because no restriction can be set on questions and viewpoints: the critic may have to call on the full range of his sensitivity and experience in the affairs of life as well as in the world of books and the resources of linguistic skill. His limitations will be his limits of skill and personality, or limits he has chosen, not limits imposed by the nature of critical interpretation" (11).

The determinism of "unifying" critical positions like those of Northrop Frye's *Anatomy of Criticism* (1956) or E. D. Hirsch's *Validity in Interpretation* (1967) answers a "[y]earning for a unity in interpretation . . . relevant to the concerns of teachers and students but not at all to that [*sic*] of writers and readers." Sparshott does not identify what he thinks *is* the concern of writers and readers. (This issue is raised by Peckham, as discussed below.) Whereas he designates the "concerns" of teachers and students as plural, he renders "that" of writers and readers as singular. He does not recognize that teachers and students are also writers and readers, just as often writers and readers are also teachers and students. To try to separate these roles as he does contradicts experience. Yet it is a common academic ploy to distance scholars from pedagogues.

For Sparshott critics like Frye and Hirsch exemplify "pedagogic totalitarianism" (12). Frye's "plea" to make the study of literature "scientific" in order to make it "respectable" makes sense for Sparshott only if "the respectability sought is to be wielded in curriculum committees and other battlegrounds of academe." Hirsch's "insistence" on the "priority" of "authorial meaning" depends on "the necessity of establishing one meaning for a text," for Sparshott "a necessity that obtains nowhere outside the examination hall and its purlieus." To this pedagogic totalitarianism and an assumed "academic norm" of "narrow dogmatism" Sparshott relates Roland Barthes's "strategies" in *S/Z* and *Le Plaisir du texte* (*The Pleasure of the Text*). Barthes's lesson replaces "Frye's and Ingarden's hierarchies of levels" with a view of the text as "the locus of intersection of as many cultural 'codes' of reference as our ingenuity may suggest" and allows us "to define the codes in any way compatible with such evidence as we elect to adduce, and to interpret in any way that pleases us the interweavings of what we thus find encoded." While there can be multiple methods of criticism, Sparshott concludes that "no one of them" is "the one method of criticism, and there is no set of methods that comprises the methods of criticism" (13).

In advocating that we not do so, then, Sparshott does specify a method of criticism by implying a particular critical aim. We must strive for a plurality of critical methodologies. We must avoid critical totalitarianism, just as we must avoid pedagogic totalitarianism, in order to reach as "full" an "understanding" of literature as we can. Although he states no explicit interest in regulating criticism, in *making* it democratic, Sparshott's exclusion of the opposite position (a critical monism assuming that one can determine one meaning for any literary work) from his plurality of critical methods amounts to a kind of regulation. To rule out any method advocating itself alone (monism) is an aim of pluralism. But through *this* exclusion pluralists attempt to ensure their own success.

However logically contradictory Sparshott's position may seem, empirically it is "appropriate"; that is, it serves his purpose, which is to exclude the exclusionary. While Sparshott does not give historical reasons to account for the appearance of arguments for pluralism as most appropriate for criticism at this time, others have done so.[2]

## John M. Ellis: Return to the Emphases
## of the Text Itself

Whereas Sparshott considers reasons for defining criticism as bad but ultimately advocates critical pluralism in showing how criticism should *not* be construed, John Ellis considers the same sort of critical diversity but explicitly justifies making normative recommendations about what critics should do on ostensibly "logical" not historical grounds. Logically, he seems to advocate the opposite of pluralism: a critical monism. Yet his so-called logical argument ultimately relies on empirical factors, as he makes historical judgments to support his own normative recommendation for criticism.

Ellis sees no progress or agreement in critical debate since the 1960s, suggesting another context for the proliferation in Pinter criticism cited earlier—critical fragmentation (16). As regards fundamental differences among critical schools, he finds no clarification of the issues involved in criticism; instead, there is "an uncertainty and confusion as to the nature and goals of our field of inquiry which has recently become more, not less, pervasive" (17). New critical positions have recently been "generally partial or peripheral rather than central, often speculative, even eccentric" (16).[3]

Ellis attributes this "perpetual state of confusion and disarray in criticism" not to historical circumstances but to "something inherent in the very question 'What is criticism?' "—to its very "assumptions" (17–18). Unlike Ralph Cohen, he does not identify such assumptions themselves as historical. Rather, he says, the "logical status" of the question makes it "slippery" and not susceptible to a single answer (18). It is *not* the kind of question that can result in "a kind of answer that would be intuitively satisfying as the thing we needed to solve the [jigsaw] puzzle," the kind of answer that "once found, it is obvious that it is the right one"; this kind of question occurs in the form of What is x? (the form of early questions posed by critics regarding Pinter's plays as "crossword" and other puzzles).

It is confusing that "we are not even sure what kind of answer we are asking for: definition, facts, or normative recommendations" (19). Ellis distinguishes between some kinds of answers that claim exclusivity, attempting to "make a legitimate claim to exclude others, and are correct or incorrect to the extent that they constitute the exclusively appropriate answer," and other kinds of answers that "do not necessarily exclude all other answers or derive their validity from being superior to all others" (19). There are, he says, two ways to "conceive of the question 'What is criticism?' ": to require "a single answer," in which case "all attempts to provide it will compete with each other," and to allow "many different answers in which the validity of one is quite independent of the validity of the others."

After stating that "[f]actual statements about criticism . . . do not compete with each other to meet a particular need best" as other factual definitions do (19)—a questionable assumption at best—Ellis proceeds to "normative statements" about criticism. Such assertions "generally recommend that we should see criticism or pursue criticism in this way rather than that" and often involve claims for exclusivity, as in "above all else, criticism is . . ." or "criticism is essentially . . ." (19–20). Constructions like *above all else* and *essentially* render exclusive "statements whose content was otherwise not necessarily exclusive." These critical definitions "represent attempts to set criticism on the right path" (20). They lead to expectations of "an intuitively satisfying, puzzle-solving answer which will take precedence over others," and these expectations are "the most likely source of the tendency to add exclusivity to normative statements even in cases where their content does not automatically require such exclusivity." But, as we will soon see, Ellis moves neither toward changing these expectations nor toward changing the question (or not asking it at all, as, say, Sparshott advocates finally). Ellis is himself striving to reach a particular empirical goal in constructing the logic of his own argument: trying to set up *his own normative recommendation* for what criticism should be and do.

As he argues in *The Theory of Literary Criticism*, Ellis claims here that "the definition of criticism implicit in the actual practice of critics is a hopelessly incoherent one" (22). While "a field of inquiry . . . must . . . focus on a kind and scope of inquiry," he submits that "the source of our problem" is that "the definition of our field, unlike the definitions of other fields, contains no unique focus for our activities" (22). This point rests on another questionable assumption: that these other fields *do* have such a unique focus. Only from outside other fields, to nonexperts, might a field appear so unified. To experts in another field, theirs may seem as "fragmented" as ours does to Ellis.

Not aware of this discrepancy of perspective, Ellis posits this lack of a unique focus as the source of too much variety of critical methods and resulting incoherence in the field of criticism (23). A need to make the incoherent coherent—to unify the disarray, as logic and reason always strive to do—motivates Ellis's own normative recommendation for criticism, which excludes several current critical practices: critics should (re)turn to letting the text "speak for itself" and to paying "close attention to *its* emphases" (24–25; emphasis added).

Ellis's rationalization for this particular normative recommendation (return to the emphases of the text itself) is that "modern critics . . . seem far more concerned to impress than to allow the text to do so, readily substituting their own ideologies and conceptual systems for those of the literary work" (25). The "result" of their various rhetorical faults, he says, "is a veritable caricature of discussion, a reduction of criticism to an entertainment for scholars, a narrowly clubby kind of discourse."

Granting that a variety of ideological concerns ("Marxism, Fr[eu]dianism, feminism, structuralism, or whatever") are at times relevant to some texts ("sometimes they obviously must be"), Ellis is nevertheless troubled when critics indiscriminately apply an "approach with a single set of concerns to texts which all have their own distinct emphases" (26). Yet Ellis fails to acknowledge that he himself is doing what he opposes in the practice of others. While he argues that "[s]train, oversubtlety, reductionism and self-dramatization are all . . . much evident in modern criticism" and that "[c]ritics, rather than literature, are seen as most central in the process of criticism" (27), he does not recognize that his own definition of "actual criticism" as "putting first and foremost the attempt to discern the unique emphases of a given text" reveals the same problems. Claiming his own critical method to be "actual" criticism or assuming its ability to see the "unique" emphases of the text indulges in "exclusive" language whose implications Ellis has so carefully detailed. Such blindness to the inconsistency of his own logic explains why such attempts as Ellis's are "commonly scorned and caricatured," as he goes on to complain.

As Ellis launches into an encomium for his own critical aim, he assures us that though "actual criticism" (the kind that he is recommending) is "often thought of as a 'narrow' pursuit, especially by the more fashionable histrionic critics . . . surely nothing is ultimately more narrow and shallow than a kind of writing which seems designed only to dazzle other members of the critical fraternity" (27). Ellis does not perceive (or, if he does, he does not admit it) that *his own exclusive emphases* have anything to do with such designed dazzling.

The New Criticism—to which Ellis allies "actual criticism"—is not "old-fashioned": "nothing will be as enduring as the plain confrontation of reader and text, the fundamental literary experience which will still be going on long after our current critical fads are forgotten" (27).[4] But he asks why so many critics now "caricature" what he regards as a "simple direct view of the task of criticism" (27). "Because surely," he answers, "to let the text take center stage pushes the critic himself out of that position, and criticism today has become more and more narcissistic" (27–28).

Perhaps, as Sparshott suggests, since no *single* aim can unify us, collectively we must maintain pluralism. But, as Ellis proposes, individually each of us must choose from among competing positions the one (or ones, Sparshott might modify) that most satisfies our own valued needs and goals. Of course it would be foolish to rule out paying close attention to *what one regards as* the "unique emphases" of the texts one is considering. Such attention is generally a *given*, an assumption that goes without stating, of any acceptable method. It would be absurd for critics to argue that their reading of a text did *not* at some stage involve a careful reading of it, a rendering of "its" emphases. But many critics today are especially aware of the degree to which their *own* emphases enter into such a rendering. While these critics aim to begin with the text, most often they want to move *elsewhere* and *beyond* so-called textual emphases to do something different with what they perceive as them (new criticism, as opposed to the New Criticism).

### Stanley Fish:
### Follow the Model of Persuasion

In "Demonstration vs. Persuasion: Two Models of Critical Activity," Fish views criticism as persuasion of others to one's own beliefs. In direct contrast to Ellis, the text is not the center of Fish's metacritical concerns; rather, one's assumptions about texts—contexts—are. As Fish "foregrounds" assumptions, his rhetoric in favor of the persuasion model of critical activity constitutes an exclusive normative recommendation (in Ellis's sense), for Fish proposes criticism as persuasion *in lieu of* criticism as demonstration. Like Ellis, he distinguishes between critical definitions based on "facts" and those based on "assumptions" (though ultimately in this essay Fish transforms assumptions into facts and vice versa). And like Ellis, Fish enjoys the use of logic in his critical arguments. Though accused of being a relativist, Fish, unlike Sparshott, who does advocate a relativistic pluralism (or a pluralistic relativism), explicitly rules out relativism as both a logical contradiction and an empirical impossibility.[5]

Even though Fish begins "Demonstration vs. Persuasion" with a demonstration of the "irreducibly interpretive" (32) debates about symbolism in Blake's "The Tyger"—mixing both demonstration and persuasion— he goes on to argue for a view of criticism as persuasion as opposed to demonstration. His own *assumptions* are "at stake" in his argument just as he says they are "in any critical dispute" (on general implications of Fish's implied game/war metaphor *at stake*, see chap. 3): "[C]ritical disputes are not, properly speaking, about facts but about the varying perspectives from which the facts will look now one way, now another; and therefore the business of criticism is not so much to demonstrate in *accordance* with the facts as it is to persuade to a point of view within which the facts one cites will seem indisputable. Indeed this is the whole of critical activity: an attempt on the part of one party to alter the beliefs of another so that the evidence cited by the first will be seen *as* evidence by the second" (31– 32). These assumptions convert Fish's initial demonstration with Blake criticism into persuasion.

Fish recurrently uses normative recommendations as argumentative moves. Constructions like *properly speaking, business,* and *whole* above suggest the exclusivity that Ellis finds characteristic of such moves. These constructions also call to mind Sparshott's arguments against fixing *properness* (propriety or priority) to one critical methodology or position at the expense of others. Fish's work often studies the so-called normal conventions of criticism, but, as he will claim here, he is also engaged in attempting to alter them. For Fish critical methods that aim to *change* critical *norms* are most "proper," most valuable, or best, and critics who propose to change criticism are most important. The contrast of models that Fish presents (32) generalizes differences between the monistic kind of criticism that Ellis advocates (defining the text's "own unique emphases" should be *the* method of criticism) and the pluralism that Sparshott favors (there can be *many* "methods of criticism" but *no* "one method"). In Fish's terms Ellis uses a demonstration model, whereas Sparshott assumes a model of persuasion.

Fish argues that "the stakes are much higher in a persuasion than in a demonstration model, since they include nothing less than the very conditions under which the game, in all of its moves (description, evaluation, validation, etc.) will be played" (33). As I discuss in more detail in chapter 3, this game metaphor suggests some common assumptions about criticism (the *competitive nature* of the game): criticism is a game of skill (not chance) in which opponents beat each other by clear thinking, wit, and command of the facts; it is not knowledge of the facts alone but also *how one plays the game*—knowledge and utilization of the rules—that enables one to win. One's prowess with words, one's rhetorical skill, and one's assessment of one's opponent (the author, the reader, another critic) lead to victory. Critics are rhetorical combatants.

Exemplifying his own rhetorical combativeness, Fish's characterization of Jonathan Culler's criticism depreciates it: "Culler's model of critical activity is one that will hold for the majority of critical performances; for it is certainly true that most of the articles we read and write do little more than confirm or extend assumptions that are already in place. But the activity that is most *highly valued* by the institution (even if it is often resisted) is more radically innovative. That is, the rewards of our profession are reserved for those who challenge the assumptions within which ordinary practices go on, *not so much in order to eliminate the category of the ordinary, but in order to redefine it and reshape its configurations*" (33; emphasis added).

All criticism (whether demonstration or persuasion, whether "most highly valued" or not) both challenges and redefines what has previously been written. But not all criticism challenges and redefines critical practice, and if we exclude what does not, we limit criticism entirely to what is (according to Fish's analysis) currently valued (in fashion). This has resulted in a kind of academic tyranny, a hegemony of theory—a condition obtaining recently when, as Fish suggests, the "most highly valued" members of our profession are those engaging in theoretical projects. Indeed, as Claude Rawson observes: "The practice of literary theory in universities has become a major adversarial, or countercultural, phenomenon, so major that it has established itself in many places as a new and more powerful Establishment" (9). As a "model," criticism as persuasion is exclusive, like an exclusive men's club, and can be equally elitist.[6]

Fish explains further why "the stakes in a persuasion model" of critical activity are "so high"; it increases the "responsibilities of the critic" so that "rather than being merely a player in the game, he is a maker and unmaker of its rules" (34). This impulse in Fish's criticism seems to model itself after entrepreneurial venture capitalism, subverting the common joke about the "stakes" in academe (Why are academic politics so vicious? Because the stakes are so small). But Fish has raised the stakes

(the rewards) without defining the risks (potential losses). His version of
the critic's activity gives critics a great deal more power than, say, Ellis
would grant them.[7] His metaphor further implies that a "player" in the
"game" can *also* change its "rules." But his own contextual assumptions,
cited in more detail below, suggest that no player is able to get *outside* the
rules (assumptions shared while playing) without also ceasing to play the
game. If a player (a critic) changes the rules of the game, he or she
changes the game (criticism).[8] By dint of this reasoning, Fish seems to
imply that he and Culler are not even playing the same game. While
Fish, it would seem, is playing hardball ("persuasion"), Culler and other
"demonstration" critics, wimpishly, prefer softball. Whereas Fish wants
to play poker with "high stakes" (rhetorical assumptions), others—
perhaps less well endowed (rhetorically)—can only afford to play penny
ante (factual statements).

Even with this persuasion model of what critics do, criticism is still
dependent on "texts, standards, norms, criteria of judgment, critical
histories, etc.," and critics still "can convince others that they are wrong,
argue that one interpretation is better than another, cite evidence in
support of the interpretations we prefer, etc." Fish claims: "it is just that
we do all those things within a set of institutional assumptions that can
themselves become the objects of dispute" (34). We have the same
"things" we had before ("texts, standards, norms, criteria of judgment"),
but sometimes their "form" has changed (34). But for one who has just
claimed that form is a function of persuasion not demonstration, what
can be the practical distinction between "things" such as "texts" and their
"form?" As Cohen suggests, the *form* of texts (their "kinds," or genres)
and all the other "things" Fish mentions (standards, norms, criteria of
judgment) are exactly what is *always* in dispute (changing) in any criticism. Form and fact are critical assumptions too.

Like Fish's other arguments about critical assumptions, here his argument about change (34–37) refers to the knowledge that one's perspective is contextually "situated" (35) or, in other words, perspectively
"limited." Knowledge that a perspective is limited is not the same as
knowing precisely what those limitations are, however; for example, the
"limitations" of one's perspective mentioned by Sparshott ("[the critic's]
limitations will be his limits of skill and personality, or limits he has
chosen" [11]). Nor is it knowledge of the exclusivity limiting normative
recommendations, about which Ellis warns us (21). Without these kinds
of knowledge too, it is unlikely that one's perspective *will* change and

that one will acquire *new* sets of facts. However possible "in theory" it is to change, if one does not recognize these limitations and limits, "in practice" one's views will stay substantially the same (persist). This charge has indeed been leveled against Fish: he is accused of not changing his position and of restating the same beliefs for years.[9]

Perhaps the charge—whether reasonable or not—bespeaks a "limitation" that Fish does not notice. Once one characterizes critical aims in Fish's terms—as persuasive not demonstrative of one's rightness—one can continually claim to make progress when others (like Fanto) will not perceive progress being made. All one does is construct arguments to persuade others of "the same old thing" (an already articulated principle) as it relates to a new subject matter (like "change") in a new guise or context. Whether or not people still *need* to be persuaded becomes of no interest. The arguments are published because they are being made by the Great Persuader, who commands attention because of his prestige and power, as based on earlier "successes." But *if* there is no clear "demonstrable" evidence (other than "earned" professional rewards [*DWCN*, 238]) that any of his work *has actually persuaded* people, then it too is of no special consequence.[10]

Fish's certainty about the nature of belief results in this platitude: "one believes what one believes, and one does so without reservation" (36). Yet Fish's own *lack* of reservation is not certainty but certitude: a *feeling* of certainty about beliefs. This feeling accompanies the criticism of persuasion just as he has been claiming that it characterizes the criticism of demonstration. So he would have us believe that any reservation about his position has "no real force": "The reservation inherent in the general position I have been arguing—that one's beliefs and therefore one's assumptions are always subject to change—has no real force, since until a change occurs the interpretation that seems self-evident to me will continue to seem so, no matter how many previous changes I can recall." By extension, when critics (such as Fish himself) believe in the rightness (or truth) of the arguments they are making, there is no way to convince them otherwise—that is, until they change their own minds.

Fish "does not mean that one is always a prisoner of his present perspective," since "[i]t is always possible to entertain beliefs and opinions other than one's own" (36). "[B]ut," he qualifies, "that is precisely how they will be seen, as beliefs and opinions *other than one's own*, and therefore as beliefs and opinions that are false, or mistaken, or partial, or immature, or absurd." This qualification may apply only to those, like

Fish, who hold their beliefs and opinions with extreme confidence or tenacity. There are many more *degrees* of belief than he suggests.

Because of this feeling about "other" beliefs, Fish goes on to claim, "a revolution in one's beliefs will always feel like a progress, even though, from the outside, it will have the appearance merely of a change" (36). (He gives no example of any such "revolution" in his own beliefs.) Fish's uses of *revolution*, *progress*, and *change* pertain to a consideration of "progress" or "lack of progress" in any kind of criticism (and, therefore, to my study of Pinter criticism). But notice the converse of his point: "from the outside" change can seem only *apparently* to be revolutionary, "merely" as a change that is not radical. This is indeed how Fish has characterized Culler's work. To extend Cohen—the *kind* of change that one perceives also reflects one's assumptions and purposes and other complex interrelations.

Contrary to earlier emphasis on the "logic" of persuasion in criticism, here Fish reveals that all that persuasion depends on are the *feelings* of the persuaded (or the unpersuaded, as the case may be). No matter what one's beliefs, it is always possible to adopt a different set of beliefs, to play the so-called devil's advocate, and to argue the opposite side (as I may or may not be doing now). One's beliefs do not ascertain the success or failure of one's arguments, one's ability to persuade—as any winning debater (like Fish) should be able to tell us. One's *audience* (their beliefs) is more important than Fish allows. Critical progress, or any kind of progress that depends on firmness of beliefs, or some other subjective apprehension of the facts, is not measurable solely as an objective entity, not something quantifiable and susceptible to validation. Indeed, as Fish argues elsewhere (e.g., *Is There a Text*; *DWCN*), the matter of progress is mediated by consensus among "interpretive communities"; hence, it is subject to communal purposes.

Despite this later emphasis on critical consensus as an indicator of change, Fish tends here to consider "progress" only from the perspective of *oneself*: for example, "If one believes what one believes, then one believes that what one believes is *true*, and conversely, one believes that what one doesn't believe is not true, even if that is something one believed a moment ago" (36–37). Fish's tone, his attitude, his felt assumptions—his "emphases"—may be wholly firm and may firmly hold him. But how do we, as his readers, *know* how firmly he actually holds these beliefs or even whether he actually holds them at all: how far he has progressed or whether he has progressed at all?

Fish's "emphases" in his argument that criticism should be seen as persuasion as opposed to demonstration may be convincing but not for the reasons he gives. *Both* models of criticism, demonstration and persuasion, are characterized by critics' statements of belief (or feeling) and contingent on logic, accepted kinds of evidence, rhetorical skill, and audience response. Critics who use them differ in *emphasis*. Moreover, whether one aims to convince others that the text says such and such, or that such and such in the text means something or other, or that these or those are the critical assumptions to hold, the beliefs/feelings of the critic as a person (as opposed to the critic as a persona) matter little to us, since many still simply assume that the critic believes/feels what he or she says; that is a conventional assumption of "traditional" criticism. And, apparently, Fish has not (yet) changed this assumption with which he too operates. But (to extend Fish) even this assumption (that trust) can change, and once it changes (to skepticism), the foundation for Fish's argument about belief weakens. In any case, Fish himself argues more recently, metacritical theory such as his own arguments in "Demonstration vs. Persuasion" and elsewhere "has no consequences for the practice of literary criticism," except for its having become another common critical practice outliving its function if not its fashion (see *DWCN*, 315–41).

### Morse Peckham: Understand the Place of Literature in Human Life

"Three Notions about Criticism" answers "three questions" which to Morse Peckham "exhaust the possibilities of questions about criticism," though he allows that others may not find his answers as "exhaustive" (38): (1) What are the kinds of critical statements? (2) What makes criticism possible? (3) What is the present state of criticism? In answering these questions, as Sparshott, Ellis, and Fish do too, Peckham reveals some of his own critical values.

First Peckham classifies critical statements into three kinds: (1) interpretational statements; (2) judgments of competence; and (3) ascriptions of value (38–40). Then he classifies the first kind—interpretational statements—into two further kinds. In one kind "the critic endeavors to determine, either from internal factors or from factors external to the composition of the work, what were the interests (or, somewhat more grandiosely, the ideology or ideologies) which governed the decisions responsible for the salient semantic attributes of the work, or at least what the critic judges to be the salient attributes" (38–39). In the other kind "the critic uses the work to exemplify his own interests (or ideologies or ideology)" (39). The two kinds of interpretational statement are, however, not entirely different: "Obviously, in the first kind the critic's interests (henceforth, 'ideologies' are to be understood) are also involved, for they govern his decisions about the interests of the writer of the work" (cf. my earlier critique of Ellis). But these two kinds of interpretational statement differ in that "exposure, in the first kind, to other interests can have an effect upon the critics' own interests, even to the extent of loosening (if not freeing) him from his bondage to them, while the second kind is unlikely to have any such corrective effect." Peckham thus suggests that the first kind of interpreter is more "open" to changing his or her mind than the second. Given these distinctions, all the metacritics discussed here—Sparshott, Ellis, Fish, and Peckham— would seem to be presenting themselves as interpreters of the first kind while they perform more like the second.

Concluding emphatically *"there is no immanent or necessary connection between any work of literature and any interpretation of the work,"* Peckham (like Sparshott) finds that the "possibilities of interpreting any work of literature are, if not infinite, at least indefinably great" (39). What he calls "the immense delta-spread of styles emerging in the last two hundred years," paralleling the spread of ideologies themselves, is "the result of the ideology that a competent writer must develop a unique style rather than developing competence in an existent style and then modifying it" (40–41). The emphasis of critics like Ellis on the importance of discovering writers' "unique emphases" has further resulted in "an equivalent delta-spread of rationalizations for judgments of competence," such as Ellis's own argument for an "actual criticism" that attends to these "unique emphases"—perhaps ironic, given his own dismay with critical disarray. Countering this critical trend, furthermore, critics are inclined "to judge that what from one determination of competence is a flaw may indeed have served the writer's interests and therefore be justifiable" (41). What results is what some have referred to as a critical game: "if one values a work of literature, it is not difficult, at least for someone trained and experienced in the rhetoric of literary criticism, either to determine that the ascription of value is justified by the writer's high competence, or that, correspondingly, an ascription of negative value can be justified by a determination of the writer's incompetence" (41).

Such critical gamesmanship leads to ascriptions of value, Peckham's third kind of critical statement. But "there is no necessary connection between judgments of competence and judgments, or ascriptions, of value," since, as Peckham uses his own changing assessments of Dickens's "major" novels to demonstrate, such judgments are "matters of personal history and temperament" (42). Ascriptions of value to literary works, like any other kinds of value judgments, of people, objects, or human activities, are "all the same kind of behavior": what Peckham terms "the value experience." At the *center* of this value experience, Peckham argues, lies "the ascription of value to oneself." (Fish's critical devaluation of Culler's project in *Structuralist Poetics* appears an act of such self-valorization.)

For Peckham literary evaluation, like psychotherapy, places the subject at the center (43). So, not surprisingly, for him the subject—the *person* doing the reading or writing—stands at the center of these debates about literary criticism. What Ellis faults as narcissism is simply a fact about interpretive behavior for Peckham. But, by making the subject "central" to all statements about literature, Peckham uses a maneuver which can only substantiate his own argument (as Sparshott, Ellis, and Fish all do too); namely, the claim that one's own interests are the source of one's judgments. This move enables Peckham to explain change in criticism in terms of the changing psychology of critics (44).[11]

On the analogy of psychotherapy, ascriptions of value in literary criticism create "value-signs" by canonizing some writers both in order to establish such normal constants and in order to ascribe value to oneself in association with others whose ascriptions of value (to oneself) one desires. In literary studies, if one values Shakespeare highly, his value reflects worth on oneself because to value Shakespeare is to align oneself with normal critical value judgments (Shakespeare is a norm against which other writers and readers are measured). Such agreements about value are "an important, even a central, factor in the totality of behavior in response to works of art, and suggest very strongly that ascribing value to others and receiving such ascriptions [are] central to the socializing process." Peckham calls these "interactional (or social) arrangements" an "*agape system*, i.e., the system of interactional and intraactional 'love'" (45). Such a "system" makes us feel that we belong to a group who values (loves) us. (For further discussion of what Barbara Herrnstein Smith calls "contingencies of value," see chap. 9.)

Peckham also considers the kind of critical statement his own essay ("and presumably the other papers in this volume") might exemplify: "If criticism is response to works of literature, then this kind is responses to responses. It can be variously called critical theory, or metacriticism. The history of such metacriticism suggests that it is an activity best subsumed by philosophy, or, to more modern tastes, such as my own, by the behavioral sciences." It would seem that such metacritical statements as those made by Sparshott, Ellis, Fish, and now Peckham, such criticism of criticism, are simultaneously interpretational statements, judgments of competence, and ascriptions of value as well. Perhaps Peckham's position suggests that this intertwining of critical aims and goals is inevitable; no matter how much we strive to separate them in theoretical analysis, in practice (including the writing of critical theory) they seem to merge.

Turning to his second question, "What makes criticism possible?" Peckham gives a "simple and obvious" reply: "we criticize literature because we criticize everything else" (45). It is simply one behavior whose meaning, competence, and value we determine, judge, and ascribe. Behavioral distinctions between "modes of apprehension" as *acts* and as *performances* are at the root of criticism (see 45–48). To criticize is to do both: to act and to perform. When such evaluations buttress practical decisions (e.g., whether to promote the department chairman), decision- or policy-makers forget their metaphoricity and regard them as literal, transforming matters of taste into objective criteria. The change of perspective transforms performances back into actions.

Fish's characterization of criticism in terms of beliefs comes to mind again when Peckham suggests the meshing of action and performance through the example of the man who is lying or the poet who presents sentiments in which he does not personally believe: "Because of this distinction between action and performance we may condemn a man for lying, but admire him for lying so well" (49). It is possible to admire another's persuasive performance and yet to disagree with the beliefs being argued, so as not to be convinced by them. To feel admiration but not conviction is to apprehend the argument as a performance instead of as an action. (When Fanto apprehends Fish's criticism more as a performance than as an action, he questions the sincerity and the value of Fish's "beliefs.")

Similarly, "[w]e can apprehend a literary work as either action or performance" (49). This distinction has consequences for one's own behavior as a critic. Seeing a literary work as *action* affects our interpretive statements about it, our judgments of its competence, and our ascriptions of value to it (49). Ultimately, "to apprehend a work as action is to facilitate our own actions as interpreters and perceivers of competence" (49). Metacritics ultimately regard other critics' and literary artists' performances as action. But as speech-act theory differentiates between performative and nonperformative verbal actions, so it can blur even this distinction between action and performance (see Ryan).

Peckham's final question "What is the present state of criticism?" is loosely connected to his first two questions through his conclusion about the centrality of critics' self-interests in critical value judgments. The present state of criticism is "very unsatisfactory" due to "an economic factor": "the infamous requirement of publication for tenure and promotion of university and, increasingly, college faculty members" (49). [12] In a rhetorical flourish, as he reaches the end of his own *published* essay, Peckham writes: "Publish-or-perish should be recognized as a policy of *publish-and-perish*, intellectually and morally. It is a policy responsible for a moral and intellectual corruption unparalleled even in the higher education establishment of this country" (49–50).

"The major explanation" of these phenomena, Peckham says, is "the peculiar place of literature (and art in general) as an institution in our culture" (50). As art and nationalism displaced religion as the prominent "value institutions" of our time, for many people ("perhaps the majority at the higher cultural level") art became "the dominating value institution." With "indications to the contrary" merely "superficial," in both "academic circles and their non-academic adjuncts (that is, for most writers and critics)," literature is still "a value institution, a source of stabilizing the self-ascription of value" (50–51). In other words, the "interpretational tendencies" criticized by Peckham show no signs of abating, and criticism continues to publicize self-interests of the critics. Critics still engage in "arguments about taste, about which it is pointless to argue."

Peckham is perhaps most damning when he observes, "such arguments are not merely analogous to arguments about whether a candidate for sainthood should be canonized or not; both kinds of arguments belong to the same category of behavior" (51). The "pietistic tone of most criticism and metacriticism" clinches the comparison: "The bulk of literary critics are to literature as theologians are to religion" (51). Since the kind of literary critics Peckham considers here are mostly academic ones, an analogy between sainthood, literary canonization, and tenuring (academic canonization) seems apt. "Publish or perish" becomes "publish and perish" as professors themselves become institutionally canonized texts.

Like the other three metacritics, Peckham concludes with a normative recommendation; in doing so he valorizes a behaviorist view of literature: "Literature, after all, is merely something that some human beings do, the deposit of a particular kind of behavior." His own critical interest, or aim, is to understand "literature's place in human life" (human behavior) and to formulate "firmly grounded" critical theories (51). For Peckham the only firm (proper) grounds for such theories are psychosocial or behavioral truths.

### Contexts of Academic and Nonacademic Criticism

Much of my subsequent examination of Pinter criticism in the body of this book concerns "academic criticism." As Rawson observes, "We live in a time when literary criticism is dominated by the academy" (8). Yet distinctions between "criticism" and "scholarship" are changing, and these activities are undergoing hierarchical shifts, with one being valued more highly than the other and vice versa, though they are not mutually exclusive. [13] Despite its institutional connections to academe, academic criticism resembles what Mary Louise Pratt calls "the one variety of criticism which survives in the realm of mass culture, namely reviewing" (181). Those who juxtapose reviewing and academic criticism generally observe that the "business" of reviewing is "evaluation," while the academic variety is devoted to "interpretation or analysis" (181). This distinction is "inaccurate," as Pratt observes, since it refers solely to superficial functions motivating each kind of discourse. Both academic and nonacademic criticism do "both things" (see 181–83; cf. chap. 9 below).

Traditionally, academic critics have sought to protect their discourse from the commercial contexts of reviewing, which is "shaped by journalism and consumerism," whereas academic criticism is "shaped by the university and by its association with elite art" (183). While "[t]he point of the move into the university was to insulate both criticism and elite art from the direct control of the marketplace, and thus to create a point of resistance to commercialization and commodification of culture," and while "[t]his strategy" has "succeeded" to a degree, economic and cultural forces have encroached upon this systematic insulation. With publications serving as academic "coin and barter" (Peckham's phrase [44]), the "publish or perish" syndrome spoils such academic ideals: "Within the university, the establishment of published criticism as the measure of determining job security, salary, and professional worth has commodified criticism anyway (though at a slight remove from money, since teaching is ostensibly the work for which we are paid)." Even though "[w]e think of criticism as working towards consensus via polemic, and of the university as fostering the free unfolding of this process" of resistance to commercial forces, certain "institutional pressures work in the opposite direction" (cf. Cain, *Crisis*; Watkins). "The equation of publishing with prestige," in Pratt's view, "institutionalizes a need for the proliferation of criticism," giving "every critic *a stake* in the idea of criticism's inexhaustibility, the potential infinity of interpretation, the need for as great a plurality as possible" (183–84; emphasis added).

The consequences of such institutionalized critical plurality include, on the positive side, encouragement to expand into "minor genres" and "mass art," and on the negative side, "overspecialization and complacency rather than consensus-oriented debate" (184). "Certainly Wayne Booth's recent characterization of criticism as a 'melee' threatening to become 'a free-for-all prizefight among blindfolded sluggers swinging at the air' [Booth, *Critical Understanding*, 6–7] rather overdramatizes what goes on in the arcadian pastures of our scholarly journals, though he is right about the blindfolds."[14] What strikes Pratt most about "the academic context" of criticism is that its "strategy for insulating elite art and criticism from commodification" has also isolated them from what happens outside the academy (184).

Focusing on "the elite canon" also associates academic criticism mostly with past literature, "as commentary long after the fact of composition." But the study of the criticism of any contemporary author (Pinter, e.g.) can alter this "tendency" to regard the "main task" of criticism as "mediating contemporary reception of past works" by associating academic criticism with "the concept of a criticism that also participates in ongoing, co[n]temporaneous artistic production" (184–85). In turn this association can discourage "[t]he tendency to sever culture from social life" (185) and reconcile academic with other kinds of criticism.

If "the commonplace assumption that what the critic does is determined by the works of art themselves" serves as "[a]nother powerful strategy reinforcing the isolation of criticism" (186), then to subvert this assumption will also undermine this strategy and reintegrate academic criticism with the "other" kind, reviewing. To vary Pratt's theme: however "elitist" critics (and even sometimes authors like Pinter) are, like "pop" art and culture, criticism "which is part of daily, unspecialized social experience" is worth "taking seriously" too. It is ironic, as Pratt claims, that "to the extent that academic criticism implies or even disseminates [the opposite view], it supports the very commercial interests it elsewhere undertakes to resist" (186).

These "commercial interests" are contexts of both academic and nonacademic criticism. They motivate the kinds of "fashions" discussed earlier: the stifling trends that Schroll perceives in Pinter criticism and that Quigley attributes to Pinter critics' limited views of language. As long as publishing is a commercial enterprise, and universities, despite their nonprofit status, compete for manuscripts on which to emboss their press imprints (as well as for funds and student populations), criticism is a kind of reviewing as well as a kind of academic discourse.

"Reviewmanship . . . is a body of techniques that enable one to mobilize the book review in the service of personal objectives. Practitioners of Reviewmanship recognize that the primary purpose of reviewing a book is to display one's talents, punish an enemy or achieve power," Lingeman tells us, listing a variety of the "stratagems" in "bygone literary wars" and further skills of this "game" (683). [15] In Lindenberger's terms, so far this chapter might be seen as a kind of extended review of parts of *What Is Criticism?*—it does quite a lot of summarizing, some niggling, and a bit of displacing, though it is not an "All-Outer"—"Notable above all for its totality of response, which manifests itself in an unmitigatingly positive or negative form" (43–44). Of course, my own primary purpose here relates to the larger aim of my book on Pinter criticism: to place Pinter criticism in critical and cultural contexts.

### Concentric/Consensus Criticism

Peckham suggests that something in the human nature and society of critics empowers their "tug of war." Allying Foucault with Marx, Terry Eagleton presents economic conditions as the source of this competition. Although, as Karel Kosík has argued, human beings make sociohuman realities like economic conditions themselves (though not the natural realities on which they are based), many people feel powerless to alter them once they have taken hold. While it may seem hard, even impossible, and perhaps undesirable, to suggest a resolution to the dramatic rhetorical struggle that *What Is Criticism?* represents, to speculate what we might do if we wanted such resolution at least implies that we possess some force to do it.

Eagleton proposes reinventing rhetoric because it "might contribute to making us all better people" (*Literary Theory*, 210). He does not define what he means here by "rhetoric" (or, for that matter, by "better people"); it "might equally as well be called 'discourse theory' or 'cultural studies' or whatever" (210). In his usage *rhetoric* seems to subsume *literature*, marking a critical trend whose influence is pervasive. As I suggested earlier, the theory hegemony has become the rhetoric hegemony. [16]

David Shumway's claim that "new literary theory is *more rhetorical* than recent composition theory" ("Unified-Field Theory," 63) conveys a competitive thrust, though the rest of his argument aims to show potential "agreement" between what Shumway sees as two disparate fields in need of unification. By speaking of "the new rhetoric" and "the new literary theory" as things already in existence, he tends to reify them even though he intends to oppose reification of what they study. Kathleen McCormick, according to her own analysis, is also "falling into these patterns" of "talking about textual features as if they did exist objectively, independent of certain conventions of reading" so as to "sound more like structuralists," which "attests both to the residual power of positivistic discourse and to the difficulty of developing new discourses" ("Introduction," 4). [17]

In their own attempts to generate "new discourses," some feminists hope to alter human nature and social and economic conditions from being predominately competitive (territorial), stereotypically or prototypically masculine ("masculinist"), to being predominately cooperative (nurturing), feminine ("feminist"). This normative impulse, outspokenly ideological, aims at no less than saving the human race from extinction. Some feminists have themselves, however, manifested a competitive attitude in their attempts to displace the masculinist Establishment, promoting one territorialism at the expense of another, championing their own feminism over other feminisms. In terms of a Marxist "dialectic," the antithesis that these "oppositional" feminists attempt to institutionalize annihilates what it opposes in the process of constructing a new synthesis based on ethical concerns for the social welfare of women. Other feminists view "androgyny" as the panacea: together people no longer distinguished in terms of male and female traits but as men and women constituting humankind will save themselves (and the world) by combining the best of both genders. This synthetic tendency is mostly cooperative, "dialogical" not dialectical, though it too must compete with what it strives to change. [18]

Some critics of modern and postmodern literature, contrary to those of Marxist and feminist inclinations, might argue against seeking dialectical or dialogical resolutions. But, like Culler and Fish, they may feel that all we can do is to recognize "what is at stake" in taking one or another side in this "tug of war" and keep on fighting for what we believe is "right." [19] Such entrepreneurism maintains the mainstream (masculinist) critical mode, however such critics seek to realign themselves otherwise with the current institutional successes (and, hence, power) of neo-Marxisms and feminisms.

Some feminist "dialogicians" are working toward an innovative, mutual cooperation, such as Bleich also advocates in *The Double Perspective* in his opposition to grading and his valorization of group classroom work. While recognizing the context of competitiveness in criticism and the ameliorative function of some critical conflicts, we can refuse to play tugs of war, aiming instead to achieve a more ethical and caring society than the masculinist critical mode has so far produced. Perhaps with rhetorical armaments, as with nuclear ones, in the context of "conventional warfare," "nonproliferation" and "mutual deterrence" can resist both annihilation and assimilation. A kind of critical eclecticism incorporates the strengths of viewpoints without having to adopt (and defend) their weaknesses. Adapting them to our own purposes, we transform them, "disarm" them, as it were. [20]

As in any conflict, any institutional "drama," if we want to participate, we must choose our roles responsibly, commit ourselves to learning and performing them, and play them to the limit, before choosing (or inventing) a new set of roles we like better, or retiring from the stage entirely. Or, in terms of the criticism-as-game metaphor, if we don't like the rules, we can either change them or play some other *version* of this game. I say another *version* not another *game* to accommodate Fish: "whatever [commentators] do, it will only be interpretation in another guise because, like it or not, interpretation is the only game in town" (*Is There a Text*, 355). Perhaps, like some students of literary studies who have switched to other fields of endeavor, we would find that, though some of the rewards may be different, the new game plan also projects some challenging goals whose realization calls more for cooperation than competition. To offset divisive rivalries for predominance among competing individuals and "schools" of critical practice, we can construct and participate in mutually collaborative projects. Such projects will enable us to develop increasingly larger interactive critical networks—*concentric circles* bridged by broader and more culturally encompassing objectives. We can replace "excentric criticism" with "concentric criticism" and "strange" or "antagonistic" texts with more "friendly" ones. Critics must reconstruct their "game" as a more collaborative and consensus-governed enterprise. How this reconstruction might enhance the ethics of criticism is a matter for later speculation (see chap. 10). My next chapter, "Criticism as Strategy" considers extensions of this metaphor to criticism and some of its implications for Pinter criticism.

# 3

## Criticism as Strategy

I'm willing to accept any challenge, any stakes, any gauntlet you'd care to fling down. What have you done with your gauntlets, by the way?—*Monologue*

The term *strategy* is widespread in a great variety of disciplines—as diverse as foreign policy studies, military science, legal affairs, business management, and literary criticism—and in both scientific and humanistic discourse. [1] Josué V. Harari sees his controlling metaphor *strategies* in *Textual Strategies: Perspectives in Post-Structuralist Criticism* as "the common denominator" in the essays collected (12). In "Critical Factions/Critical Fictions" he cites dictionary definitions of *strategy* and *stratagem*: "*Strategy* [fr. Gr. *strategia*. See STRATAGEM] 1. The science and art of employing the armed strength of a belligerent to secure the objects of a war. 2. Use of stratagem, or artifice. . . . *Stratagem* [fr. Gr. *stratos* army and *agein* to lead] 1a. An artifice or trick in war for deceiving and outwitting the enemy. 1b. A cleverly contrived trick or scheme for gaining an end. 1c. Ability to devise cunning plans to gain an end. 2. obs. A violent and bloody act. [Slaughter; execution.]" (Harari, 32, citing *Webster's International Dictionary*). Then he presents "the various critical strategies at play" (68) among such writers as Roland Barthes, Jacques Derrida, Paul de Man, Michel Foucault, and Gilles Deleuze. In his final section, like Booth (as cited by Pratt in chap. 2), Harari compares criticism to boxing: "It remains to inscribe these strategies in a more global framework, to put them in the ring of criticism as it were, and to determine how the rounds are to be scored. It is not a matter here of declaring one critic the winner and another the loser—in this game, everyone is eventually a loser—but of defining precisely *what is at stake*: in this case a definition of a postmodern critical attitude and a perspective on the critical implications it brings forth" (Harari, 68–69; emphasis added). Harari's phrase *what is at stake* is characteristic of poststructuralist criticism and theory. [2] Such definitions of so-called conventional and postmodern critical attitudes aptly describe some recent Pinter criticism.

The more "traditional" stance has "confidence in the text" and "takes the text at face value: it hides nothing and has nothing to add beyond what it declares explicitly" (Harari, 69). Such criticism provides "a transparent communication, an order to things, an ideology, and a truth. Thus when it attempts to reconstruct and explain a work, criticism becomes a reassuring operation" (69). This attitude characterizes much early critical writing about Pinter and some writing still being done, as we will see in later chapters.

Such a "satisfied attitude" contrasts to the "much more problematic" one which Harari considers "today's representative critical view" (69). Derrida's conception of the text as a concealer of "the rule of its game" results in a critical stance that, in the words of René Girard, tries "to discover what the work omits as much as—if not more than—what it includes" (69, 69 n.78). For Derrida and Girard, Harari says, a text is "constituted more by concealment than by revelation," and "critical activity is structurally linked to this concealment" (69–70). Such criticism has "two immediate corollaries, namely, (1) that critical activity does not receive its legitimacy exclusively from the text being commented upon, and (2) that critical discourse can no longer aim at completely mastering a text" (70). Despite the negations in these corollaries, supposedly they provide "a profound and . . . positive rethinking of the nature of the critical activity" (70). This rethinking has been attempted in recent Pinter criticism, as we will see in a moment.[3]

As we would expect from our previous metacritical discussion in chapter 2, while there may be an indefinably great variety of critical attitudes, those that Harari defines are two broadly "opposing" ones. While he says that he himself aims "to present and explain the various problematics at play in post-structuralism," he also says that he recognizes the strategic impulse of his own critical presentation: "all criticism *is* strategic. To the question: how should the critic approach knowledge? I know of only one answer: *strategically*. The power and productivity, the gains and losses, the advances and retrenchments of criticism are inscribed in this term: strategy, reminding us of its obsolete—obsolete?—definition: 'A violent and bloody act.' In the game of knowledge, method has become a strategy: the 'violent and bloody' agent by which criticism *executes* the work and in so doing, paradoxically, canonizes it" (71–72). As Harari does here, stressing the strategic value of critical presentations actualizes the metaphor of criticism as strategy common in many poststructuralist writings: rhetorically, it pits critic against author, text, and other critics.

Two writers have recently applied this metaphorical conception of strategy to Harold Pinter's writing. Exemplifying what Harari calls "today's representative critical view," Guido Almansi and Simon Henderson see "Pinter's idiom" as an "essentially human" one of "lies and stratagems" and, as such, as a *competitive* mode. In the so-called paradoxical logic of deconstruction, they view Pinter as "unreliable and conscientious about advertising his unreliability" *and* "honest in revealing his dishonesty" (13). They reject those critical approaches to Pinter that regard him as "avant-garde," those that habitually "search for a meaning and a message," and those that "search for motivations, for psychological or psychoanalytic causes, for some kind of intellectual or emotional rationale that could help us explain why these strange beings, the Pinterian heroes, behave as they do (a *normal* key for their *abnormal* behaviour)" (14–16).

Almansi and Henderson reject the role of the critic as "the motivemonger who tries to join the dots and complete the picture, filling the gaps in the overall view, adding motivations to the character's actions, causes to his emotions, pretexts to his whims, reasons to his ideas, fuel to his passions" (17). Instead they stress "the role that strategy—rather than psychology—plays in [Pinter's] characters' behaviour": "Pinter criticism has a better contribution to make—through our understanding of the *strategic* purpose of dialogue rather than through our involvement with the characters' *emotional* needs" (18; emphasis added).

This direction (aiming to understand dialogue as strategy) is a reaction to earlier Pinter criticism, comparable to Quigley's emphasis on the "interrelational" function of dialogue. Citing Barthes, Almansi and Henderson observe: "The death of the author in post-modernist times has given rise to a corresponding birth of the reader" (18, 102 n.8). They explain the changing reception of *The Birthday Party*, for example, in terms of this development in criticism: "It is significant . . . that *The Birthday Party*—despite its initial failure—should, over the years, have become a commercial success, for this is a play which, more than any other on an English stage, heralded the triumphant emergence—or perhaps renaissance—of the reader-*participant* who contributes to the meaning of the text, and the belated exit of the passive reader, the reader-*consumer*" (19). The "excitement" of Pinter's text, they propose, "lies in the mental speculation it provides, not in the dull text itself" ("Nothing is duller *per se* than a piece of Pinterian conversation"); Pinter's text, they suggest, "is like conceptual art, where the focus lies on our reaction to the object, not on the object itself" (19).

In words strikingly like those of Harari on the "game" of criticism cited earlier, Almansi and Henderson describe contemporary writing as "strategy": "One clue to reading the text is to recognize that all the plays are apparently given over to the singleminded preoccupations of *strategy*" (19). Thus, Pinter's reader or audience member, like Pinter and his characters, "must be cunning, aiming to penetrate diagonally in the cleft between expression and emotion, in the fissure between what is uttered and what is meant" (21). They justify "the dishonest obliqueness" of their "post-modernist" approach to Pinter:

> We do not pretend to crack any linguistic or psychological or symbolic or allegorical or anthropological or psychoanalytic code, for the very good reason that we do not believe any such general code exists (and, if it were to exist, it ought not to be broken, the penalty being the destruction of the text). We are inviting the readers to fight with an antagonistic text which refuses to take a collaborative stance with anyone: hence we are urging them to *a battle that can only be lost* (like Jacob fighting with the angel). Pinter's plays are powerfully persuasive, provided that we do not ask ourselves the final question: what (truisms apart) is it that we hope to be persuaded of? In this respect Pinter's plays are post-modernist texts, rejecting all conciliatory blandishments of an audience, all friendly gestures towards readers ever so willing to suspend their disbelief. The plays are meant to create bafflement, irritation, fear, a general sense of impotence, feelings of helplessness, a seething resentment, an acrid hostility. (21; emphasis added)

In terms again recalling Harari, Almansi and Henderson oppose Pinter's text to "[t]he Romantic text," which "went out of its way to seduce the passionate reader into sharing the exhilarating experience of its heroes"; in contrast, they observe, "the post-Romantic writer, and Pinter in particular, requires brave spectators who are ready to face the vacuum of their own intelligence, the failure of their own perspicacity, the brutality of their own emotions" (22). Citing Pinter's description of the audience's laughter at a production of *The Caretaker* as "a mode of precaution, a smokescreen, a refusal to accept what is happening as recognisable," they agree that the audience's avoidance is strategic: "a simple defence mechanism, a Freudian resistance not so much against the text as against their reaction to the text."

Almansi and Henderson previously disavow an interest in psychology and psychoanalysis, but they also *deny* issuing "a manifesto of anti-psychologism" (18). Here they find such metaphors consistent with their own emphasis on strategy. Yet, against the concept of defensive strategy found in psychoanalytic descriptions of behavior, unlike Peckham (as discussed in chap. 2), they prefer a more philosophical approach. They emphasize the dishonesty and cynicism of people in general, finding Pinter the inheritor of "part of this great lesson of cynicism." Despite their own use of a psychoanalytic metaphor ("defense mechanism"), then, they argue that Pinter's plays "can be seen as violently anti-psychological, and hence impervious to most traditional critical approaches" (23).

With this move they judge it futile "[t]o search for psychological plausibility, behavioural congruity, confessional eloquence or epistemological clarification" in Pinter's plays; futile to pursue "the quest for social realism, psychoanalytic symbolism, anthropological allegorism or ideological commitment": "Such searches and quests," they say, "satisfy the critic's vanity but dull the reader's sensitivity to the text." Instead, they feel that "Pinter is clearly playing a different game, one meant for poker-faced hustlers and card-sharpers, not for bingo players or crossword enthusiasts." As critics, their aim is "to be as devious as he."

These metaphors recall language in which reviewers first described Pinter and his plays. In such early criticism Pinter was compared to a "magician" and said to have "tricks" up his sleeve, called a "trickster" and a "conman," and mistrusted as devious in his "gamesmanship" and "sleight of hand." When reviewers compared his plays to crossword puzzles with missing clues, they regarded them (inappropriately, many have argued) as problems demanding definitive solutions (what Ellis calls what-is-x? questions).

In contrast to these reviewers of the early 1960s, Almansi and Henderson admire Pinter's gamesmanship. This change parallels already cited changes in critics' attitudes toward Pinter's ambiguity: what was previously considered a fault now appears a virtue. Whereas at first Pinter was chastised for creating insoluble puzzles, later they were considered appropriately "postmodern." Rejected as "incomprehensible" in the fifties, praised as "avant-garde" in the sixties and seventies, Pinter began losing his "avant-garde" status in the late seventies and early eighties, moving into the "mainstream." With the advent of postmodernism and poststructuralism, critics began to see him as less revolutionary and more part of the status quo. But even this perception of Pinter is changing as his more explicit "political" interests move him to the forefront of controversy in the nineties (see chap. 8).

### Rhetoric of Strategy/Strategy of Rhetoric

Harari's conception of criticism as strategy—"All criticism *is* strategic" (72)—applies to Almansi and Henderson's book on Pinter. Whether critics aim to be oblique and devious, as Almansi and Henderson claim to do, or whether they aim to reveal Pinter's "meanings" and "messages" more directly, as more "traditional" critics do, all critics *are* writers. A common rhetorical term for their intention is *aim* or *purpose*; from a rhetorical angle all writers have some aims or purposes (Kinneavy, 48–72). Like other kinds of writing, criticism too has rhetorical contexts, and, like other writers, critics choose rhetorical devices strategically to achieve their goals according to their purposes.[4] As we have already seen in chapter 2, critical writers say that they aim to achieve or accomplish specific tasks, for specific purposes, for specific audiences (both real and imagined), in specific contexts, out of specialized interests. And just as the metaphorical language employed by early Pinter reviewers was rhetorical in purpose, so is more extended, academic Pinter criticism. Criticism is rhetorical: goal-directed, interested; in short, strategic.

From this vantage point we can read Gale's review of Almansi and Henderson. After describing the spread of approaches to Pinter's work since 1969, Gale observes that these approaches "have ranged from thematic (Gale) to Freudian (Gabbard), mythic (Burkman), linguistic (Quigley), production (Sykes), and existential (Kerr). There have been historical, structuralist, computer-analysis, and reader-response studies" (143). Though "[t]his output does not mean that there is nothing new to be said about Pinter, of course," Gale concludes that "Almansi and Henderson's *Harold Pinter* cannot be justified on the grounds of providing important new insights." While "interesting," it is "not . . . indispensable" (144). Yet Gale himself places this evaluation of Almansi and Henderson, who reject the "thematic approach" to Pinter, in the context of his own "strategic" interests in this particular approach when he acknowledges his own thematic "bias" (see chap. 5 for further discussion).

Rhetorical distinctions between "writer-based" discourse and "reader-based" discourse can sharpen the various classifications of writing by and about Pinter. In "writer-based prose" writers assume that readers already understand what they have to communicate, whereas in "reader-based prose" writers write more with readers in mind. Writer-based prose, more private in its symbolism and meanings, is less accessible to understanding than reader-based prose.[5] Pinter has said that he writes *only* for himself ("Writing for Myself," 175). Whether or not this is so (and his emphasis was likely hyperbolic to indicate his priorities at the time), many have felt that Pinter aims more to satisfy his own needs as a writer than theirs. In this sense Pinter's writing has been more "writer-based" and "writerly" than "reader-based" and "readerly," though, with regard to his most recent work, this distinction is becoming obsolete as well.

Though "aims of discourse" do "overlap," Kinneavy separates them "in order to study them in a systematic manner" (60). Likewise, while he acknowledges that the "modes of discourse" also "overlap," he argues that "in a given discourse there will often be . . . a 'dominant' mode" (37). When the "aim" of such discursive modes is "scientific," furthermore, "narration becomes history, description becomes analysis or description, evaluation becomes criticism, and classification becomes theory."[6]

Kinneavy's *Theory of Discourse* "rests on the assumptions of New Criticism"; it is "essentially moralist and could lead its adherents away from genuine pluralism" (Hunter, 279, 280). His "uncritical acceptance of the claims of formal logic" leads him to "overlook the rhetorical foundation" of both informative and scientific referential discourse, his theory neglects "situational and intersubjective" contexts in advocating the so-called objective theory of literature, and his hierarchical positioning of aims renders the persuasive aim least significant "and probably arranges the others, in increasing importance: expressive, literary, referential" (281, 285). With regard to "overlapping aims," Kinneavy questions the efficacy of mixing aims and tends toward a singularity of aim that accords privilege to "the positivist, the monist, the scientist" at the expense of "the artist and rhetorician" (286); to resolve these difficulties Hunter advocates a theory of writing based more upon reading than speaking, on what he calls "enhanced literacy" (287).

Extrapolating from Hunter, we can view critical writing in general and writing about Pinter's plays in particular as a kind of "enhanced literacy." Such writing is produced with mixed aims, results in mixed modes, and can be distributed through mixed media. Books and articles on Pinter are mixtures of historical and personal narrative, analytic description, evaluative criticism, theoretical classification; their contexts are often both academic and nonacademic. As with any given discourse, while the medium in which writing about Pinter's plays is communicated at first may seem singular (e.g., a written speech by Pinter), dissemination through a variety of media will mix these contexts, as when his now often cited speech presented first to a "university" audience in 1962 was later circulated to a broader audience through publication in the London *Sunday Times* ("Between the Lines") and then revised and recirculated to a more "elite" community of both academics and nonacademics through publication in *Evergreen Review* ("Writing for the Theatre").

Some of the writers' aims and modes may seem more dominant than others *to some readers* depending on their relative perspectives. Often we take a portion of a piece of writing about Pinter's plays "out of context" when we see it as a passage of description or evaluation or history or theory and compare it to other passages of this kind in others' writing. And we characterize an entire piece of writing as more in one "critical mode" than another (as, say, an example of "linguistic" or "psychoanalytic" criticism) if its writer states that he or she intends to use one such "strategy" more than any other, or if *we* see the piece of writing as *related* to others *in kind*.

My own classifications of writing about Pinter's plays begin with critics' *stated* aims and modes, but of course these categories are ultimately interpretive—related to my own knowledge and interests and habits of perception and to interpretive communities to which I myself belong. My groupings of Pinter criticism are instrumental; they are meant more for convenience than as absolute, unchanging, or unchangeable. They are not irrevocable. Whether or not others find them useful too depends on more than my skill in presenting them: it depends also on commonality or intersections of knowledge, experience, perception, purpose, and sense of community. Anyone else's willingness to share my categories is a result of such interrelations.

As cited earlier, Almansi and Henderson deconstruct the contradictions of Pinter's stance: he is "unreliable and conscientious about advertising his unreliability" *and* "honest in revealing his dishonesty" (13). Such critical oxymorons represent the futility of any attempt to determine whether Pinter (or any other writer deemed postmodern) means what he writes or says. Some mixture of both skepticism and trust (skepticism/trust) characterizes so-called postmodern interpretation.

Meaning—both in the sense of interpreting writers' aims from their discourse and in the sense of interpreting larger texts within our cultural discourse—becomes a moot issue. To make this claim is, however, to say something meaningful about the nature of meaning as it is often regarded today.

Generally, postmodern investigations (including now "post-contemporary interventions") do not claim to *aim purposely* to resolve the issue of meaning. One of their tenets is that the issue of meaning *cannot* be resolved. Attention presumably turns elsewhere. But in such criticism the language or "operation" of contradiction "resolves" the problematical interpretive unresolvability. By expressing paradox these critical writers attempt to confront the problematical. By a trick of discourse, suspending former rules—or, in Derridean parlance, putting these concepts "under erasure" (~~literature~~; ~~criticism~~)—they raise such problematical concepts *as* problematical. Of course, a Derridean position is a position, and a Derridean reading is a reading from a position, as any critical reading (unless confused) is. And a *deconstruction* of a Derridean ~~position~~ is a reading of a position from a position. But Derrida has even put "the concept of the *position*" under erasure and would rather "leave *open*" discussion of "this question" (*Positions*, 93–96).[7] There are common ground rules in the postmodern critical inquiry—commitments to intellectual positions shared by writers who wish to be associated with one another. These commitments, like those motivating criticism written at any other time, still affect critical writing. Fidelity to sets of principles and persuasions still influences a writer's aims and methods and the statements ultimately published. Writing on Freud's famous Wolf Man analysis, sidestepping paradoxes of his own rhetoric, Fish asserts: "*One who has learned the lesson of rhetoricity does not thereby escape the condition it names. . . .* [O]ne cannot get to the side of rhetoric" (*DWCN*, 552–53).

Writing is rule-governed modes of behavior, and genres are classes of writing defined by specific operations—classifications that change as certain characteristics change or are perceived to change. Rules of rhetoric are generic rules applying to the analysis of writing behavior, so in analyzing writing rhetorically we borrow terms from rhetorical analysis. Rhetorical terms like *context, aim, purpose, audience, stance, attitude,* and *strategy* are used descriptively and analytically across a variety of disciplines. But writing considered as a kind of verbal performance widens what Mailloux calls "rhetorical action," and modes of analysis from other fields such as linguistics, psychoanalysis, cognitive psychology, and philosophy come "into play." Allying semiotics with discourse analysis within various cross-disciplinary paradigms, for example, critics and scholars are attempting to provide insights about a common human endeavor. Such various "fields of play" provide a powerful arsenal of rhetorical weapons against what critics perceive to be the strategies and tactics of a writer like Pinter. Working at what some regard as "his" game, they put Pinter "in play."

### Pinter as "a Working Man": The Power of Authorship

While Pinter is not generally inclined to discuss the criticism of his plays, David T. Thompson acknowledges Pinter's special "delight" in providing "information" for *Pinter: The Player's Playwright*, a study of (in Thompson's words) "very strong [creative] connections between Pinter's work as an actor and his plays" (viii, 126). Though Pinter admitted recognizing "a connection between his work as an actor and his plays," he himself "could not precisely analyse" it.[8] Thompson aims "to explore the connections between actor and playwright acknowledged by Pinter" especially "to refute the line of attack" against Pinter's plays as *merely* playable exercises for actors (3). Let us explore one of these connections between actor and playwright from another angle.

Pinter has said that he regards himself as "nothing more than a working man" ("Speech," 3). As a working man, he has had to develop strategies of finding work in order to make his living. In this respect he appears no different from many of the rest of us working people. For most of us no matter how poor or wealthy we may have become—and of course these terms are relative—there are times when what we do is immediately connected to earning money to pay the rent. Making a living, first as an actor and then as a playwright, was an early preoccupation of Pinter's, and Pinter's early professional career as an actor and writer was marked by this concern. Beginning in 1949, for about ten years, often through handwritten letters, Pinter pursued contacts at BBC Radio and Television in order to secure acting jobs and writing commissions. From 1958 to 1960 the BBC Radio Department reviewers' written reactions to the synopses for *Something in Common* (a radio play that Pinter proposed writing but apparently never completed and that the BBC eventually dropped), *A Slight Ache*, and *A Night Out* document some heated controversies about the value of Pinter's writing at that time. Yet Pinter and his supporters persisted. With the aid of producer R. D. Smith, script editor Barbara Bray, and assistant head of radio drama, Donald McWhinnie (over the objections of Val Gielgud, head of radio drama), from 1958 to 1960, *A Slight Ache* and *A Night Out* were submitted, commissioned, accepted, and produced.[9] Starting in 1959, with the successful broadcast of *A Slight Ache* on the Third Programme, and increasingly after the radio success of *A Night Out* and the stage success of *The Caretaker* in 1960, Pinter obtained paid interviews promoting his career as a playwright. Radio, television, and theater producers began courting Pinter. When he turned to writing screenplays for films, mostly adaptations of others' novels (starting with *The Servant* [1963]), he began making a more substantial income than he was making from writing plays. He is still engaged in the more lucrative ventures for film more than in work for the stage.[10]

Pinter's strategies as a working man provide another context for understanding his attitudes toward his plays and the criticism of them. As a professional writer, Pinter has something in common with the professional writers in universities and colleges whom we call "academic" literary critics or scholars and with the other professional writers or "nonacademic" critics, the journalists who interview him or review his plays for the "popular" press. "Independent" or free-lance writers and those employed by newspapers, magazines, or academic organizations— all do work of "mixed modes." Some academics teach so that they can do their research; some write so that they can teach; some have a more integrated approach to their work, seeing themselves as professionals who both write and teach, thus achieving a balance in their priorities. Playgoing is part of the *work* (not "merely" pleasurable entertainment, or play) for many critics in the academy as well as for the writers for the more popular press. Whether or not they "love" their work, they all must develop strategies in their development of their careers. They do their writing in this larger professional context. In this context of professional "life and death," Harari's description of critical method as a "violent and bloody" agent executing and, paradoxically, canonizing the literary work may seem apt; this view makes criticism appear less whimsical, less playful, and more "deadly" serious an enterprise than his play metaphors do. Despite my own playful use of these metaphors, I know that putting Pinter "in play" involves a great deal of hard work, and sometimes even strife.

The opposite of play is not work, but reality (Freud, "Relation"). A way to reconceive the relation between work and play is not to see them as opposites at all, but to see them as complements, whereby work and play *enable* each other. Likewise, writing is both work and play; when engaged in the act of writing, on various levels and to various degrees, writers experience both pain and pleasure, struggle and enjoyment. One could extend this double perspective to playwriting (as Pinter himself has done).[11] This view also pertains to critical writing about plays. There is a mutual relationship between the playwright and the critic by which each one enables the other. When viewed this way, playwright and critic appear less competitive and combative, and "strategy" gives way to cooperation, even collaboration.

## Power and Strategy Relations of Authorship

Though it is obvious that one reality of the writer's occupation is economic, we do not always remember that as working people—those who make their living from writing, whether employed by others or "self-employed" (free-lance)—all writers are "working class," if not always "lower class," as, it is often pointed out, Pinter (whose father was a tailor) began. For many the "profession" of teaching writing and literature has become close to a lower-class occupation in terms of widespread unemployment and noncompetitive wages; for others, both inside and outside the academy, writing is a lucrative "venture," earning its practitioners large incomes and raising them to higher economic class status.

Like our economic status, our political status is a function of our relation to other members of our society, and it is a relation of power. Whether our society is constituted by other members of our academic group—our colleagues within and without our own colleges and universities, in our own country and elsewhere—or whether it is constituted by members of some other group or community, our relation to one another is characterized by power: who has got it (or is perceived to), who has not got it, who is trying to get it. In both academic and nonacademic communities writing and especially publication are recognized as means of achieving power because of their economic value. Publications result in earning power—grants, subsidies, promotions, prizes, royalties, and so on; the resultant enhanced intellectual power and prestige yield even greater earning power (e.g., endowed academic chairs). In any project analyzing published writing, power must be a topic of concern.

Critical strategies are means of acquiring and maintaining power. Michel Foucault differentiates "power relations from relations of communication which transmit information by means of a language, a system of signs, or any other symbolic medium," yet his definition of "a relationship of power" seems broad enough to *include* such communication relations within it ("Subject and Power," 786 & 789). According to Foucault:

> what defines a relationship of power is that it is a mode of action which does not act directly and immediately on others. Instead, it acts upon their actions: an action upon an action, on existing actions or on those which may arise in the present or the future. . . . [A] power relationship can only be articulated on the basis of two elements which are each indispensable if it is really to be a power relationship: that "the other" (the one over whom power is exercised) be thoroughly recognized and maintained to the very end as a person who acts; and that, faced with a relationship of power, a whole field of responses, reactions, results, and possible interventions may open up. (789)

Extending Foucault's definition of power relations metaphorically to critical relations (or the relations between and among critical strategies and strategists) highlights contexts of criticism and scholarship of Pinter that would perhaps otherwise be overlooked.

For Foucault the author is "a certain functional principle by which, in our culture, one limits, excludes, and chooses" ("What Is an Author?" 159). Harari observes that from Foucault's point of view, "as a principle of order and selection," the author is "a principle of power, but one which is always presented—and this is the ultimate strategy of power—as being only an instrument of knowledge" (44). In this sense critics and scholars are also "authors"; as instruments of knowledge they wield power through their discourse, "not only an object of power but . . . the decisive *stake* of power" (43; emphasis added).

Foucault coins the term *agonism* in describing the "reciprocal incitation and struggle" between "the recalcitrance of the will and the intransigence of freedom" that he sees "at the very heart of the power relationship, and constantly provoking it" ("Subject and Power," 790). Commenting on this "neologism," Foucault's translator Leslie Sawyer observes that, based on the Greek word *agon* meaning "a combat," *agonism* implies "a physical contest in which the opponents develop a strategy of reaction and of mutual taunting, as in a wrestling match." Other metaphors used by Foucault in describing relations of power are *interplay* and *game*; for example, "In this *game* freedom may well appear as the condition for the exercise of power (at the same time its precondition, since freedom must exist for power to be exerted, and also its permanent support, since without the possibility of recalcitrance, power would be equivalent to a physical determination)" (790; emphasis added).

In the "interplay" or "game" of criticism and scholarship, there are parallel relations of power. Power relations and their social roots inform the interactive cultural contexts of academic and nonacademic criticism, indicating intersections between these modes. The same writers often contribute to "popular" magazines and newspapers, radio and television programs, and literary and academic journals.[12] "Relations of power and relations of strategy" permeate all these kinds of criticism. Since academic freedom (as tied to tenure or job security) and freedom of the press and other constitutional rights to speak freely are "guaranteed" preconditions of the exercise of power in academic institutions and in the communications industry in the United States, these are concepts that many academics and journalists or free-lance writers evoke or emulate when they seek to foster conditions favorable to free expression in their working environments. But even in democratic institutions there is also what Foucault calls the "possibility of recalcitrance," as any academic or journalistic writer experienced in confrontations with colleagues and editors knows well, either our own "recalcitrance" or theirs.

Perhaps the dream of inventing what Foucault calls "a winning strategy" (794) is felt by every writer who writes about Pinter's plays. Perhaps every writer who writes about writing attempts, in some way, to triumph over it, to become *dominant*, rather than *dominated*. And perhaps Pinter himself senses this when he reacts to *criticism* of his plays with the dictum that all that matters is what happens in the *plays*. The struggle between the critic and the author is one that Pinter seems to regard as a form of insubordination on the part of the critic. From Pinter's standpoint some critics of his plays, or of criticism of them, must seem perversely recalcitrant, obstinately insubordinate.

But, as Foucault observes, "it would not be possible for power relations to exist without points of insubordination which, by definition, are means of escape" (794). The very act of writing a book about others' writing can provide such a means of escape. It is one writer's declaration of freedom from the domination of another's text. Yet the act of writing about others' writing still allows their writing to dominate ours. And so our writing is "about" both our own and theirs. This relation produces what I would call an "oscillation effect" between subjectivity and objectivity (or between the personal and the social) in critical writing.[13] For Pinter critics like Almansi and Henderson, Foucault's perspective on "the locking together of power relations with relations of strategy" (795) applies to Pinter's plays; it is useful for interpreting the relationships between his characters. For critical theorists it is a tool for explaining the discourse of criticism.

The term *hegemony* is fashionable, by now a cliché, in discussions of the theory, practice, and profession of literary studies; these topics dominate the pages of many books and journals, resulting in what I have (fashionably) called a hegemony of theory ("theory hegemony"). Since even such terms as *hegemony* can function in criticism "hegemonically," no matter what our aims and our modes and media of inquiry and communication—whether in the classroom or in print, whether in newspapers, magazines, or academic journals—all of us engage in rhetorical strategies of social and cultural consequence. Fish's denials that there are "theoretical consequences" to his own and others' recent critical positions (*DWCN*, 315–41) raise more pertinently the question of whether or not the consequences that there are are *important* or "of value." Despite congruently virtuosic arguments against "critical self-consciousness" (*DWCN*, 436–67), we do still need to subject our practice, our theories, our hopes, and ourselves to careful scrutiny. The "checks and balances" in criticism are not only each one of us, but one another.

### Pinter's Dramatic Techniques as Strategies

Partly as a result of the influence of writers like Derrida and Foucault, in the 1980s it became fashionable to regard the techniques of writers like Pinter as "strategies." Like Dukore (*HP*, 2), Almansi and Henderson are developing a metaphor that Lois G. Gordon first used in *Stratagems to Uncover Nakedness* in 1969 (see chap. 6). Before Almansi and Henderson published their "post-modernist" investigation of Pinter, in 1981 Thomas F. Van Laan described Pinter's techniques similarly when he called Pinter's "handling of the relationship between the dramatist and his audience" a kind of "manipulation." Van Laan takes a decisive stand on the issue of Pinter's "experimental," "avant-garde," or "innovative" strategies, or whether Pinter is a "traditional" or a "nontraditional" playwright, as we will see in chapter 4.

It is reasonable to suggest that Pinter's playwriting has *both* traditional *and* innovative features; it is neither "basically" traditional nor "basically" innovative, but both at once, simultaneously. Pinter reuses some dramaturgical traditions "with a difference," while breaching others and inventing new modes. Though like some critics, Quigley stresses Pinter's continuity with previous drama more than his difference (*MSOW*), others emphasize the opposite. Pinter criticism tends to oscillate between the double sides of this question too, and it is part of a much larger question of critical and cultural change or, in Fish's term again, consequences (see chap. 10). From one perspective Pinter uses a strategy of "open form" in *The Birthday Party*: "the apocalyptic transformation of a modern 'Everyman' into a nonrational creature in a destructive society" (Thaler; cf. Raben); from another perspective "[t]he loss of traditional forms, paradoxically, reduces the impact of the experimental ones which are so thoroughly recorded. It is only in context that the avant-garde can be perceived as experimental: . . . without Rattigan, Pinter now seems highly conservative" (Woods, 170).

A historical reading of how critics and scholars have described Pinter's dramatic techniques—his strategies as a playwright—suggests that, no matter what terms the analysts apply, certain issues persist (cf. Quigley, *PP*, 4). Among the most resilient concerns in commentary on Pinter's techniques are these: his control and mastery of his material through form and structure and the relation of his techniques and themes (or form and content); his use of reality versus his use of fantasy (or related oppositions such as realism/expressionism and objectivity/subjectivity, invoking such terms as *suprarealism* and *hyperreality, naturalism, absurdity*, and so on); his use of language (including dialogue, pauses and silences, poetic techniques, musical qualities, vaudevillian routines, ritualistic rhythms, verbal games or stratagems, psychological defenses or defensive strategies, class-specific dialectisms, among other features); his use of symbolism; his ambiguity or use of ambiguity; his comedy or use of comedy; his characterizations or characters; their theatricality and the theatricalism of other aspects of his plays; and the responses of his audiences and critics. As the last-mentioned issue is my own central concern, I see these other issues in relation to it. What seem to change (and, hence, to be of consequence) are not simply the issues—they proliferate, of course—but the writers' attitudes toward them, their ways of perceiving the issues and of describing them. The issue of Pinter's "ambiguity" is a common denominator of Pinter criticism. My next chapter chronicles changing attitudes toward what critics perceive as his ambiguity, elegantly turned "semantic uncertainty."

# 4

## Pinter's "Semantic Uncertainty"

## and Critically "Inescapable" Certainties

LENNY. Well, some people would envy your certainty. . . .—*The Homecoming*

When Austin Quigley descried a lack of progress in Pinter criticism as due to "the uncertainty that has characterized responses to Pinter's work" (*PP*, xvii), he seemed to suggest that a sign of critical progress is the *reduction* of uncertainty. An uncertainty about interpretation still characterizes much Pinter criticism.[1] Debates about uncertainty recur frequently not only in commentary about Pinter but throughout much contemporary criticism. Changing attitudes toward uncertainty evinced by some Pinter critics parallel currents and crosscurrents influencing dramatic theory and criticism.

Susan Sontag's *Against Interpretation* was "well received because her ardent attack upon the objectivism of traditional exegetical practice highlighted the contradiction that exists between modern literature and traditional interpretation when the latter reduces the polyvalence of the 'open work' (*opera aperta*) to an ostensibly pre-given meaning, hidden in the text or to be sought behind it" (Jauss, "Literature," 135).[2] An early reader of Barthes, Sontag imported this French critic's writings to the United States when, in 1982, she published *The Barthes Reader*. American academics similarly influenced by French criticism joined the "against interpretation" movement. Culler's optimistic claim in "Beyond Interpretation" that "[t]here are many tasks that confront criticism, many things we need to advance our understanding of literature, but one thing we do not need is more interpretations of literary works" (246; *Pursuit*, 6) has raised much debate.[3] Like Sontag's early manifesto urging an "erotics of art" (an attempt to recover our sensory experience by attending "to form rather than content"), both poetics or literary theory ("the study of problems about the nature of literature: its forms, its components, their relations" [Culler, *Pursuit*, 218]) and semiotics (the identification and description of the "conventions" and "operations" of "signification" [48–49]) tend "to exchange the great realism of New Critical methods for the great abstraction of a theory whose purpose, as Tzvetan Todorov once noted, is to perfect its own discourse" (Ulmer, 557). Deconstruction is "a vigilant reaction against [a] tendency in structuralist thought to tame and domesticate its own best insights"; it aims at "dismantling a concept of 'structure' that serves to immobilize the play of meaning in a text and reduce it to a manageable compass" (Norris, 1–2).

In "Writing for the Theatre" Pinter says that "there can be no hard distinctions between what is real and what is unreal, nor between what is true and what is false. A thing is not necessarily either true or false; it can be both true and false" (1:11). But Hayden White writes, "Stories are not true or false, but rather more or less intelligible, coherent, consistent, persuasive, and so on. And this is *true* of historical, no less than of fictional, stories" (492; emphasis added). Despite his willingness "to bear the label of radical relativist in matters having to do with *historical knowledge*," in claiming to be a "genuine pluralist" (486)—a proponent of "true" pluralism—White does not regard his own account of critical theories in the same terms.[4] Culler speculates that *truth* may play "an indispensable role in argument and analysis" because of its "persistent duplicity": "Truth is both what can be demonstrated within an accepted framework and what simply is the case, whether or not anyone could believe it or validate it" (*OD*, 154). Even as Cain observes that "[t]he intellectual . . . is not naturally a questioner and skeptic, is not necessarily responsive to or interested in change, but rather 'craves certitude' and is prone to accept half-truths," his own use of *half-truths* implies a belief in some "whole truth" (*Crisis*, 10).

As critics develop the "uncertainty" issue in writing about Pinter's plays, they encounter similar contradictions. My chronicle of changing views of Pinter's "ambiguity" begins with Richard Schechner, Alfred E. Rickert, and Robert L. Tener, then moves through a debate about *The Dumb Waiter* in *Modern Drama* involving Charles A. Carpenter, Austin E. Quigley, and Thomas F. Van Laan. After this excursion through academic Pinter criticism, I show how my own experience of a (nonacademic) production of *The Dumb Waiter* has enhanced my understanding of responses to the play and how it relates to this literary critical debate. Quigley's more recent formulation of Pinter's drama raises the issue of uncertainty to the level of Heisenberg's uncertainty principle and Einstein's theory of relativity, suggesting some far-reaching contexts of Pinter's dramatic world.

Such metaphors empower critics as they transform uncertainty into certitude. When they build metaphors into interpretive strategies, critics formulate "concrete abstractions" generalizing from their own particular experiences of ("interactions" with) texts being interpreted and thus fulfill their own felt needs as audience members and readers. The value of these strategies—their truth-value for other critics—is mostly their usefulness in manufacturing more "certain" interpretations.

The following discussion of Pinter criticism shows several critics both engaged in skeptical questioning and concerned with change, but still craving certitude while negotiating a mine field of obstacles to "truth," not the least of which is the concept of the "essential truth" about Pinter's plays and dramatic phenomena in general. Calling critical belief in such "truth" into question, I urge greater tolerance of uncertainty to forge humanistic change.

### Changing Views of Pinter's "Ambiguity"

The earliest and perhaps most confident discussion of uncertainty or ambiguity in Pinter is Richard Schechner's "Puzzling Pinter," published in 1966. Schechner argues that "the *essential* characteristic of Pinter's work is its conceptual incompleteness" (177; emphasis added). Though Pinter presents "insoluble riddles," he differs from "that other great riddler, Pirandello. Pirandello built his plays around contradictions, Pinter around conceptual incompletion. We cannot know in Pirandello; we shall not know in Pinter" (184; cf. Rickert, 30). Before Wolfgang Iser discussed indeterminacy and reading, before poststructuralist hermeneutics, Schechner writes, "The information we are given should be sufficient. The structure allows for gaps. To be prompted into filling them— either with thematic speculation or realistic detail—is to be misled" (182). Anticipating Almansi and Henderson's "post-modernist" account of Pinter, discussed in the previous chapter, Schechner warns critics away from explaining Pinter's "action" realistically so as not to deflect attention from "the moves and counter-moves [of the characters], and the thickening web of strategies."

By the seventies Pinter's "ambiguity" was already a cliché of criticism. In 1971 Alfred E. Rickert described a trend: "there is a growing body of Pinter criticism full of contradiction. Everyone has his explanation of a

Pinter play, and the problem of puzzling Pinter has become so great that some critics have taken the position that it is impossible for us to know a Pinter play. We cannot explicate his work; we can only react to it, because he consciously and deliberately constructs his plays to create an unknowable world" (30). In 1973 Robert L. Tener argued, "[N]o one has pointed out that Pinter varies a theme central to Ionesco's and Beckett's dramas": "the relationship between man and reality as expressed by man's myth-making tendencies and as seen in his language" (175). "Everything is uncertain," and Pinter uncovers "the semantic uncertainty which underlies experience."

Today some would perhaps modify this statement to read that *nothing* "underlies" our experience and that, rather, it is we who impose structure on it. Projecting our own "semantic uncertainty" onto what we experience (live, read, and write), it is we who are uncertain. In part as a response to modern and postmodern writers—Ionesco, Beckett, Barthes, Derrida, Foucault, Borges, Calvino, Fowles, Pinter—we are able to see this "inescapable truth" about ourselves.

"Semantic uncertainty," however, is Tener's label for "the Pinter formula," which "contains two conflicting themes":

> one, a bare sketch of values anchored to a middle or lower social class perception of reality and of human behaviour by the monotonous linguistic habits of the speakers and the commonplace situations; and two, a rich texture of ambiguity sutured to the primitive, inner, dark, mysterious, emotional biological man by what he fears, often some unknown external hostile force or agent reflected in a line or action or situation ultimately affecting all the characters. The situations occur within a room, and both—the room and the situations—interact with the characters. The interaction is revealed through the linguistic habits of the characters. The result is a room-situation-character-language relationship which is continually developing throughout the time of the play. (176)

As if the metaphor *formula* could help *predict* structure, texture, and theme in Pinter's plays, its usage militates against this perception of ambiguity. Like any formula, "semantic uncertainty" bespeaks an aim to reduce *thematic* uncertainty to *critical* certainty.

The *Modern Drama* debate involving Carpenter, Quigley, and Van Laan about *The Dumb Waiter* symbolizes a shift from the positivistic objectivism of the New Criticism and structuralism to the essentialism of nominal pluralism and poststructuralism. Vis-à-vis their own somewhat conflicting interpretations of the same play, these critics register a certainty in the rightness of their methods and findings at odds with some of their own interpretive principles and hermeneutic pronouncements regarding Pinter's work.

Publishing in 1973, the same year as Tener on Pinter's "semantic uncertainty," Carpenter faults Pinter criticism for taking *The Dumb Waiter* too seriously as an example of "terrifying Absurdity" and hence overemphasizing its "menace" at the expense of its comedy; previous critics "have drastically misunderstood the play." "Actually it is a mockmelodramatic farce," "an hour's worth of sheer, rich fun." The "blinders" resulting from earlier critics' "preconceptions of profundity" caused them "to misread clear-cut stage directions, to overlook giveaway lines of dialogue, to miscalculate obvious indicators of tone—in general to resist perceiving the depths (or heights) of frivolity that the play achieves" ("Absurdity," 280). Critics who detect "portentous reverberations" in such events as Ben and Gus's debate whether to say "light the kettle," "light the gas," or "put on the kettle" and their attempts to fill orders for such exotic dishes as "Ormitha Macarounada" (1:141–43, 152) have "simply overreacted" in as "ludicrous" a manner as they. "Instead of reflecting the arbitrary, alogical meaninglessness of the Camus-Sartre universe in the manner of *Waiting for Godot*, [*The Dumb Waiter*] establishes its own singular world: a nutty, unlifelike, non-alogical world of farce." Instead of depicting Heideggerian "dread" ("a generalized sense of hysteria prompted by the mere chaotic nature of things"), it is "mock melodrama" and a *parody* of absurdity (280–81).[5]

Yet *The Dumb Waiter* has *something* serious about it: Ben's "irked rejoinder" to Gus's repeated queries—"What's one thing to do with another?" (1:161)—is "one of the few things in the play that can be taken seriously" (Carpenter, "Absurdity," 282). Ben is echoing "one of Harold Pinter's many warnings to critics," this one from an interview that Pinter gave about his film *Accident*: "The most we know for sure is that the things which have happened have happened in a certain order: any connections we think we see, or choose to make, are pure guesswork."[6]

Pinter's text describes Ben's attitude in his repeated rejoinder to Gus's questioning the connection between "Who sent" the matches and "Who" is upstairs as nervous (*"nervously"*). Ben may be nervous (as well as annoyed, bothered, or disgusted [irked]) because of the *implications* of "one thing" having "to do" with "another," since Gus implies *a connection* as opposed to *a lack* of a connection between what Ben may have at first considered unconnected events or between what Ben may now *surmise* to be connected events (He *has* just spoken to someone upstairs, whose voice he may recognize [1:156]). This reading infers a connection between Ben's attitude and his knowledge or lack of knowledge about the two events.

Though Carpenter generalizes the significance of Ben's rejoinder, connecting it to Pinter's statement about *Accident*, he also points out, "it would be ridiculous to grant Ben much intellectual acumen" (282). But there seems to be *some connection* between Carpenter's own "intellectual acumen" in tying Ben's lines to Pinter's "serious" statements about *Accident*—which, unquestioned, has in part spawned the responses by Quigley and Van Laan discussed below—and the prominence of the theme of uncertainty in Pinter criticism.

Far more important to Carpenter than this motif of critical uncertainty are aspects of the play's *certain* lack of seriousness. He argues that the play's "astounding finale" (1:164–65) is one thing that "certainly cannot be" taken seriously. As this sequence "absolutely defies critical gravity," "[a]ny feasible hypothesis" resulting from a "search for rational explanations" of it must be "fraught with improbability" (282–84). But, Carpenter supposes, even though "[l]ike the whole play, the last hovering image roguishly exposes the absurdity of dread," today's critics "have to say something else—perhaps the asininity of funk" (284–85).[7]

Perhaps challenged by Carpenter's admonition against searching for "rational explanations" of the end of *The Dumb Waiter*, Quigley bravely (and gravely) enters the debate with his 1978 *Modern Drama* article. In describing *The Dumb Waiter* as "a puzzling play which is rendered even more puzzling by its abrupt termination at precisely the point at which we feel that something decisive is finally about to happen," Quigley reminds us that the play's "final tableau" is "climaxed not by a gunshot, nor by the lowering of Ben's gun, but by a long, silent stare." To surmise Gus's subsequent murder is "interesting but irrelevant speculation" (1).

Moving from the audience's uncertainty about Gus's fate to other ambiguities, Quigley considers the general epistemological issue of uncertainty and the characters' relative attitudes toward their "incomplete" knowledge. Against Carpenter, "the seeming trivia of the play" acquire "a distinctly nontrivial function," and "the initially trivial" become "ultimately central" to what Quigley perceives as the play's epistemological theme of uncertainty (7; cf. 11 n.2).

Quigley's move here resembles the Derridean deconstructive strategy whereby the "marginal" or "supplemental" becomes "central" or "crucial," reversing a prior hierarchy of values.[8] Uncertainty permeates the world of *The Dumb Waiter*: "The incomplete nature of [the characters'] knowledge of their professional situation might seem abnormal and bizarre, but placed in the context of the issues which the audience has accepted with laughter early in the play, it becomes a suddenly recognized norm. And by the same token, the similarity between the conclusion and these earlier [apparently trivial] events renders them no longer simply humorous, but disturbing examples of a world shaken suddenly loose from the security and certainty of its assumed moorings" (7).[9] As Quigley extends this epistemological issue to "our" world, he recalls Schechner: "the worrying point . . . established by these incidents is that we do indeed operate all of the time on information that is from one point of view or another disturbingly incomplete" (7). But he goes beyond Schechner: "In the context of the play, not having sufficient information upon which to base specific actions becomes only a special case of the wider problem of anyone ever having sufficient information upon which justifiably to base any action" (8). Quigley reassesses the play's title, finding a "further implication" to be that "like the dumb waiter [*sic*] itself, [the characters] are governed and controlled by forces beyond their ability to know and understand. The strings by which the dumb waiter is manipulated and controlled are no more visible and no more understandable than those which control not only the environment but also the behavior of the characters onstage" (9). For Quigley "[t]his is the final and climaxing dimension of the themes of incomplete information and displacement of cause from effect that permeate the play" (9–10). Pinter undermines "the tacit dimension of understanding." As the "trivial" becomes "crucial," Quigley argues, "[t]he various attempts by both characters to explain the unexplained, to unite cause with effect and effect with cause, to transform the recurringly bizarre into the basically reasonable, gradually transcend the limited context in which they occur." The characters' attempts at sense-making make more sense in paradigmatic terms borrowed from Frank Kermode: people's efforts "to make sense" of their life "span" through "fictive concords with origins and ends, such as give meaning to lives and to poems" (10, citing Kermode, 7).

Quigley agrees with Carpenter; Pinter's "undermining" of the "tacit dimension of understanding" cannot adequately be described by "that much abused term, the Absurd." But he gives different reasons for the inadequacy of this label. While the play *focuses* on "the incompleteness of the characters' knowledge and control," it does not *end* by *asserting* the consequent *uselessness* of "the pursuit of knowledge and the exercise of control." Rather, *The Dumb Waiter*, Quigley argues, "demonstrates . . . the danger of losing sight of the inevitable incompleteness and inexactness of our knowledge in almost all situations in which we find ourselves involved." So Quigley generalizes again from the plight of the characters to that of the audience: "For the audience in the theatre, the organization for which Ben and Gus work remains appropriately and disturbingly offstage." Through this interpretive interpolation he transforms "the play itself" into "a manifestation of its own thematic concerns" (10).

Apparently unaware of his own critical intervention here, as he "makes sense" of Pinter's play, Quigley projects back onto it the "thematic concerns" that he considers "its own," himself displacing cause from effect: "Our belief in the existence of the organization, in its control of the situation in general and of the dumb waiter in particular, remains for us, as well as for Gus and Ben, a necessary but unconfirmed surmise— resting, as always, upon incomplete information" (10). Undermining "the tacit dimension of understanding" creates what Quigley calls the audience's "epistemological impasse." But the critic's "epistemological impasse" also is reflected back upon itself (as Quigley's own later view of Pinter will suggest). Instead of "a denouement of a theatrical murder," the audience "finds itself . . . staring uncertainly at the two transfixed characters, who are also staring, equally uncertain, at each other" (11). With this last image Quigley registers both the self-consciousness and the ambiguity of twentieth-century art forms. Turning "the play's focus" away from meaninglessness to meaning by making *The Dumb Waiter* manifest "its own thematic concerns," Quigley "turns the screw" of interpretation of *The Dumb Waiter* (and Pinter's plays in general) one more turn. [10]

With another twist Van Laan judges most previous commentaries "rather unsatisfactory" (494). "Instead of analyzing the play as Pinter wrote it," he complains, "most commentators rely on distortions and fabrications—or, at best, conclusions based on guesswork—to *concoct a new play of their own making*" (emphasis added). Though adept at using *The Dumb Waiter* against its other commentators, he never notices how his own commentary is implicated in the process he himself defines, even as my metacommentary "inevitably" is here.

Van Laan's own "concoction" of *The Dumb Waiter* questioning the so-called legitimacy of "filling in" (495) recalls Schechner's admonitions against "filling" Pinter's "gaps." The first variation on a "sequence of three occasions during which Ben calls attention to an item in his newspaper" (1:130, 131–32, 163–64), when Ben reads to Gus about a girl who killed a cat and they decide her brother really did it, is "crucial," Van Laan argues, because Pinter uses Ben and Gus "to mirror his audience," creating "a burlesque version of the commentators, a built-in before-the-fact put-down of their similar act of 'filling in' in order to make a presented situation conform to the sense of reality the viewer has brought to it" (495–96). The second variation, when Ben reads nothing aloud, may imply "that people like Ben and Gus (and most of his commentators) scarcely need *any* objective data to inspire them when making pronouncements about the reality external to their minds, that their 'responses' may not be responses at all but self-activated and self-gratifying perceptions, relying almost exclusively on internalized stereotypes" (496–97). Van Laan excepts from this generalization not only himself but "[t]wo commentators" on the play who "have managed to avoid sounding like Ben and Gus identifying the real murderer of a cat" (497): Carpenter and Quigley. Although at first he seems to *accept* both "concoctions," ultimately Van Laan *rejects* Carpenter's and Quigley's in order to make his own.

Carpenter "properly makes fun of the typical responses" to the play but his account is flawed. Not only does he fail to recognize Pinter's burlesque of commentary, but "his own ultimate response is questionable and troublesome, for," as Quigley has already pointed out, "he refuses to take the play seriously," distorting "what is *in actuality* a profound piece of drama" (Van Laan, 497; emphasis added).

While Quigley does take the play "very seriously," providing "the best reading of it yet to appear," still "[e]xcellent as it is," it is "not entirely satisfying" for two main reasons: (1) like the other commentators on *The Dumb Waiter*, Quigley provides "considerable explanation of what the characters are going through during their final stare, and while what he has to say is far subtler than the usual thing, it nonetheless borders upon 'filling in'"; and, "far more important" (2) "like his brilliant and indispensable book, *The Pinter Problem*," Quigley's article on *The Dumb Waiter* "may very well make a bit too much sense": "[B]y clarifying the real action of the play as thoroughly as he does and by ignoring some of its more refractory elements, Quigley domesticates it almost as effectively as do those who turn it into familiar melodrama" (497–98). This deconstruction puts the commentator of the play in a "no win" situation: one cannot explain the "uncertainty" experience without being accused of reducing it to certainty—"too much sense."

As I have been saying about Tener's reduction of Pinter's writing to "the Pinter formula" and these other critics' formulaic extensions of uncertainty to "proper" interpretive procedure, given what commentators still generally aim to do—*to make meaning out of experience* (reading, theater, art, other events)—this sort of reduction would seem inevitable. As we will see, Van Laan cannot escape reducing Pinter's plays to "too much sense" either. But another way to regard this reduction (in each case) is to consider it as an *enhancement*. As in the chemical reduction occurring when metals are derived (purified) from ores, to some degree critics attempt to "concentrate" the "essence" of Pinter's plays. And like the reduction in entropy, or disorder, occurring when a compound precipitates from a solution, this critical concentration (or "essentializing") *reduces* uncertainty. Paradoxically, then, some *reductions* of Pinter's "puzzling" plays simultaneously *enhance* them by increasing their intellectual value, or enlarging their worth as intellectual "currency."

As reducing bauxite to aluminum increases its value, a "critical strategy" can have economic value in the academic marketplace. And as for an owner of a metal processing plant, for a critic value comes not only from what is produced but also from the method, the "operation." If it is reproducible, replicable, capable of extensive duplication, like a metallurgist creating a new "refining" process, a critic is "in business." To extend Len's metaphor of *scum/essence* in *The Dwarfs* (see n.7): a result of criticism—symbolic interpretations—is the "scum" skimmed off and either discarded or "sold" as "waste"; the valuable "essence" desired from the literary-critical transaction is thus the "by-product." From Pinter's viewpoint critics' "guessing games" are a "waste of time" (Gussow, "Conversation," 43): the *play* is its *own* essence; its value is self-contained or contained within it and not something extractable.

By reading *The Dumb Waiter* as a play about the dramatist's chosen relationship with his audience—by seeing this topic as *central* to the play—Van Laan engages in a common postmodern reduction/enhancement of literature: It is about itself. This varies Quigley's notion that the play manifests "its own thematic concerns." But Van Laan anticipates objections to the circularity of this common thematic rendering: "All dramatists establish some kind of relationship with their spectators, but as long as it is the traditional—and comfortable—one in which the dramatist serves us as trustworthy and unobtrusive presenter of the material, we are not likely to notice the relationship as part of our experience of the play" (498–99). In *The Dumb Waiter* Pinter alters "the traditional model" so that "his relationship to us becomes *a central element* of the drama" (499; emphasis added). The *proper* way to regard *The Dumb Waiter* is to see it as a play that *mocks* the very "responses it encourages us to make" and makes us "far more conscious of our responses as such and of ourselves as responding beings than is normally the case when we are watching a play" (499).[11] *The Dumb Waiter* thus becomes "a *commentary* of sorts *on our role as spectators* while watching any play"; it enables us to notice our own meaning-making activities: how "by making connections of various kinds, we always *contribute* to the *shaping* of the meaningful events presented to us in the theater" (499; emphasis added).

As his commentary *remakes* Pinter's play *into* commentary, Van Laan considers the consequences of what he calls Pinter's "manipulation of the audience," turning the screw still further: "But since Pinter prompts us to reflect on our contributions to shaping his play's *action* rather than to discerning the *meaning* of that action, his manipulation of the audience in *The Dumb Waiter* . . . calls into question the conventions of traditional drama and the familiar assumptions about reality upon which these conventions are based."[12] As Van Laan countervails such "familiar assumptions" as "the laws of reason" (499), he recalls Carpenter's earlier objections to "rational explanations" of Pinter's play. This context puts Van Laan's earlier criticism of Quigley for making "too much sense" into stronger terms: it makes what Van Laan labels Quigley's critical traditionalism inappropriate to Pinter's plays.

Turning the screw now a complete circle, Van Laan generalizes from the single Pinter play to drama overall: "Pinter's manipulation of us in *The Dumb Waiter* asks us to question the validity of the traditional conventions of action in drama, but he probably does this only in passing, for he seems to be *after bigger game*" (emphasis added). What is the "bigger game" that Pinter is after? What is Van Laan's own larger target? "*The Dumb Waiter* seems to ask, does an event acquire only its meaning from the way we connect data, or does it also acquire, through this process, its very existence?" (500). Echoing his own opening gambit against "conclusions based on guesswork," Van Laan quotes Pinter's interview with Taylor, coming full circle back to Carpenter: "The most we know for sure is that the things which have happened have happened in a certain order: any connections we think we see, or choose to make, are pure guesswork."

Van Laan finds a "lesson" for reading *all* of Pinter's work in this discussion of reading *The Dumb Waiter*: "[W]hatever legitimacy 'filling in' may have elsewhere—and its legitimacy for any dramatist remains undemonstrated—it is for Pinter at best a very risky process." For Van Laan, Pinter's "very essence" is his *defiance* of "our expectations about life and/or drama" through "dizzying dislocations in which a stylistic mode that we have grown comfortable with [naturalism] abruptly gives way to a strikingly different one [stylization]." Such "atypical effects" as "the bizarre behavior of the dumb waiter, or Mick's surrealistic speeches, or the non-transition-like transitions of *The Homecoming*" substitute for "the coherent action" of traditional plays. "[T]hese effects—and not some action that we have ourselves invented—constitute the *proper* focus of our interpretive powers and *appropriately* engage our efforts to discern meaning and significance" (500; emphasis added).

As Van Laan issues these particular normative recommendations for reading Pinter, he *connects* the so-called atypical in Pinter's plays with his "handling of the relationship between the dramatist and his audience" (500–501). Van Laan's conclusion extends his metaphor of the game (Pinter "seems to be after bigger game"): "In keeping with our usual role as spectators at a Pinter drama, we have become a part of his play. He has, in other words, been playing with us and playing us in order to make sure that our responses get called into play and into *the* play—that they become not just passive adjuncts to the dramatic experience but active and indispensable elements of its total design" (501).

While I myself appreciate Van Laan's enhancement of Pinter, I also recognize this appreciation as *both* a cause *and* an effect of my own immersion in reader- and audience-oriented critical inquiry. My leaning functions projectively on Pinter's plays and commentary about them. Whereas Van Laan sees himself as understanding what he regards as a "preoccupation" and an "interest" of Pinter's, I see both myself and Van Laan as *also* projecting our own critical preoccupations and interests on Pinter's plays (and on Pinter criticism)—and, hence, finding them there. As we enhance Pinter's plays, we reduce both them and commentary about them to allegories of our readings. [13]

Carpenter, Quigley, and Van Laan say nothing explicit about interrelations between the "texts" that they have concocted for *The Dumb Waiter* and particular actual performances of the play. Recent interest in performance study allying academic scholars with theater professionals suggests the rich possibilities of exploring such multiple interpretations in performing plays.[14] As Carlson observes, "The concept of the supplement, as theorized by Derrida, provides a new way of thinking about several of the key paradoxes which bedevil theories of performance as illustration, translation, or fulfillment [of the dramatic text]" ("Theatrical Performance," 9). As both surplus and replacement, the phenomenon of performance exemplifies "this double dynamic."

## A "Supplemental" Reconstruction of
## *The Dumb Waiter* in Performance

*The Dumb Waiter* has not been produced on stage as often as some of Pinter's other plays. So I was delighted to attend a performance of *The Dumb Waiter* in a London pub in the summer of 1982. This "lunchtime theatre" performance at the Finborough Arms began with a sandwich on the way in, ordered from the playbill's "Lunchpack Menu," listing also "Ormitha Macarounada" and "beer (with crisps)." (Balancing paper plates and cups throughout the performance further realized this metaphor of food being served.) Upstairs from the pub proper, the play was performed on a make-do stage by two actors on brief reprieve from a West-End production of *The Sound of Music*.

Their renditions bespoke definite ("certain") interpretations of their roles, accentuating Ben's assertive dominance and Gus's intermittent subservience. This Gus (Nicholas Lumley)—alternately passive and inquisitive, his interrogative mode punctuated by dependence and attendance on Ben's commands—and this Ben (Graham Fawcett)—continually annoyed by Gus's every question and gesture (no matter how slight), by his very presence—were an "odd couple": more like mismatched domestic partners than professional killers. This portrayal underlined the comic dimension discussed by Carpenter; it was very funny and evoked much laughter, especially from me.[15]

I found this production both poignant and thought-provoking as well as funny. Ben's treatment of Gus—as if his every gesture, his very being, were gratuitous, unnecessary, superfluous, absurdly *de trop*—took on a more serious dimension when Gus's superfluity in the process being dramatized on stage—his (hypothesized) replacement by another "killer" after he would be gone—became *both* a critical (crucial) assumption necessary for understanding *and* a critical (interpretive) consequence of my own response to *this particular theatrical interpretation* of the play.

Gus is *replaceable* if he does not behave *properly*, or according to Ben's (and/or "Wilson's") purposes. To extend the domestic metaphor, there is a kind of separation or divorce this "couple" is about to experience as a result of their incompatibility. They just don't get along, and their various conflicts (such as that about whether one says "light the kettle" or "put on the kettle") comically and ominously dramatize this "fact" of their lives.[16]

My own experience and understanding of such discord enables me to elaborate the domestic metaphor in reconstructing this production. But whether a pair are life partners, business partners, partners in crime (the hit men most presume Ben and Gus literally are), roommates (as Davies and Aston are, for a while, in *The Caretaker*), old friends (as Hirst and Spooner would have themselves in *No Man's Land*)—even author and critic or academic colleagues—merely varies this experiential gestalt. Each of us builds versions of *The Dumb Waiter* out of metaphors selected from (associations to) our own experiences. Everyday or common experiences form (if only in part) "bases" for our critical understanding, "grounds" for our eidetic reductions or enhancements of dramatic ambiguity, "foundations" for structures we impose. As Van Laan suggests, what "underlies" our interpretations of current experience is prior experience. It serves as "scaffolding" for our ideas as we rationalize the "unfamiliar." Critical metaphors drawn from experience ("literary" and other kinds) supply important sources of understanding. As Culler intimates, such "stories" make the "incoherent" cohere.

On a literal level critics often see Ben ("the senior partner") as an agent of an organization; "Wilson" seems to be the boss. Then, in symbolically hierarchical readings, Ben stands (in) for some microauthority figure: the "top banana," even (as I have suggested) a husband, wife, or other partner; and "Wilson" for some macroauthority figure: He, They, God, the Supreme Author or Organization Man. In Van Laan's "concoction" the microaction (literal) and the macroaction (figurative) merge: the conflict is between a supreme author (Pinter) and his audience (us). This reductive enhancement stresses that, like Gus (and Ben), we are all "dumb waiters," whose uncertain destiny may be at some other's apparent bidding and at still another's actual doing. Though we are "participating," someone else "calls the shots."[17]

These allegorical reconstructions—whether epistemological or some other kind—relate to our own situations. That so many people *do* fill in (even if only momentarily) the murder of Gus, the expulsion of Davies, the punishment of Stanley, or the sexual background of Ruth (or any number of other omitted endings and beginnings) signals their own humanness: their meaning-making authority. Interpreting a play (even while we are watching it)—connecting unconnected dots, crossing un-crossed t's, "filling in" gaps—does rationalize the irrational, but in this respect it merely resembles what we do with our other experience, which we have also learned "to interpret." As Carpenter, Quigley, Van Laan, and the rest of us question one another's procedures for meaning-making, we only substitute more or less sophisticated versions of the same.

Though to some it may appear arbitrary or improper, a theatrical production reproduces a play so as to recreate (for an audience) a so-called meaningful experience, just as any reading of a play ("critical" or other-wise) attempts to do. While fashionable, denying the importance of meaning to dramatic experience can also appear as a kind of meaning-mongering. [18] To stop "filling in" missing dramatic details, as Van Laan seems to advocate, limits the procedure of making meaning for this experience. Yet, closing Pinter's "openness" in his own way, Van Laan first plugs the holes with theory and then turns theory into a dramatic theme.

At the Finborough Arms, it seemed (to me, though not necessarily to Gus) that Ben was *hiding* not only his knowledge of what was going on (however limited it is), but also his own sense of his *lack* of knowledge. (Critics seem to hide the latter more than the former.) While Gus appeared sensitive to Ben's discomfort yet ignorant of its source, Ben seemed extremely jumpy, defensive. I imagined that before the action begins, Ben has been asked to keep an eye on Gus (perhaps when the car stopped [1:135]), that there are already some doubts about Gus's ability to function. [19] In the midst of their "linguistic" argument, Ben asks Gus, "Who's the senior partner here, me or you?" and when Gus acknowledges that Ben is, Ben says, "I'm only looking after your interests, Gus. You've got to learn, mate" (1:142). Along with his lack of readiness to follow Ben's orders, Gus's recurrent questions and his express repugnance about the girl previously killed (1:146–47) could imply his unsuitability for the job. In the course of the play he does not "learn," or if he does (during the final stare), this learning occurs possibly too late for him to benefit from his knowledge: he is facing Ben's pointed gun. At some time (in plays, in life) there may not be another chance to act "appropriately" toward "authority." Even though we, like Gus, may have passed earlier "tests" (1:162), we too may fail an ultimate one. There may be no "next time." Imaginatively extending the end of the play creates dramatic afterlife.

The image of Ben, who presumably should know but may not, as *hiding, concealing* the "real meaning" of the action from Gus (for whatever motives) serves audiences and critics as an icon for Pinter, the author.[20] Like Ben, the "senior partner," or "Wilson," the author Pinter, they feel, is concealing the "real meaning" (of the movements of the dumbwaiter, of other events of the play, of the relationship between author and audience, of Life). When, like Ben, Pinter has protested that (no "prophet") *he* does not know these "true" meanings (once finished revising and rehearsing, he too enters the audience), critics have argued that Pinter protests too much.

Some interaction between Pinter's plays (as texts and theater experiences) and their audiences and commentators occurs; however, the causes and effects of the interaction probably cannot be pinpointed. Yet Pinter enables what we must (on some "level") already know, the so-called familiar—the same old thing, the traditional, the conventional—to interact with what we do *not* already know, the so-called unfamiliar—the different, the new, the innovative, the nontraditional, the unconventional. As the unfamiliar becomes recognizable, some would rather reject it. They become "uncertain" about what they know.

Perhaps no one can be certain exactly where Pinter's thematic "preoccupation" or "interest" begins and our own ends; the most we can do, as Pinter has suggested, is "guess." With "informed" judgment we can arrive at a qualified certainty—a certitude (a feeling of absolute sureness or conviction) at best—if indeed *certainty* is what we are after (as so many disclaim). If not, we have to learn how to cope with uncertainty.

### Critical Reformulations as Metaphors for Critical Progress

Quigley's *Modern Stage and Other Worlds* extensively reformulates his critical position on modern drama, Pinter's included; but, reminiscent of Tener's "Pinter formula," this "reformulation of the issue" (226) verges on the formulaic as Quigley aims to present a means of reading modern plays in "appropriate" ways. Like Van Laan's, Quigley's tendency toward defining what is appropriate in dramatic criticism is prescriptive; some approaches are more "proper" (right for the purpose) than others.[21] For Quigley at this juncture Pinter's plays exemplify "[t]he drama of inquiry in a pluralistic universe" (262) and are most "appropriately" approached philosophically. The experiential aspect of drama and theater gives way to intellectual inquiry as Quigley defines the "proper" role of the critic as theorist (philosophical worker).[22] Yet, some critics feel, Pinter mocks such a notion in Teddy's only long speech, cited below, calling into question the philosopher's ability to "see" any more *appropriately* than anyone else.

Nevertheless, Quigley extends Van Laan's insights, engaging "tradition" and "novelty," claiming that "these issues of relating old and new" acquire "a peculiar structural and thematic importance" in Pinter's play *Betrayal* (*MSOW*, 221). To explain Pinter's "extensive use of well-made-play elements" alongside the unconventional, Quigley uses scientific paradigms, elaborating on both the "uncertainty theme" and Schechner's earlier concept of Pinter's use of "incomplete information": Quigley's "enhancement" of Pinter extends Van Laan's: "The disturbing events in Pinter plays characteristically serve to remind us that the explanations we rely on in our daily lives tend often to be incomplete and that we frequently resort to rounding them out with guesses based upon not clearly justifiable assumptions. Consequently, further inspection of a situation is likely to generate not clearer explanations but more confusion, as our guesses and assumptions fail to stand up to further scrutiny" (223–24). Pinter dramatizes "Heisenberg's uncertainty principle in scientific inquiry," which suggests that "our methods of explanation can in part constitute the data to be explained" and provides "an alarming potential for circularity in our explanatory activities." Such circularity occurs in scientific analysis of matter into particles in accordance with Einstein's theory of relativity: "the proliferation of new particles might well result from the methods used to locate them. That which is to be explained in part results from, and is in part constituted by, the method of examining and explaining it."[23]

As we become involved in our "explanatory activities," most often we disregard this "potential for circularity" and feel as though, somehow, we have circumvented the problem. As I do in allegorizing the Finborough Arms production of *The Dumb Waiter* (I see retrospectively), while making meaning of *Betrayal* Quigley manifests the same ability to repress cognitive awareness of "the hermeneutic circle." Pinter's treatment of certainty and uncertainty reverses "one of the basic thematic consequences of the well-made-play structure . . . the reinforcement of an attitude towards the nature of explanation, experience and truth that is easily accepted as the only reasonable one" (Quigley, *MSOW*, 224). This attitude is "not . . . the only possible attitude, nor the only reasonable attitude, towards such things. And although it provides the basis for one mode of explanation in Pinter plays, it is by no means the dominant one, nor the one that gives the plays their disturbing and disorientating quality" (224). In contrast, what Quigley defines further as Pinter's attitude duplicates parts of Quigley's own earlier theoretical argument by favoring pluralism over dualism or Hegelian dialectics. "[T]he key point is that the characters, like the dramatist, are persistently engaged in a struggle not so much to locate the truths that underlie inherited structures, as to create the kinds of structures that will embody acceptable truths" (225). Given Van Laan's concern with audience, one could extend this "struggle" to its domain and, given my concern with critics as members of the audience with specialized interests, to critics as well.

As Schechner was doing in conceptualizing Pinter's "conceptual incompleteness," Tener in devising "the Pinter formula," Carpenter in turning absurdity into farce, Quigley first in employing "the tacit dimension of understanding" and then again in relating structural, thematic, and textural "conventions" and "innovations" to epistemology, Van Laan in playing with "Pinter's play with the audience," and as I am doing in structuring "critical strategies"—so we are all trying "to create the kinds of structures that will embody acceptable truths." The "theme of uncertainty" becomes the certain theme of both Pinter's plays and commentaries on them. And yet, in an important way, it remains the uncertain theme.

Van Laan shows himself "filling in" omitted details of *The Caretaker* ostensibly to illustrate the risks of doing so with *The Dumb Waiter* and other Pinter plays and drama in general. But this interpolation *enables* him to construct his interpretive stance. Quigley seemed unaware of his own earlier intervention in *The Dumb Waiter*. Perhaps now he would readily acknowledge the logical circularity of his views that Pinter explores "social interaction in the context of certainty confronting and negotiating with doubt, doubt negotiating with other doubt, and certainty with other certainty" and that the "key issue" of Pinter's plays is "the peculiar mode of interaction established between the commonplace and the unusual, the traditional and the experimental, the practical and the epistemological" (224–27). Of course these "factors" seem to "achieve a startling structural and thematic embodiment" in the "complex" play he is about to examine, *Betrayal*. They duplicate his own "reformulation" of the relationship between modern stage conventions and attitudes toward a "process of explanation" leading "back towards itself": this "dramatized recognition of the inescapable interaction for characters, for dramatist and for audience, of things known and the ways of knowing that help generate them." Such an interactive circularity seems "inescapable": once one has turned the screw of interpretation far enough, it seems to unscrew itself, to deconstruct. And yet I say "seems" inescapable, for I cannot be certain it *is*. This uncertainty is an effect of my own immersion "in" Pinter's plays and contemporary criticism and theory. In poststructuralist, functional terms, it would be called a reading-effect.

The arguments about *The Dumb Waiter* and Pinter's other plays are "recapitulated" in the "philosophical" debate in *The Homecoming* (3:68–69). Like this play's philosopher Teddy, some critics do not want to get "lost in it" (3:77–78); yet, we do get implicated by the very stuff of our inquiry.[24] The "intertextuality" of Quigley's engagement with modern plays, philosophy, linguistics, and criticism; the "intersubjectivity" of his reading and rereading of Pinter through his own experience (reading and otherwise) and his reading and rereading of other writers through this reading of Pinter; Pinter's "inquiry" (William James's, Goodman's, Quigley's): where does it all "begin" and where does it "end?" We have Said's "beginnings" and Kermode's "endings"; but to extend Lenny, "Philosophically speaking," *what* are they? What have we got and what are we "going to do with" them? Where are we "going to take" what we have gotten "hold" of? We have all these reverberations of "the table leg"—the supposedly *certain* thing—the "thingness" of texts. Themes, rituals, games, fantasies, and dreams: this is the "stuff" criticism is made of, as critical Teddy boys strive to maintain "intellectual equilibrium," a "way of being able to look at the world."

As Norman N. Holland once wrote, "Any critic is first and foremost a member of the audience. . . . A critic experiences the work of art initially as anyone else does" (*Psychoanalysis and Shakespeare*, 314). Critical theorists question how closely "specialist" and "nonspecialist" aesthetic encounters do resemble one another. Still, a "recognition of the inescapable interaction . . . of things known and the ways of knowing that help generate them" escapes many critics, as it does other audience members, characters, directors, and dramatists. If this "recognition" is dramatized by Pinter in his plays and felt dramatically by critics, we redramatize it in our commentaries. Put into terms that would antagonize any playwright, especially Pinter: as we "make" and "remake" the plays, "formulate and reformulate" them, we critics would seem the playwright's certain "doing" and "undoing." *We* would seem inescapable. I say "would seem" because to say "are" would give us critics a privilege that we do not always have (however much we crave it).

If plays endure (both as theater and as texts), it may be in part also because critics' work returns readers to them. But when readers do turn back to dramas like Pinter's after having read criticism of them, or turn to them first with criticism in hand, these texts are *altered* in the reading by the writing about them. They are reread after they have been rewritten. Such interactive alterations of Pinter's work by Pinter criticism (and of Pinter criticism by Pinter and by other Pinter critics) seem inescapable, no matter how hard each of us may try to escape noticing them.

As this critically "inescapable" certainty, this certitude, becomes a platitude, Pinter criticism, and dramatic criticism and theory along with it, progresses, advances, as it were. Critical progress is metaphorical in that it occurs *through* metaphors—new ways of seeing—chosen by critics to substitute for (the experience of) plays.[25] As plays are both aspects of our environment and productions involving other people, to regard them experientially is to interact with them in ways that create what Lakoff and Johnson call "mutual change" (230): we change them and they change us, and through our criticism of them, we change one another. Perhaps we can realize that "the way we have been brought up to perceive our world is not the only way and that it is possible to see beyond the 'truths' of our culture. . . . But metaphors are not merely things to be seen beyond. In fact, one can see beyond them only by using other metaphors" (239). (*In fact* is no less a figure of speech than Gus and Ben's *light the kettle*.)

When we accept other critics' metaphors as truths, we are saying, "We understand" in these particular terms. Their metaphors, their new ways of seeing the dramatic world—and critical strategies built on them— become effective means to control the uncontrollable, name the unnameable, master the unmasterable: to know this unknowable but still inescapable member of our universe of discourse. As critics, we work to control, name, master, and know, but never can we escape language. Though we may strive to get "beyond" it, we cannot. Would we (who work and play in language) be more *happy* if we could? Or is a portion of our happiness the price of our knowledge?

An enhanced sense of the language of drama and theater incorporates nonverbal as well as verbal performance. It enables people to "understand" these phenomena through a variety of structures—metaphors— in new ways, if no more or less *certainly*. If the *inability* to reach certain understanding has become for some a new inescapable critical certainty, this certitude founds new critical enterprises through which they hope to advance, at least intellectually.

Pinter's most recent political plays may stimulate some of us to scrutinize where we, the human race, are heading. As we critics attempt to bridge the still vast chasm between invented categories of "experience" (personal, emotional, intellectual, psychological, social, economic, political, ethical, professional, cultural, semiotic) and myths of "knowledge" (objectivist, subjectivist, experientialist, perspectivist, stereoscopist), *do we know* where we are going with the new structures, the new strategies? Even if progressing *uncertainly*, we venture exploring "mysterious" interrelations of life and drama, experience and knowledge. Whatever paths we choose entail heavy risks and responsibilities, so we must proceed carefully, tempering our quest for adventure and fun with social purpose. Before setting out toward new "discoveries," new "worlds," we are wise to examine where we have already been: paths already taken. We must try to understand why people have chosen these routes to knowledge about Pinter as well as what they have learned. My next four chapters are such an inquiry.

# II

## Some Strategies of Pinter Critics:

### Themes, Rituals, Games, Fantasies, Dreams

# 5

# Thematic Tactics and Ritual Ruses:

## Searches for Meaning

TOM. I've often wondered what "mean" means.—*Tea Party*

In *Ways of Worldmaking* Nelson Goodman discusses the phenomenon of "ordering" through "groupings and arrangements" as our "only" way of "hand[ling] vast quantities of material perceptually or cognitively. . . . Whatever else may be said of these modes of organization [e.g., the decimal periodization of historical time and the marking off of daily time], they are not 'found in the world' but *built into a world*. Ordering, as well as composition and decomposition and weighting of wholes and kinds, participates in worldmaking" (13). Critics participate in making what they call "Pinter's world" as they order it into "meaning" and "form" in the course of decomposing or "analyzing" it. Whether or not others are prone to perceive these orderings—these categorical analyses—as "true" or "useful" and as "enhancements" or as "reductions" of the experiences of Pinter's plays depends on how well any reader's and writer's orientations and needs match.

Thematic and stylistic analysis is perhaps the most widespread means of making sense of Pinter's plays and other literature and criticism too.[1] Quigley's *Pinter Problem* "orders" Pinter criticism using thematic metaphors, as if he were answering the question What are the recurring themes of Pinter criticism? My own approach construes critical approaches *as metaphors* for Pinter's plays ("Pinter's plays as themes, rituals, games, fantasies, dreams"), and I classify or arrange the metaphors via a controlling play motif ("tactics," "ruses," "maneuvers," "language games," "role-playing," "feminist ploys"). *Theme*, *motif*, and *metaphor* are closely connected terms in literary critical analysis. Critics often use *theme* to denote a topic, subject, idea, or concept; *motif*, a repeated theme; and *metaphor*, a concept substituting for and replacing something else. Thematic interpretations are thus metaphorical or otherwise figurative, even though we often take them literally.

## Thematic Tactics:
## Steven H. Gale

In *Butter's Going Up: A Critical Analysis of Harold Pinter's Work* and related writings, Gale uses what Peck calls "residual New Critical close-reading strategies" (49) to trace Pinter's "thematic and stylistic developments" (Gale, *B*, 87). Gale chronicles changes in Pinter's "unique emphases" (Ellis's phrase discussed in chap. 2). Gale's "central aim" is to analyze, describe, and evaluate Pinter's work: to "demonstrate that [Pinter's] continual development as a dramatist is an important factor in his increasing popularity" (*BGU*, 5). (See opposition to locating thematic sources for Pinter's "fashionable reputation" cited in chap. 1.) Gale aims to define the "basic" concepts with which to begin understanding the plays, conceptualizing and compartmentalizing them in simple terms so as to gain control of them.

Unlike some New Critics, however, Gale uses the biography and published statements of the author and others' interpretations in his critical analyses. Extending the first chapter on Pinter's biography, in the rest of *Butter's Going Up*, Gale links events in the author's life, topics about which Pinter has expressed interest and concern, and the intentional content of his work and incorporates other critics' pertinent insights. This approach illustrates the kind of "overlap" that Kinneavy mentions in discussing "aims" and "modes" of discourse (37), resulting in what Beale would term a "functional" mutation of discursive strategies (48–49).[2]

In his review of Almansi and Henderson's "post-modernist" reading of Pinter, as cited earlier, Gale declares what he calls his own particular "bias": "I believe that works of art are created to convey some sort of intellectual or emotional meaning" (143). What Pinter has said about a variety of concepts provides Gale with clues to the intellectual or emotional meaning of the dramas, and they become "complex collections of interrelated themes" (*BGU*, 17). Gale himself makes Pinter's plays meaningful by interrelating "sets" and "subsets" of "themes" and "concepts." He defines five "basic concepts" in Pinter's dramas—love, loneliness, menace, communication, and verification—and four distinct stages in Pinter's "thematic evolution from generalized to particularized menace," ending with Pinter's concern for a particular "aspect of the verification problem," memory, and "a new element," "a sort of omnipresence of experience" (*BGU*, 174–76). The "plays of memory" introduce "a dif-

ferent kind of love . . . a more 'romantic' love." Gale extracts Pinter's
"ideas" (or—in the case of love, loneliness, and menace—emotions
suggested by the characters' experiences) from various nondramatic contexts and reduces often emotionally ambiguous character relationships to
these more precise terms. This mode of reducing and enhancing Pinter's
meaning is reproducible, as Gale and others have demonstrated pro-
lifically.

The source of Gale's title is two lines that he considers "among the
most important in all of Pinter's work": in *The Dwarfs* Mark says, "I see
that butter's going up," and Len responds, "I'm prepared to believe it,
but it doesn't answer my question." In chapter 6 Gale observes that "not
only" are these lines "the key to this particular play, but they provide an
insight into most of the concepts [Pinter] investigates in all his drama.
. . . [They] express much of the content of the Theatre of the Absurd,"
relate to "Pinter's previous comments about verification (i.e., something
may be true and at the same time irrelevant)," and set a "standard" of
comparison rendering "many seeming enigmas . . . clear, though possibly unanswerable" (114). Yet, in chapter 11, on "technique," we learn
that this "vital exchange" was "deleted" from Pinter's "original version"
of the play in subsequent editions from 1965 on (263). It is unlikely that
Pinter would delete or allow to be deleted lines that he himself considered
"among the most important" in all his work.

Thus, though in *Butter's Going Up* and elsewhere Gale also analyzes
Pinter's stylistic development, he subordinates style to content. Maintaining the focus of his dissertation on "thematic change," he devotes far
more space to themes than to techniques. In chapter 11 of *Butter's Going
Up* and his other discussions of Pinter's technique, he regards style as
Pinter's means of exposing and exploring particular themes. Like others,
Gale suggests the technical influences of Pinter's work in other media on
his work for the stage.[3] But in his writing published thus far, he gives
content more importance than form by making it more prominent
throughout his analysis. Gale regards Pinter's plays as "statements" of
Pinter's "concepts" about life: "In essence the author explores the various
aspects of a question through a series of minor works and then writes a
major play which sums up his thematic conclusion. He then begins
another set of plays, which will in turn lead to another major drama"
(*BGU*, 5–6).

In *Butter's Going Up* Gale says that he interprets the plays without
reliance on other disciplines (6), but he does draw on common (or tacit)

knowledge of general psychology and existential philosophy for his names and definitions of Pinter's themes and concepts, generally favoring psychology over philosophy. Gale's understanding of psychology presented in the book derived from college courses and was motivated by a general interest (interview with author). His acquaintance with existentialism at this time is less specifically documented. He usually qualifies Pinter's so-called existential aspects (81, 177, 236, 251); for example, "Kerr supports his claim that Pinter is the quintessential existential playwright by the same reasoning" that Esslin uses to place him in the Theatre of the Absurd—"Pinter has joined form and content" (251). Moreover, though "[e]xistentially it could be said that Ruth is continually in the process of 'becoming'" (154), Lenny's challenging Teddy on "all this business of being and not-being" (3:68) is a "burlesque of existentialism" (143). After eleven pages and no further allusions to the existential, Gale concludes: "In summary, the actions of the characters in *The Homecoming* have their center in psychological needs" (154).[4]

As "Pinter's concern" shifts from actual menace in the early plays to its "derivation" in *A Slight Ache* and subsequent plays, the events of his plots become less important than the characters' "psychological reactions" to them, for the action springs from the characters' emotional needs (82). "[T]he essence of the thematic change" in Pinter's work from 1957 to 1968 is this growing importance of "the focus on need" and "a simultaneous deemphasis of the requirement for a material sanctuary"—the room (156). In thematizing the "content" of Pinter's plays from 1968 to 1975, Gale recognizes its subjectivity (175–76). Distilling the texts into "themes" and "concepts" and gradualistic "stages" of development, however, neutralizes their powerful affective impact on audiences and readers. Moreover, while stating that Pinter's more recent "subject matter" requires an "understanding" of "subjectivity," Gale himself does not acknowledge in *Butter's Going Up* that this subjectivity might also apply to exegesis of Pinter's work, such as his own "analysis." Instead he stresses its interpretive objectivity, verifiability, and validity: all summed up in a pedagogical caveat that he calls "Gale's Law of Provability" (interview with author). Even though earlier he has claimed that there are five "basic concepts" in Pinter's plays, as the book develops, he adds a *sixth* concept, memory, to the list. Of course any such list would grow longer as "Pinter's interests" develop, though, as I suggest below, the "basic concepts" proliferate too with critics' own proliferating interests and change with their own changing perspectives.[5]

Not only does Gale regard "the biographical fallacy" and "the intentional fallacy" as "themselves fallacies" and thus of "limited applicability," but he considers facts about the author's life, statements made by the author, as well as details from the texts—anything applicable if it helps one to understand the plays. While "accept[ing] the premise that a work of art must stand on its own," Gale says that he is "willing to consider other sources that might increase his insight into the work. Other approaches are amplifications or alternates and not contradictory, for they focus on specific interests or elements—and the critics' ultimate concern is still with what and how the dramas mean."6

Following the first chapter on Pinter's biography, Gale extrapolates from details of Pinter's early life given in Esslin's *Peopled Wound* to explain the menace in the "comedies of menace" (18). When Gale describes changes in Pinter's "emphasis" in later plays, however, at first he offers no personal biographical grounds, instead establishing and supporting his interpretations of "the meaning" of Pinter's later plays with Pinter's own remarks about "love and the lack of love," or "need." Since Pinter does not explain his use of *love*, Gale bases his discussion on dictionary and psychology textbook definitions (see *BGU*, 18–19; cf. "Writing," 89 n.6). He extends Pinter's generalizations and abstractions about some of his plays to explain the rest of his canon.7

Gale reiterates general critical acknowledgment of Pinter's stylistic "economy." Textual changes (detailed in lengthy footnotes) show that Pinter moves "toward subtlety and poetic expression," resulting in greater vitality and "an emotional flow instead of attempts to delineate"; yet "[t]he newer pieces are as emotionally effective as Pinter's earliest writing, though in a completely different way and effecting quite a different response" (274–75). Gale does not substantiate this claim, however; textual evidence cannot explain entirely how and why responses to Pinter's newer plays differ from his earlier ones. People encountering a Pinter play for the first time still have responses similar to those that people had before.8

Reviews of *Butter's Going Up* praise the book's comprehensiveness and particularly how Gale organizes Pinter's writing into periods (*Choice*), groups (Styan, 303), or recurring "basic concepts" (J. R. Brown). But the detailed analyses are "overly padded with plot and character summaries" (*Choice*) and "plodding" (Styan, 303); Gale's writing style "ponderous" and "pedestrian" (*Choice*), "heavy and necessarily repetitive" (B. Brown), and improper or "infelicitous" (Styan, 302). Gale has the "vice of restating the commonplaces of Pinter criticism exhaustively" (302). Though it produces "several original insights" (*Choice*), Gale's analytic method raises recurrent reservations.

It is "infuriating" that Gale "lets Pinter largely speak for himself," Styan says, criticizing Gale's "sense of what a play is and does." By emphasizing " 'the meaning' of Pinter's plays, " he argues, "[Gale] hardly suggests he is the critic to tackle Pinter, the experience of whose plays are of the theatre theatrical, and not the least like deciphering the small print in some insurance policy. . . . Pinter's plays do not have meanings any more than Shakespeare's or Neil Simon's, but when they are working well on the stage, they offer us refulgent insights" (302). The crux of this "complaint" is Gale's "working method": failing to suggest any "dramatic reason" for the plays' actions and "any intended response from an audience," his analyses "will not pass for dramatic commentary"; "[a]ll the old inadequacies of 'literary criticism' when applied inappropriately to drama are apparent, and the method serves neither to help the actor nor to make the reader want to see the play" (302–3).[9] Though Gale's generalization about Pinter's changing relocation of menace "bravely" relates the plays to one another, he "is more at home with the jargon of 'themes,' another of the Aristotelian straitjackets that sit uneasily on an author who said that he distrusted definite labels" (303). It is "especially alarming" that the introductory chapter on "Basic Concepts" precedes "the analysis of text," and Gale overemphasizes "the notion of 'verification' "; yet the account of "the early concept of 'menace' " is "admirable," and Gale's chapter summarizing Pinter's techniques is "most useful."

The subjective variability of these reviews matches that of reviews of Pinter's plays. While J. R. Brown also values the book for this chapter, unlike Styan, he likes the introductory chapter on Pinter's "basic concepts." In contrast to Styan, Bernard Brown praises Gale's "handling of [the] 'verification principle' " and his emphasis on "the epistemological problem" in Pinter. But whereas Bernard Brown is unhappy with what he regards as Gale's failure to integrate or survey other "critical approaches" to Pinter, especially the "existentialist and psychological approach" that he sees Gale suggesting in places, J. R. Brown highlights Gale's consideration of "several opposing views of the plays . . . without arguing for any single view"; and, similarly, Styan gives Gale "the virtue of urging no particular thesis, placing no weight on anthropology or psychoanalysis" (302).

Despite the mixed criticism, according to Duke University Press

*Butter's Going Up* has been a "very good seller." Two positive evaluations published on the inside of the dust jacket explain this popular appeal. Despite Gale's own judgment of the difficulty of two "major" Pinter plays, *The Homecoming* and *No Man's Land* (*BGU*, 138, 220), Kimball King still finds the book "sophisticated yet simple like Pinter's best works." Kenneth Gros Louis also praises the book's simplicity. Both attribute its readability to Gale's thematic approach: "This book is a useful addition to previous criticism because the author uses a thematic approach" (K. King); "[Gale's] discussions . . . belie the complexity of the material he is dealing with. . . . While . . . obviously fully aware of the puzzling aspects of Pinter, he does not give the reader the sense that the puzzles are insoluble" (Gros Louis). [10]

Two published reviews follow suit. Styan calls the book "the plain man's guide to Harold Pinter, a Pinter handbook" (302), and J. R. Brown, who praises Gale's "clarity and ease," adds that "[h]is commentaries will make a reader wonder how anyone could have been puzzled, disturbed, or irritated by a slow-moving, very considerate, very expert dramatist." In "Pinter's Progress" Noel King could be alluding to the simplicity of Gale's thesis about the shift from actual menace to its psychological derivation when he says: "The *simplest* definition of the change in Pinter's work is to say that the menace has been relocated" (250; emphasis added; cf. 247).

As he does in *Butter's Going Up*, in his essay on *Family Voices* Gale also relies on what he can discern about Pinter's life experience. He begins by citing a 1975 letter in which Pinter gives family responsibilities for declining Gale's invitation of a visiting writer position just a few months before the press reported Pinter's extramarital affair with Lady Antonia Fraser: "Pinter's plays exhibit the same ambiguity regarding the concept of family that the dramatist has displayed in his personal life" (146). [11] To use the reasons given in the letter as the only ones or to take them literally or thematically and as proof of Pinter's attitudes toward private aspects of his own life, however, loses sight of their public function. After this justification for the importance of the family theme in Pinter's work and after citing Pinter's explanation that "[c]ertain facts like marriage and the family . . . have clearly ceased to have any meaning" for Ruth in *The Homecoming* (153), Gale builds his argument on more textual grounds. [12] Applying Pinter's description to Flora of *A Slight Ache* as well as Ruth, Gale asks, "How does Pinter define family . . . so that we know what it is that has ceased to have any meaning for these women?" In contrast to his seeking clues to Pinter's definition of love in a dictionary and a psychology text, as he did before, in defining Pinter's concept of family, here Gale relies on the letter and Pinter's dramatic texts and other critics' interpretations of them. The "central" point of *Family Voices*, he concludes, is, ironically, the *unimportance* of family (163). This makes the "concept of family" paradoxically *important*. Without explicitly trying, Gale deconstructs "the concept of family" in *Family Voices*, but, no poststructuralist, he still relates the play to stages in Pinter's "essential" thematic development.[13]

Slicing Pinter's canon with "the concept of family" enables Gale to elaborate his argument in *Butter's Going Up* that the change in Pinter's "thinking" parallels "the difference between describing a symptom and discussing a disease" ("Harold Pinter's *Family Voices*," 152).[14] But *Family Voices* presents a further shift in Pinter's "emphasis" from focusing on "[r]elationships between individuals, family members or otherwise" to scrutinizing these relationships "through a gauze of time and memory"; Pinter's main "interest" has become "the nature of reality, how relationships affect and are affected by time and memory" (156).[15] As he explains the interrelations of time, reality, and memory in Pinter's plays in another article, Gale decentralizes each of these themes or subjects and offers a more complex point of view on the plays than he did in *Butter's Going Up* ("Nature," 202–3).

Personal and professional background and individual values may account in part for Gale's attraction to a "thematic approach" to Pinter. As an undergraduate college student, Gale aspired to be a medical doctor like his father. Pursuing a "premed" concentration at Duke University (1958–63), he was particularly drawn to the precision of science and mathematics.[16] This penchant for methodological exactness may partially explain his statement that "a scientific approach" to literature is "perfectly legitimate." He discovered such an approach after receiving his M.A. in English from the University of California, Los Angeles (1963–65), when he was studying for a Ph.D. in English at the University of Southern California (1965–70): one of his professors, William Templeman, impressed him by continually directing the class to analyze "how [literary texts] meant and what they meant" (interview with author), showing him "what to look for" ("Acknowledgments," *BGU*).

Gale's choice of Pinter as a topic for his dissertation was accidental. Having planned throughout graduate school to do a publishable edition of some letters by James Agee, he had to find another topic because they were destroyed. With little time left he settled on doing a dissertation on Pinter's plays after being stimulated by some assignments on *The Homecoming* for a graduate course with Emil Roy, since Pinter's "themes and style," as Gale puts it, "appealed to me." Sustained immersion in Pinter's work led to much greater interest and appreciation of the playwright's talent. Yet, at the beginning, "with absolutely no guidance" from his dissertation committee or "anybody" else: "I had to go out and sit down and try to work things out myself. And so I taught myself just by doing. My approach was, if I understand what the thing's about, there won't be any loose ends, unless they're there for a purpose."

Despite emphasizing Pinter's exploration of emotional need rhetorically in *Butter's Going Up* and his other writings, in 1982 Gale himself still did not find Pinter's plays particularly moving emotionally, either in reading or in seeing them on stage. His knowledge was generally based on reading them, since he had relatively little opportunity to see them staged. On the occasions that he had seen productions of Pinter's plays— for example, a production of *The Homecoming* in Los Angeles—he mostly enjoyed their comedic effects, laughing throughout the production of *The Homecoming*. [17] The concern with literary analysis has predominated even in Gale's initial experiences of Pinter, distancing him from more primary emotional involvement. In reading a Pinter play for the first time, he said in 1982, he maintains "openness" to the experience, to whatever "associations" may come to mind, but early on he attempts to parcel out the play's "meaning," to "place" various aspects of the play in "pigeonholes." Explicitly using the figure of a desk, he compared reading with sorting the "themes" of the play into the desk's pigeonholes. [18]

Yet Gale's own personal interest in the value of family life, the centrality of his own immediate family to his daily concerns, has enhanced his particular sensitivity to some of the issues about which he sees Pinter to be most concerned. He may be projecting his own attitudes and personal feelings toward his own family in understanding both Pinter the playwright and Pinter the man. Alluding to Pinter's letter citing family responsibilities mentioned earlier, Gale said:

> I believe that his family is important to him. . . . In a sense I see that [conflict between family and professional obligations] in myself. There's nothing more important to me in my life than my family. I can't imagine my life without my three kids. And yet, far too often I'm guilty of not giving them the attention that they should have or

giving them the time, because I want to be, I have to do other things, in order to be able to be with them at all or supply them with education or food or whatever it is. So I don't think that one thing really necessarily contradicts the other. It's ironic, it's sad, but maybe there's nothing that can be done about it either. They [family and such conflicting obligations] [are] not necessarily mutually exclusive. [19]

While the subjective reasons for Gale's insights about Pinter and his plays may constrain these insights, they do not diminish them. Quite the contrary, sensitivity to relations perceived between literature and the "themes" of their own lives enables critics to articulate literary "meaning."

Gale's description in his *Bibliography* of his own *Butter's Going Up* as "[t]he most complete study of all of Pinter's work available" (87) reflects his own hopes for it. He wanted to write "a book about Pinter that would be the book that anybody who worked on Pinter would have to refer to," one that "would contain all the basic ideas" about Pinter's plays, from which, no matter what "direction" would be taken, "everything would start." In other words he wanted to write *the* standard reference work— everyone else's point of departure: "My desire was first to create as comprehensive and complete a study as possible."

These hopes were somewhat frustrated by the seven years it took for his dissertation, completed in 1970 and then revised, submitted to, and accepted for publication by Duke University Press in 1971, to reach its published state. Later Gale did update the chronology to 1975 and some other lists of events and secondary source references to 1977. But the delay may have led reviewers to think that Gale was repeating ideas of others, though when he presented them, he thought that the ideas were fresh. As we have already seen, though in 1977 the reviewer for *Choice* still found some of his "insights" to be "original," noting his "advantage" of "being up to the moment," in his 1978 review Styan criticizes Gale's "vice of restating the commonplaces of Pinter criticism exhaustively" (302). In sharp contrast, Hinchliffe's bibliography for a revised edition of his Twayne monograph presents this "vice" as a virtue: *Butter's Going Up* is "[p]robably the most complete collection of information to date"; it "follows up every clue exhaustively" (*HP*, 28).

The aim to write "the basic book" in any field is the *dream* of many scholars. They want to become the *standard* or the *norm* in their fields, the "touchstone" against which all other related writing is measured: to be consulted by everyone else. A dream that perhaps goes beyond even economic rewards, this is a dream of *power*. For some this dream does "come true," if only temporarily, since most standard reference books are eventually superseded—in the study of American literature, one might think of F. O. Matthiessen's *American Renaissance* and other revisionist works, such as the feminist rewritings of the canon by Judith Fetterley or Jane Tompkins (*Sensational Designs*). The relation between such books can be seen as a relation of power and strategy, in Foucault's sense as discussed in chapter 3.[20]

Being a point of "departure"—a "basis" for others' work—means that others have to *differ* from you, leading to what Derrida calls "différance"—difference, deferment—and deference. Yet some may find Gale's thematic interpretations of Pinter's writing *so* basic that they can only agree with them. Rather than to disagree for the sake of controversy alone, or to agree blandly, perhaps they bypass him so as to produce new (different) material of their own. *Butter's Going Up*, like the bibliography, may be consulted more frequently than cited and thus perhaps not "seminal"; if it germinates new themes and even new approaches, it may do so somewhat indirectly.[21] When Almansi and Henderson, who offer a postmodernist approach to Pinter (as discussed in chap. 3), attack the "basic" value of Gale's thematic approach obliquely (as they do everything else), they cite *Butter's Going Up* only once: in comparing Eric Berne's "Let's You and Him Fight" game to Pinter's characters' "love triangles" (Almansi and Henderson, 32, 103 n.25; cf. Gale, *BGU*, 127). *Butter's Going Up* includes chronological and alphabetical lists compiling factual information regarding Pinter's writings; first performances of his plays and their casts and directors, productions directed by Pinter, roles acted by him, and awards given to him; and an extensive annotated bibliography. Within a year Gale published the volume-length bibliography, updating some of these lists. As over ten years have passed since publication of both books, it is perhaps time to revise and update not only the lists but, as Almansi and Henderson argue more recently, the approach as well.

Many academic dissertations on Pinter written in the seventies pursued thematic approaches; since then, despite much outcry, academic Pinter scholars still use them in their theses and publications.[22] As Gale does in his essay on *Family Voices*, many other critics retrospectively investigate themes in Pinter's past work thought to be most prominent in his most recent work, rereading and rewriting the former in terms of the latter and Pinter's contemporaneous public statements. Pinter's most recent plays have been viewed by Pinter himself and others as "political," and discussions (and questions about) the "political implications" of all his work are already appearing (see chap. 8). So, despite new critical trends, thematic approaches persist, especially for beginning students or new scholars of Pinter, who may find their "simplicity" helpful. Searching for meaning and cataloging formal stylistic changes are a "staple": a *stable* feature of Pinter criticism.

"[A]fter all," Gale still feels, "the thematic approach is the broadest and draws on, and is applicable to, the widest range of subjects, techniques, etc.—it really is all-encompassing. . . . Some critics who make important contributions using other approaches [e.g., Burkman and Quigley] still occasionally find it useful to take the thematic tack." The view that there is such a thing as "the thematic approach" or that any one approach encompasses *all* is debatable, as we will see. Burkman's ritual approach is an *instance* of thematic criticism, while some "psychoanalytic" and "linguistic" critics (including Esslin and Quigley) interpret Pinter's multiple "themes" or "meaning" through strategies quite distinct from Gale's and Burkman's; Susan Melrose rejects hermeneutics entirely for a "semiotics of performance."

Yet, given the link between academic pedagogical necessities and criticism, books and collections of essays interpreting Pinter are in demand in academic libraries. Obvious institutional factors such as requirements for tenure and promotion and the quest for academic prizes and endowed chairs perpetuate the "glut" of thematic criticism in the academic marketplace. Though Scott oversimplifies the impetus of early criticism of Pinter's plays in America as a search for "moral significance," this "approach to Pinter" has indeed "reached industrial proportions" (12). Instead of abating, thematizing has gotten a second wind through some critical theorists' unintentional perpetuation of "the New Critical legacy of 'interpretation'" (Cain, "English," 103 n.10).

### Ritual Ruses:
### Katherine H. Burkman

Burkman's *Dramatic World of Harold Pinter: Its Basis in Ritual*, a book said to exemplify "myth criticism" of recent drama (Willeford, 956), is the first full-length study of the ritual metaphor perceived in Pinter's work.

If "Pinter's drama employs ritual to approach the mysteries of life" (*DWHP*, 17), Burkman uses ritual to demystify Pinter. "Certainly," she discovers, "Frazer's *Golden Bough* kings offer an excellent metaphorical clue to the ritual sacrifices at the center of Pinter's dramas" (16–17). Sir James George Frazer's interpretation of the succession to the priesthood of Diana at Nemi "helps to explain" (61) Pinter's dramatic world.[23] The "menaced priest" becomes "an illuminating image" for Pinter's so-called comedies of menace—*The Room*, *The Birthday Party*, *The Dumb Waiter*, and *A Slight Ache*—and for Pinter's film *The Quiller Memorandum*. Reading Pinter's plays "in the light of the ritual rhythms which structure them" (10) transforms Pinter's so-called absurd meaninglessness into what Burkman terms "ritual meaning" (49). Defining Pinter's use of rituals redirects critical attention to positive spiritual values in his dramatizations of the "riddling nature of man" (91). Through her own ritual ruses, to echo Hamlet: by indirection Burkman finds direction out.

In ritualizing Pinter, Burkman claims: "At the center of the action of most Pinter plays is the *pharmakos*, or scapegoat, of ancient ritual and tragedy, the victim whose destruction serves in a special way to re-establish certain basic relationships in the family or community" (12). In her terms the ritual "metaphorical clue" yields the following "solution" to Pinter's puzzles: his plays are about "a seasonal ritual"—the *agon*, or the battle between the old god and the new god in "contention for the priesthood of Nemi" and the Golden Bough (51, 64). In *The Birthday Party*, *A Slight Ache*, *The Caretaker*, *The Homecoming*, and *The Basement*, "the old king-priest-god invariably must suffer death or banishment (Davies, Teddy, Edward—all must be sacrificed), either to be reborn as the new spirit of spring and life (Edward becomes the matchseller, Stanley becomes the new creation of Monty and Co.) or to be replaced by a new god (Teddy is replaced by Lenny and Joey, Law is replaced by Stott, Davies loses the battle to the young gods already in possession, Mick and Aston)" (134).[24] The same ritual also helps Burkman to explain "man's ambivalent relationship with woman" as dramatized by Pinter (91). "The role played by Pinter's women is also clearer if their place as fertility goddesses in the ritual is understood. . . . The new god must receive a welcome and be joined with mother earth if life is to continue" (134).

Speaking of the "patterned words" of Pinter's characters as "word games," Lois G. Gordon (discussed in the next chap.) calls them "a ritual that protects" and "the religion of everyday life" (*S*, 3). Similarly, Burkman regards the rituals of daily life performed by Pinter's characters as their protective measures against it. But she still assumes that the "daily secular rituals" in the plays "protect" the characters from "an awareness of life" forced upon them by the plays' "echoes of sacred sacrificial rites." She contends that "beneath the daily secular rituals which Pinter weaves into the texture of his plays . . . beat the rhythms of ancient fertility rites, which form a significant counterpoint to the surface rituals of the plays and which often lend the dramas their shape and structure" (10).

Barnet, Berman, and Burto summarize "ceremonial" kinds of primitive rituals on which contemporary critics thought literature based as well as the literary "theme" of "the importance of ritual in daily living" but conclude that the "question of [the] origins [of much literature in ritual]" is "debatable" (95). While reviews of *The Dramatic World of Harold Pinter* tend to praise Burkman's detailed exegeses, they question the exact nature of the connection that she draws between ritual and the plays. Gale finds "the element of ritual" in Pinter's plays "obvious" and the book a conscientious explanation of "what ritual means in the context of each play." "By its nature [Burkman's] study is self-limiting, but it provides a legitimate alternative reading of the dramas when presented with valid evidence from the plays. Unfortunately some of the readings are forced" (747). While Gale criticizes Burkman's "tacked on" Epilogue for making "no effort to place [*Landscape*, *Silence*, and *Night*] in the pattern of rituals (though they could be made to fit)," he praises it, "[i]ronically," for containing "some of the best readings of the plays . . . as [Burkman] does not try to restrict the works to her theme."[25] Reflecting values of his own work, he criticizes Burkman's overall "presentation" as "arbitrary and . . . not always logically structured" and her failure to account for "chronology" and to recognize "Pinter's development as an artist." Mainly he opposes the general impression conveyed: "that Pinter creates ritual for its own sake rather than as a means of conveying his meaning, placing the emphasis on too literarily conscious a level, as though the dramatist is simply trying to recreate specific rituals."[26]

James Hurt also complains of "theoretical confusion" in Burkman's "method" (285). Citing "the curious confusion and ambiguity at the center of the book, despite individual passages of excellent analysis," he explains: "If the rituals of *The Golden Bough* are only convenient metaphors for clarifying Pinter's themes of self-destruction, competitiveness, and sadomasochism, why insist so heavily upon detailed and sometimes tenuous analogies? If there is a substantial connection between the rituals and the plays, what is it?" This confusion is "most damaging" in Burkman's analysis of *The Birthday Party*, where it seems she is "translating the most obvious facts about the play into an irritating jargon." Burkman's book "for all its merits" suggests "a warning to those who come after of the difficulty in putting one's finger on the quintessence of Pinterism" (284). Nevertheless, Burkman's often cited ritual analysis of *A Slight Ache* in chapter 3, published first as a separate article in *Modern Drama*, is "the most illuminating criticism in the book" (286).[27] The whole book is "[c]learly a labor of love," whose "greatest virtues are [her] recognition of the depth and subtlety of Pinter's plays and the sometimes searching individual analyses which grow out of that recognition" (287).

Kent G. Gallagher seems most sympathetic to the Frazerian approach. Recognizing that Burkman's investigation is "analogical," he claims: "she moves one step further than the psychological critics who perceive dark Freudian and Jungian rhythms behind Pinter's recurrent familial and social rituals." In contrast to Gale's purported failure to treat Pinter's plays as theatrical cited above, Burkman includes a chapter on "Pinter in Production" (chap. 6): even if the "referent" of Burkman's "analogical schema" may be "the *lingua obscura* of subtextual ritual," her "textual criticism" is "rooted in a close and sensitive evaluation of the scripts as drama."[28]

Both Burkman's "referent" and her "textual criticism" reflect her educational training in literature and theater. She attended Bryn Mawr College (1951–52) and majored in English at Radcliffe College (1952–55), receiving an M.A. in English and a Certificate in Education from the University of Chicago (1955–56). After teaching high school English and Drama (1956–63), she also had professional training in acting and directing in New York City (1960–64). Following further graduate studies at the University of Iowa (1964–65) and Indiana University, Bloomington (1966), she received a Ph.D. in Theatre from Ohio State University, Columbus (1966–68). The archetypal criticism of Northrop Frye and the dramatic criticism of Francis Fergusson in the sixties were seminal influences on her own criticism, especially her belief in the roots of all drama in ritual. She also had subsequent experience with the role of dramatic performance in education and some background in psychology.[29]

Most often Burkman links ritual and psychology in directing and writing about Pinter's plays. Her early work on Pinter deemphasizes the psychological in favor of the mythological, using Frazer more than Freud as the key to Pinter and generally showing that the ritual nature of drama transcends the psychological and that ritual is ultimately more important than psychology in Pinter's plays. Even Freud based features of his theory of infantile sexuality—namely, the Oedipus and Electra complexes—on ancient mythic dramas, considering initiation rites in *Totem and Taboo* and the mythological origins of religion in primitive people's infantilism in *The Future of an Illusion*.[30] Updating and extending her ritual insights to Pinter's more recent plays, from *Old Times* through the three plays in *Other Places*, and Pinter's film adaptation *Turtle Diary*, Burkman has achieved more balance between ritual and psychology. Her more recent writing extends some of her earlier observations about oedipal rivalries structuring relationships between Pinter's men and women characters (*DWHP*, 90–118). In "Harold Pinter's *Betrayal*" she considers "the oedipal rivalry of the men over Emma" in *Betrayal* as a new manifestation of Pinter's "theme of betrayal as communication" (506–7). On *No Man's Land* in "Hirst as Godot," she notes again (as she does in her analysis of *A Slight Ache*) Freud's interpretations of dreams involving water and rescue from drowning as dreams about (re)birth.[31]

For Burkman, doubling in drama also has both mythological and psychological significance. Psychologists who deal with doubling, like Otto Rank, explore its sources in ritual and often use ritual metaphors. In discussing Pinter's doubles, Burkman observes: "By portraying the doubles as characters who are independent of the protagonists yet a part of them and as mysterious outer forces as well, Pinter offers a vision of life that has both psychological and spiritual dimension" ("Death and the Double," 143). She presents a potentially positive interpretation of this dual dimension: "In their dramatic encounters with death as a double, Pinter's characters must confront and accept their mortality if they are to arrive at any meaningful kind of existence." Although she often cites the "ambivalence" of Pinter's characters' attitudes toward one another (especially the "love-hate relationships" between fathers and sons, between men and women, and between the "doubles"), her interpretations tend to stress the positive side of an ending (renewal, rebirth, and communication) rather than its opposite (spiritual failure, destruction, or even death). A sense of the spiritual dimension of ritual generally provides Burkman with an upbeat frame of reference for resolving Pinter's paradoxes, softening their psychological edges.

"Displacement in Time and Space" concludes that "Pinter's dramaturgy in [*Family Voices, A Kind of Alaska,* and *Victoria Station*] draws us into the characters' [psychic] disorientation about realistic time and space, from which stance we, too, may feel terribly lost, but at the same time more able to seek a new way" (11). *"Family Voices* and the Voice of the Family" renovates Gale's deconstruction of family as a "cause for destruction" in the plays after *The Lover*: Burkman can find "a play suffused with sexual betrayal a family-affirming drama . . . [p]artly because the characters care very much about each other as family. Their very betrayals, wounding as they are, are desperate attempts at c[o]mmunication; they betray one another, paradoxically, to find that which is authentic within the family" (172).

Burkman's reading of *No Man's Land* in *The Arrival of Godot* focuses more on "death-in-life" than on deliverance, though the issue of "man's salvation" still figures in her thematic rendering of the play (117–24, 125). But in this book Burkman places discussion of *The Homecoming* after the chapter on *No Man's Land*. This positioning highlights Burkman's interpretation of the earlier play as Pinter's "drama of arrival" ending "modern man's and woman's exile" and "celebrat[ing] an authentic arrival of Godot" through "the savior figure" Ruth (125, 126).[32] As Burkman says, in conclusion, speaking allegorically of the driver in Pinter's *Victoria Station*: "The old god/king has become as irrelevant as Victoria Station where he must be stranded. The new god/king sits still in his cab, his sleeping passenger a part of his own potential awakening. Ruth has left her American family, the driver has left his wife and child at home, and the controller leaves all logic, all his dying values behind as with a leap of faith, he sets forth in search of Godot" (159). Or, as she puts it later in "Displacement in Time and Space": "Although his forthcoming journey to other places, the unspecified dark park by which the Driver is parked, is undertaken with an ambivalent rage, the Driver's new-won Beckettian disorientation about realistic time and space offers the possibility of reorientation to the Controller, making the play a kind of third act in *Other Places* that leads the audience to this more hopeful stance" (10–11).

Such optimism may be a projection of Burkman's own personal philosophy onto Pinter's plays. Though Burkman is dedicated to family, the Burkmans' own "religious 'observation' and practice of 'rites' is negligible": "It is hard to say what is of value to me in my religious heritage, but it has more to do with ethnicity and history and identifying as a Jew than with anything religious at all. In fact, one of my friends who knows me well thinks I write about myth and ritual because it fills a gap [created] by my lack of religious observance. So I don't place a high value on religious observation or identify much with religious rite. I enjoy some

religious rites—we make a great occasion of Passover—but that's all"
(letter to author).

From 1966 to 1968, when she was working on *The Dramatic World of
Harold Pinter*, Burkman felt that myth criticism was controversial and
that it was risky to undertake it. Though aware that she was "going out
on a limb" (in her words) and that some reviews would respond more to
the approach than to the working out of it, she has described herself as a
person who always writes what she wants without concern for the difficulty of getting it published. So, despite the critical risks, she has
persevered. Even though reviews of her first book, as we have seen,
criticized her use of ritual, since the early seventies she continued to
publish criticism of Pinter (and other dramatists) from her interdisciplinary perspective combining ritual and psychology.

Several other critics build on Burkman's ritual approach to Pinter's
work.[33] A graduate student whose master's thesis was directed by Burkman, Kelly Belanger finds that Burkman's "application of Sir James
Frazer's theory to *A Slight Ache* has provided valuable insight into Pinter's
characterization of [the ancient need for] renewal"; since this need "des-
perately . . . persists today," reading "the matchseller as a fool character
[lends] a new perspective to the [play's] structure and meaning" and
transcends "the initial sense of shock and despair that modern tragi-
comedies often instill in audiences" so that we "can eventually emerge to
meet the world of order and reason refreshed and enlightened" (43, 40,
50). Leslie Kane extends Burkman's thesis about "the central place of
ritual—in particular that of the scapegoat" in Pinter's drama to explain
his "identification with Jewish cultural experience" as depicted in "patterns of exclusion, expulsion, and literal or metaphoric extermination,
coupled with a heightened sensitivity to alienation, the ironic inversion
of prayers and rituals, anti-Semitic stereotypes, Gematryia—the nonverbal Jewish preoccupation with the numerical value of words—excre-
mental imagery, focus on betrayal and the depiction of drifters who avoid
detection and identification as Jews" ("Weasel," 19–20).

Burkman's own *Arrival of Godot*, according to Flannery, represents "a
newer stage of [ritual] criticism." Instead of regarding the meanings of
plays as based in ritual, Burkman sees the plays as presenting "a framework for thinking about, or imaging, their ritualistic structure and
underlying symbolism." Like the anthropologist Victor Turner, she "locates the source of power in the plays she discusses precisely in their
capacity to move audiences towards a state of liminality [timelessness].

. . . Burkman demonstrates . . . that ritual is a means of providing a ground in which the individual fates of men and women are less important than their participation in communities which enable them to become more than individuals" (543–44).

Further instituting this view of ritual, in the summer of 1986, the University of Pittsburgh's Department of Religious Studies began publishing the *Journal of Ritual Studies*, soliciting writing "from scholars in religious studies, anthropology, sociology, psychology, performance studies, history, and other disciplines that treat ritual in any of its various forms," so as "to encourage scholarly collaboration on the topic and its allied subtopics" ("Professional Notes"). Like Burkman's own more recent collection of essays, *Myth and Ritual in the Plays of Samuel Beckett*, such collaboration promotes critical strategies using ritual (ritual ruses) to redirect literary and cultural study toward positive communal values.

# 6

## Psychoanalytic Maneuvers:

## Smoke Screens against Recognition

The speech we hear is an indication of that [which] we don't hear. It is a necessary avoidance, a violent, sly, anguished or mocking smokescreen which keeps the other in its place. When true silence falls we are still left with echo but are nearer nakedness. One way of looking at speech is to say it is a constant stratagem to cover nakedness. —Harold Pinter

Katherine Burkman initially located the "basis" of Pinter's plays in "ritual action," arguing more recently that at an "allegorical level" Pinter "transcends psychology, and characters who might have become case histories gain archetypal resonance" ("Death and the Double," 134–35). Alan Bold claims that "[i]n a Pinter play the characters act ritualistically rather than realistically" (8). But as for many other critics, for Gerald Nelson "everything happens psychologically in a Pinter play," on the level of "psychic action" (38). Burkman's sacrificial victim Stanley (*DWHP*, 23–38), via "infantile regression," enters "the bosom of the family," becoming figuratively a child—"the perfect victim for anyone who wants to tell him what to do" (Storch, 706; cf. Schiff). Such differences of emphasis as those between ritual and psychology often reflect differences of both critical ideology and personal response.

It is difficult, probably even impossible, to penetrate critical defenses: "Psychoanalytic theory has shown that an artist/writer is always an artist/writer-in-transference: the material with which she works, be it stone or paint or word, is invested with desire before and as soon as she works with it. The reader-cum-critic's position is then vastly complicated, for she is subject to the effects the work produces in her as reader, and at the same time committed to the analysis of these effects as critic" (Wright, 177). As I analyze the strategies of psychoanalytical critical writers-in-transference, I recall my own experience, complicating my position even more, though I hope not compromising it.

### Lois G. Gordon:
### Pinter's Stratagems to Uncover Nakedness

Gordon's *Stratagems to Uncover Nakedness*, published in 1969 and reprinted in 1970, is one of the first monographs on Pinter, the first Freudian interpretation of Pinter's plays, and the first application of Eric Berne's transactional analysis to them. Distinguishing between Pinter and Beckett, Gordon counters presentations of Pinter's work by Martin Esslin in "Parallels and Proselytes" in *The Theatre of the Absurd* (1961) and Walter Kerr in *Harold Pinter* (1967), who argue, respectively, that Pinter presents universal "absurd" themes realistically, symbolically, and poetically and that he presents existential themes existentially.

Though Gordon describes Pinter's characters' word games as rituals that protect them from their own "primitive and repressed feelings" (*S*, 3, 5), generally she perceives ritual as less archetypal in Frazer's or even Jung's terms than Burkman does and more in terms of Freud and Berne, who provide her key to Pinter's "familiar but puzzling" idiom (1). The "dramatic force" of Pinter's characters comes from "the heart of their emotional life," which Pinter lays "bare," rather than from "the manner in which they symbolically represent philosophical dilemmas": "Pinter is not primarily a symbolic or philosophical writer. Although questions about ultimates and absolutes may be abstracted out of his plays (as such truths are contained in all great art) there is something more immediate and essential in his work that resists allegorical or philosophical categorization" (2).[1] Berne's transactional analysis analogically explains the more "sinister" purposes motivating Pinter's characters' apparently "banal" exchanges (3), while Freudian psychoanalysis exposes relations between what they say and do and what they feel (11, 61–62).

Though Pinter's "faithful reproduction of the nuances of ordinary speech" and "his impeccable recording of its hesitations, repetitions, and incoherences" are admirable, the basis of Pinter's "linguistic mastery" is his ability to reflect "the manner in which language disintegrates as internal impulses threaten and the speaker grows less assured of his patterned behavior" (3). Pinter uses "the increase of verbal wastefulness, the pointedness of clichés, the preponderance of *non sequiturs* in word and deed, and the punctuating and final silences" to chart "the faltering of word games" (3–4). In contrast to Burkman's later stress on ritual *action* as the basis of Pinter's drama, Gordon argues: "Ultimately in Pinter's work, the disintegration of normal language becomes a measure of dramatic tension, and, in a sense, drama exists at the level of language, as opposed to plot. In effect, exposition, crisis, and denouement are marked by verbal congruity, dissolution, and final resolution" (4).

Pinter's 1962 speech at Bristol University, in which Pinter defines speech as "a stratagem to cover nakedness," is Gordon's source for the metaphor that she uses to explain his plays. Citing Pinter's expressed distrust of language, Gordon describes his plays as "a careful carving of the truth of character beneath the stratagem of words." But this linguistic "paradox" explicates only "part of the Pinteresque," leaving "unaccounted for one essential ingredient—the mysterious, grotesque menace, that element of the bizarre, the extraordinary, the seemingly unreal, which always intrudes and disrupts Pinter's people somewhere about the middle of the play." To sum up the "pattern" of Pinter's plays in "simple" terms: "The 'intruder's' appearance initiates the breakdown of the patterned words and games, the habitual stratagems to cover nakedness. It also challenges the serenity and security provided by the room, whose arbitrary structure in effect parallels the habits of word and deed. At last, as the internal menace is fully projected externally, language disintegrates, and the so-called victim is expelled from the room; he finally exhibits himself in all his mental nakedness" (5). From this perspective Gordon explicates several of Pinter's plays: *The Room, The Birthday Party, The Dumb Waiter, A Slight Ache, The Caretaker, A Night Out, The Dwarfs, The Collection, The Lover*, and *The Homecoming*. Her treatment of the later short plays is much briefer than the others.

Stanley's oedipal "dilemma" is "at the heart" of *The Birthday Party* and the crux of "all of Pinter's work": "man is born with certain natural drives, and, as he grows up, he bears the burden of repressing what society then labels his illicit impulses. Unless he can do this, the Goldbergs and McCanns will erupt periodically to punish him for his original sin, his instinctual energies" (28–29). Even though mostly psychological, "man's" dilemma is also existential: "if he acts upon his instincts, his deeds will terrify and haunt him; his only alternative is to attempt a constricting life out of the fear of what is inside. The great paradox is that what is inside is not simply the free and lusty energy, indulgence of which might at least bring pleasure, but the inhibitions of society as well. Guilt (the internalization of society) *and* the raw instincts live unhappily side by side" (29). This combination of psychological and existential perspectives on *The Birthday Party* anticipates Esslin, discussed in the next section, and Gale, who cites Esslin often as well as Kerr and also acknowledges and sometimes qualifies Gordon's views.

Decisions about where to locate a play chronologically in Pinter's career have consequences on critics' reconstructions of Pinter's developing themes and techniques. Unlike Esslin, who analyzes *The Dumb Waiter* after *The Room*, and like Gale, Burkman, and Gabbard (discussed later), Gordon analyzes *The Dumb Waiter* after *The Birthday Party*. Her insight that "Pinter's humanization of the so-called menace marks an important aspect of his dramatic development" is contingent on this assumed order of composition. "Not only is the figure less terrifying in the next few plays, but by *The Caretaker* and *The Homecoming*, Pinter omits him entirely and is able to give bolder emphasis to his subject: the struggle within the warring personality" (19). Gordon does not identify the unseen operator of the dumbwaiter as such a "primal figure" as Riley, so in *The Dumb Waiter* "Pinter omits his usual third-party intruder" (29). Given the posited chronology and the sense of this omission, Gordon argues that "Pinter returns to the pattern of *The Room* and *The Birthday Party* in introducing the third-party figure" of the Matchseller in *A Slight Ache*; moving from *The Birthday Party* to *The Dumb Waiter* seems to be an advance; and from *The Dumb Waiter* to *A Slight Ache* a regression.[2]

When Gordon argues that in *The Caretaker* "Pinter sets aside the specifically sexual and the bizarre and concentrates upon the difficulty of maintaining human relationships because of the self-interest that prompts most communication" (40–41), she also anticipates one of the "themes" that Gale later notices (a need for love): the dynamic of the three characters' "role-playing" is based on their loneliness, resulting in a "sort of free-floating fear of general upset" (43). As she remarks that *A Night Out* and *Night School* continue the "tendency toward a more direct rendering of character motivation" begun in *The Caretaker* (50), while in the three subsequent television plays, *The Dwarfs*, *The Collection*, and *The Lover*, Pinter again raises "[m]ajor questions" about identity and the function of social behavioral patterns as disguises for "erratic inner compulsions" (51), Gordon further anticipates Gale's thesis about Pinter's "thematic development" (cf. Gale, *BGU*, 97–98).

For Gordon *The Lover* is "Pinter's least interesting play, as it diagrams multiple aspects of personality" (52). "More effective" when he merely suggests the various dimensions of the fragmented mind," Pinter "over-simplifies a complex situation" in *The Lover* when he "draws two people who, in terms of psychological portraiture, are shadows by comparison with his other couples."[3] Yet *The Homecoming* expands the acting out of fantasies "with a finesse and ingenuity only suggested in Pinter's early work" (53). While *The Homecoming* "again treats the struggle for power and sexual mastery beneath the ritualized games of daily life," it has "a primitive quality, as Pinter reveals, both in action and imagery, the uncontrollable, bestial underside of man."[4]

In her introduction Gordon observes that Pinter "has tried to realize dramatically the complexities of consciousness and the irrational welter—'the seething cauldron,' as Freud named it—that lies beneath it. This is a grand attempt," she continues, "considering the inevitable limitations that the dramatic form places on an exposition of interior self" (11). Concluding, she describes this irony: "Eden is not innocent, nor civilization corrupt; the latter is an endless round of banal responsibilities, the former—to use Freud's phrase—'a seething cauldron' of sexual intrigues. Things are not what we suppose; but then, if they were, we would have no need for Pinter and his stratagems" (61–62).

Reviews of *Stratagems* have singled out Gordon's use of Freudian psychology as either a strength or a weakness or both. On the positive side the reviewer for *Choice* finds her "frame of reference" an effective means of elucidating "the struggle in Pinter's plays between infantile sexuality and an inhibiting society," contrasting it to Walter Kerr's use of existential philosophy: "Rather than develop general theses about man's estrangement, she examines specific characters and situations and notes the high degree to which Pinter's plays are dream works in which the external world of menace is a projection of the characters' inner turmoil." Hinchliffe (whose own monograph on Pinter was first published two years before hers) regards Gordon's introduction as "excellent" because she explains that though Pinter's plays call for "symbolic interpretations," as Hinchliffe restates it: "Pinter's repudiation of such interpretations is supported by his characters, for Pinter, essentially, is dealing with people not patterns, and the disorders of his characters are the product of *daily* conflicts not cosmic upheavals or political confrontations" (450; cf. Gordon, *S*, 3).

On the negative side, however, Hinchliffe describes his own "sense of unease" at the title of Gordon's "63-page pamphlet" as exacerbated by the knowledge that she "is married to a psychiatrist" (449–50, citing "About the Author," in *S*, flyleaf). Though Hinchliffe himself suggests that his response to this knowledge might be "irrational," he changes tack, arguing that Gordon's "method of attack" might be more productive if she did not omit *Tea Party* and *The Basement*. There is some weakness in Gordon's method, he suggests. After repeating her words (quoted above) verbatim: "Thus Mrs. Gordon sees Pinter as trying to realize dramatically Freud's 'seething cauldron' which is far from easy considering the limitations drama puts on expositions of the interior self," he locates "difficulties" in Gordon's *"leitmotif"* of *"emasculation,"* based on (in her phrase) "the Freudian interpretation of the Oedipus Myth." Her interpretation of this "pattern" in *The Homecoming* conflicts with Pinter's text as Hinchliffe perceives it and with productions that he has seen. Assessing Gordon's evaluation of *The Lover* as Pinter's "least interesting" play and anticipating Styan's criticism of Gale, Hinchliffe argues that *The Lover* may be least interesting "from Freud's point of view but on television and in the theatre it is simply stunning": "The real danger of this method" is its inability to account for "what happens in the theatre." As far as he is concerned, "Mrs. Gordon's stratagem has transferred the plays from the stage to the couch and turned Pinter's people into patients" (450).

This complaint about Gordon's application of a Freudian approach to Pinter's plays illustrates a common reaction to any use of this approach, given the general critical attitude toward Freudian criticism in 1971: "A Freudian critic is in some measure a follower of Freud; he generally praises a work to the degree to which it recognizes the things (*e.g.*, the Oedipus complex) that Freud recognized. Freudian criticism often veers into biography, finding in the literary work clues to the author's personality, and explaining the work in terms of the occurrences in the author's childhood" (Barnet, Berman, and Burto, 31). Whether or not critics relate textual features to the author's childhood, as Gordon generally does not, the claim that psychoanalytic literary criticism is "reductive" is often a battle cry against the use of psychoanalysis in any context, even the therapeutic one that in part stimulated Gordon's Freudian frame of reference.

After receiving her B.A. from the University of Michigan in 1960 and her M.A. from the University of Wisconsin in 1962, while teaching English at the City College of New York (1964–66), Gordon wrote her Ph.D. dissertation on the dramatic language of Beckett (University of Wisconsin, 1966). She moved to the University of Missouri, in Kansas City, where she taught English (1966–68) while her husband, Alan, was chief of psychiatry at Munson Army Hospital. She read Alan's books both when he was a resident in training at Albert Einstein College of Medicine in New York City (1964–66) and later when he was in the army. Fascinated by a performance of *The Caretaker*, she read Pinter's plays and wrote *Stratagems to Uncover Nakedness* from a psychoanalytic perspective on relations of characterization and language.[5]

"Harold Pinter—Past and Present" and Gordon's entry on Pinter in *Contemporary Dramatists* ("Pinter, Harold"; see chap. 9 below) both mention other works of Pinter's (screenplays and poetry) in passing: the former covers Pinter's plays through *Silence* and *Landscape*, the latter through *Hothouse* and *Betrayal*. "Harold Pinter—Past and Present" repeats Gordon's earlier thesis that "[u]ltimately Pinter's plays are stratagems to *uncover* nakedness" (89), modifying and extending it to Pinter's more recent plays, including now both *The Basement* and *Tea Party* as transitions to an important change in Pinter's writing. Along with other "changes mark[ing] new techniques in Pinter's work," the characters have "two alternatives in coping with the ordeal of ordinary experience: They can attempt the games that people play, but if they do, a kind of breakdown ultimately results. Or, they can abandon themselves to the world of fantasy and silence, in which case they must suffer total isolation" (95, 98). Pinter portrays "pure being" in these dramatizations of relationships between men and women through "more poetic" language (98–99). Elsewhere Gordon observes that Pinter "has most frequently marked the breakdown of the games people play by exposing their outbursts of suppressed inner violence. But these [and other] trademarks, associated with his filmscripts as well as his plays, are absent in [his film] *The Go-Between*" (Gordon, "*Go-Between*," 81).[6]

Despite his denial of any "particular interest in psychology" and a claim not to have read Freud (Bensky, 29; Packard), Pinter himself has commented favorably on Gordon's work. She sent him copies of both *Stratagems* and "Harold Pinter—Past and Present" before meeting with him in 1971. During their expected "hour" meeting, which actually lasted several hours, Pinter said that he found an existential focus on his plays incorrect, and he was very receptive to Gordon and her work; he told her, "You really understand my work." Pinter was even encouraged by Gordon's writing. Preparing the bibliography following Gordon's subsequent essay on Pinter in *Contemporary Dramatists*, the publisher listed *Stratagems* with his approval.

Neither Gordon's past interpretations of Beckett nor her subsequent work on Pinter and other writers (e.g., Donald Barthelme, Robert Coover) are as psychological as *Stratagems* is. In discussing Coover, however, Gordon does observe that, like contemporary physics, "[t]he social sciences, especially psychology and the work from Freud and Jung through Deleuze, Goffman, and Laing, have also radically altered traditional notions of reality, specifically in the areas of human behavior and thought process" (*Robert Coover*, 3). While she notices that Coover has cited Freud as one of several important influences on his work (13), Gordon draws this comparison: as in Coover's world, "[i]n Beckett's and Pinter's worlds, the individual is ruled by inner and outer forces that defy his best efforts to construct games or stratagems to endure time. . . . [But] Coover is closer to Yeats, Woolf, and Joyce in restoring to man the redemptive imagination—and, in a unique sense, the games that it constructs—as the means toward comfort or despair" (8). Unlike Burkman and other myth-ritual critics, Gordon does not find in either Pinter's dramatic world or his stratagems to uncover nakedness the more comforting means of this redemptive imagination.

### Martin Esslin:
### *Not* a Psychoanalysis of Harold Pinter

Anticipating prevalent antagonism to Freudian criticism reflected in objections such as Hinchliffe's and complaints against scholars "imputing motives to artists" (P. Hall, 80), in *The Peopled Wound: The Work of Harold Pinter* Esslin presents his "psychoanalytical" focus as purposely thematic, not biographical. His aim is "*not* to give a psychoanalysis of Harold Pinter or to probe his subconscious motivations but merely to explain the *impact* and *effect* on audiences who obviously respond to the subconscious content of much that would otherwise remain enigmatic and inexplicable."[7] Esslin demonstrates (as Gordon and Gabbard would before and after him) a greater interest in analyzing the minds of Pinter's characters (however "archetypal") as if they were real people with real and understandable motivations. Psychoanalytic "themes" are a main source of audience response to Pinter's plays; Pinter's poetic artistry as a writer and his sense of the theatrical as an actor and a director account for most of the rest of his success as a playwright.

A recurrent emphasis throughout this monograph on Pinter is the ultimate ambiguity of Pinter's dramatic world and the uncertainty of any interpretation of his plays. The three levels of interpretation of *The Birthday Party*—social, existential, and psychologically archetypal—allow for "many others," for "there is *no contradiction* between these different aspects" (90).[8] As Gallagher suggests in reviewing Burkman's *Dramatic World*, Esslin's recurrent emphasis on the universal symbolism of Pinter's "archetypes" and "dream images" is a mixture of Jung and Freud. The "insistence on universality" distinguishes archetypal criticism from "Freud's 'typical symbols' which were to be interpreted within a specific cultural context" (Wright, 69). Yet the complementary emphasis on "the realism, the reality of the concrete situation portrayed" in Pinter's plays still accommodates Freud.

Interpreting Pinter's more recent plays in the second and third editions of *The Peopled Wound*, Esslin has extended both his perspective on Pinter's ambiguity and his tendency to construct tripartite interpretations mixing "realistic" and "symbolic" or "archetypal" levels or "planes" of meaning. In the fourth edition at times Esslin still suggests Pinter's continuing universal archetypal significance (cf. 195, 204); however, in discussing the plays new to this edition, Esslin implies that Pinter's ambiguity is lessening. Some plays are characteristically ambiguous, some not. This suggests a change in Pinter's overall attitude toward reality beginning with *Betrayal* (205–24).[9]

In the introduction to *The Peopled Wound*, dated September 1969, Esslin asks: "Is there any justification for a monograph on an author who, at the time it was being written, had not yet reached the age of forty?" (8). In his 1972 preface to the second edition, he observes that his monograph has appeared in English, American, German, and French editions, showing that "the interest in this important playwright is undiminished and that the demand for a comprehensive study and analysis of his work . . . really exists," and cites "the astonishingly large amount of queries and requests for help which I have received from students, academics and theatre people who, in one way or another, were working on or with the plays of Harold Pinter" (11). He further justifies his subsequent editions on the basis of Pinter's "increasing" professional activities (12–13).

*The Peopled Wound* consists of five chapters: "Chronology of a Career," "Background and Basic Premises," "Analysis" (through *Silence* and *Go-Between*), "Language and Silence," and "Evaluation." The chronology of Pinter's career is "built up from the main dates of decisive events in his life, illustrated by quotations from his own recollections contained in interviews with him which have occasionally appeared in periodicals, and with quotations from characteristic reviews of important performances of his plays" (9). In compiling this list Esslin had help from Pinter, who checked this "factual data." For the second edition Pinter clarified some of the "biographical details" (11), and he also checked the chronology for the fourth edition. Each of the subsequent editions updates the chronology and (to a degree) the selected bibliography. The revision of the bibliography in the fourth edition is somewhat expanded by "the most important new critical books on Pinter" (e.g., Gale, *BGU*; Quigley, *PP*; Gabbard, *DS*; but still not Burkman, *DWHP*; Gordon, *S*), but "the extensive bibliographies now available" rationalize excluding translations and periodical articles, "as keeping up with the masses of new material would have enlarged the book beyond reasonable bounds" (13).

Subsequent editions have maintained the same structure as the original *The Peopled Wound*, with new sections on *Old Times* (2d ed.); *Monologue, No Man's Land*, and very brief mention of *The Proust Screenplay* (3d ed.); and *The Hothouse* (the published version), *Betrayal, Family Voices, A Kind of Alaska*, and *Victoria Station* (4th ed.). The second edition also adds a group of photographs of productions of Pinter's plays in Great Britain and elsewhere, augmented in subsequent editions. So that the fourth edition would remain up to date with productions of Pinter's *Other Places*, first produced at the National Theatre's Cottesloe in October 1982, Esslin examined scripts of *Victoria Station* and *A Kind of Alaska* well in advance of their theatrical premiere. The fourth edition lists these plays in its updated chronology and includes analyses of them; its preface is dated over half a year before they opened. Thus Esslin's analyses of these new plays were written for *Pinter: The Playwright* even before the plays opened on stage and were reviewed as productions, reversing the customary order in dramatic criticism. In terms of the *business* of criticism, by "scooping" them, Esslin clearly has an advantage over other Pinter critics. His own relationship with the playwright, originating in the late fifties and developing mostly during Esslin's tenure as the head of BBC Radio Drama (1963–77), makes his work on Pinter tend to seem "authorized," though, Esslin insists, it is not (8–9). If not authorized, it appears to be privileged. [10]

Almansi and Henderson assert:

> Of all the critics, Martin Esslin is perhaps the most consistently guilty of 'pigeonholing Pinter' and taking his heroes at their word.
> . . . He is, we believe, at once the most perceptive of Pinter's critics and the playwright's worst enemy. On the one hand, he recognizes the need to maintain the proper sense of pluralistic ambiguity in his

readings. . . . At the same time, however, he appears to want to seal what he calls the 'open wound' in Pinter's plays—that which Pinter leaves deliberately unexplained. . . . He tries to satisfy a craving for comprehension . . . to meet a critical requirement that was once vociferously demanded by the audiences (though not any longer, we believe; like Picasso's, or Stravinsky's, or Joyce's, Pinter's outrage has become the norm of respectability). (71–72)

In defense against this critique Gale calls Esslin's Pinter study as "periodically updated" still "one of the best" books on Pinter (rev. of Almansi and Henderson, 143).[11] Other reviewers have also praised the chronology of Pinter's career, the discussions of unpublished materials, and the chapter on "Language and Silence" in the various editions of Esslin's Pinter monograph. But there has been far less of a consensus on the critical importance and value of Esslin's analysis of Pinter's oeuvre.[12] The main bones of contention have been Esslin's attitude toward interpreting Pinter and his "methodology": his "psychoanalytical" approach. (Some are even skeptical of Esslin's continually emphatic denial of interest in Pinter's motives.)

Whereas for Gilman Esslin's "method" is "the extremely conventional one of providing detailed summaries of the events of each play and then moving on to elucidate and make interpretations" (35), for Kalem Esslin's attitude in using this very method is the book's strength: "To take a hard line on the 'meaning' of a Pinter play is like taking a hard line on the meaning of a sunrise. In his play-by-play analysis, Esslin displays a winning humility. He is never arbitrary about imposing interpretations" (60).[13] Gilman agrees with other reviewers that "Esslin is a reliable guide to what happens" in a Pinter play "[i]f you aren't familiar with [it]." "(He is especially valuable for his summaries of discarded or unfinished plays and those written for TV but altered for the stage.) But once past that we enter the realm of Esslin's ideas about Pinter, and what is needed is a critique of *them*, or rather of what Esslin does with them" (36). So Gilman criticizes Esslin for offering interpretations of Pinter's work while praising Pinter's own refusal to do so. Esslin "stuffs the categories he has erected with possible meanings and theoretical significances," and "in nearly every case" his interpretations are "either clearly wrong, or right but reductive." Like many other reviewers, Gilman is *sure* that *The Homecoming* is "'about' something other than an Oedipal situation" and that *The Caretaker* "is more (or less) than a metaphor for the relations of fathers and sons."

Despite differences of emphasis qualifying its general value, some appraisals of Esslin's use of a psychoanalytical focus are positive: "Esslin's technique is Freudian, but it is used with restraint and intelligence" (Luddy); "[i]n approaching the substructure of Pinter's dramas, Esslin is appropriately psychoanalytical" (Kalem, 60). But more numerous negative assessments reveal strong biases against using Freudian psychology to explain Pinter, faulting Esslin for inconsistency (as Gilman suggests, in interpreting Pinter at all) and/or reductiveness. Whereas Barranger praises Esslin for fulfilling his promise to leave "the central mystery of the Pinter play . . . intact throughout *The Peopled Wound*" (476), Rusinko finds him *unable* to resolve Pinter's enigmas and to explain his mysteries, *despite* "the promise of the perceptive background chapter," *because* of the psychoanalytical approach (rev., 114–15).[14]

With respect to Esslin's claim that he uncovers in Pinter's work "archetypal" themes to which audiences respond: reviewing the fourth edition, Frances Hill notices that "Esslin implicitly raises a question he might in fairness have tackled. He claims that *The Homecoming* is based on an Oedipal theme, with Ruth in the end becoming both mother and whore to Max's sons Lenny and Joey. This theme gives the play 'universal' power and interest, he says. But why should the 'universal' appeal of repressed male longings be felt by an audience's female members? . . . The question is not at all trivial, since Esslin believes that *The Homecoming* makes more explicit a theme running through all Pinter's previous plays and accounting for much of their power." Emerging from more recent critical awareness of the effects of gender on audience response, such questions put Esslin's psychoanalytic Pinter criticism in a larger cultural context (see chap. 8).

In a 1986 interview with Robert Bly, Esslin attributes his perspective on drama to his practical work:

> In 1960, after I had spent twenty years in what I would call political broadcast journalism [for the BBC], I became Assistant Head of the Drama Department at BBC Radio, and then Head of it in 1963. That twenty years as a political journalist was especially good training for my actual profession, which is theater—or drama, rather. I spent sixteen or seventeen years as Assistant Head and

Head of the BBC Radio Drama Department, which is the largest theater in the world. We produced something like a thousand to fifteen hundred productions a year on radio. Of course we had a very large dramaturgical department, which was called the BBC radio drama script unit. There were ten to twelve people reading the thousands of scripts that we were getting. I was in a way the top decision maker in this process. So in that sense, for sixteen or seventeen years I was, in fact, presiding over the largest dramaturgical department in the world. (20)[15]

Esslin's practical professional training and experience as a dramaturge helped to develop his breadth of "general" knowledge: "a thorough knowledge of dramatic literature, a thorough knowledge of how plays are produced and directed" and "knowledge of languages"—in addition to German and English, "Ancient Greek and Latin . . . French, Italian, Spanish, Hungarian, and quite a bit of Russian"—as well as knowledge of "other peoples' cultures and ways of life" (19–20). For Esslin "an ideal dramaturg would be a kind of Renaissance man who knows everything. Now, while I'm not claiming to be that, that was my ideal aim in training myself." He does *not* mention having acquired knowledge of or a commitment to any one particular academic specialty or critical methodology.

Just as psychological "character analysis" is a strong interest in Esslin's work as a dramaturge (22), so it is a prominent feature of his writing on Pinter. In *The Peopled Wound*, to explain the thematic significance of Pinter's character relationships, Esslin loosely borrows "archetypal" strands from philosophy ("the existential") and psychology ("the psycho-analytical") through the "analysis" in chapter 3 and then focuses chapter 4 ("Language and Silence") on the "function" of Pinter's technical use of language, pauses, and silences in the structure of his dramas.[16] Though his critical elasticity might seem a methodological inconsistency, Esslin's own published views of criticism tend to justify eclecticism.

For Esslin criticism is "a search for subjective truth": "I for one feel that even in the 'higher,' scholarly context the usual dictionary definition [of *criticism*], on the lines of 'the explanation and analysis of works of art or literature,' is already too exact and specific. The term after all is, quite legitimately, applicable to such a variety of different, albeit related, activities, that even such a definition seems to narrow it down too much. There are many different types of questions to which the answers might be regarded as instances of a critical activity" ("Search," 199–200). The questions that Esslin himself seems to ask recurrently about Pinter's work are the conventional What is it about? and How does it achieve its effect?[17]

Esslin opposes "the quest" of "a more scientific, positivist age" to "discover laws of criticism in analogy to the discovery of laws of nature by the natural sciences," considering "[t]hat analogy . . . equally fallacious and even more harmful" (201). Criticism that assumes "that there could ever be such a thing as a truly scientific framework for our 'discourse on art'" is "misguided": "For science is concerned with establishing objective truths, verifiable facts, immutable causalities. But the arts, above all literature, are concerned with *subjective* truths, *subjective* experience and the subjective causality which creates a different, *subjective* reaction to the same object, in different individuals. There can, thus, be no absolutes in criticism" (201–2). "Does that mean that there is no generally accepted body of knowledge in this field, no generally established standards?" Esslin asks. "By no means: but these generally accepted standards, these widely held convictions merely have the status of a *consensus*, not of an absolute truth" (202). The "two kinds" of such consensus are "about minimum standards of *craft*, on the one hand, minimum standards of *taste* on the other," *neither* being "absolute."

Esslin's own practical professional experience illustrates the mutability of taste:

> When, in my capacity as head of the BBC Radio Drama department, I had editorial responsibility for accepting or rejecting plays out of the one to two hundred manuscripts sent in every week, I was reasonably certain that the ones I turned down were verifiably not worth doing, were certainly below acceptable standards; I remained, nevertheless, equally certain that their unacceptability, their verifiable badness, was so only within the context of prevailing tastes, prevailing expectations, prevailing conventions. Those conventions, that consensus, I was equally well aware, are in constant flux, subject to constant almost imperceptible change. But one has only to look at the bulk of old films, read the best-sellers or even some of the "classics" of yesteryear, to realize how radical that change is over longer periods. (203)

Even given this "awareness of the absence of standards of judgment independent of local, cultural, historical, social, and other specific circumstances, and hence of the impossibility of applying absolute criteria of any kind," we can still "reason about works of art within an ordered logical framework: *we must merely be aware of the relativity of that framework itself.* . . . If there are no absolute standards of judgment, similarly there are *no absolute standards of critical methodology*" (203–4; emphasis added). If the "many differing intentions behind critical activity" lead to "a multitude of differing methodologies and techniques by which texts are approached, analyzed, explained and discussed," Esslin continues, "Each of these, in my view, is valid, so long as it is recognized that each deals with a different aspect of a wide and multifarious subject matter and can yield results only in relation to the intentions that originally motivated its formation" (204–5). Thus it would be "valid" (not "inconsistent") to analyze "archetypal themes" and "language and silence" in the same book.

For Esslin, "[s]een as a dialectical process—as discourse, debate, exchange of reactions, impressions, views—resulting from widely varying interests and intentions, criticism clearly is a *collective* endeavor which will at best produce a *consensus*, sometimes long-lasting, sometimes short-lived, about individual works, problems, techniques or values" (206–7). Though concluding that a "major" social function of criticism is "the dialogue between the communicator and the recipient of the communication" (209), recalling Fish (as cited in chap. 2) Esslin nevertheless insists: "those who contribute to the dialectical process . . . should believe in the absolute truth, the supreme rightness, of their own ideas" (205).

As the "recipients" of Esslin's "communication" on Pinter, some reviewers have not been so impressed by its "supreme rightness" as Esslin himself may have been when he wrote it. It is "somewhat plodding" (*Booklist*); his "terminology"—*metaphor, ambiguity, archetype*—is more "a coercion toward acceptance, an instrumentality of adult education" than helpful in differentiating Pinter from "all the other writers whose work is metaphorical, ambiguous and archetypal too," and his judgments of Pinter's work originate in "theories of literature instead of full encounters with it" (Gilman, 36).[18] Such discriminations reflect both individual and group taste. But (as Esslin tells us) both kinds of taste are temporary; they can change. So John Peter demonstrates in reviewing the second edition of Esslin's book three years after reviewing the first. Now its "shortcomings" are only "relatively minor," it is "more attractively titled," and it is "a blessed relief" from Baker and Tabachnick's *Harold Pinter* ("Beckett and Friends," 79). Esslin's theory of criticism renders the "truth" of *all* these judgments equally "subjective."

## Lucina Paquet Gabbard:
## A Psychoanalytic Approach

*The Dream Structure of Pinter's Plays: A Psychoanalytic Approach*, the most extensive application in English of Freudian psychoanalysis to Pinter's plays, considers Pinter's texts as dream-texts, interpreting the meaning of the plays (the "subtexts" or "latent content") beneath the plots (the "manifest content"). Like Gordon and Esslin, who try to demonstrate the unity of Pinter's canon, Gabbard groups the plays around "the oedipal wish—the classic theme of all great literature and the universal problem of all mankind"—and organizes them in groups of variations on this wish: "punishment dreams" (*The Room, The Birthday Party, The Dumb Waiter*, and *A Slight Ache*); "anxiety dreams" (*A Night Out, The Caretaker, Night School*, and *The Dwarfs*); dreams centering on "the wish to have mother" (*The Collection, The Lover, Tea Party, The Basement*, and *The Homecoming*); and further retrospective "punishment dreams" resulting from the fulfillment of the wish for mother (*Landscape, Silence, Old Times*, and *No Man's Land*) (see dust jacket; 38–40, 275). Whereas Gordon considers *The Birthday Party* most crucial, for Gabbard *The Room* is "the key dream" in the "dream series" of Pinter's plays.

Like the earlier psychological critics, Gabbard defines the plays' developing "thematic emphases" (40). But, uniquely, she observes that whereas the earlier plays represent the fear of punishment and anxiety with which "man" perceives the future, the later plays demonstrate his "depression" as he contemplates his memories of his earlier self (273). While earlier critics compared Pinter's plays metaphorically to dreams (calling them "dreamlike" and highly "symbolic") and even considered his "stratagems" as a playwright, they did not associate these dramatic strategies with aspects of Freud's "dream-work"—psychic processes disguising the "latent content" of a dream—as Gabbard does. She builds the analogy into an extended definition, applying it precisely, as she offers explanations of "condensations," "splittings," and "displacements" to show significant interrelationships among characters, events, images, symbolism, and whole plays. She indicates unconscious features of Pinter's creative process as well as his conscious methods of revision.

As with both Gordon and Esslin, in reading this book some reviewers found the psychoanalytic approach a source of irritation: for example, "Pinter scholars . . . will, no doubt, find it irritating and suggestive by turns"; "non-Freudians will like the book as little as anti-Freudians" (Jiji,

115; *Choice*). Jiji expresses particular disappointment that Gabbard neglects "[l]ater developments in psychoanalytic thought, such as ego psychology and the study of object relations, which might have been useful" (116).[19] But when the use of psychoanalysis or the kind of psychoanalysis used are not insurmountable problems, reviewers regard Gabbard's work highly. For example, Luddy, who also appreciated Esslin's *Peopled Wound*, finds Gabbard's book a "classic Freudian analysis of Pinter's output," demonstrating "a consistent and ordered pattern of inner structure in his work," and considers her "summary of Freud's theory of dream structure" to be "a model of clarity"; he also admires Gabbard's "sense of meticulous detail" and finds her analysis illuminating.[20] In contrast, her harshest critic, Moleski, describes *The Dream Structure* as "a purely mechanical decodage" ("a pastiche of translations of Pinter's language and situations into the terminology of developmental phases, psychic topography, etc. . . . a book not too dissimilar in spirit from the *Traumbuch* against which Freud set his project in the *Traumdeutung*"); Gabbard "[s]uspend[s] the difference between drama and dream" in order to "resolve" Pinter's "obscured causalities, enigmatic motives, elusive if not phantasmal frames of reference" (291).

Like Esslin, Gabbard professes pluralism: "In general, no one of these interpretations or determinations is any more valid than another. However, one determination may be more meaningful or more recognizable to one individual than another, depending on his associations. To discover increasing numbers of interpretations, whether they be realistic, symbolic, or psychological, is to demonstrate the universality and power of the play. The principal focus of this study is on the various overall interpretations of the plays that overdetermination allows and comprises" (23). Nevertheless, she still "privileges" the psychoanalytic. This "inconsistency" troubled me when I first reviewed the book; perceiving "some difficulty in this book's definition of its own worth," I argued: "[T]here is no doubt as to which interpretations Gabbard favors; her nonpsychoanalytic renditions of the plays are generally more like plot summaries than interpretations. She regards the psychoanalytic reading as the 'hidden' meaning of the plays, its deepest (least superficial) meaning. . . . This disparity between the validity of the approach and its usefulness does confuse her stance toward the plays" (Elliott, "New Solutions," 240–41). Strongly interested in psychoanalysis myself at the time, however, I concluded: "But the readings are so interesting in many cases, especially to those already psychoanalytically inclined, that this inconsistency might escape Gabbard's readers" (241). It was also noticed by Jiji, however: "despite the lip service to multiplicity and ambiguity found best phrased in the conclusion, the dogmatic style throughout seems to reflect a naive insistence on her views as scientifically validated. This view is unjustified" (116).

One of Gabbard's sources for these "views" was Norman N. Holland's *Dynamics of Literary Response*, which directly raises the issue of "validity," arguing that "psychoanalytic psychology offers a more valid and comprehensive theory of inner states than any other" (xv; cf. *Psychoanalysis and Shakespeare*, 318–19). Gabbard softens this stance when she says in *The Dream Structure* that although the book analyzes the latent meanings hidden beneath Pinter's dream-plays, she does not claim greater validity or importance for her interpretations over others. But what Jiji perceives as "lip service to multiplicity and ambiguity" is more central to Gabbard's evolving sense of personal and professional identity than any critic could guess.

How educational training and some other personal and professional experiences led Gabbard to modify Holland in such a way as to create these inconsistencies is a complex story. Her "first love since grade school" was the theater, and eventually she developed an interest in acting and dramatic literature, continuing these interests in college and graduate school, where she became most concerned with dramatic character. She received her B.A. in Speech and Dramatic Art from Louisiana State University in 1942, her M.A. in Theatre from the University of Iowa in 1947, and her Ph.D. in English from the University of Illinois in 1974. Marriage to E. Glendon Gabbard (later chairman of the Theatre Arts Department at Eastern Illinois University) and the Second World War intervened between her first two degrees. Raising their two sons and part-time teaching preceded her work on her doctorate. Her interest in Freud and the psychoanalytic approach to literature first emerged when she was studying Ibsen and encountered Freud's interpretation of *Rosmersholm*. After the children were born (1948, 1949), Gabbard became more deeply interested in psychology, reading "widely on the psychological development of the child, seeing it primarily as a source of guidance in rearing my children effectively." Psychology and literature dominated conversation in the Gabbard household; eventually, the eldest son, Glen, became a psychiatrist on the staff of the Menninger Clinic, which he now directs; Krin earned a Ph.D. in comparative literature and teaches at the State University of New York at Stony Brook.[21]

Gabbard's own experience as an English teacher began in the early fifties, when she started teaching part-time to supplement the family income while her husband worked on his doctorate in Theatre at the University of Iowa. After he completed this degree in 1954, they returned to Eastern Illinois University, where he resumed his position as professor of Theatre Arts and director. From 1954 to 1968—fourteen years—she taught part-time "on a temporary basis" in the English department because an antinepotism law prohibited her from having a regular position. After it was eliminated, she was "hired for a regular tenure-track position with the provision that I would begin work immediately on thirty hours beyond the Master's." Beginning this advanced study in the summer of 1969, she enjoyed it so much that she continued through the doctorate.

Gabbard became "particularly fascinated" by the "ambiguity" of Pinter, Beckett, and Albee, choosing Pinter's work for a dissertation topic partly because of the "challenges" that she felt it presented: "puzzles that I wanted to unravel for myself."[22] Interested in "the psychological mechanism of projection," at first she planned to explore how Pinter's characters use projection. Her *own* tendency to project led her to read Freudian psychology "right into Pinter's plays." Recalling her parental experience with child psychology, *The Dream Structure* treats Pinter's characters not as fully developed adults, but as childish adults, adults with unresolved neuroses. Yet "Freudian psychology is built upon the fact that these early childhood experiences are to such a large extent the controlling forces in the unconscious. . . . [I]n dreams, the surface content of the dream springs out of current events which relate and connect with earlier events that trigger strong emotions. But at bottom there's always that residue of emotional and traumatic experiences from early childhood and infancy which infects the current responses." Methodologically speaking, "if you're dealing with a psychoanalytic approach to a character, there's no way that you can *not* go back to childhood."[23]

Refocusing her interest from projection to Freud's work on dreams, Gabbard still had difficulty finding "some kind of overall organizational pattern" or "framework" to explain Pinter's plays until she had what psychoanalysts call an "Aha!" experience. One day, reading *The Interpretation of Dreams*, she "stumbled upon this part about dream sequences, and it just came to me like a flash, how perfectly that fit with Pinter's plays. . . . The pieces of my puzzle that I had worked out individually, all of them began to take shape into a . . . kind of unified, whole." It seemed "almost uncanny" when she "discovered" the connection between Freud's structure of sequences centering on "one dream thought" and Pinter's plays: "Now, of course, I recognize this tendency I have to see what I'm reading in terms of what I have *just* read, and so part of this *fit* was in my perspective, but it did seem that way to me. All these wishes . . . and the way they worked, punishment dreams, anxiety dreams . . . just exactly the way Freud lays it out in *The Interpretation of Dreams*. . . . The two just came together like a perfect fit."[24]

Despite her long-developing interest in a psychoanalytic approach ("the most interesting approach to me at the time") and despite the enthusiasm following her "Aha!" experience, Gabbard felt ambivalent: "[I] really did not think . . . that this [approach] was going to be any more valid, *or better*, than anybody else's. . . . But what I did think was that it was different, it had not yet been fully explored, and it was as valid. But I really didn't think—in fact, when I did it I never dreamed anybody would think [the book] was *good* enough to publish. . . . I really had no idea that this would ever be published because I had great inferiority feelings because I was so advanced in years at the time of my Ph.D. work" (emphasis added). Equating validity with value or worth, even self-worth, Gabbard "didn't consciously think that [her psychoanalytic approach] was in any way better than anything else"; "if I was being defensive at all," she told me, "it was because I may have thought that it wasn't as good."

The book received some strong praise, yet Gabbard was discouraged by the negative criticism. Though she "probably" had "a blocking out mechanism" about some of the more negative reviews—"I think that I distance myself from them and try not to let them disturb me"—one review did disturb her deeply and inhibited her pursuit of a psychoanalytic approach in her writings for some time afterward. "I find that some people are unable to accept Freudian analysis, but that is a general refusal to accept Freudian theory, not just a rejection of my analyses of Pinter's plays," she recognized; yet she was "conscious of the fact that there was a time, a period where I wondered if the psychoanalytic approach wasn't just a big red flag to some people, and that either they didn't understand it or they were threatened by it, or they felt that it was old-fashioned— Freud was old-fashioned—and they'd gone on beyond that, and I consciously think that, and that maybe it was an obstacle to having my work accepted." Gabbard strategically attempted to overcome such professional pitfalls by muting the earlier Freudianism and turning (at least temporarily) to other approaches in her academic writing.

Yet, though she "found other approaches interesting," gamely, Gabbard did use psychoanalysis again in some of her more recent writings on Pinter (and, to a lesser degree, Albee), encouraged by "letters and comments from people maintaining my Freudian approach opened up Pinter for them for the first time. Interestingly, I usually receive this kind of positive response from theater people—actors and directors who are interested in studying the characters for performance." Her former student at Eastern Illinois University, actor and director John Malkovich, who directed the Steppenwolf Theater Company productions of *The Caretaker* in Chicago (1978) and New York (1986), has described *The Dream Structure* as a "great influence" (Shewey). Prompted and encouraged by director Terry Schreiber, who consulted her about a production of *Betrayal* for the Syracuse (N.Y.) Stage Theatre in 1981, Gabbard wrote an article extending the perspective of *The Dream Structure* to *Betrayal*. "The Depths of *Betrayal*" reiterates her view of "the banality of the play's manifest content" as "a defensive mask for the unconscious anxieties of its characters" (228) but draws on the work of Anna Freud, Charles W. Socarides, and Theodore Lidz, as well as Freud.[25] But Gabbard's most recent essay on "various kinds of reversals" in Pinter's plays, "The Pinter Surprise," makes no further reference to psychoanalytic sources.

Gabbard's reactions illustrate Peckham's "*agape system* . . . of interactional and intraactional 'love,' " through which critics want to feel valued (see chap. 2). Even though Gabbard knew that "[t]here's no such thing as a perfect book," when she wrote *The Dream Structure* she still "wished" that it would be perfect. "I was so crushed that someone would be so totally negative toward it," she said, laughing. "I was unprepared for that. As I say, I knew that it wasn't perfect, although I wished it might be. And I really wished that people would like it and respond favorably to it. I'm sure that's natural." She wanted others to approve of her work "as an extension of" herself, and when someone did not, it was "a crushing experience." "Look what you invest in a book," she explained further: "Fourteen hours a day for long periods of time. There's so much of yourself, you know, that goes into a book. I think it would be a very strange, unusual person who would not wish for it to be well received."

Besides ambivalence about the psychoanalytic approach and a wish for general approval, there were strong feelings that Gabbard was not inclined to discuss in detail publicly. To cite them only in general terms, they concern how women academic critics and their books differ from men academic critics and theirs; for example, a man could choose the same topic and approach that a woman does, but his attitude toward the work might be different from hers because of differences in their professional situations and their attitudes toward these situations. While Gabbard's reluctance to record her feelings about her own past professional situation may be "a personal idiosyncracy" (her phrase), equally reticent about connections between their personal lives (even their personal impressions) and their professional work, many scholars share her reluctance to "go public." It is "unprofessional" to declare such connections publicly; people fear exposure and, in some cases (though not, apparently, Gabbard's), even possible retaliation (from colleagues and even from the playwright). This institutional taboo in part explains some of her attitudes about criticism in general, her avoidance of criticizing others, her own felt need for greater assertiveness, and her desire for personal privacy. Such a concern for critical propriety seems to have motivated the pluralistic defensive posture that Gabbard took regarding the validity of her psychoanalytic approach as well.[26]

Another source of confusion for several readers of *The Dream Structure* (including me) is the ambiguity of what Dearlove calls "the dreamer's identity" (126). Gabbard rules out working with the author's mind: "Freud insists that the dreamer's cooperation is necessary to any accurate interpretation of the private symbolism of a dream"; since Pinter's cooperation was not feasible, she makes "no attempt to psychoanalyze Harold Pinter" but aims "to identify the universal elements of these plays as dreams that, in turn, provide insight into everyman's inner self" (16–17). Regarding the characters as representations of "everyman," her approach identifies what she calls the "latent dream-thoughts" of the characters, though she could enlist their "cooperation" and analyze their minds no more than Pinter's. Moreover, as she makes even fewer direct references to the audience (as discussed further below), she appears not so concerned with the reader's mind, including her own. For example, Gabbard writes, "*The Room* is opaque and abstruse until attention is brought to bear on the unconscious content, or latent dream-thoughts, which lie beneath the surface" (25). On first reading these lines, I queried in my margin: "*whose* 'latent dream-thoughts' are these?" "Who is the dreamer in your book?" I later asked her in person.[27] "I laugh when you ask that question," she replied, "because the first draft that I brought to my thesis adviser, that's the very question he asked. He said, 'Who's the dreamer, have you considered that?' And, of course, the answer that I had is 'The dreamer is Harold Pinter.'" This statement contradicts Gabbard's strong emphasis in the book otherwise, quoted above. When I asked whether the dreams that she defines are "the author's dreams," Gabbard reiterated, "Yes. These are the author's dreams. And *I* am interpreting them." Nevertheless, she was still unwilling to reveal publicly her reasons for the book's denial, for insisting that she "wasn't trying to psychoanalyze Harold Pinter." She would only go so far as to say, "I'll let you deal with it from your own thoughts about it. I mean you can take any critical attitude toward it you want, but [she laughed] I don't know that I want to talk about it."

Since Gabbard attached no imagination, no mind, explicitly to the dreams that she was analyzing in the book, readers and reviewers of *The Dream Structure* (such as her thesis adviser and Dearlove, Jiji, and I) had no way of knowing to what mind the dreams were connected for her. Just as Gabbard had felt she could not talk to Harold Pinter, the person who wrote the plays (the "dreams") on which the book (the "dream-analysis") was based, reviewers and most other readers did not talk to the person who wrote it. I had surmised that Gabbard was dealing with the characters' dreams. "I did try," she told me (six years later when we did talk), "that's the way I tried to get away from it; I tried to deal with the characters because I didn't want to try to deal with Pinter or myself as the dreamer." At this point Gabbard was still not willing to say "These are my own projections"; yet, as I pointed out to her, she is saying just that when she observes theoretically (in her conclusion and elsewhere) that interpretations derive from individuals' associations to the plays. While she could agree that it would seem that the dream interpretations were her own projections, she was still not willing to (in her words) "come right out and say that." She was still unwilling to confront this means of "defense" (her word) against her personal attitude toward her work.

Gabbard's persistence suggests an aspect of general critical experience. Wishing not only to relate to others but to protect themselves as well, writers disguise their need for privacy through critical conventions like using a general pronoun instead of *I*. These critical conventions parallel fictional conventions like the creation of characters substituting for the person of the author and for people whom he or she knows. In "The Relation of the Poet to Day-Dreaming," Freud says that creative writers disguise aspects of their fantasies so as not to repel others. Critical writers disguise their personal experiences too. But using a psychoanalytic critical approach makes critics especially aware of this analogy between their own defensive strategies and those of creative writers: "That's why the first thing I shot back to you [after receiving your letter] was 'I don't want to be exposed,'" Gabbard reminded me. "I felt that I was more vulnerable than the others [to be interviewed] because I had taken the psychoanalytic approach. . . . And yet I had this basic trust that since you were also interested in psychoanalysis that you would understand this."[28] Extrapolating and generalizing from her understanding of her own attitude "that a person wants to protect his own privacy," Gabbard described Pinter as sharing an impulse to create "a protective smoke screen" with "all writers who tend to be ambiguous and obscure at times," like Eliot, who admitted that his own obscurity was due to omissions through which "he was protecting himself." Once this issue of the need for privacy in her criticism emerged, Gabbard and I broke through a barrier to understanding her emphasis on the "equal validity" of her psychoanalytic methodology (its being no more or less valid than other critical viewpoints).

"Enlightened" by our discussion, Gabbard admitted, "I do think it's the most important way of looking at it; . . . it *is* more valid than the rest in a sense. . . . I *do* think and thought [when I wrote the book] that the psychoanalytic approach is perhaps more important than all the others, if you want to really get at the truth. . . . I think that it does uncover things that other approaches don't even get close to. I do believe that." Both "the truth" and "validity" are contingent on a great number of personal and social factors. As Gabbard clarified more recently, "I cannot say that my perception or interpretation is universally more valid even though it may be so for me personally" (letter to author, 9 Oct. 1988).

Even though Gabbard valued most an approach illuminating life's "psychological realities" (*DS*, 36), her reaction to a taboo against relating professional and personal contexts of her work created inconsistencies between her theoretical pronouncements and practical interpretations. A main source of these defensive inconsistencies was her "reluctance . . . to be assertive, . . . a conflict within me . . . of not wanting to put myself on the line in a very strongly assertive way for what I believe" out of a fear of being "put down." Wishing not to be perceived "as trying to be as good as everybody else or better than anybody else because I had grown up thinking I wasn't," she compared her feelings about herself as a critic to her feelings about herself as a woman facing professional and other social domains of male domination. This reluctance to be assertive also seems to have motivated her denials in the book about whose dreams she is interpreting.

"Projecting" her own responses on "the audience," Gabbard refuses to say *I* throughout *The Dream Structure*: her substitutions of objective pronouns and passive constructions make it seem that she is not talking about *her own dream-thoughts* (or "associations") to Pinter's plays. For example, discussing *The Collection*, she writes: "The audience, of course, realizes that the truth will never be known. . . . The audience have been amused and delighted with the subtle interconnecting relationships and deceptions. . . . The audience feel intellectually adequate and satisfied" (147).[29] But she *was* talking about *her own* thoughts and feelings; rereading the passage on *The Collection* from which I have quoted, Gabbard declared: "I must have meant *I*, that's what *I* thought." Though, when pressed, Gabbard admitted that she understands her own interpretations of Pinter's plays to be such projections, nonetheless, her desire to protect both her own personal privacy and that of Pinter still overrode her Freudian critical assumptions. To extrapolate from Holloway, an explanation of such an inconsistency in this critic's discourse is the force of some contradiction not only in her experience of the work but in her own sense of self.

Gabbard's own perception of "the uncanny fit" between Freud's dream interpretation theories and Pinter's plays—her "Aha!" experience cited earlier—exemplifies a "primary process" inspiration, creatively drawing on the unconscious sense of a connection suddenly made conscious. Using the secondary process in working out the connection, shaping and unifying her presentation of her analysis of Pinter's plays, Gabbard defended against or disguised some of her own unconscious impulses or associations to the plays. By suppressing these (or camouflaging her own identity as the "dreamer" or the reader) and by suppressing Pinter's identity (the playwright as dreamer) as well, she found a more comfortable intellectual mode of expressing her own responses to the plays, disguised as "the audience's" view of "the characters' latent dream-thoughts." The discrepancy between the subjectivity that her psychoanalytic approach aims to illuminate and Gabbard's own observance of conventionally objective critical decorum results from her own discomfort with self-disclosure, projected in her emphasis on protecting the author's privacy.[30]

If "one of the sources of what people call [the absurdists'] 'obscurity' is this wish to disguise what they do recognize" of themselves in their own work, it results in "a lot of shaping with the secondary process," Gabbard said. While the obscurity of Pinter's "private symbolism" may or may not suggest "deliberate disguise," she could "understand why [the writers] feel the way they do about us [scholars], because we dig and pry . . . but a symbol unexplained can . . . create some obscurity for somebody trying to unravel it all and make . . . the pieces all fit together."

In my own attempt to "depuzzle" *The Dream Structure,* I have been digging and prying in the manner that Gabbard describes, trying to make the pieces all fit together. But however much the book has been praised for its clarity by reviewers, some measure of the obscurity of its author's own private symbolism must remain inaccessible to such intrusions. Gabbard's unusual ability to analyze her own motivations is of course to some extent still limited by scholarly taboos, cultural and personal inhibitions, her later perspective, the professional context of our interview and correspondence, and perhaps other unidentified factors. Yet, despite/because of all these limitations, together we were able to "piece together" a plausible story of how she formulated and practiced her psychoanalytic critical strategy for understanding Pinter's plays as dreams. By examining Gabbard's psychoanalytic strategy in so much detail and with so much welcome help from the author herself, I have tried to engage as well as to define the intersubjective contexts of reading and writing critical texts. Such personal and social relations both underwrite and undermine the playing out of critical conventions.

### Recent Trends in Psychoanalytic Criticism of Pinter's Plays

Applying the motivational psychology of Paul Diel to Pinter's plays, Daniel Salem confronts the task of "psychoanalyzing Pinter" shunned by earlier critics like Gordon, Esslin, and Gabbard. *Pinter ou le masque de la vérité* extrapolates Pinter's repressed wishes and fears from his characters' dramatized ones; his repressed ambivalence and anguish about his own Jewishness in an alien, hostile (Gentile) world motivate tensions and ambiguities characterizing human relationships with others in his plays.[31] Like many previous commentators, Salem attributes Pinter's perspective to his childhood and adolescent experiences during and after World War II. But he takes into account Pinter's more recent adult experiences also as he argues that Pinter's characters' ambivalences about their identities and their need for protection from self-disclosure reflect the author's own more current wishes and fears. Actual events and dreams related by Pinter in available interviews and in his published and unpublished work, such as his poetry and the manuscript of his unpublished novel *The Dwarfs*, as well as unpublished interviews that Salem himself did with Pinter's acquaintances, close friends and colleagues, and with Pinter himself, contribute to a psychological composite of the author, which is compared with detailed analyses of his characters' psychological motivations.[32]

Salem's interest in such relations between Pinter's life and work began when he worked as a journalist for the bbc, giving him access to Pinter. (See the preface to *Pinter ou le masque de la vérité*. Neither this book, the published version of a doctoral thesis at the University of Paris, nor his Master's thesis, *Harold Pinter, dramaturge de l'ambiguité*, has been translated into English.) As Salem sensitively and humanely speculates about how Pinter's personal experiences relate to his art, he adds another perspective to psychoanalytic investigation of Pinter's plays, one that has itself been previously "repressed" and that, despite this taboo status, deserves attention.[33]

Other psychoanalytic Pinter criticism follows recent developments in French psychoanalysis, especially the revisionary work of psychoanalyst Jacques Lacan and the cross-fertilizing influences of Roland Barthes, Michel Foucault, and Jacques Derrida.[34] For example, whereas both Gabbard and Salem apply more classical Freudian concepts of repression and projection to understanding *Betrayal*, Linda S. Wells uses Lacanian-Barthesian strategy to uncover the "underlying" subject of Pinter's characters' infidelities: "the more universal conflict between self and other" (23). Though *Betrayal* may address the question that Wells frames—"can one act because of self-interest and still be harmoniously united with another?"—she seems to ignore an important poststructuralist lesson about *critical* transference. Her analysis of Pinter's characters' relationships and projections employs categories from Barthes's *Lover's Discourse* to *fix* Pinter's text as "*really* a discourse on failed love" (30; emphasis added) without considering the intersubjective ramifications of this discourse for his audience and critics. If "*Betrayal* demonstrates that the menace of autonomy prevents these characters from being really honest with each other, for they fear that honesty would mean the end of their fragile but essential social structures" (30), what does it demonstrate for the critic— for Wells herself? Wells suggests that in *Betrayal* "[w]hile the impulse is to move toward others who offer love, the obsession with the self and the impulse to manipulate and dominate destroy the very relationships which are sought and insure the alienation which is most feared" (30). She could be writing about a main impulse of critics and the threat to their relationships with other writers.

## "Validity" in Psychoanalytic Interpretation:
## Another Strategy

Patrocinio P. Schweickart offers a heuristic perspective on some of the problems of validity raised about psychoanalytic Pinter criticism in particular and about psychoanalytic criticism in general. In "Reading Ourselves: Toward a Feminist Theory of Reading," she offers "another approach to the problem of validation, one that is consonant with the dialogic model of reading" based on the relationship between the feminist reader and the woman writer. If "the validity of an interpretation cannot be decided by appealing to what the author 'intended,' to what is 'in' the text, or to what is 'in' the experience of the reader," then we can regard "validity not as a property inherent in an interpretation, but rather as a *claim* implicit in the *act* of propounding an interpretation. An interpretation, then, is not valid or invalid in itself. Its validity is contingent on the agreement of others." Borrowing from Jürgen Habermas to interpret Adrienne Rich, Schweickart observes that for Rich "to read a text and then to write about it is to seek to connect not only with the author of the original text, but also with a community of readers. To the extent that she succeeds and to the extent that the community is potentially all-embracing, her interpretation has that degree of validity" (56, 62 n.43).[35]

The same perspective that Schweickart applies to the validity of interpretations can be applied to the validity of interpretive strategies: to the extent that the community potentially accepts such a strategy as psychoanalytic criticism, it has that degree of validity. The validity of "a psychoanalytic approach" is not static, but changing. In 1983 Styan concluded that "the audience" may provide "the only valid area for the application of psychology to the art of the drama" ("Psychology," 265). In an important reassessment of psychoanalysis in literary study by Françoise Meltzer (*Trial{s}*), Peter Brooks describes the "embarrassment" and "malaise" persisting in psychoanalytic literary criticism (334). Shlomith Rimmon-Kenan sets forth a new direction in psychoanalytic literary criticism focusing on "discourse" and emphasizing "rhetorical structures" and "textual strategies" and their "investment . . . with desire, power and other aspects of subjectivity" *rather than* "the personality of the artist, the creative process or the psyche of the fictional characters." Though thus aligned "with structuralist and post-structuralist oriented studies," it goes "beyond" them "in restoring *the human dimension* . . . not 'in the raw,' as in traditional approaches, but through the traces it leaves in the text, as activated by its reading" (xii; emphasis added).

If such newer psychoanalytic maneuvers appear more valid now than the older ones did, more "potentially all-embrac[ed]" by members of some academic communities, we must allow for the effects of such contextually contingent revision in reading and rereading earlier critics on Pinter like Gordon, Esslin, and Gabbard and more recent ones like Salem, Wells, and Woodroffe. Features of such critical discourse—rhetorical structures and textual strategies—are produced through complex interactions of personality and creative and social processes, all of which are constantly in flux. Effacing "the human dimension" of such interactions through theory may serve to ensure critics' self-protection, insulating them from scrutiny by themselves and others, but it also obscures the relations between their own choices of structures and strategies and those made by other creative artists. This erasure guarantees critics' privacy by relinquishing their social responsibilities as ethical human beings.

# 7

# Some Other Language Games:

## Linguistic Parlays and Parleys

MICK. What's the game?—*The Caretaker*

Ludwig Wittgenstein defines "language games" both throughout his treatise *Philosophical Investigations* and in the "Preliminary Studies" for it, *The Blue and Brown Books*, where he writes: "Language games are the forms of language with which a child begins to make use of words. The study of language games is the study of primitive forms of language or primitive languages. . . . [W]e recognize in these simple processes forms of language not separated by a break from our more complicated ones. We see that we can build up the complicated forms from the primitive ones by gradually adding new forms" (17).[1] The criticism written about the language of Pinter's plays is one of these "more complicated" forms whose "primitive" roots may still remain recognizable. Critics engage in complicated language games instrumental in producing subsequent developments in and suggesting new directions for future investigations of Pinter's language.

In "Language and Silence," chapter 4 in *The Peopled Wound* (and its subsequent editions), Martin Esslin asserts: "A true understanding of Pinter's use of language must . . . start from an examination of the function of language in stage dialogue generally—and indeed from considerations of the use of language in ordinary human intercourse itself" (234–35).[2] After a very brief historical survey of how language functions on the stage (235–36), he concludes that Pinter significantly extends Chekhov's technique of " 'oblique' dialogue" in which the text hints at a hidden subtext (236), comparing the closing scenes of Chekhov's *Uncle Vanya* and Pinter's *Birthday Party* (236–38). For Pinter, Esslin argues, "People interact not so much logically as emotionally through language; and the tone of voice, the emotional colour of the words is often far more significant than their exact meanings, by their dictionary definition. . . . What matters in most oral verbal contact therefore is more what people are *doing* to each other through it rather than the conceptual content of what they are saying" (239). Esslin does not define explicitly how this idea relates to his psychoanalytical, existential, and archetypal interpretations in the longer section of "analysis" (chap. 3); yet his use of spatial metaphors throughout this discussion echoes his earlier use of Freudian theory of the unconscious (or "subconscious," as Esslin also says).

In addition to verbal elements in Pinter's "armoury" such as tautologies, repetition, and associative structures, Esslin investigates Pinter's use of his characters' nonverbal behavior, especially their pauses and silences (234, 239–40). Like some other playwrights, Pinter has discovered a "highly significant aspect of drama": "Only when it was recognized that the verbal element need not be the dominant aspect of drama, or at least that it was not the content of what was said that mattered most, but the action which it embodied, and that inarticulate, incoherent, tautological and nonsensical speech might be as dramatic as verbal brilliance when it could be treated simply as an element of action, only then did it become possible to place inarticulate characters in the centre of the play and to make their unspoken emotions transparent."[3] Esslin's main point is that Pinter does not use such linguistic devices merely to ridicule them; rather, "they do in fact illuminate the *mental processes that lie behind* the ill-chosen or nonsensical words" (240; emphasis added). Esslin reiterates the position several times that their language *hides* the characters' true thoughts and feelings. While Esslin says *also* that "in each case superficially similar quirks of language may serve quite different dramatic functions" (240), he does not build on this brief acknowledgment that the "dramatic functions" of Pinter's dialogue are multiple, focusing ultimately on their "essential" thematic value or content.

For example, in considering a linguistic controversy between Mick and Davies in *The Caretaker* (Davies refers to Aston as "a funny bloke," and Mick takes issue with the meaning of *funny* as Davies uses it [2:58–59]), Esslin's recurrent interest is the "existential" significance of their argument: "A disagreement about the meaning of a term has become a fundamental, existential contest of wills. Words, thus, are of vital importance. And yet, it is not so much the words themselves as the existential situations they conceal and reveal. . . . it matters little whether Mick's or Davies's interpretation of the word 'funny' is the correct one[;] what is essential and existentially important is that Mick makes Davies accept *his* definition of the word's meaning" (251–53).[4]

Even though Esslin also argues that Pinter's dramatic language is repeatedly "the medium through which a contest of wills is fought out, sometimes overtly as in the disputes about the correct expression to be used or about the correct meaning of a given word or phrase, sometimes beneath the surface of the explicit subject matter of the dialogue" (253), his other statements suggest that Pinter uses language more referentially: for example, regarding Pinter's "search . . . for the area of reality that lies *behind* the use of language" (253). In the penultimate passage quoted, Esslin appears to subordinate the notion of the inexplicit "sometimes" being "beneath the surface of the explicit" to a more overarching concept of language as a *medium* of character conflict. Esslin's analysis of particular passages of dialogue *also* observes the *interaction* of the characters *through* language as the central import of Pinter's plays. Nevertheless, he still concludes by extending his spatial metaphor for the referential relation between form (text) and content (subtext): Pinter's "hallmark" is a "density of subtext beneath the sparseness of the text itself" (265).

Aiming to find "a path . . . that leads beyond the generalizations which governed the field a decade ago" (xix), in *The Pinter Problem* Austin Quigley acknowledges that Esslin's chapter on "Language and Silence" in *The Peopled Wound* is "the most extensive attack so far on what [Esslin] recognizes as the major problem of the field: the complete rethinking of our approach to Pinter's language" (*PP*, 24). But as Esslin says that the "function" of Pinter's language has previously been "misunderstood" (234), so *The Pinter Problem* corrects what Quigley regards as a continuing misunderstanding of how language functions (pluralistically).[5] For Quigley's purposes, while Esslin's analysis of Pinter's plays demonstrates his ability "to perceive a variety of uses for language, . . . it is instructive to follow through the difficulties Esslin encounters in trying to reconcile his interpretative activity with generalizable theoretical positions" (25).

Before presenting his "interrelational" solution to the problem of Pinter's language, as a theoretical context for establishing "controlled contact between [observable] details of [Pinter's] language and responses to those details" (32–47, 33), Quigley moves from dissecting Esslin's work as an example of "temporary critical failure" (29) to locating suggestions of an alternative approach in some "piecemeal observations" from other critics who establish "that Pinter's language functions in a new way" (30). Pursuing "the significance of the language . . . in terms of its appropriateness to the situation in which it is used" ("an illuminating direction" suggested by Bert O. States), Quigley discovers "a whole new set of questions" about Pinter's characters: "to what extent is the situation independent of the language uttered? how is a character to decide what is appropriate language for that situation? is the question of appropriateness a given or is it open to negotiation? what if two characters disagree over what is appropriate at a given time? what kinds of issues are raised by such events?" (31). These questions clarify "the distinctive functions of language in Pinter's work" so as to avoid "the limited and limiting reference theory assumptions" of Esslin and others. The "major difficulty" of these critics—"reconcil[ing] perceptive comments on Pinter's work with general theoretical statements about the ways in which the things perceived are present in the language" (32)—has, Quigley argues, stifled investigation: "Progress is unlikely to occur when accurate observations are required to interact with inaccurate generalizations. Instead of fruitful interplay between data and hypotheses, which is fundamental to the development of further data and to the refinement of hypotheses, there has been a lack of interaction between incompatible elements, and the field has stagnated. The process of discovery has subsided into a protracted rediscovery of inadequate theoretical positions" (32–33).

In using notions of Wittgenstein, other philosophers of language, and linguists to lead Pinter critics in a new direction beyond this impasse, Quigley himself engages in sophisticated language games with other critics. As Quigley posits the so-called interrelational function of Pinter's language, his approach is itself instrumental. He attempts to reactivate a "field" that he sees as "stagnated" when he articulates and interprets the linguistic interactions of Pinter's characters in a more "controlled" manner consistent with theoretically "accurate" generalizations about how language works (32–33). Since Quigley invents the name of the "interrelational" language function in order to perform his analysis of the plays in the context of such theoretical generalizations, the term is "appropriate" for his own conventional, rhetorical purpose. But the ramifications of Quigley's parlaying of past work on Pinter's language into this new "field of play" are multiplex.

To counteract "dualistic distinctions in an area in which pluralistic distinctions are essential" (27; cf. 40), Quigley introduces and builds on Wittgenstein's notion of how language games function through a " 'multiplicity' " of " 'use' " as opposed to "a 'given' or 'normal' function" and how " 'new types of language, new language-games' " emerge.[6] Asserting that "[a]ny attempt to contrast Pinter's language with some given core of normal language is . . . fundamentally misguided," Quigley proposes that instead we "look at Pinter's language from exactly the same point of view that we should adopt in approaching all language use; we must begin with Wittgenstein's suggestion that we: 'Look at the sentence as an instrument, and at its sense as its employment'" (*PP*, 46).[7]

A salient theoretical point of Quigley's study is "that language is not so much a means of referring to structure in personal relationships as a means of creating it" (66). Recognizing this general principle enables him to achieve important perceptions about ongoing development or change in Pinter's character relationships. Quigley's insights about "the structural and textual implications of the interrelational function of language" in *The Room*, *The Caretaker*, *The Homecoming*, and *Landscape* demonstrate how Pinter dramatizes characters' "developing relations" through "duologues"; both the "internal structure" of these "major units" and "the external patterns that develop between them" are significant, unifying features of Pinter's dramaturgy (75, 78–79). These interrelated structures affect the "texture" of the plays and thematic implications of the characters' changing relationships.

The questions that Quigley raises about Pinter's characters (quoted earlier) also apply to his critics. Substituting *critic* for *character* in these questions highlights interactional relationships between *critics*—their "intertextuality."[8] To what extent is the *critical* situation independent of the language uttered? how is a *critic* to decide what is appropriate language for that situation? is the question of *critical* appropriateness a given or is it open to negotiation? what if two *critics* disagree over what is appropriate at a given time? what kinds of issues are raised by such events? The debate between Esslin and Quigley about Pinter's language illustrates such linguistic interactions among critics and suggests the kinds of issues raised by critical investigative controversy.

Metacritically, Esslin's point about "stage dialogue" is also apt: "[T]he element of action, the inter-action between the characters, their reactions to each other . . . constitute the truly *dramatic* element in stage dialogue" (239). As with Quigley's passage on characters, we can substitute *critics* here for *characters* and *critical* for *stage* so as to make the point that the interaction between critics, their reactions to each other, constitute the truly *dramatic* element in critical dialogue. In multiple ways and on intermixed levels of consciousness, language serves as strategy both to maintain desired—dynamic—critical relationships and to enforce needed interactional—effective—critical change.

## A Subtext of the "Subtext"

A main issue raised by Quigley but apparently misunderstood and contested by Esslin involves "dualistic distinctions" using such terms as
*subtext*. *Webster's New World Dictionary* (2d college ed., 1982 printing)
lists two definitions of *subtext*: "1. the complex of feelings, motives, etc.
conceived of by an actor as underlying the actual words and actions of the
character being portrayed[;] 2. an underlying meaning, theme, etc." In
the first sense *underlying* means motivating; whereas in the second one
*underlying* suggests referentiality. But these usages are not mutually
exclusive, and slippage occurs between the two senses. Psychoanalytic
reconstruction of the "latent" content "underlying" the "manifest" content of dreams, symptoms, and other psychopathological phenomena
engages both definitions of *subtext*, resulting in some confusion.[9]

To show how critics use this spatial metaphor to indicate some content
*underlying* or *beneath* or *behind* the play text, Quigley momentarily foregrounds "the notion of a subtext" to explain the larger theoretical issues
raised by any such distinctions between language and thought:

> The danger of words like "behind" or "underneath" is that they
> deflect an intended contrast between two levels of the language into
> a contrast *between the language and something else.* Control of the
> "something else" is then lost by contrasting it with everything that
> is available as evidence. . . . It is a logical error to set up a contrast
> between the textual data and an abstraction from that data. . . . The
> notion of a subtext loses all utility if what it deals with cannot be
> spoken of as a product of the linguistic data. The meanings referred
> to are either linguistically specified or they are not there; how else
> could we divine their existence? Ultimately the search for a subtext
> and the need for a symbol have a common foundation but the misuse
> of both concepts has led criticism away from rather than into the
> Pinter play. (14–15; see 15 n.39)

Quigley points out that Esslin moves from distinguishing between
" 'what is being said and what lies behind it' " in his comparison between
Pinter and Chekhov to explicating a passage from *The Birthday Party* "in
terms of '. . . the complete contradiction between the words that are
spoken and the emotional and psychological *action* that underlies them.
Here the language has almost totally lost its rhetorical, informative
elements and has fully merged into dramatic action' " (*PP*, 25, quoting

Esslin, *PW*, 2 1 1–1 2). "The crucial point" for Quigley is "the direction in which Esslin's distinctions take him": moving away from the text rather than into it, "Esslin arrives at a distinction between informative and noninformative language" (25).

"It is no coincidence," Quigley asserts, "that the form/content dichotomy reemerges in Pinter criticism because the same [reference] theory of meaning is at issue, and the same barrier to progress is encountered. . . . The barrier to progress in this area is the seeming impossibility of finding a controllable second term with which to contrast what is felt to be characteristic of non-Pinter language. With alarming regularity, this second term refuses to emerge in any adequate form" (34). For Quigley it is a "theoretical error" to regard Pinter's language that way: "Contrasts between text and subtext, what is said and how it is said, the language and what lies behind it, prose and poetry, the meanings of the words and the meaning of the language, surface meaning and association of meaning. . . . Such distinctions are either not logically contrastive or they contrast all that is available as evidence with 'something else,' which is not available for inspection, analysis, or demonstration" (34). To sum up: "Suggestions that Pinter's language conveys something other than the meanings of his words, that Pinter shows that language can be used to convey what it cannot say, that it is not the words that count but the subtext, that Pinter has transcended the boundaries of language—all are based upon a separation of meaning and use" (*PP*, 46).

Defining "the interrelational function" of Pinter's language (47–67), Quigley starts from "an important key to the puzzling dynamics of the Pinter dialogue" (50): Pinter's often-cited account of how he and his friends dealt with threats encountered outside a Jewish club just after World War II.[10] This narrative is "naturally seized upon by cause-oriented critics as an indication of why Pinter should write plays dealing with latent menace" (47). But, more importantly, it illustrates how a verbal event supplanted a potentially threatening physical one, suggesting "the nature of the power invoked by the dialogue" and ways in which "relationships are subject to verbal negotiation, even verbal imposition" (49). The purpose in analyzing the "stages" of this recounted "verbal event" is to "shed light on the social activity within the plays" (48–49). By realizing how social relational forces constrain what one character says at one time and another time and what various characters say to one another, we can understand previously puzzling, obscure statements in Pinter's plays (50). Help from J. R. Firth with explaining "the source of the peculiar tension generated by Pinter's language" and illustrations of some limitations of Firth's explanation through an analysis of such tension in Pinter's play *The Dwarfs* enable Quigley to reach this conclusion: "The language of a Pinter play functions primarily as a means of dictating and reinforcing relationships" (50–52).[11]

When he names this linguistic function "interrelational," Quigley is renaming the "interpersonal" function of language defined by M. A. K. Halliday as one of three functions of language.[12] Quigley substitutes "interrelational" for "interpersonal" so as "[t]o avoid the implication of a personality given in advance." This stresses Halliday's own awareness of the significance that "for certain forms of literature . . . since personality is dependent on interaction which is in turn mediated through language, the 'interpersonal' function in language is *both* interactional *and* personal" (53, 53 n.40; emphasis added).

For Quigley, at the time a neophyte scholar proposing to redirect established Pinter criticism, whatever the "subjective bases" for his own disagreements with Esslin and others, such a belligerent tone as we see Esslin using against him later would scarcely have succeeded with expert readers. As when criticizing Esslin's and others' use of *poet* and *poetry* to describe Pinter and the language of his plays as another instance of confusing language with what it is not, at times Quigley uses ironic understatement, hyperbole, and other witty rhetorical devices to drive home his argument: "Unless the evidence deceives us all, Pinter is a dramatist"; "The unanalyzed in Pinter's work is a product of temporary critical failure, not of some metaphysical, ultra-valuable, unanalyzable characteristic located behind, above, or beneath the text of the plays" (*PP*, 28; 29). But usually Quigley's own expressive mode tends more toward the coolly objective tone associated with philosophical rigor: "The coining of a name for this function of language does not reduce it or Pinter's plays to something single or something that is simply repeated from one play to the next. The abstract term serves to provide a perspective from which to view the variety and subtlety of the work of a major writer. With this general statement about Pinter's work established, it remains to test its validity by seeing to what extent it interacts with details of individual plays" (55).

Quigley redefines unverifiability as "not simply a device for creating audience uncertainty" but as "a thematic consequence of plays that deal with truth and reality as negotiable concepts" (*PP*, 71). But while Quigley views "truth" and "reality" as such negotiable concepts for

Pinter's characters (94), it is not clear to me that he consistently operates with the same interactive notions in testing the "validity" of a critical concept. Like other terms that Quigley discusses (*comedy of menace, Pinteresque*), *verification* and *unverifiability* are descriptive, thematic terms resulting from "[a]ttempts to categorize Pinter's plays" (*PP*, 274). Elsewhere Quigley describes "the unverifiable" as "a dangerous critical instrument both because it encourages a premature cessation of analysis and because it can end up converting all plays into the same play."[13] Like *verification* and *unverifiability*, *validity* is also dangerous when used without an awareness of its instrumentality. Moreover, while Quigley's concern "to test" the "validity" of the term *interrelational* may make *The Pinter Problem* sound rather objective, it may also make reading the book a dull experience for a reader with interests invested in a very different sort of critical account.

## Quigley's *Pinter Problem*:
### Esslin's Review

In his review of Quigley's *Pinter Problem*, Esslin castigates the book. This review is (in Lindenberger's terms cited in chap. 2) an "All-Outer," a "totality of response . . . in an unmitigatingly . . . negative form." Given the compatibility of several of their insights about Pinter's language, we would now be more shocked by Esslin's relentlessness (as I myself was on first encountering it) if we had not already noticed Quigley's characterization of Esslin's views as exemplary of "theoretical inaccuracy," "inappropriateness," "inadequacy," "error," and "failure." Perhaps more than "the crucial point" of Quigley's argument, these rhetorical terms appear to have stimulated the force of Esslin's rebuttal. But while Esslin retaliates against perceived injuries in Quigley's presentation, he plays a different language game than Quigley: "verifiable" evidence and theoretically "sound" generalizations figure less in Esslin's work in general and in this review; he sounds much more "subjective" or "impressionistic" than "scientific" or "philosophical."

Hesitating to identify *The Pinter Problem* as "*academic*," because to use this term "in a pejorative sense" would be to belittle other more "genuine contribution[s]" to knowledge, Esslin calls it " 'dry-as-dust-pseudo-scholarly' . . . only too symptomatic of what pressures to publish at all costs produce, books, that is, which seem to have no *raison d'être* beyond the fact that they can be added to a *curriculum vitae* as evidence that their author has burnt the midnight oil with utmost diligence" (102). Quigley merely plays an academic "game": "is Pinter really a *problem?* . . . The problem consists merely in that Mr Quigley had to have something to write about. So he had to find a problem" (102). Vivid sarcasm, hyperbole, and other rhetorical "stratagems" eventually culminate in what Lingeman calls an "indispensable Last-Line Put-Down" (684): "Much real illumination and insight is derived on both sides of the footlights from much genuine scholarly criticism. Discovering the obvious at enormous length is, however, of no use at all" (Esslin, rev. of *PP*, 105).

Quigley's criticism of the notion of subtext (14–15, 46; quoted above) is a particularly sore point for Esslin: "Mr Quigley has discovered something which he thinks no one has discovered before him, namely that language has not only an informational function but also an 'interrelational' one. In other words, he has stumbled across the hitherto unheard of truth, that what people say to each other has an effect on their relationships." Despite this charge that Quigley undeservedly claims originality, Esslin adds: "To buttress this discovery—for a pseudo-scholar of this type cannot make any statement without an authority—he invokes Wittgenstein and J. R. Firth. What he has failed to notice is merely that none of the other critics whom he has consigned to the dungeons for stupidity [has ever] doubted this for a moment, and that in fact the term *subtext* stands precisely for this aspect of the matter" (103). Esslin vigorously defends the theatrical importance of the word *subtext*:

> In the almost three hundred pages of the book, Mr Quigley gives hardly any evidence that he has ever been to a theatre, has ever seen a play or, indeed, has ever spoken to an actor. Had he done any of these things, he would have found that his problem was, in fact, a pseudo-problem. Any actor could have told him—and Harold Pinter writes from an actor's standpoint and experience—that, when speaking any lines in a play, one has to be aware not only of the dictionary meaning of the sentence one utters but, above all, what its effect will be on the character to whom it is addressed and what the *intention* is in which it is addressed. That is what Mr Quigley calls the 'interrelational aspect of language' and what actors call the subtext. (103–4; cf. 105)

In "Language and Silence," as we have seen, Esslin tends to contrast text and subtext; he does not define the practical theatrical meaning of *subtext* explicitly. Nevertheless, here he claims to have stated it "very clearly" as he responds dramatically to Quigley's disposal of the chapter, concluding that "Mr Quigley, who was merely reading it to find fault, did not notice it because he was not trying to understand what was being said, merely to confirm that his self-made terminology was not being employed" (104). "Having proved that there is no such thing as a subtext," Esslin adds ironically, "he then fills a further 200 pages with a detailed explication of the plays, which, as any actor or director could have told him, is merely a very laborious and boring exposition of the subtext of four of Pinter's plays . . . and at that neither very perceptive, nor even wholly accurate." The invective expresses symbolically Esslin's angry indignation in response to his sense that Quigley neglects remarks in *The Peopled Wound* potentially compatible with the "interrelational" function of Pinter's dramatic language.

To use a so-called dualistic distinction: in my own view Esslin's pique is quite evident "behind" or "beneath" and "in" the text of this review; in both senses cited earlier from *Webster's*, as qualified by Quigley, this feeling is both related to its language and its subtext. But such expressed resentment of Quigley (if that is what it was) was not *conceptually* behind or beneath Esslin's review (its "meaning" or "intention"); it is not *separate* from it. To be more precise, in accordance with *both* Quigley's theory of the "interrelational" language function *and* Esslin's comments on the actors' subtext, Esslin's feelings (in part) *motivated* his discourse and are still "present" (palpable) in his language. Only in *this* sense do they lie "behind" or "beneath" or "at the bottom of" it. They are extratextual or metalinguistic features of Esslin's discourse: part of the *situational context* of both the review and Esslin's "role" in writing it.[14]

Esslin gives few of what Quigley calls "observable details of the text" to support his arguments. A dominant purpose in writing the review seems to be to defend his own work against what he perceives as Quigley's attack on it. His defense is particularly aggressive: a new offensive or counterattack. His language "resymbolizes" the relationship that he perceives between himself (as reviewer) and Quigley (as reviewed), just as my own description of this relationship as an *embattled* one "resymbolizes" it.[15] Confronting Quigley, it seems to me, Esslin sees an opponent trying to wrest power away from himself and tries to take it back: to wield it to his own advantage in the service of his own argument. Criticism thus impelled may satisfy the so-called territorial imperative said to motivate most of Pinter's "selfish" characters, but it will not (in any positive way) promote investigative progress of the kind that Quigley repeatedly espouses. Its psychological energy is not directed toward building a more potent *community* of knowledge.

### The Complementary Supplementarity of Critics

If I understand his purpose—his "intention"—Quigley has perceived other critics (including Esslin) as stymied by a "problem," which he (acting as a kind of philosopher-guide) is trying to diagnose and resolve, so as to enable other Pinter critics to forge ahead. As he shows established Pinter critics the way "to move out of the trough in which [they have] labored for over a decade" (31), the problem that Quigley may *not* have perceived is how his apparent "arrogance" (Nightingale, "Human Zoo," 71) might make them feel. Though Quigley may be more concerned with their ideas than their feelings, nevertheless, when such feelings *do* motivate critics and enter their writing relatively unchecked (as in Esslin's review), they may *impede* the "progress" of a critical community, rendering Quigley's rhetorical method of logical argument counterproductive.

To answer Quigley's questions about dramatic characters that I have extended to critics: as the situation of Esslin's review motivates it symbolically, the language of the review does appear to "depend on" the reviewer's "subjective" responses to external ("objective") circumstances, generating a new psychosocially symbolic event accessible to apprehension and definition ("resymbolization"). The critic, his or her peers, and other readers decide what is appropriate language for a situation according to their own present and projected future purposes and in the context of critical conventions and innovations. The question of appropriateness of critical language is only a given if taken as such, for otherwise it could still be open to negotiation. And if two critics disagree over what is appropriate at a given time, they can opt to ignore these disagreements, to battle them out in print, or (as I advocate in this book) to cooperate however they can: by establishing how their purposes match and other points of mutual agreement amidst their disagreements, and, I think even more importantly, by understanding more precisely how their more general positions relate to each other and to the gamut of their pertinent other views about language, literature, criticism, theater, and theory. Finally, the kinds of issues raised by controversies about what is *appropriate* in various kinds of criticism are like issues raised by clashes among Pinter's characters: psychological and social as well as epistemological.

Ultimately, such issues are resolvable only through fluctuations in community consensus. As critics, we hope to *build* a new consensus, not merely to tear old ones down. If we are to build stronger new structures, we must understand the effects of our work on our relationships with those providing the building materials.

Critics, like other people, have to get along—to communicate—if they are to advance the work of criticism. Often in criticism, as in other human activities (such as Pinter's plays, according to both Esslin and Quigley), the assumption of a *failure* to communicate precludes diagnosing communication problems *fairly*, prematurely foreclosing any potentiality or possibility for resolving them, learning from them, moving on (progressing). What appears at first sight to be a mere quibble about the "right" meaning of a word symbolizes a more crucial critical issue. The common attitude that one critic is right (proper, etc.) and the other wrong (improper, etc.)—in the usage of *subtext* or in reconciling local observations with theories of language and meaning—is a crux of the problem as I see it. Such matters are not simply "either-or" issues. Esslin's answer to Quigley forcefully demonstrates (however unintentionally) not only the "appropriateness" of *both* Quigley's *and* Esslin's understandings of Pinter's language but the consequences of each one's failing commensurately to practice what he preaches theoretically: what people say to one another has an effect on their relationships; language is an instrument of people's relationships with one another (see Quigley, *PP*, 32–47). As Halliday indicates, moreover, through language people also assert their own personalities (however much, as Quigley cautions, these may be in flux).

Yet, as Esslin states in "Language and Silence," what-people-say-and-how-they-say-it—their "language and silence"—influences their relationships. [16] As Quigley states, language even creates the structure of relationships. However convincing a concept "the interrelational function" of language, the language through which Quigley presented his revision of earlier work on Pinter's language (Esslin and others exemplify "inappropriateness," "inaccuracy," "inadequacy," "error," and "failure," however "temporary") may have been more objectionable to Esslin than "the crucial point" that Quigley was making about language. In terms of the sort of style/content dichotomy that Esslin assumes, the mixture or combination ("fusion") of the how/what in *The Pinter Problem*—the rhetorical manner in which Quigley presented ideas that (however mistakenly from Quigley's viewpoint) Esslin regards as similar to his own—may have antagonized Esslin and provoked his sarcasm.

By interweaving Quigley's and Esslin's perspectives and reading them in the context of their individual purposes as critics, I have tried to document their complementarity as well as their supplementarity. In the script that I would prefer to be writing about Pinter criticism, they would play roles as protagonists rather than as antagonists. "Apparently small refinements in procedure and vocabulary," Quigley still believes, "can introduce new perspectives that have large consequences for our capacity to understand and interpret" (letter to author, 29 Aug. 1989). But it is still necessary to introduce such new perspectives in ways that encourage and enable others to recognize not only their novelty but also their consequentiality. These ways may require further "small refinements in procedure and vocabulary" to have "large consequences for our capacity to understand and interpret," or even to have any effect at all.

If Quigley had been able to impress Esslin with the importance of following his more instrumental theory of language instead of perpetuating referential applications of concepts like subtext (whether literary critical or theatrical and psychological)—unless the issue was merely a red herring—Esslin *might* have felt more receptive as a reviewer. Even though Quigley devoted more pages to the perceptions of Esslin than to those of any other critic (a *compliment* to Esslin), the interrelational function of Quigley's language still apparently provoked Esslin's defensive belligerence. Quigley's appeals to Wittgenstein and other language philosophers and linguists may have functioned for Esslin as what Lingeman calls "The Avant-Garde Dismiss" (684). Had Esslin attempted to compare his own views about Pinter's language with Quigley's thesis more carefully, looking beyond what he regards as a displacer's invocations to Wittgenstein and Firth and "fault"-finding words like *error* and *failure*, had he been able to acknowledge how the subjectivity of his own negative responses to Quigley may have affected his judgments, he might have considered writing a different kind of review, one that could have contributed more substantially to investigation of Pinter's use of language.

Given common spontaneous human responses to it, the "right"/ "wrong" approach may serve less to stimulate than to depress cycles of critical investigation. As most teachers know, students do not like being told that they are "wrong." When in the position of readers reading a new book instructing them about their own work, critical writers, no matter how long out of school, resemble students; we might be more successful in convincing them of "new perspectives" if we were to exercise greater tact in commenting on and judging ("correcting") their past performances as we attempt to add to and likely even to supersede them. All "revisions," like all rereadings, are not necessarily either more correct or equally misread, but from a variety of critically purposive perspectives they may become both. Deciding which versions are "right" or "more right" or "better" or "best" is as instrumental a procedure as any other language game.

### The "Subjectivity"/"Objectivity" of Book Reviews and Authors' Responses

Of course, the so-called subjective bases of Esslin's writing—his own particular biases—seem more accessible principally because he did *not* disguise them in so-called academese. While most expert readers are sensitive enough to read "through" such reviews as Esslin's—to perform an "interactional" analysis of his discourse—this kind of review is an anathema for many academics, who, like Quigley, are persuaded by arguments marshaling "verifiable" evidence rather than by innuendo or attack. According to his own account of criticism, Esslin's review of Quigley's book is "not a matter of objective, but merely one of subjective truth"; yet if "literary criticism is discourse about discourse and is thus itself a branch of literature" ("Search," 211, 210), do we judge Esslin's review of Quigley's book and Quigley's book by the same criteria that we use in judging Pinter's plays?[17] Most conventional critics still consider book reviews and plays different genres of writing, and the so-called objective criteria used to establish the use-value of these forms generally differ, even if the contexts affecting value judgments of them are similar (see chap. 9 for further discussion).

Among the "multitude of skills" needed "to talk well on a subject like literature" are "cool detachment as well as passionate intensity of feeling" (Esslin, "Search," 200). These skills are also necessary for effective discourse about criticism. As we noticed in chapter 2, Lingeman exposes "Reviewmanship" as "a body of techniques that enable one to mobilize the book review in the service of personal objectives. Practitioners of Reviewmanship recognize that the primary purpose of reviewing a book is to display one's talents, punish an enemy or achieve power" (683). From a different perspective, in "On Being Reviewed," Esslin himself argues: "Emotive language, rudeness, the obvious desire and indeed need to injure, are sure indications of the reviewer's own insecurity, envy or subconscious awareness of his inferiority. Equally the implied assertion of an unquestioned superiority of the reviewer over his target proclaims similar insecurities" (22). Reviews with such "fairly infallible tell-tale signs . . . need not be taken too seriously," but they do "give amusing insights into the psychology of their writers. And often it is sheer envy which triggers off this kind of snobbish reaction" (22, 23). "What is most important in all reviews, including the most unfavourable ones," Esslin concludes,

> is that the actual argument, the line of reasoning of the book, should be based on a fair exposition of the content. If that rule is observed even the most merciless review is acceptable, for it gives the reader the opportunity of actually judging for himself whether the condemnatory judgement is actually justified. . . . [T]he crux of the matter: the core, the sole *raison d'être* of a book review must be the fair and perceptive exposition of the book's content. The judicial aspect, the effort to assign the book its place in a hierarchy of values within the existing literature, is important but, to my mind, secondary. In the floodtide of publications—many of them produced without any deeper necessity beyond the academic treadmill's incessant demand for published material—which makes it impossible to read all the relevant material in even a fairly narrowly circumscribed field, the book review is an essential instrument of communication and information. . . . Reviewers may often be vain, unfair, unperceptive and even downright perverse, but they perform an immensely important, an essential function. (23–24)

Quigley has permitted me to quote him on his initial "amusement" in response to Esslin's review of *The Pinter Problem*—"[i]t didn't strike me as a serious argument in terms of anything I had to say." For Quigley to have regarded it "as a serious review," he said, "it would have to have . . . addressed the issues that I was addressing. . . . And as it didn't, I didn't." To his mind Quigley has already replied to Esslin's review because in the review Esslin offers no arguments that Quigley has not already discussed in *The Pinter Problem*. Preferring to make no further public comment on Esslin's review (or reviews by others), Quigley was "wary of being unnecessarily unpleasant to someone who is well down the line of his career, has done useful things, and doesn't need any flak from anybody, who's had a venerable career and deserves the generosity of the next generation; I'd like to extend him that generosity."[18] While a laudable gesture, such "generosity" may have resulted in part from the taped interview situation in which Quigley and I were engaged; it may have inhibited Quigley's further public disclosure of his personal responses to reviewers like Esslin, thus recalling the "privacy" issues discussed in my previous chapter.

No matter how public its medium, no review is wholly impartial, for subjective and intersubjective factors motivate all reading and writing, all "public speaking." Critics are responsible for understanding how such factors may be affecting their perceptions of someone else's work. They must come to terms with their own subjective engagement and acknowledge it (at least to themselves) so as both to arrive at fair (if not impartial) assessments of their colleagues' work and to share what they have learned from such self-examination with others.

For Quigley "books have two lives: one is the life of the instant review, which seems to me to be finally not a very important life; and the second life of the book is the important one; that is, who's reading it five years later? who's still talking about it? who's put it on their book lists? And if you ask yourself Whose *reviews* are on everybody's book list? of course, the question is ludicrous. The reviews have died away. They are a very rough-and-ready guide from sources whose reliability is open to debate. Which doesn't make them useless. They're used in that context." This viewpoint resembles Pinter's own position on his plays—The text speaks for itself: "The notion somehow that your book lives and dies on its reviews perhaps comes from an earlier year, an earlier age, an age that is perhaps to some degree perpetuated by the tendency of tenure-review committees to want to see reviews. And I've argued myself about the foolishness of this many times. And I say, 'Look, if you want to know what the value of this book is, don't [read the reviews] . . . go read the book.' " Obviously, as both Esslin and Quigley suggest, a review substitutes for reading a critical book *no more than* a critical interpretation or scholarly study substitutes for experiencing a play; yet a review can also provide both guidance and a dialogic opening for other readers. My own resurrection next of some other "dead" reviews of *The Pinter Problem* aims to achieve a more balanced review of its reception.

### The Reception of *The Pinter Problem*: Beyond Esslin

Most of the other reviews of *The Pinter Problem* that I have examined offer strong positive evaluations of the book.[19] As would be expected, none gives unqualified approval, and there are substantial disagreements, as well as degrees of consensus about certain flaws in Quigley's argument, method, or style of presentation that might appear to substantiate some of Esslin's complaints. Quigley's own claims for the importance of his "solution" to "the Pinter problem," however, do have strong support: *The Pinter Problem* "will turn criticism of Pinter and all modern drama in new directions" (*Choice*); it "breaks new ground" (Buck); its "emphasis" is "more focused than what has gone before," it poses new "important and potentially enlightening questions," and "[i]n many respects it is as good as anything yet written on Pinter" (Gale); it is "a valuable, or one might say an invaluable, contribution not only to the study of Pinter but as a model for future explorations of other, especially contemporary, playwrights" (Hammond, 45); it is "unquestionably one of the best critical works on Pinter to have been published in English," "it abounds in fresh, remarkable insights into the nature of Pinter's stagecraft," and it presents "a myriad of brilliant observations which explain fully almost every one of the alleged incongruities that numerous critics have chosen to read into the plays" (Imhof).

But even in these positive reviews, the qualifications and disagreements are striking. Among "several" of the book's "flaws," the reviewer for *Choice* notices first: "Quigley is extraordinarily ungenerous with earlier critics; implicit is the idea that earlier interpretations will be invalidated—in fact, many are nicely validated, but from a different point of view." This reviewer is also distressed that Quigley's "detailed analyses" are so "mechanical." Hammond grants Quigley's argument that "there are 'different ways in which language can carry information'" as clearly exemplified and his rejection of "the 'reference theory of meaning'" as "sound reason" accompanied by "very impressive support" from theories of Wittgenstein and others; whereas Hudson judges Wittgenstein's "rejection of the reference theory" based on "[h]is injunction about the sentence as an instrument" (cited earlier), "though influential over philosophers in the 1950s," to be "flimsy" and "a ridiculous view of language." Hammond claims that Quigley's "conclusions" are "actually reached, not merely declared, and exciting as well as instructive" (46); whereas Gale observes that it is "not clear" why Quigley "feels that no one has made this discovery [that language functions pluralistically in Pinter's plays] before" and that "[u]nfortunately Quigley insists on 'something new' as though his insistence alone will bring it into being" and "simply asserts that certain things are so" in his explication of Rose and

Bert's relationship in *The Room*" (784, 785). Though Imhof declares Quigley's style "clear and easily accessible" (427), as for Esslin, for most of the other reviewers, it was a detraction (cf. Buck; Gale, 786; Nightingale, "Human Zoo," 72).

Imhof also praises the verifiability of Quigley's interpretations of the plays (427) without acknowledging Quigley's own ambiguous attitude toward interpretive verification discussed earlier. In contrast to Imhof, though he declares Quigley's "interpretation of *The Dwarfs*" to be "fine," Gale concludes, more generally, that "Quigley's interpretations occasionally are contradictory and often do not show clear understanding of the plays" (786). For example, though finding "[t]he examination of *The Caretaker* . . . more credible" than that of *The Room*, Gale describes the chapter on *The Homecoming* as "a combination of valid insights and misreadings," himself making some debatable points about "communication" and "Max's use of language"; without giving any further specific explanation or supporting evidence, while granting Quigley "an understanding of how language works in [*Landscape*], in terms of patterns," Gale still claims, "but he does not understand the play" (786). Read instrumentally, this claim implies: "understand the play as I do." (Cf. *Choice*: "the discussion of *Landscape* is not as convincing as the discussions of the other plays.") A context for Gale's further point that "Quigley obviously does not study the play as a dramatic form, and more attention should be paid to *how* the play means rather than what it means, given existing criticism" (785) is his own *Butter's Going Up*, about which reviewers made similar observations.

Quigley's analysis of "Pinter's use of language in his youthful confrontations with broken milk bottle wielders" (cited earlier) is for Gale one of the book's "most promising" parts; it is "well done" and "both informative and logically presented" (785). As with Burkman's epilogue in his review of her *Dramatic World* (cited in chap. 5), however, Gale calls Quigley's conclusion (discussed later in this chap.) "tacked on" (786). Moreover, though agreeing that a study of Pinter's plays from the viewpoint of "theoretical linguistics" is long overdue—as Imhof suggests that Quigley's critical terminology emerges more from communication theory (the *relational*) than linguistics (429)—Gale questions Quigley's "contention that *The Pinter Problem* is a linguistic study," which he claims "has not been borne out by the text" (apparently because he could not find sufficient "attention" to "language"—or "the way the words work"—and "linguistics" per se in the analyses); "the commentary comes to no meaningful conclusion regarding Pinter's language" (786). Gale's notion of what constitutes "linguistics" could differ radically from what he calls Quigley's "liberal definition" (786); but Gale does not explicitly define either one. Yet, in concluding, he still regards Quigley's "premise" as "valid" and indicative of "the direction in which a segment of Pinter scholarship needs to develop" (786). The book is "a legitimate addition to Pinter studies" because "[t]he attention to Pinter's use of language from a linguistic point of view is important, and [it is] an area which has been slighted." But Gale registers "disappointment . . . that *The Pinter Problem* will serve to show others what needs to be done instead of having done it."

Hinchliffe—who observes that Pinter's language "justifies Professor Quigley in forcing the matter of linguistics upon us in the context of the plays" (933)—nevertheless concludes by citing "Dr Leavis's admonition that language in the full sense eludes the cognizance of any form of linguistic science" as a warning "particularly relevant to drama," without defining either how Quigley can be "forcing" anything on us or what "language in the full sense" is. Hinchliffe suggests a resistance to linguistics paralleling his earlier resistance to psychoanalysis by repeating the Leavisite bias that even if "[t]he desire and need to bring about an interaction between linguistics and literary criticism is both honest and urgent . . . drama seems the very last context for such a marriage" (935).

Further exemplifying these reviewers' unfamiliarity and discomfort with linguistics, Hudson charges that Quigley "has borrowed the authority of linguistics and linguistic philosophy for the impression of analytical rigour they give, rather than because they have any logical bearing on the critical task at hand." Having located "a precedent" for Quigley's "emphasis on broken patterns of communication . . . in the work of psychiatrists, psychologists and sociologists like R. D. Laing, Eric Berne and Erving Goffman," Hudson considers it "a pity that Professor Quigley has read so much linguistics, and so little of the psychology that now seems nearer his chosen home."

Each reviewer has his or her own complex of reasons—psychological and social, ideological and nationalistic, as well as philosophical and aesthetic—for making such judgments. The particular organ in which a reviewer is writing may also affect these judgments.[20] Overtolerance of "Reviewmanship" apparently countenances publishing questionable judgments without the kind of evidence accompanying the scholarly arguments under review. Self-serving evaluations often displace more serious debate. Gale's review cites "a British bias" in Quigley's "limited" bibliography, acknowledging however that "in a study of this sort not much more is needed"; yet, this opening enables Gale to promote his own G. K. Hall bibliography, at that time still in press (786). Similarly, Imhof, who also published a bibliography of Pinter criticism, in the same year as *The Pinter Problem* (1975), cites these "some sixty typed pages" as "a fact to provoke the assumption that critics have left no stone unturned in Pinter-land"; yet, in support of Quigley, Imhof adds: "in spite of this heavy bulk of material, several—to an appreciation of Pinter's plays crucial—problems have, surprisingly, remained unresolved" (427). Without explaining how, he claims that Quigley "provides conclusive evidence that a good deal of commentary on Pinter has, in fact, to be discarded as rubbish" (cf. Trussler, 13).

Rather than to dismiss one another's work as "rubbish," we can try to understand factors contributing to judgments with which we may not agree so that we can show how our judgments relate to one another in terms of both how we make them and what purposes they serve in our own and others' lives. Like reviews that they might later provoke, rhetorical choices in first books (and reviews of them) would seem motivated to some degree by insecurity (or its reaction-formation, overconfidence), as well as ambition and enthusiasm. Such motivations may be expressed only obliquely in books and articles; yet we must still take them into account in "receiving" and evaluating statements in part incited by them. Some would discount (devalue) reviews because such motivations have apparently affected (infected) their aims, causing evaluative distortions. But we must understand that, to various degrees and with varying effects, these dynamics produce all criticism and scholarship under review.

### The Making of *The Pinter Problem*

Quigley's personal and professional experiences have enabled him to combine interests in drama and Pinter's plays with interests in linguistics and philosophy of language. He grew up in Northumberland, in the north of England, and, contrary to Esslin's assumption that Quigley appears never to have attended the theater, he did so frequently. While growing up, he lived "within easy reach of the community and professional theatres of Newcastle and Sunderland. There was a thriving new theatre in Nottingham when I went there to University, and graduate school at Birmingham University kept me close to Nottingham, Stratford, and Birmingham theatres and within a short train ride of the theatres of London's West End." His preface to *The Modern Stage and Other Worlds* (perhaps in response to Esslin's critique of his first book) relates: "My interest in the theatre goes back as far as my earliest memories. As the child of a village schoolmaster, I found myself at an early age behind the scenes of the school's drama productions; as a youth in the north of England, I was quickly introduced to the boisterous worlds of music hall and community theatre; as a university student and subsequently a university teacher, I exchanged the regional theatres of Newcastle, Leeds and Nottingham for the major theatre centres of London, Europe and North America" (xv). His interest in the theater began in the late fifties and developed through the sixties, along with "Pinter's career": "Harold Pinter's work first appeared on the London stage at about the same time that I began to take a serious interest in drama. The controversy that quickly surrounded his work attracted my attention and has retained it ever since" (*PP*, xiii). While Quigley was still in grammar school (high school), he was intrigued by reports of John Osborne's *Look Back in Anger* from his future brother-in-law, a college student in London, from whom he also borrowed a pirated copy of *The Dumb Waiter*, which first appeared ("legally or not") in "some magazine." The first performance of a Pinter play that he saw was the 1960 ABC "Armchair Theatre" telecast of *A Night Out*.

Quigley started training in literature at the University of Nottingham in 1964 at the age of twenty-one. During this training he became "very impatient" with "the kind of thinking" that he encountered in criticism: "It seemed to me so often impressionistic, unhelpful, likely to tell us more about the critic than about the text." After becoming "quite dissatisfied with what it would be like spending a career studying and teaching English," he decided to do graduate work in linguistics instead at the University of Birmingham. After two years of studying this discipline (1967–69), "trying to see what it could do, what it couldn't do," however, he "quickly began to feel that linguistics was really not going to provide me with what I hoped—that is, a better way of thinking about language, life, truth, reality, fiction, plays, poems." At first it had seemed "an obvious step, for if literary people couldn't talk about literature and the language of literature in the ways that I could find satisfactory, then maybe the linguists would be able to do it better." But he realized that this scientific study of language as "the study of

elements within sentences" had "siphoned off" the issues relating to
language that interested him most: "obviously a great deal going on in
literature is interaction—among sentences—so if you wanted a grammar
at all it has to be a text grammar not a sentence grammar." When Quigley
first began studying linguistics, this (as he ironically termed it) "particularly startling discovery" had still not "really made much impact" on
the field; "It has since." (For more recent application of discourse analysis
to Pinter's plays, see my discussion of Burton below.) A fortuitous
connection between linguistics and Pinter occurred when Quigley's professor John Sinclair selected a passage from Pinter "as a way of showing
the kinds of information that you get out of language that derive from
sentence interaction rather than from sentence components."[21] Though
he shared with Sinclair an interest in discourse analysis, neither Quigley
nor Sinclair had developed it much then. "I became very dissatisfied with
what linguistics at that time was able to do. And I was moving into a
kind of steady search—and a foolish search—for the basic discipline."

Quigley's next step was to regard linguistic theories as "largely unanalyzed philosophies of language"; investigating this field led to a
continuing interest in the writings of Wittgenstein and recognition that
"there is no basic discipline (as we have all discovered by now)." Having
learned "that there was no base, and that underlying the philosophy of
language would be another set of metaphysical assumptions about the
nature of humanity and the world and so forth that you end up with in
endless pursuit," Quigley discovered that, unbeknownst to himself, he
had been engaged in a "process" of "theorizing," had "become a theorist."

By the time he began his doctoral studies at the University of California, Santa Cruz, in 1969, Quigley was "very interested in how language
works" but also maintained "a great deal of interest in the theatre,
considerable interest in Pinter, an interest in how drama and literature
[move] in terms of how one can discuss their language, and an interest in
positioning, theorizing." When it came time for him to write a dissertation, he had already "been following Pinter criticism, and watching
Pinter plays, and seeing them in the theatre, thinking about them, and it
was quite clear that there was a problem with dealing with his work that
linked up very nicely with the kind of intellectual interests and nonin-
tellectual interests that I had been developing over the years, and the two
converged."

As Quigley explains in the preface to *The Pinter Problem*, the director of
his dissertation, John M. Ellis, guided and encouraged "the development

of this project" and most particularly his development as a theorist (xiii).[22] While his own interest in Pinter began ten years before his encounter with Ellis, during the year that Quigley took to write his dissertation, "The Dynamics of Dialogue" (expanded and published as *The Pinter Problem*), he discovered that Ellis shared his theoretical interests in Wittgenstein, philosophy of language, and literary criticism. Though, as a professor of German literature, Ellis "had no professional interest in the English theatre," he had "strong personal interest" in it. The work with Ellis was "a very good intellectual experience of the best kind, where you don't become an apprentice or a clone . . . but you get to be someone pushed to do your own thinking." There continue to be striking similarities, I would add, in Quigley's and Ellis's attitudes toward the use of logic in critical argument.[23]

Quigley attributed his understanding of Pinter's language not to "a particular relationship or a particular situation, [but] just [to] the range and texture of lived experiences." While he regarded his own experience growing up in England as helpful in understanding Pinter, he emphasized more general, practical roots of the theoretical side of this understanding: "I think the element of negotiation in dialogue has been clear to me for as long as I remember. . . . And because I have the conceptual framework that comes out of theory and out of Wittgenstein to be able to talk about how language is used . . . there may then be an interaction between whatever sophistication I have for conceptualizing language usage of the kind that Pinter is doing—an interaction between the capacity to conceptualize and a long-term fascination with that element of language in relationships."

At first Quigley could not locate an explanation for his understanding of Pinter merely in his personal social experiences. There did not appear to him to be "some one class of phenomena, some local relationships that made the difference in any particular interpretation of any particular play" of Pinter's that he has published; "all" of his personal and professional experiences pertained, but "none of them specially." The experience that Pinter reported to Bensky, which occurred outside "a Jewish club, by an old railway arch," however, did recall "a *class* of experiences" involving "boys' clubs":

> For him [Pinter] it was localized to being a Jew in working-class London. For me it was if you lived, as I did, in the north of England, there is a number of small villages. Villages tend to have a certain

degree of competition with each other. I grew up to play soccer a great deal all over the north of England, and if you were from another place, you were likely to be challenged, in a way that's not at all uncommon here—it's a matter of the same in New York City. . . . So that kind of situation I dare say was not at all uncommon, where you run into the leaders of another group and some muttering did take place and a certain amount of threat is offered and you kind of address them, and the negotiation of a truce through some quick interchange of that sort would work.

Quigley tended to downplay this conjunction of his personal experience of social competitiveness with Pinter's: "So that type of instance was . . . [familiar to] anybody growing up in anything other than upperclass England at that time, and probably is the same way in England now." But particular personal social experiences of this kind (involving interrelational negotiation with others) form some basis for Quigley's own critical understanding of the way that language works in Pinter's plays, for other audience members' more intuitive recognition of what is happening in the plays, and for other critics' willingness to accept Quigley's more sophisticated, theoretical analysis of how Pinter's dialogue works: their common ground (however much it may be also, as Pinter has said, a "quicksand").

Pinter's "broken milk bottles" account serves Quigley and others who cite his interpretation as a kind of shorthand description of the dynamics of Pinter's character relationships as enacted through dialogue. Its appropriateness seems directly proportional to its commonality with their vividly remembered experiences as children and adults. If, as Quigley stressed, the typicality of his own experience as an English youth is more important than the unique singularity of any particular "club" experience of this kind, then the accumulation of similarly typical, vividly intense experiences may explain the strength of the familiarity with this mode of Pinter's language for other members of Pinter's audiences too, an aspect of its "universality."

Despite his "academic approach" to Pinter's plays, Quigley's interest in them is "recreational and experiential" as well as professional, particularly since he became interested in the theater professionally only after having experienced it recreationally. Regarding his more emotional responses to Pinter's plays: "regularly" he becomes "quite moved by" the experience of the plays in reading and in the theater; "if I didn't, I don't think I would be writing about them." While he admitted that "the capacity to respond to what is happening to [the characters] is deepened by more extensive relationship to the plays," I would add that this capacity to respond to the plays is deepened also by more extensive personal social experience and intensive exploration of their interrelations. "If there's something of a large emotional consequence that's happening in my life at the time I go to a play," Quigley elaborated, "I can find myself responding in a slightly skewed way to the texture of the play by foregrounding the elements that interact with me, that seem to be the points of contact with my life—when I'm preoccupied with something, fascinated by something where I will just react to something in [the direction that] my own personal relationships are going." Responding more critically is "trying to find the right balance . . . to set out to deal with one's own responses" and to "try to lose the thoughts of yourself." Recognizing the complex connections between his personal social experiences and his interpretations of Pinter's plays, though regarding "no single" experience as "privileged above all others at the time when the interpretation was being done," he still noticed the "counterpoint" to this position: that "all of them in fact contributed to a particular interpretation." Yet in Quigley's view "the range, the texture of one's own experience is simply a mode of access to the plays which one transcends" through interpreting and theorizing.

In contrast to the viewpoint of Esslin, who stresses the importance of "subjective truth" in literature and criticism (considered a form of literature or creative writing), and that of Richard Ohmann, who emphasizes "the social relations of criticism," Quigley foregrounds the *interactivity* of individual and social purposes in criticism. "I don't want to use the *subjective/objective* distinction. . . . What matters is the negotiated, agreed-upon reality base for this particular mode of interaction."[24] Linked to Quigley's notion of the interactivity of individual and social in experience is his view of the relation between "conventionality" or "tradition" and "innovation" or "novelty" in modern plays (elaborated throughout *MSOW*). His own usage of dualistic distinctions like *conventionality/ novelty*, *right/wrong*, *accurate/inaccurate*, and (I would add) *appropriate/ inappropriate*, recurrent throughout his critical writing, are helpful for "public" purposes; they are "public language games," dependent on (a concept that I suggested) negotiated usage. In making such distinctions he upholds Wittgenstein's view that "because words serve many purposes in many language games, they have many kinds of significance"; "it would be very difficult to pin down exactly what *novelty* is or exactly what *conventionality* is so that that exact definition would hold for all future language games in which the words emerge."[25] Terms such as *"conventionality* and *novelty, exactness, precision, accuracy, truth, reality, certainty, right, wrong . . .* [like all other words] are used for contextual purposes. . . . [T]hey are all instrumental distinctions, for certain purposes, and those purposes are contextually variable. Therefore, the function of the word is contextually variable." Moreover, "[m]ost of these words that have a built-in value judgment of one kind or another, about the usefulness or lack of usefulness about a particular line of inquiry, or a particular approach, or a particular statement" require Wittgenstein's "governing principle": "a useful critical statement is one that would . . . enable you to go on. That is, what you're doing all the time is untangling conceptual knots. So that if you untangle a knot, you've not suddenly arrived at the definitive truth about the issue that you're exploring, you've simply arrived at a point where it's possible to continue to explore."[26]

*The Pinter Problem* concludes by citing "literary criticism's neglect of the functional plurality of language" and Quigley's disappointment that "a similar neglect" characterizes "the recent history of linguistic study in general" (275). Regarding further theorizing based on "the syntactic patterns that occur within individual sentences" as a conceptual dead end, Quigley advocates investigating "[t]he relationship between sentences in discourse and the relationship between syntactic form and semantic function." While championing Wittgenstein's ability to transcend "[c]ertain semantic assumptions about language . . . [apparently] built into literary criticism and into our culture," Quigley notices the failure of literary critics to assimilate Wittgenstein's later writings and recognizes the pertinence of Pinter's own comments about "the relationship between language, time, and reality" to understanding the instability of the so-called common ground. He urges us to approach Pinter's plays *not* "with a belief that truth, reality and communication ought to conform to certain norms" but with the realization "that all of these concepts are, like any others, moves in language games" (275–76). To understand Pinter, it follows, we must understand these "moves."

But just as Pinter's characters strive for social adjustment, "negotiating not only truth and reality but their very freedom to engage their preferred identities in the environments that surround them" (276), so do his critics. If "an awareness of, and an ability to describe, the interaction of sentences in dialogue is indispensable" for understanding Pinter's plays, as Quigley argues (275), this awareness and this ability are just as crucial for understanding critical dialogue about Pinter's plays.

## From Structuralist Moves to Semiotic Conventions (Signals to Signposts)

The last sentences of *The Pinter Problem* elaborate the metaphor of Pinter's characters' "linguistic battles" (276–77). Not only can the "weapons" change, but the *modes* of discursive "strategies" can too. It may be culturally significant that one of Pinter's most recent characters to relinquish such weapons for a different mode of talk is a relatively unsocialized woman (Deborah, in *A Kind of Alaska*), that key figures of abuse and oppression in *One for the Road* and *Mountain Language* are women, and that several of the academic critics who have taken up Quigley's "challenge" to linguistic study of Pinter are also women.[27] There are, of course, also important studies of Pinter's language written by men, such as Andrew Kennedy's *Six Dramatists in Search of a Language* and "Natural, Mannered, and Parodic Dialogue." These are not, however, strictly speaking, what Quigley refers to as "discourse analysis." *Six Dramatists* (like Quigley's *Pinter Problem*, a dissertation published in 1975) defines Pinter's theater or comedy of "mannerism" and tries to describe the relationship between naturally mimetic features of Pinter's dialogue and stylized or mannerist ones. Extending this perspective in the 1979 article, Kennedy cites Quigley supportively ("Natural," 45 n.1), but, more exclusively structuralist in his approach, Kennedy is principally concerned with *patterns* in texture and style.[28]

## Discourse Analysis: Deirdre Burton

Deirdre Burton advances Quigley's own investigation by pursuing a sociolinguistic "discourse analysis" of Pinter. "Making Conversation" and a revised version of this discussion in *Dialogue and Discourse* both use Pinter's revue sketch *Last to Go* to illustrate the potential benefits of "the analysis of conversational data" for "linguists working on stylistics and literary texts" ("Making Conversation," 188). *Dialogue and Discourse* adds extensive analysis of *The Dumb Waiter* from this perspective, while "Conversation Pieces" extends this analysis to focus on "transaction management," a particular aspect of discourse analysis, or "the linguistic examination of the organization of spoken and written texts" (86).

"Making Conversation" demonstrates "how an analyst of play-talk can benefit from linguistic analysis of real-talk" (200). Burton attempts to resolve two "problems" that have interested Pinter's critics throughout his career: "First, why does this dialogue sound/read like a real conversation? Second, how do we know so much about the interactants in the dialogue?" (191). In answering these questions, she draws upon "a substantial body of linguistic writing that presents aspects of rule-governed behavior of conversationalists": most notably, the work on "shared knowledge" by William Labov; on "repetition" by Gail Jefferson; and on "phatic communion" by John Laver (191, 200 n.2). Burton's analysis of Pinter's characters' conversation illuminates their recurrent "strategies" for "making more conversation" and how their discomfort during "the whole interaction" is a function of the manner in which "phatic communion co-occurs with psychological insecurity" (198). Particular "rules of conversational analysis" show Pinter illustrating S. I. Hayakawa's explanation of "'the prevention of silence'" as "'an important function of speech'" (199, 200 n.8).[29]

Burton's "stylistic study" of Pinter's *Dumb Waiter* further exemplifies what I mean by cooperative criticism and helps to explain some observations about the play discussed in chapter 4. While criticism, like other forms of human interaction, depends on *both* competition *and* cooperation, Burton illustrates the effectiveness of a cooperative rhetorical mode. Strategically but cooperatively, she develops Quigley's lead in *The Pinter Problem* by citing "'the dominant interrelational function' [of language] as opposed to any simpler referential function to be found in all Pinter's works" in building a rationale for her own focus on the conversational interactions between Ben and Gus (*Dialogue and Discourse*, 69–70). In her later analysis of *The Dumb Waiter* in "Conversation Pieces," noting the importance of *transaction management information* as one of "at least three types of 'information'" characterizing "all conversational exchanges," she explains pertinently: "Conversations are subtle cooperative productions, and ultimately it is the responsibility of the good discourse analyst to represent fairly and delicately the intricacies of the work that goes into the making of any conversational exchange" (86–87). Citations of Quigley mentioned above in *Dialogue and Discourse* (69–70) and immediately after this quotation in this essay (87–88) exemplify the benefits of regarding critical dialogue as such conversational exchanges and following "a global conversational rule, which [Grice] names the *cooperative principle*"; for "the successful conduct of linguistic interaction is possible only on the basis of a joint commitment to the communicative objective" (Elam, 171).[30]

Burton differs strikingly from most other previous Pinter criticism that I have read in another way: she gives her interpretations less priority than the analysis itself. While offering her own interpretations simply as reasonable illustrations to locate larger theoretical issues, she presents them as specific instances of an academic critic's own "casual and intuitive" reading-responses to the text under analysis and as evidence of a teacher's attentiveness to those of students ("Conversation Pieces," 88–89).

As Quigley has said about linguistics, discourse analysis is important both for what it can do and for what it cannot do. Burton admits that it cannot "say everything one wants to say about a text"; yet what it does tell us, it says "very precisely, clearly, rigorously and consistently" ("Conversation Pieces," 108). Discourse analysis demonstrates "how artefacts are made, why it is that large numbers of readers respond to similar effects in any text, how to locate those effects where they *must* be—in the organization of the language of the text itself" (108). Burton's powerful "descriptive apparatus" (109) for analyzing discourse in Pinter's plays does advance Quigley's quest for such a path to improved understanding of Pinter's language. But her structuralist orientation neglects how "those effects" also result from more interactional/intersubjective factors influencing response.[31]

As Burton and others move beyond Quigley's seminal work on Pinter's language, they are modifying his language games with newer language games, putting into practice the very principles on which discourse analysis is based.[32] As sociolinguists suggest, critical discourse (critical language games) involves strong skills in social negotiation, both inside and outside the academic classroom. Such work is an important critical signpost, a guide to kinds of relationships that critics could foster through mainly cooperative rather than merely competitive stances toward one another's work.

### Semiotics of Performance: Susan Melrose

Among the most recent criticism of Pinter's plays from a linguistic perspective is that termed "semiotic" or "semiological."[33] Paralleling Burton's project, a strong pedagogical impetus motivates much of this work. As some of these efforts are the result of collaborative research, like

Burton's they also promote cooperative criticism. Melrose's analysis of two productions of Pinter's *No Man's Land* (Peter Hall's at the National Theatre in 1975, as later filmed by Granada Television, and Roger Planchon's Théâtre National Populaire at Villeurbanne in 1979–80) illustrates recent tendencies and trends in theater semiotics, as summarized by Bassnett: "reception theory on the one hand, with emphasis on what happens in the interaction between performance and audience, and the mechanics of acting on the other, with emphasis on the physical rather than the psychological processes of creating theatre" (82).[34] Melrose's invention of an elaborate notational system for comparing the English and French productions of *No Man's Land* was necessitated by her previous experience with this "slippery" Pinter text, which "short-circuited every method of staging analysis" that she had attempted in four years of study with Patrice Pavis and Anne Ubersfeld (217–18).

Like Quigley, Melrose borrows her view of Pinter's language from M. A. K. Halliday, who "rejects the hierarchical metaphor of deep and surface, and attempts to take on language as social interaction" (215). This "replaces the intuitive approach of the hermeneute" with another reading practice, systematically evaluating and classifying textual items in terms of "three basic functions: experiential or ideational, interpersonal, and textual."[35] But since Melrose finds "the textual function—the way in which the human speaker links together his verbal message" of most particular interest and relevance to reading drama, despite her emphasis on language as "social interaction" and acknowledgment of the importance of audience reception, she specifies details of text in relative isolation. Nevertheless, she suggests that complex dramatic texts such as Pinter's require multiple critical approaches to establish how divergences in performances and audience response are linked to translations from the English, directors' "staging practice," and "socio-cultural factors" (218).

If Melrose could *embrace* hermeneutics instead of rejecting it—that is, incorporate it in her theory—she might be able to explain the *interactivity* between functional levels of text and audience response. Her methodology could then relate "intuitive" and psychological components of audience response to "experiential" or "ideational" and "interpersonal" levels of Pinter's performance-text (and other such texts) more substantially than she claims to do. By neglecting relations between "paralinguistic" signs and audience members' affective experiences of the play, she overlooks an important source of interpretive or hermeneutic information.[36]

Closing her article on what she calls "a highly digestible note," Melrose defines the "theatrical focalized theme" that Pinter seduces "us" with the scrambled eggs and toast served to Spooner at the beginning of the second act of *No Man's Land*. "We" feel the hunger and the thirst in responding to *No Man's Land*, she suggests. For an approach that champions the central role (function) of the audience, there is a striking absence—a deferral—in Melrose's theoretical presentation. How does who "we" are relate to what we contribute to these textual language games? How are we their subject(s)?

### Cultural Implications and Limitations of "Language Games"

Melrose highlights the degree to which Pinter's drama is a transcultural, transmedia phenomenon.[37] A recently published study of Pinter's screenplays and films by Joanne Klein, like some studies of his radio drama (Esslin, "HP's Work"; Imhof, "Radioactive"; and Salmon), further stresses the importance of examining the interrelations of Pinter's work for various media, as do Noel King and others.[38] Klein also defines the game motif in all this work, while Almansi and Henderson "play" upon it too.

Several academic theses and dissertations have examined the play motif and "theatricality" in Pinter's work from a variety of angles. Elin Diamond's *Pinter's Comic Play* and David T. Thompson's *Pinter: The Player's Playwright* are two recently published. As Quigley observes in reviewing *Pinter's Comic Play*, Diamond offers an illuminating survey of sources of Pinter's "conventional comic strategies" and an "ingenious explanation" of how these may engender audience ambivalence, though she does not base her insights on a "global theory" of comedy (514).[39] In contradistinction to Dukore, whom she sees as making "a rigid distinction between the funny and the unfunny," with "each play analysis identif[ying] the moment 'where laughter stops,'" Diamond asserts: "Stacking character confusion against audience uncertainty, Pinter places unverifiability at the center of our experience of the comic" (13, 217 n.9). Though, as Quigley notices, this stress on "the unverifiable" may curtail analysis and convert "all plays into the same play" (rev., 514), Diamond illustrates complex, parodic relations between Pinter's plays and their cultural antecedents in such diverse forms as comedy of manners, melodrama, music hall, television soap opera, and gangster film. As mentioned in chapter 3, Thompson reveals "very strong connections" (61) between

Pinter's playwriting and his personal experiences as an actor in repertory plays in the fifties, though, as Vincent Curcio complains, "the question of whether or not Pinter's world of negotiated unknowable reality is interesting and profound, or truncated and shallow, is never really engaged."[40] For resolution of this question, on the side of Pinter's depth, there are the detailed analyses of his recent plays in performance by Richard Cave. (See, however, chap. 9 below.) Pinter's "theatricality," "metatheatricality," or use of "the postmodern performance principle" is a current subject (cf. Hornby; Rao; Van Laan; and work in progress by Garner).[41]

Somewhat echoing Pinter's description of one of the "two silences," the "torrent of words . . . speaking of a language locked beneath it," Ed Berman, the director of Inter-Action, a community-arts project based in London since 1968, has eloquently written: "Locked within all of us is a social language learned in childhood. This is a language of behaviour based on the rules of children's games. These games are usually abandoned as an active pursuit in early adolescence. The language remains within us, however, as a major formative influence and touchstone in our adult intellectual, social, and emotional relationships and as one of the filters through which we sift the world" (quoted in Barker, 232–33).

Reducing everything to "language games" (or "play" or "theatricality") or even inventing new ones like a "global" performance "notation"— however these models enhance our understanding, fuel our articles and books—neglects some *other* important aspects of experience: *people play such games as part of larger social events and enterprises.* By attending to some neglected social features of Pinter criticism in this book, I am trying to readmit the "social purposes" of criticism that Bleich argues have been omitted from what he calls this "ludic mentality" in criticism. Some of the neglected "social items" that Bleich mentions are the very same ones that I have been noticing here—"the writing of the text, the reading, the reviewing, the enjoying"; these "items always occur in small multipersonal circumstances" generally overlooked in traditional criticism ("Intersubjective Reading," 419–20). By exploiting the metaphor of language games as far as I can take it, however, I have been trying to underline the *social connection* between my own past and present writing on Pinter and that of others. Yet my own current work also tries to "lead away from the philosophy of language games, paradox, mystery, and self-justifying ludic mentality" and "toward a rationality of multiple voices and common interests, toward readings 'responsible for the meaning of each other's inner lives'" (420; cf. *DP*, 17–26).

So as to reactivate a stagnated cycle of investigation, Quigley follows Wittgenstein. Others may be following Pinter in *No Man's Land*, who is echoing Eliot prefiguring Beckett's *Unnamable*: "You must go on, I can't go on, I'll go on." Pinter cites these lines apropos of going on in a nuclear age, where global self-annihilation ("in twenty-five years at the outside") is a plausible prospect, a very real threat ("A Play," 20). My next chapter shows how literary and critical endeavors concerning the cultural politics of class and gender enable us not merely to "go on," but to examine and even to revise our desired goals in doing so. Through such alternative investigations as those discussed next, we move from looking at Pinter's plays as "signals" for interpretation—as complex sign systems calling forth specific responses—to seeing them also as "signposts," as clear indicators of broader social and communal change.

# 8

## Cultural Politics

The Russians and Americans love each other
They place a golden eternity ring
    On each other's finger
They swear they will cross the last tape
    Fucking each other—
And leave the rest of us up to our ears in shit
—"Partners," by Harold Pinter

In her 1973 *Plays, Politics, and Polemics*, Catharine Hughes does not include any plays by Pinter. Yet as an epigraph she gives a familiar quotation from Pinter—"The [*sic*] thing is not necessarily either true or false; it can be both true and false." Repeating this quotation in her conclusion, she adds: "If it is the element of doubt, of gray, in Pinter's plays that lends them much of their fascination, it is the absence of doubt—the unwillingness to entertain its possibility—that cripples many, perhaps most, of the plays in the theatre of controversy. For to exclude doubt too often means to exclude the very conflict that is the essence of drama. Pursuing his polemic, the playwright all too frequently becomes its prisoner" (183). Now that he has turned toward more overt political concerns in his own plays, has Pinter become the prisoner of polemic too? No matter how polemical his nondramatic writing and remarks in interviews and speeches have become, a subtle "gray" area even in Pinter's most recent work for the stage may reserve a particular freedom from polemics: a space or quality recognizably "Pinteresque."

### Pinter and Politics

Though acknowledging a "shift" toward political drama in Pinter's recent dramatic works *One for the Road*, *Precisely*, and *Mountain Language*, some critics question whether it is genuine. Judging the authenticity of any such change of direction is more complex than giving an account of

Pinter's views or of his dramatic plots. Such judgments are contingent on the perspectives of the critics, on their particular politics or ideologies. From different critical vantage points, Pinter's politics can seem to have undergone a radical shift on the one hand, while maintaining a somewhat conservative stance on the other. This double perspective on Pinter's shift to political drama reflects current conflicts in cultural studies between those writing from mainstream positions and those espousing Marxist, neo-Marxist, and post-Marxist views.

A feature of the academic study of drama and theater may have engendered the problem of assessing Pinter's position and classifying his plays. As Marvin Carlson documents, "a continuing point of debate in modern theatre theory has been over whether the theatre should be viewed primarily as an engaged social phenomenon or as a politically indifferent aesthetic artifact; a significant amount of contemporary theoretical discourse can still be oriented in terms of this opposition" (*Theories*, 454). Carlson's own historical account of twentieth-century theater details the opposition between theater based on Brechtian theory and practice ("political theatre") and theater based more on the theory and practice of Artaud ("absurd theatre," "theatre of cruelty"). [1]

Critics have difficulties "placing" Pinter and his drama because he crosses the "standard" boundaries delineated by such binary oppositions. At various stages throughout his career, Pinter himself has characterized his work in some of these terms, and Pinter's plays have been championed by one "camp" or another, leading to early critical claims that he is *either* a "social realist" *or* an "absurdist" *or* that his work is an oddly idiosyncratic mixture of *both* strains. It has been commonplace to quote Pinter's statement "what goes on in my plays is realistic, but what I'm doing is not realism" ("Writing for Myself," 174). Critics' different responses to this "paradox" inform controversies about how to assess any developments in his career. [2]

The social realism perceived in his most recent work complicates the problem. Though Pinter dramatizes political concerns more overtly in *One for the Road*, *Precisely*, and *Mountain Language*, this "new interest" has strong roots in Pinter's early "comedies of menace" with their representations of individuals anxiously confronting the forces of social authority. What *political position* Pinter represents through his plays is difficult to situate on a conventional Left/Right spectrum. As we will see, Pinter gravitates less toward specific political ideological affiliations (rejecting even their terminology) than toward thinking matters out on his own, though he does ally himself with organizations that support his particular inclinations.[3] If a label is necessary for purposes of identification—and I am not so sure one is—I would call Pinter a social democrat and an advocate, even an activist, for peace, international human rights, and freedom of expression; his current political activities and his plays dramatize concerns with the protection of human rights and unilateral disarmament. Perhaps the most conspicuous shift, however, involves his characterization of the source of these concerns as an unquestionable political "reality."

Throughout most of his career it has been "against the grain" to discuss Pinter's drama as "political." For example, Henkle points to the relative isolation of Pinter's characters; "[t]he possible political dimensions of plays like *The Birthday Party* are remarkably abstract, and the sources of our response to them lie much more in our *personal* anxieties" (185).[4] But, in Germany, where *The Dumb Waiter* premiered in 1959 and *The Caretaker* was performed in 1960, the initial critical popularity of Pinter's plays was partly due to an appreciation of their social relevance. Describing the first performance of Ionesco's *Rhinoceros* at the Düsseldorf Schauspielhaus, where *The Caretaker* also played, Esslin observes: "the German audience instantly recognized the arguments, used by the characters who feel they must follow the trend, as those they themselves had heard, or used, at a time when people in Germany could not resist the lure of Hitler. . . . Rhinoceritis is not only the disease of the totalitarians of the Right as well as of the Left, it is also the pull of conformism" (*Theatre of the Absurd*, 150–51). Though Pinter has recalled spectacular choruses of "boos" accompanying his opening night curtain calls in Düsseldorf ("Between the Lines"), some Germans, focusing on the lower-class status of Davies, regarded *The Caretaker* as relevant socioeconomically.[5] In England, following *The Caretaker*, Taylor grouped Pinter with the "Kitchen Sink" playwrights—social realist and working-class drama of "the Angry Young Men," John Osborne and Arnold Wesker—in *Anger and After*, first published in May 1962.[6]

Yet, in talking about the politics of such drama with Harry Thompson in 1961, Pinter rejected its dramatic viability (9). When Bensky gave him another opportunity to discuss his political concerns in 1966, Pinter himself tended to deemphasize their importance to his early work. Though qualifying the impression that he was "indifferent" to politics and indicating that his political consciousness was still developing, he nevertheless questioned the relevance of politics to his social role as a playwright, focusing on his violent dislike of politicians and political ideologies and how such violence characterized his life and his work. Perhaps as a result, the theme of violence has been discussed repeatedly in Pinter criticism.[7]

By the late sixties Esslin was still trying to sort out connections between Pinter's personal act of conscientious objection in 1948, when he was eighteen years old, and political aspects of his drama (*PW*, 24–27; *PTP*, 36–39). In 1971, when Gussow raised similar questions about his political (ir)relevance, Pinter replied by criticizing the "totally meaningless, hypocritical" language of "politicians": "Politicians just don't interest me. What, if you like, interests me, is the suffering for which they are responsible. It doesn't interest me—it horrifies me!" He offered comments on Vietnam, South Africa, and China as evidence that he is "very conscious of what's happening in the world. I'm not by any means blind or deaf to the world around me. . . . I'm right up to the minute. I read the papers. I have very strong objections to all sorts of things" ("Conversation," 133–34). Yet these objections still did not enter his plays directly.

Anderson compares Pinter with Arnold Wesker and Edward Bond in terms of their similar lack of popularity in England ("This," 447). In 1979 Pinter alluded to the "very, very strong *young* wave of political playwrights" currently popular in England to help explain what he saw as his poor critical reception there (Gussow, "I Started," 7). The next year Pinter told Barber that he found himself in the "odd position" for a writer of being "really quite unpopular in his own country, when he is apparently of interest elsewhere. I have a suspicion," he said, "that fashion at the moment is with the young political Left. I'm never going to be a young political Left. I'm afraid it's a bit too late!" ("Precise Words"). As Pinter also told Gross, "my last three full-length plays [*Old Times, No Man's Land,* and *Betrayal*] have hardly been performed at all in this country, outside London" (27). About this time (1980) Pinter produced and published *The Hothouse,* a "heavily satirical" play which he had "discarded" as worthless earlier (Bensky, 28–29). Though Pinter described his decision to produce *The Hothouse* "rather quietly—at the Hampstead Theater Club" in terms of having "a bit of fun" (Gussow, "I Started," 5), later remarks suggest that (for a variety of reasons perhaps) Pinter was also now ready to produce more overtly political work.[8]

At the University of East Anglia in 1981, ending his brief talk, Pinter directly addressed the difficulty that he was encountering as a "nonpolitical" writer: "I think it must be very much easier for other people, particularly people, writers who write from a very political point of view and are able to incorporate their politics in one way or another into their work. I do happen to have strong political views but they simply do not come into my work as far as I can see." Asked whether this avoidance of politics as a subject in his plays was "deliberate," Pinter said, "Of course not. It simply doesn't work out that way," adding: "I am myself a convinced nuclear unilateralist but I don't see there is any—there is no way I can write a play about it. It's simply something that would never occur to me, I suppose, any of these considerations. . . . I am sure that some writers do—can very easily and properly sit down and write plays from a political kind of ideology. I am unable to do that." Yet, as another audience member suggested in East Anglia, after having "obviously achieved what [he] set out to," Pinter can now "use the success . . . to help" dramatize sociopolitical and ethical issues.

Pinter began to "help" first by reassessing publicly the political implications of the work that he had suppressed earlier and then by writing and producing new plays. Talking about the 1982 American premiere of *The Hothouse*, he told William Gale that whereas *The Hothouse* "would have been taken as a fantasy, as something remote and surrealistic" when it was written in 1958, "I felt that was not the case then, and I *know* it is not the case now. In 1982 it cannot be denied that it fits in with the facts of life today. The real political hypocrisy and brutality are now blatant. We cannot be fooled by them any longer" (A-16).[9]

Pinter's most recent dramas—*One for the Road*, *Precisely*, and *Mountain Language*—present today's political "facts of life" more starkly. *One for the Road*, written in 1983 and first produced and directed by Pinter in 1984, dramatizes political torture. *Precisely*, a dramatic sketch that Pinter read before an audience at New York University upon accepting the Elmer Holmes Bobst Award in Arts and Letters in December 1984, satirizes nuclear war bureaucracy. *Mountain Language*, first published and produced in 1988, dramatizes institutionalized abuses of sociopolitical prisoners and their distrust of their guards' apparently feigned ultimate tolerance, satirizing effects of censorship curtailing individual freedoms.[10]

Pinter's more recent perceptions of the political relevance of his early work further counterbalance the critical commonplace that it lacks such relevance. In "A Play and Its Politics," a conversation between Pinter and Nicholas Hern in 1985 published in the Grove Press edition of *One for the Road* the next year, Pinter explicitly discusses the change in his attitude toward authoritarianism between his early plays (e.g., *The Birthday*

*Party*, *The Hothouse*, and *The Dumb Waiter*), all written in 1957–60, and *One for the Road* and *Precisely*. Though he actively considered "the abuse of authority" in writing the earlier plays, he says, they "use metaphor to a great extent, whereas in *One for the Road* the deed is much more specific and direct": "I don't really see *One for the Road* as a metaphor. For anything. It describes a state of affairs in which there are victims of torture. You have the torturer, you have the victims. And you can *see* that two of the victims have been physically tortured" (8). *One for the Road* is "brutally real: my earlier plays were perhaps metaphors for states of affairs in various respects. This is not a metaphor about anything—it's just a brutal series of facts" (back cover). As when discussing the germination of his earlier plays in other interviews, in "A Play and Its Politics" Pinter further explains the impetus for such violent acts of "actual physical brutality" as rape and murder in *One for the Road*. As well as citing the general context of torture "quite commonly" practiced in "at least ninety countries now" throughout the world, both "Communist and non-Communist," he recounts the more particular circumstances stimulating him to write it: his knowledge of torture and inhumane prison practices in Turkey and his anger at the insensitivity of two young Turkish women toward their own country's violations of human rights. His own active membership in Campaign for Nuclear Disarmament led to his awareness that members of a counterpart organization in Turkey (the Turkish Peace Association) have been inhumanely treated (12–14).

This "new direction" in Pinter's playwriting grows out of Pinter's long-standing engagement in some social activities against human rights abuses. As early as 1974 Pinter wrote a letter to the London *Times* to draw attention to the plight of Soviet internee Vladimir Bukovsky. Pinter told Gross, in 1980, "While we're talking now . . . people are locked up in prisons all over the place, being tortured in one way or another. I'm quite raddled with these kinds of images, with the sense that these things are ever-present" (25). Several months after his 1981 visit to the University of East Anglia, in the summer of 1982, with his wife, Lady Antonia Fraser, Pinter helped to coordinate "The Night of the Day of the Imprisoned Writer," described as "a charity occasion to benefit the all-too-many writers of the world who are now in prison" (Owen, 24). Pinter's claim for the "very positive effect" that this International PEN benefit could achieve seems deflated by his account of a previous benefit for the imprisoned Czech writer Václav Havel: "On my 50th birthday last year [10 October 1980] the National Theatre were kind enough to put on a

play of mine [*Landscape*] for one night and the proceeds from that were for
Havel's family. The awful thing is that now, a year later, nothing has
changed for him" (Owen, 25). Despite this recognition, Pinter persisted
in his efforts.[11]

Pinter represented International PEN again on behalf of imprisoned
writers in March 1985, when, as vice presidents of English and American
PEN, Pinter and Arthur Miller visited prisons in Turkey. On 23 March
1985 the two writers held a joint news conference in Istanbul to protest
Turkish human rights abuses. During the five-day visit to Turkey, they
talked with over "100 Turkish intellectuals, with former prison inmates,
politicians and diplomats," expressing International PEN's concern with
"'the dignity of its members throughout the world'" (Gursel; cf.
Kamm). At the opening ceremonies of the 48th International PEN Congress in New York, on 12 January 1986, it was reported that "almost 450
writers on nearly every continent are known to be confined" (McDowell).

In a postscript to the interview with Hern, written after he returned
from Turkey, Pinter points to support that the United States gives
military regimes like Turkey (24). While he clearly protests human
rights violations in *One for the Road*, those abused in the play comprise a
family (a man, his wife, and their young son) whose national and social
identity is not specified. Going beyond the imprisoned writer, the play
embraces all prisoners of conscience and others whose rights are being
violated by "the State" throughout the world and their loved ones. The
play "could take place in totalitarian countries in Eastern Europe or South
America," but, Dukore argues, "the many approving references to religion ironically exclude Communist countries, where the interrogator
would be unlikely to call himself a religious man, to declare that God is
on the side of the state not the dissidents, or to claim that the state's
business is to cleanse the world for God" (*HP*, 132–33). To me Nicolas's
religious references seem fanatical (not merely "approving"), as associated
these days with Middle Eastern countries; yet, I would stress that the
setting could still be almost anywhere in the world today, where, unfortunately, such religious, ideological, and other "anti-intellectual" fanati-
cism is all too widespread.

Vis-à-vis such experiences and concerns, it appears, Pinter's perspective on the political themes of his earlier plays has sharpened. In the
February 1985 interview with Nicholas Hern, comparing those plays
with *One for the Road*, Pinter alludes to a "run-through" of a television
production of *The Dumb Waiter*: "It was quite obvious to the actors that

the chap who is upstairs and is never seen is a figure of authority. Gus questions this authority and rebels against it and therefore is squashed at the end, or is about to be squashed. The political metaphor was very clear to the actors and directors of the first production in 1960. It was not, however, clear to the critics of the time . . . that it was actually *about* anything" (7). [12] "*The Birthday Party*," Pinter tells Hern, "which I wrote more or less at the same time, in 1957, again has a central figure who is squeezed by certain authoritarian forces," and "*The Hothouse*—which actually followed quite shortly, the next year, I think—is essentially about the abuse of authority" (8). (Pinter told Bensky that he wrote *The Hothouse* after *The Caretaker* [28], but his note to the published text confirms his statement to Hern.) When Hern suggests that, retrospectively, the early plays would appear to reflect Pinter's "unease about the Hungarian Revolution and the Soviet annexation of East Europe," Pinter qualifies this view somewhat: "Except that one doesn't normally write about today, but yesterday—or even the day before yesterday" (9). His own "political act" of conscientious objection resulted from being "terribly disturbed as a young man by the Cold War. And McCarthyism. . . . A profound hypocrisy. 'They' the monsters, 'we' the good. In 1948 the Russian suppression of Eastern Europe was an obvious and brutal fact, but I felt very strongly then and feel as strongly now that we have an obligation to subject our own actions and attitudes to an equivalent critical and moral scrutiny."

Even though *One for the Road* did not represent "a sudden crystallisation of [Pinter's] political sensibility" as Hern at first thought, since Pinter had been a conscientious objector as a teenager and thus "involved in political acts from early on," nevertheless, "in 1958," critics saw Pinter's plays "as having no relation to the outside world at all"; his plays were, Pinter recalls, "dismissed as absurd rubbish" by most critics (10). "[F]or many people," Hern speculates, "it must have seemed that you've been operating on this political level invisibly" (11). Pinter recapitulates his political attitude: "I wouldn't say that my political awareness during those years was dead. Far from it. But I came to view politicians and political structures and political acts with something I can best describe as detached contempt. To engage in politics seemed to me futile. And so, for twenty years or so, in my writing I simply continued investigations into other areas" (12; cf. "Radical," 6).

As Mel Gussow has observed more recently, "In retrospect . . . [Pinter] can identify the political content in his plays, which he can trace back to

'The Birthday Party' and 'The Dumbwaiter.' Linking 'The Birthday Party' to 'One for the Road' and 'Mountain Language,' he said they all dealt with 'the destruction of an individual.' " The idea for the "knock" on Stanley's door in *The Birthday Party*, Pinter said, "came from my knowledge of the Gestapo. The character of the old man, Petey, says one of the most important lines I've ever written. As Stanley is taken away, Petey says, 'Stan, don't let them tell you what to do.' I've lived that line all my damn life. Never more than now" ("Pinter's Plays," C22).[13] Whereas, retrospectively, Pinter presents his most recent plays as a more overt development of a generally underestimated aspect of his earlier ones in "A Play and Its Politics," in another more recent interview he explains the change that *One for the Road* signifies more emphatically: "It certainly represents a permanent change in me as a citizen of this country . . . a man living in this world. It's been happening for a very long time. In other words, I've become more and more political over the last 10 years— more politically engaged. And now I'm profoundly engaged" (Drake, 6).

Whether or not this "change" will indeed prove "permanent" remains to be seen. So far what Gussow calls Pinter's "politicization" ("Pinter's Plays," C17) has raised "anxious murmurings from his devotees that, by taking on the mantle of Amnesty International, he may lose the touch of genius with which he illumines the despair and the power games of less obviously charged situations" (Carne). In assessing this "new phase in Pinter's oeuvre, a departure into the realm of political debate, even propaganda," Esslin still asks: "To what genre do Pinter's anti-torture tracts belong?" To consider *Mountain Language* "straightforward *documentary drama*" is problematic because "the aestheticism . . . the beautiful way in which it is done, undercuts the documentary quality. Real torture is much more messy, much more sordid" ("Mountain Language," 76, 78).[14]

### Pinter's Shift to Political Drama:
### An Alternative Critical View

As if anticipating these concerns, in *British and Irish Political Drama in the Twentieth Century*, David Ian Rabey observes: "The merging of social drama into political drama is an easy transition and may cause problems of classification (as in the work of Osborne and Wesker)" (2). Rabey makes no mention of Pinter. Though *British and Irish Political Drama in the Twentieth Century* was probably in press at the time that Pinter published

*One for the Road* and *Precisely*, even on the basis of these short works and *Mountain Language*, Rabey still might not have included Pinter, given this definition of the aims and styles of the genre:

> "*Political* drama" emphasizes the directness of its address to problematic social matters, and its attempt to interpret these problems in political terms. Political drama communicates its sense of these problems' avoidability, with implicit or explicit condemnation of the political circumstances that have allowed them to rise and continue to exist (just as Brecht identifies *The Rise of Arturo Ui* as *Resistible*). In perceiving social problems as avoidable, political drama is necessarily diverging from the worldview that the agents of the status quo would seek to impose for the continued smooth running of society in its present form. (1–2)

Whereas Rabey takes "*social* drama as that which purports to act as an impartial report on social relations, or to focus on specific social abuses, without stepping over into an attack on the fundamentals of the society in question," he takes "*political* drama as that which views specific social abuses as symptomatic of a deeper illness, namely injustice and anomalies at the heart of society's basic power structure" (2). Whereas otherwise it might seem that *One for the Road*, *Precisely*, and *Mountain Language* could be classified as political drama, Pinter's attitude toward social change, as he describes it to Hern, does not fit "Leftist" concepts of the attitude and kinds of change that a political dramatist advocates.

Pinter does not seem to perceive social problems of the kind he dramatizes as "avoidable." When Hern asks "whether a play like *One for the Road* can really have any effect," Pinter explains: "[R]eason is not going to do anything. Me writing *One for the Road*, documentaries, articles, lucid analyses, Averell Harriman writing in the *New York Times*, voices raised here and there, people walking down the road and demonstrating. Finally it's hopeless. There's nothing one can achieve. Because the modes of thinking of those in power are worn out, threadbare, atrophied. Their minds are a brick wall" ("A Play," 20). Whereas Pinter recognizes hegemonic paradigms governing institutional abuses—"the modes of thinking of those in power"—he gives no indication that solving the problem must involve a change in what Rabey identifies as the "basic . . . structure" of power; indeed, he denies that *any* solution is even plausible. "But," he adds, "still one can't stop attempting to try to think and see things as clearly as possible."

In her interview with Pinter, Drake observes that Pinter "feels artists don't influence politics much": "The only thing that will influence politics," Pinter said, "certainly in this country [America], and in my own country, is the voters. I do take the point that if I say something someone might listen. At the same time, I don't talk as an artist; I talk as a man. Everyone has a quite essential obligation to subject the society in which we live to moral scrutiny" (6). Pinter defines his own position quite clearly: "My own view is that the appalling danger that the world is in at the moment has to do with a schism that has actually been manufactured. I'm referring to Them and Us. To inhabit rigid and atrophied postures like these has led to the present danger." The McCarthyite distinctions between political-economic systems (Communists and non-Communists) that he objects to in "A Play and Its Politics"; national alliances (Eastern Bloc and Western Bloc); classes (bourgeois and working class, or, more generally, the Haves and the Have-nots); and even political ideologies (Left and Right): Pinter rejects all such polarizing binary oppositions. "I was 15 when the war was over, so that one emerged out of that and lurched through adolescence into manhood as it were, with the weight of all that and the further reverberations—such as The Bomb and the Iron Curtain, McCarthyism here, repression in Eastern Europe. There seemed to be no end to it. But there is an end to it. There's an end all right. My view, incidentally, is that that end is going to come. . . . I think it's inevitable, yes." Ironically, he concludes, with (mock?) upper-class panache: "And on that note I shall have a glass of champagne."

In contrast, Günther Klotz defines the "internationalism" of "recent progressive British drama" to include such recurrent themes as "the combined efforts of monopolies, governments and military commanders to keep themselves in power and to enlarge their control by enforcing maximum profits" and "socialist reality" (36, 39). There are "a new strategy of anti-imperialist drama and a new type of production as well as reception in the British theatre, a new type of play which offers something constructive for people to identify with, the feeling of a prospective integration of the individual in a new common cause which is not an abstract idea but, in some parts of the world, tangible reality" (39–40). This is not the same "tangible reality" that Pinter has been describing and dramatizing.

For Pinter, altering his earlier emphasis on reality as relative and unverifiable: "All we're talking about, finally is what is real? What is real? There's only one reality, you know. You can interpret reality in various ways. But there's only one. And if that reality is thousands of people being tortured to death at this very moment and hundreds of thousands of megatons of nuclear bombs standing there waiting to go off at this very moment, then that's it and that's that. It has to be faced" ("A Play," 21). Thus intending to confront his audience with this "one reality," Pinter has been critical of their unwillingness to face it, despite his own awareness of "that great danger, this great irritant to an audience" of "agitprop" ("A Play," 18). Pinter has not suggested any "constructive" measures for his audience to take against the atrocities dramatized in *One for the Road* and *Mountain Language* or those implied in *Precisely*. As he has said about spectators' responses to his other plays, any response is their own individual responsibility (cf. "Radical," 5).

Several people walked out midway through performances of *One for the Road* that I attended in New York City and Portland, Oregon (see *Other Places* and *No Holds Barred*). Apparently, some could not tolerate the physical and verbal abuse on stage. Portland's Sumus Theatre management received complaints about the play's language, not the political issues it raised. Since the performance of *One for the Road* that I saw in Portland was a benefit for Amnesty International, it was preceded by a short speech about the aims of this organization, delivered by its local president, Arden Benson, who encouraged the audience to sign petitions in behalf of individual political prisoners, directing us to such petitions, as well as leaflets, in the lobby. In this way the theater management provided opportunities for purposive political action that Pinter's play does not directly prescribe, though they are activities likely to merit his approval, since Pinter himself is a member of Amnesty International (Drake, 6).

Rabey further distinguishes "the comparative aims and styles of political *drama* (plays) and political *theatre*" by citing Sandy Craig's "working definition," which attributes the difference to a playwright's stance toward the audience:

> the important feature which distinguishes political plays from political theatre is this: *political plays* seek to appeal to, and influence, the middle class, in particular that section of the middle class which is influential in moulding 'public opinion'. The implication of this is that society can be reformed and liberalized, where necessary, by the shock troops of the middle class—and, of course, such people are influential in campaigns for reform. But further, political plays

in bourgeois theatre implicitly realize that the middle class remains the progressive class within society. *Political theatre*, on the other hand, as embodied in the various political theatre companies, aims—with varying degrees of success—to appeal to, and be an expression of, the working class. Its underlying belief is that the working class is the progressive class within society. (Rabey, 6, quoting Craig, 30–31; emphasis added)

Political theater tries "to produce plays that arouse a wider and deeper awareness of the necessity and of the possibility to change the present society," Günther Klotz also observes. "In its struggle against imperialism and against the set-up of the commercialized institutions and media of communication, the progressive drama had to change from the social criticism of the breakthrough [e.g., Osborne's *Look Back in Anger*] to a theatre looking for alternatives. . . . No longer can a progressive drama be effective if it continues to imitate life in a naturalistic way, in serving the old liberal aims of education and entertainment, of moralizing and edifying. What is required is a drama as medium of social movement" (40).

Though Pinter himself comes originally from a working-class background (his father was a tailor), he has, through his own professional success and his second marriage to Lady Antonia Fraser, risen through the middle class into the upper class of English society. Though his first few plays featured working-class characters loosely modeled on people encountered during his experiences as a struggling actor, these dramas were presented first to university audiences. After *The Caretaker* Pinter became more upscale, appealing to upper-middle-class audiences. Some of his later characters could *attend* what Rabey calls "the legitimate, established theatre" (ix). If Pinter's political plays do not count as political theater, it is also because his customary audiences—"bourgeois" or "elitist"—are not politically progressive.

The distinguishing "political" issue involved in "cultural analysis on the left" is "how to acknowledge and comprehend the tremendous capacity of patriarchal and capitalist institutions to regenerate themselves not only in their material foundations and structures but in the hearts and minds of people, while never losing sight or despairing of the power of popular organization and struggle to resist and transform them" (Batsleer et al., 5). Joining the "professional" classes (as an actor, writer, and director), Pinter has worked within our "patriarchal and capitalist" cultural institutions (what Klotz calls "the commercialized institutions and media of communication"—theater, radio, film, television, and print) and become a phenomenal commercial success. This success is sometimes cited as a symptom of Pinter's "cop-out"; he has become a symbol of the "mainstream," the kind of theater to which "alternative theatre" is an alternative.[15] Yet "whilst the tradition of academic Marxism which is now a familiar feature of literary criticism provides an ideology, a vocabulary and enough internal disputes for the committed critic of political theatre, the alternatives to *that* alternative are less clearly formulated and the continuities between one group and another largely uncharted" (Anderson, "This," 452).

Unlike most other Leftist critics, who regard Pinter as a mainstream, commercial playwright and would term him *"boulevard,"* West-End, or "Broadway bound," Klaus Köhler argues that Pinter's position is "the position of a bourgeois dramatist at variance with the sacrosanct beliefs of his class[;] the direction of his criticism is clearly anti-bourgeois. Rather than invite compliance with an untouchable status quo[,] [Pinter] discredits the illusion of possible harmony and integrity under imperialist power structures." With their "individual activities of consciousness warped by the ideologic strategies of the 'Welfare State', [Pinter's characters] are unable to take stock of themselves and the world around them." Their alienation and "estrangement" result from "a repressive canon of bourgeois ethics and politics." But there is an important difference between Pinter's "distancing effects" and Brecht's contention that " 'the present-day world can only be described to present-day people if it is described as capable of transformation.'" With other "congenial late bourgeois writers," Köhler argues, Pinter "shares . . . an unresolved dualism of rejection and doubts as to the alterability of what is rejected" ("Establishment," 324–25).

Köhler concludes "The Establishment and the Absurd" (published before Pinter's *One for the Road* and the interview on its politics) by citing Pinter's repeated expressions of "his indifference to political issues" (326). But in both his plays and his public pronouncements Pinter has never been unequivocally indifferent to politics (cf. Dukore, *HP*). Köhler's more specific contention that "[c]rucial problems of the present-day class struggles in Britain are absent from [Pinter's] plays" is even qualified by rereading *The Caretaker* from the perspective of Sahai, for whom it dramatizes consequences of urbanization for the lower and would-be middle classes. Yet, as Köhler recognizes, "[Pinter] has also stressed the

general social significance of his theatre" (326). [16] Pinter presents "model
situations from a micro-sociological perspective. Beyond all ambiguities
they set forth a perpetual fight of opposites, not so much between
the privileged and the unprivileged as among the representatives and
camp-followers of the bourgeois regime today." From this perspective,
"[b]y exposing [his characters'] fruitless navel inspection, self-laceration
and incapacity for purposeful action[,] [Pinter] analyses the social and
moral make-up of a class destined to perish by its own contradictions."
But despite this "[t]renchant debunking," Pinter still refuses "to en-
visage any constructive commitment," Köhler concludes, and "this basic
inconsistency . . . narrows the extent and impact of Pinter's critique."
This opinion of Pinter's social and political range suggests a current
strategy of some cultural criticism "on the Left": to devalue any author who does not espouse a Marxist and/or feminist ideology. Pinter
is being "rewritten" by critics sympathetic to Marxism and feminism
(as we will see). To become successful "social strategists" themselves,
these critics rewrite Pinter so as to enact their own scenarios for social
change. [17]

A position somewhat different from Köhler's informs C. W. E. Bigsby's "Politics of Anxiety: Contemporary Socialist Theatre in England."
Melmoth defines Bigsby's perspective succinctly: "the truly subversive
dramatist is relativistic and anarchistic rather than programmatic, a
farceur rather than a commentator or, as Bigsby puts it, 'not Arden but
Orton, not McGrath but Pinter'" (Melmoth, 954). As neither Bigsby
nor Melmoth was able to take into account *One for the Road*, *Precisely*, and
*Mountain Language*, I wonder how these plays might modify their views.
In all three plays Pinter suggests no particular solution to problems of
culturally institutionalized oppression that they dramatize; but he does
implicate his audience in these problems viscerally. Finding solutions (if
there are any) is up to us—audiences and voters—and our governmental
officials (elected or not). Pinter may have placed little stock in our ability
to solve such social and political problems, but at least he has given us the
opportunity to "try to think and see things as clearly as possible" too, to
subject "reality" to intense "moral scrutiny."

While accepting Pinter's viewpoint that *One for the Road* is "not
metaphorical in the same way that *The Dumb Waiter* and *The Birthday
Party* are," Judith Roof points out that "the concreteness of the portrayal
of abuse also conveys larger ideological metaphors (the family, the father).
Its realism, thus, is not only a realism of detail and behavior, but also a

rendering of the context, of the ideas in whose name horrors are perpetuated" (11). If, in *One for the Road*, "[t]he central place of the subversive
stare . . . suggests that an unauthorized watching—a kind of seditious
theatre—is a way of opposing political oppression" (17), so the final
silence of the Elderly Woman in *Mountain Language*—an unauthorized
*refusal* to speak—subverts linguistic oppression by "the State."[18] Though
Pinter suggested that an impetus for *Mountain Language* was his visit with
Arthur Miller to Turkey, the play was advertised falsely as "a 'parable
about torture and the fate of the Kurdish people' "; while Pinter accepts
that it is about torture, he denies both that it concerns " 'the fate of the
Kurdish people' " and that it is " 'a parable' " (Pinter, " 'Mountain Language' "; cf. Gussow, "Pinter's Plays," C17). From Pinter's own "point of
view," as already noted, "it is about suppression of language, and the loss
of freedom of expression . . . [and] therefore . . . as relevant in England as
it is in Turkey" (C17; cf. "Radical," 6).

"While the 'clear vision' Pinter proposes may make a more intelligent
populace," Roof argues further, "it too is complicit in the maintenance of
the power relations it dissects. Awareness must be accompanied by a look
back at the forces which conspire to construct us all within a dominant
ideology which obscures problems in the interest of maintaining status
quo" (17). Yet in "[u]rging a different way to see"—and different ways to
hear and to feel as well, I would add—like Beckett's *Catastrophe*, Pinter's
political plays do "propose a theatrical model for that seeing different
from the analytical disengagement of Brecht's alienation-effect. Commit-
ting theatre to political action in a most direct way, Pinter and Beckett
involve both stage and audience in an enactment of the oppression theatre
embodies and exposes."

### Pinter's Future as a Political Dramatist

We do not know how Pinter's own beliefs in the political prospects of vast
social change will develop. We do not know, as he himself has said that he
does not know, how long he will continue to write political plays, or
anything else ("A Play," 18–19). "I won't, I'm sure, continue to write
plays about politics," he has insisted, "unless an authentic image comes
into my mind which demands to be written. But I've no such plans and I
can't write out of ideological *desire*. That, almost invariably, is artificial.
Dry. Manufactured. In other words, I've no idea what I'm going to write
and I don't anticipate that I shall continue to write political plays as such.

I don't know what my future is as a writer" (Drake, 6).[19] But while he may not know his "future as a writer," Pinter does predict his "future . . . as a man," and that is: "To continue to ask some very straight questions about the society in which we live, without fear or favor. In other words, I don't give a damn how many people I offend."

"My attitude toward my own playwriting has changed," Pinter told Gussow. "The whole idea of a narrative, of a broad canvas stretching over a period of two hours—I think I've gone away from that forever. I can't see that I could ever encompass it again. I was always termed, what is the word, 'minimalist.' . . . Maybe I am. Who knows? But I hope that to be minimal is to be precise and focused. I feel that what I've illuminated is quite broad—and deep—shadows stretching away." Reporting his answer to a Sussex University student's question about whether he could ally his current interests with "characters as [he] used to write them, people called Meg and Max"—"I don't think I can any longer"—he reserved this opening: "I don't want to cut myself off from all experiences likely to come" ("Pinter's Plays," C22).

On 3 October 1989, after his reading at the 92d Street Y, when asked by Gussow if he had reconsidered the change in his attitude, Pinter said: "It is not a matter for me to reconsider. Nothing would give me greater pleasure than to write any play, of whatever length. I don't think length is in any way so important anyway, but one thing about the act of writing is that it is an act of—essentially an act of freedom, as I understand it, so it's great to write any way, if you can do it. I just find it more and more difficult." "I'm only concerned at the moment with *accurate* and *precise* images of what is the case," he added. In response to Gussow's opening statement that Pinter has "always been a political playwright" and his question about whether Pinter could trace "a serious interest" in "the world of politics" from *The Birthday Party* through *Mountain Language*, Pinter replied:

> in the early days, which was thirty years ago, I was a political playwright of a kind. But I then took a break from being so for about seventeen years. And I wrote a lot of plays between 1970 and 1985 which can't be said to be political plays—things like *Old Times*, *Betrayal*, *Landscape*, and *Silence*, which were concerned with memory and youth and loss and so on . . . they didn't take place and didn't concern themselves with social or political structure, whereas the earlier plays did. . . . My early work was I think full of games

and jokes and so on, but I think the distinction I would make between those plays then and these plays now is that I'm afraid that for me the joke is over. I can't see any more jokes. I can't play any more games. So I therefore find that I'm writing shorter and shorter pieces which are more and more brutal and more and more overtly naked, you see.

Though admitting that the theater may "affect the world in which we live" only a "little," Pinter explained: "But that little is something, and I respect the power, the correspondence between theater and audience. . . . I always have hated propaganda plays . . . agit-prop. . . . But I still feel that there is room, there is a role somewhere, for a work that is not following, pursuing, the normal narrative procedure of the drama, and it's to be found, and I'm trying to find it." Criticizing the "debased language" pervading American and English governmental statements about Central America, Pinter stated: "I just want to make the facts *absolutely clear*, and it's as I see myself not only as an actor and an entertainer, but . . . I'm also a citizen of the world in which I live, and I take responsibility for that, I really *insist* upon taking responsibility and *understand* my responsibility quite precisely as *actually* trying to find out what *the truth is*. And what actually happens. And so [what] I've found is that we're really at the bottom of a *blanket* of lies which unfortunately we are either too indifferent or too frightened to question."[20]

If Pinter does keep on writing plays—however minimalist, serious, and factually truthful—critics cannot rule out further developments that might alter assessments of what Köhler terms "the extent and impact of Pinter's critique" (326). Pinter may continue to widen his breadth while further deepening his insight into human social relations and global politics.

Signaling such a development perhaps, Pinter has written some new screen adaptations dealing with a variety of sociopolitically relevant subjects: *Reunion* (based on Fred Uhlman's novel about Stuttgart in the 1930s and 1980s), *The Heat of the Day* (based on Elizabeth Bowen's novel about wartime London), and *The Handmaid's Tale* (based on Margaret Atwood's novel about a Christian fundamentalist regime in America).[21] *Reunion* is "a story of friendship between two boys—one a German aristocrat, the other a German Jew, beginning in 1932 and ending a half century later, when the Jewish man comes to terms with his belief that his friend has let him down"; the film's American director, Jerry Schatzberg, describes "the relationship" between them as the project's appeal (Van Gelder, "Togetherness"). According to writer-director Paul Schrader, Pinter has also written a screenplay adapting Ian McEwan's *Comfort of Strangers*, a novel "set in Venice—about a vacationing young British couple whose lives are sort of taken over by a local couple," reminiscent of *The Servant* (1963); "full of innuendo and subtext," it is reportedly "quite close to the kind of thing Pinter writes for himself. Though it's an adaptation, it has the same themes and cadences of his original work, that element of dominance in relationships between men and women that is very Pinteresque" (Van Gelder, "Pinteresque Pinter"), that is, in the broadest sense—very political.

On 3 October 1989, when Pinter related his current project of writing a screenplay of Kafka's *The Trial* to people's distorted memories of it "as a political book" reminiscent of Arthur Koestler, he explained: "I simply wouldn't be interested in writing a screenplay of *Darkness at Noon* because it's so specifically of its time and place"; whereas "the nightmare of [Kafka's] world is precisely in its ordinariness, and that is what I think is so frightening." But, though chairman of the Arts for Nicaragua Fund in Great Britain, writing "a specific play about such a[n immediate political] situation" as Nicaragua "is not something I could possibly do." Yet, like many of Pinter's past remarks, this one should not be taken as "final and definitive": what Pinter foresees now that he could not "possibly do" does not rule out what he may actually do in the future.

## Sociological Role-Playing and Class
## Consciousness in Pinter: Ewald Mengel

Ewald Mengel is a West German whose early recognition of the political implications of "face-to-face encounters" between Pinter's characters draws in part upon Erving Goffman's concept of "strategic interaction" and theories of the German sociologist H. P. Dreitzel.[22] Showing the relevance of personal, sociopolitical, and academic contexts of Mengel's rewriting of "the Pinteresque" can in part redress the effects of what Jeffrey Sammons calls "the campaign against individual response in literary studies" (11).

Basing his analyses of Pinter's plays on sociological role theory, Mengel repudiates "all metaphysical and symbolical speculations" about Pinter's connections to "the so-called 'Theatre of the Absurd,'" seeing it rather "as a socio-pathological phenomenon . . . arising immediately from the interactions of people in 'face-to-face' situations." He sums up this pattern of conflict in Pinter's plays: "At the beginning of each play the distribution of positions and roles seems to guarantee a stable and well-ordered social reality as a pre-requisite for the following interactions. But after a while, Pinter's characters begin to behave in a strange and disturbing way: they show a tendency to leave their roles and confound 'role-expectancies', not only of their partners in the interaction, but also of the spectators, who, of course, also expect them to behave according to their roles." Thematically, Pinter demonstrates "that reality is nothing fixed or firm, but may be redefined within the process of interaction, so that, at the end, a new kind of reality is established." "The paradoxes of communication and the distortions of the interaction" in Pinter's plays result from "the constant struggle of the figures to undermine each other's position and to define reality in their own way." Mengel claims that Pinter's approach to the absurd produces his spectators' "alienation" from the reality of his characters: "The more [the characters'] relationships are depicted in this absurd condition, the more reality itself becomes impenetrable for the spectators." This "gradual process of alienation" pervades most of Pinter's plays through *No Man's Land* (*HPD*, 273–75).[23]

Mengel's interpretation of *The Homecoming* in his published dissertation elaborates on an earlier thesis that he wrote as a student in a seminar taught by Paul Goetsch, who later directed the dissertation. The following interpretation of *The Homecoming* exemplifies Mengel's later strategy for rewriting Pinter: "In *The Homecoming*, Pinter again shows that the antagonisms of society also invade the family home. The interpretation focuses on the distribution of positions within the frame of the family and the various fights which are triggered off by the homecoming of Teddy and his wife Ruth. By assuming the role of a prostitute Ruth tries to liberate herself from the suffocating domestic roles as wife and mother. The absurdity of the play lies in the fact that Ruth's attempt to liberate herself leads her into a still greater dependency" (274). Köhler takes issue with this rewriting of *The Homecoming*: "Ruth, once a 'model for the body', is obviously tired of the doubtful respectability connected with her husband's station. Throwing in her lot with his family *she does not accomplish an act of emancipation* but one of adjustment at a level more consistent with her nature" ("Establishment," 320; emphasis added).[24] There is no explicit evidence *in* the play, however, that will enable us to determine *with certainty* whether or not Ruth is a prostitute at heart, as Köhler implies, or is, for a variety of other reasons, playing that role, as

Mengel argues. These interpretations are not mutually exclusive. Ruth may be playing the role so well because she can easily identify with it.[25] Just as Köhler's interpretation is a product of his own personal, cultural, and ideological assumptions about Pinter's plays, about literature and life in general, so are Mengel's. Literary interpretations "resymbolize" such factors, rewriting literary texts in terms of critics' own particular experiences, goals, fantasies, and fears.[26]

Mengel's interest in sociological role-playing and Pinter's plays grows out of his personal, social, and professional history. His maternal grandfather had little or no formal education: born around the turn of the century near the Polish border, he spent all of his childhood in the country and, during the First World War, had to flee with his family to the north of Germany, where he found refuge in a little village called Hohenholz, which had no school.[27] Mengel's father spent seven years fighting as a soldier in the Second World War on the Russian and the French frontiers, barely escaping with his life; after the war he worked his way up into the civil service as a railway clerk. After high school (1963–68) Mengel himself enlisted in military service, serving in the Bundesgrenzschutz Bad Hersfeld from 1968 to 1969; when the Russians entered Czechoslovakia in 1968, he helped guard the West German border with East Germany. Though elders in his village advised him to "stick to the village and do some farming or something," recognizing the vivid differences between his options as a West German youth with a working-class family history and without advanced education and as a university graduate, with the support of his parents, who had very little money but "invested" what they had in his future, Mengel pursued his studies. After study at the University of Giessen (1969–71) and the University of Newcastle upon Tyne (1971–72), he earned his Ph.D. in English and German language and literature at the University of Freiburg (1972–75) and did a postdoctoral thesis (*habilitationsschrift*) at the University of Bamberg (1984), where he has taught since 1979 and held the Heisenberg grant since April 1988. In becoming a university teacher and scholar, Mengel broke with his family history, enabling him to enjoy the material pleasures that a university career can afford: to rise into the middle class. But his attitude toward future achievement is still not typically "bourgeois": "I simply didn't think of [my educational career] in terms of money, or in terms of house-building, or money-accumulating; I always thought in terms of qualifying for something more . . . I still stick to that."

During the late sixties through the midseventies, when Mengel went to college and graduate school in West Germany, he was "interested by the German Leftist movement." At the time he began studying Pinter's work in a seminar with Goetsch at the University of Freiburg, he was actively seeking a politically and socially relevant topic. He chose to write about Pinter's plays because Goetsch suggested a sociological approach to Pinter that Mengel found compatible with his own experiences and interests:

> I think you'd have to take one thing into consideration, which might be relevant. We [studied Pinter] in a time that all the students were rather rebellious. It was the student movement which started along in '68, in Paris, Berlin, and Heidelberg, and Amsterdam, and I grew up in an atmosphere which was very rebellious and in which there were many critical ideas abounding. I think this atmosphere somehow led to a discussion of Harold Pinter, because he was the one who from a Leftist point of view was not relevant at all. And in that atmosphere—everybody was looking for somebody, a Leftist writer, who was saying that he wanted to revolutionize society—he [Pinter] wanted to do something else; there was this man Harold Pinter, who seemed to be, well, rather conservative; he seemed to be not relevant to society at all. And it was this anger which I think started me off. Is he really that relevant? In a way is he not irrelevant, socially irrelevant? And I wrote this paper before I became really involved in him, saying "Well, here's some sort of bourgeois writer who doesn't have anything to say at all." And then I started to think about him, and I think it was Goetsch's idea, it was this idea he had about Pinter which really set me off. . . . He suggested that something might be *in* Pinter which nobody has recognized so far; there might be a *social* dimension in Pinter which one could get at by using the approach of sociological role theory. So he suggested to me to study sociological role theory and try to find out what Pinter was like from that point of view. It was what I did.[28]

While Mengel was working on his dissertation, his own awareness of the differences between the world in which he moved as a university student and his earlier environment may have heightened his sensitivity to role-playing in Pinter's plays: "dealing with Pinter for him was an existential question, because he was trying to find out about role-playing himself.

The approach he chose made him aware of so many everyday situations in which he had to play roles" (Goetsch, interview with author). Mengel was prone early on to see his experience in terms of class distinctions and to rewrite Pinter's plays from this perspective:

> I think in a way I'm predestined to take that point of view [sociological role-playing] because I've put a lot of attention to the analysis of people's behavior as far as their class or their position is concerned. I think you could say that I'm predestined in a way. I know that people behave differently when they are on a rather low level of society, when they have a low position; they have to because they have less education, less money, less prestige, and less self-confidence. And Pinter's . . . one of the English writers who really makes that a subject of his plays. There's what I see in him, here's what really attracts me to a play. He's the one who shows that people are not people but there are different classes of people and that as soon as people get into contact, the class position comes into relevance.

It was Mengel who directed my attention to Michael Owen's interview with Pinter and Lady Antonia Fraser about their social activities in behalf of political prisoners cited earlier. Mengel was both amused and disappointed that Pinter would engage in such a charity benefit, complaining that the article gives "the impression that Pinter is a writer of the English upper class": "this is something which I find rather strange about him. This is something which I can't tolerate, I'm sorry about that. But the impression that I got from that article is that he is . . . someone from the lower classes moving slowly into the upper classes by having success and, I don't know, he seems to be determined on having success at all means, and this is the point where I don't take him seriously anymore." Pinter should not be giving readings for charity, Mengel argued. He should not "compromise himself" by performing for "token clubs now popular in England" but should "keep quiet. Shut up. He shouldn't give in to sentiment by responding" publicly, he should be writing. Moreover, Pinter should not be writing explicitly political plays: "Everything Pinter writes is political in a way. It's *highly* political, but it's *indirectly* political. This is good, so, it's good the way it is. As soon as Pinter becomes *outspokenly* political, or charitable, I don't like him." Though for these reasons Mengel did not at first like *The Hothouse*, he remained "really keen on what [Pinter] writes in the future."[29]

Mengel was stating his own mutable preferences here. But, given Pinter's eventual writing of *One for the Road*, *Precisely*, and *Mountain Language*, it does seem that Pinter himself has reached a similar conclusion: for a writer opposed to social and political injustices, talking is not enough. Unlike Mengel's preference for the "indirect" politics of Pinter's earlier work, however, as we have seen, Pinter has become much more explicitly political in his work and his life, even concentrating more on his political activities and on giving readings and taking part in meetings ("talk") than on writing.

Rather than compromising his purposes as a writer through these activities, Pinter is *redefining* his purposes through them. *Both* social enterprise ("public" readings and meetings) *and* individual pursuits ("private" writing) are necessary for human survival. Contrary to what he himself said early on, Pinter is not *either* "writing for myself" *or* "writing for the theatre"; he is doing *both*. As writers like Pinter continue to write both for themselves and for others, they encourage progress toward social justice and even world peace.

### Pinter and Sex

As with politics, Pinter's attitudes toward love and sex have especially intrigued critics and scholars.[30] Critics' attention to the relations between these aspects of his private life and his work perhaps peaked with publicity connecting Pinter's adulterous love affair with Lady Antonia Fraser to the subject of his play and film *Betrayal*. Gale, who also cites the affair in another context (*BGU*, 15 n.6), reports that Pinter's "first love affair" occurred when he was thirteen and that another love interest distracted him from study at the Central School of Speech and Drama in his early twenties (8; cf. Bensky, 19). Pinter has described his memory of such times: "I did have a pretty strong association with a girl in my early teens. But anyway, it was all rather different then. There was this dark world of sex which took place in mists and rain, in alleys and on park benches under trees. I remember it with a very special fondness; I hope for the sake of the young that it still exists somewhere" (Gross, 25). He went on to tell Gross: "I think there's a good deal of love about in some of my plays. But love can very easily go down the wrong path and be distorted as a result of frustration in all kinds of different ways." The resulting tension drives the sexual politics of Pinter's plays.

My own initial interest in Pinter focused on this topic: my first essay on Pinter's plays, written for a graduate seminar in 1968, was called "The Power of Pinter's Women." As with this title, there is a tendency to render greater "power" to one sex or the other in Pinter criticism. In the same year that I wrote the seminar paper, Hinchliffe published "Mr. Pinter's Belinda," viewing sexuality as central to many of Pinter's plays and describing the women as filling the roles of mother, wife, mistress, and whore.[31] The relationships between Pinter's men and women characters are among the most controversial aspects of his plays. Critics often present extremely contradictory interpretations of these characters' motives, as I documented in my 1973 dissertation (Elliott, "Fantasy behind Play"), where, extrapolating from parallels between my own responses and published criticism, I speculated that the sexual gender of interpreters significantly affected their readings.

More recently published critical accounts have also seemed particularly prone to masculinist and feminist ploys. In "Notes toward the Archetypal Pinter Woman," for example, Thomas P. Adler summarizes some "recent psychologically oriented criticism of Harold Pinter's women" but argues that the view of Pinter's women as "victimizers of their men" in the Freudian oedipal pattern is shortsighted; though some of these women do "exercise power and strength primarily to control and emasculate the man," often, Adler claims, "the Pinter woman craves dominance as her only means of achieving the psychological wholeness and integration she desires and demands for herself as a person." The result is "a fairly uncommon pattern in modern drama, in which the man willingly chooses to relinquish his own position to permit the woman to flower, acquiescing to the female's needs to help her attain complete fulfillment as woman" (377). While Pinter was indebted to Strindberg "for the male/female tensions and configurations" in his plays, "unlike Laura [in Strindberg's *The Father*], a Pinter woman does not require a man to lose before she can reach completion" (385). Pinter often provides through his male characters what his female characters do need: "a man who understands the necessity for accommodation, the necessity for sometimes subordinating, perhaps even diminishing, the self so that the woman might be fulfilled as woman."

Thus Adler's interpretation of Teddy's motivations in *The Homecoming*, which also refers to some of Pinter's other male characters, serves to illustrate masculinist assumptions, whereby by dint of a *man's* decisive efforts a woman is saved "[f]rom a worse fate."[32] Though Adler offers support from other critics for this view and though it seems consistent with Pinter's own emphasis on the "great deal of love" in *The Homecoming* and on Ruth's relative freedom (Gross, 25; Gussow, "Pinter's Plays," C22), it conflicts strongly with many other readings, which generally agree with Free's opinion that "Teddy is pathetic and ineffective" ("Treatment," 4).[33] Yet, like Adler, John M. Warner allows that in his "seeming indifference to his wife's prostituting herself," Teddy may reflect "rather a determination not to impose his will on her, a desire to let her 'be' herself and not the object of his will" ("Epistemological," 353). Such interpretations of Teddy's motivations are wish projections of (would-be?) "liberated males."[34]

Recently, there have been enormous interest and publishing activity in feminist and gender-oriented criticism and theory relating to language and literature, women's studies, and cultural analysis of men and women in society. Many respected scholars establish the prominent influence of gender and sexual orientation in reading and writing about literature.[35] If feminist criticism "recognizes how theories can have serious consequences, how reading can involve great stakes" (Schilb, 107), ideological and ethical factors affect the theoretical premises as well as the practical findings of feminist criticism, just as ideology and ethics influence other critical or theoretical strategies. As we have been noticing otherwise, personal and social factors coalesce in critical stances "genderwise" too.

### Elizabeth Sakellaridou's Feminist Ploys:
### Toward a Balance of Sexual Power

In *Pinter's Female Portraits: A Study of Female Characters in the Plays of Harold Pinter*, a revision of the dissertation "Masks of Women" and the first book published on Pinter's women characters, Elizabeth Sakellaridou charts Pinter's "constant effort to overcome . . . obstacles" in portraying "complex" women characters (122), clarifying if not resolving the puzzling sexual politics dramatized in his plays. She argues that Pinter's presentation of women develops from an androcentric (or male-centered), at times even misogynistic viewpoint in his early plays to a kind of androgyny and a "gradual integration into one unified whole of the initially-split female image" (11). Strategically enacting the aims of a feminist criticism, Sakellaridou portrays Harold Pinter as a writer trying to humanize his characters, one who equilibrates male and female discourse while growing to develop and reveal humane compassion for them.

Pinter's early male characters' fragmented projections of women as mother/wife/whore anticipate "a gross distortion of the feminine person-ality, silencing of the woman's opinion and her isolation from a male-dominated society" characteristic of many of Pinter's later women charac-ters and due to "strong male interference" in their lives (18). As early as *A Slight Ache* (1958), however, Pinter's female characters "begin to emerge as autonomous entities and to develop independently from the male characters' conception of them" (71). The "all-male plays" forestall "his other endeavour to present the male and female principles on equal terms": unlike the men characters in these plays, when the women characters "speak for a cause," at least until *A Kind of Alaska*, they "always remain unmistakably feminine . . . always stand as representatives of the feminine cause, never of universal human values" (120). Despite this, with the "asocial, ahistorical and deeply human approach" of Pinter's playwriting between 1967 and 1974, coinciding with his adapting and/or directing work by Joyce and Proust, "Pinter's characterisation becomes fully androgynous as all the characters gain equal importance, irrespective of class or sex barriers. . . . Female characters . . . do become serious and honest illustrations of the human condition from the femi-nine point of view" (140). Pinter's work for stage and screen from 1978 to 1982, including *Betrayal, Family Voices, A Kind of Alaska*, and a screen-play for John Fowles's novel *The French Lieutenant's Woman*, marks "a final stage of fullness and perfection," where "[h]is women attain full human dimensions and a solid unified character" as "an independent, autono-mous entity" (178). But the 1984 play *One for the Road*, through the "regressive nature of its stylistic tactics and dramatic devices," raises some afterthoughts about the subsequent impact of Pinter's expressed "new faith in the political mission of his art" on his future plays (211).

To account for the changes that she perceives in Pinter's female (and male) characterizations, Sakellaridou points out that Pinter's "successive marriages to two highly individual, emancipated women," Vivien Mer-chant (in 1956) and Lady Antonia Fraser (in 1980), "may have" influ-enced elements of his work. She wishes, however, to treat this "aspect of Pinter's life" with "extreme caution and delicacy because of its very private nature" (14/10).[36] Sakellaridou speculates that "a woman who shared her life with the playwright for some twenty years would enter his work in one way or another, though perhaps in well-disguised form" and acknowledges "other information" informally obtained suggesting that "Vivien Merchant, despite her amiable and charming personality, was probably a possessive and jealous type of woman," but she also asserts that this information, though "in a sense a relevant discovery, which might become a key to the understanding of Pinter's heroines," must be "discarded or left to the discretion of a future biographer" because of the "demands" of "decency" ("Masks," 14–15). Obviously this version of Sakellaridou's work *includes* it. To discard the information would be to omit it entirely, as indeed *Pinter's Female Portraits* does (cf. 10). This discarded hypothesis may illuminate why *competition* between men and women is less central to Pinter's plays and film adaptations after the dissolution of his marriage to Merchant and his subsequent marriage to Fraser.

*Pinter's Female Portraits* maintains the view that Pinter's "insistence on stressing his distance as a creative writer from both his mother and wives might suggest a continuous struggle to shake off a deeply felt feminine influence. It is remarkable that a similar attitude is often manifested in the behaviour of his men characters to their women" (15/11). Whereas Pinter's dramatic and theatrical presentation of women was initially "dictated by a prevailing masculine discourse, which produces collective—archetypal or stereotypic—female figures in the models set by patriarchal society," Sakellaridou argues: "This initial biased sexist attitude follows a steady, though often uneven, evolution, until it eventually crystallises into a gentler, *totally androgynous* vision" (15–16/11; emphasis added).

In presenting her critical terminology, Sakellaridou anticipates "critical controversy": "Obviously the adoption of any position on [the exact degree of androgyny in an author's work] depends on the extent to which one is prepared to pursue the nuances of androgyny. The problem is especially acute in drama, where the absence of a narrator and of a direct authorial intervention makes it harder to decide where the writer's sympathies lie" (15). Though she herself apparently views an "androgynous companionship" as "ideal" (124), whether or not or when Pinter comes to share "an androgynous standpoint" (14) is perhaps not so "unmistakable" as she repeatedly claims. It is perhaps not "the exact degree of androgyny" or its "nuances" that need differentiation so much as the degree to which critics' own views of Pinter's characters are (to appropriate her phrases) "just mirror-images" of themselves, feminists' and nonfeminists' own "fantasised wishful projections" (12).

Carolyn Heilbrun defines *androgyny* as "a condition under which the characteristics of the sexes, and the human impulses expressed by men and women, are not rigidly assigned. Androgyny seeks to liberate the individual from the confines of the appropriate" (*Toward*, x). In a more recent essay not cited by Sakellaridou, "Androgyny and the Psychology of Sex Differences," Heilbrun observes that increasingly few feminists advocate androgyny, concluding: "Androgyny is a necessary stopping place on the road to feminism" (265). Some feminists argue "that the basic frameworks of logic and rationality are not universal but gender specific, that discourse as traditionally conceived is male" (Graff, 259). Binary oppositions associated with male and female like objectivity and subjectivity are not products of biological determinism so much as cultural myths collectively believed and taught.

More recent debates in "feminist criticisms" are also pertinent. When Toril Moi situates Virginia Woolf's "crucial concept of androgyny," she observes Woolf's understanding "that the goal of the feminist struggle must precisely be to deconstruct the death-dealing binary oppositions of masculinity and femininity." Moi opposes Heilbrun's distinguishing androgyny ("the concept of an 'unbounded and hence fundamentally indefinable nature'" [*Toward*, xi]) from feminism, siding with Woolf and Julia Kristeva in stressing "that a theory that demands the deconstruction of sexual identity is indeed authentically feminist" (14). Mary Jacobus writes: "The gesture toward androgyny is millenial, like all dreams of another language or mode of being; but its effect is to remove the area of debate (and the trespass) from biological determination to the field of signs; from gender to representation ('words' not 'things'). And in holding open other possibilities—otherness itself—such writing posits 'the difference of view' as a matter of rewriting" (39). Regarding *A Kind of Alaska* as Pinter's "metaphor for the politics of femininity," Ann C. Hall reads the play as "a metaphor for the position of woman in the patriarchal structure"; psychoanalytic and feminist critics not cited by Sakellaridou (Jacques Lacan, Luce Irigaray, and Teresa de Lauretis) buttress Hall's argument that "through the play Pinter demonstrates the politics of femininity, the intolerant attitude of patriarchy toward feminine difference." From the vantage point of both deconstruction and Lacanian psychoanalysis, such interpretations of sexual difference raise rather complex problems: "When literature turns from experience to psychoanalysis for an answer to the riddle of femininity, psychoanalysis turns the question back to literature, since it is in language—in reading and in writing woman—that femininity at once discloses and discomposes itself, endlessly displacing the fixity of gender identity by the play of difference and division which simultaneously creates and uncreates gender, identity, and meaning. 'The difference (of view)' which we look for in reading woman (reading) is surely nothing other than this disclosure, this discomposition, which puts the institution of difference in question without erasing the question of difference itself" (Jacobus, 24). In her recent rewriting of Pinter and other contemporary British playwrights, Sakellaridou herself goes "beyond gender boundaries" and the term *androgyny*, borrowing Derrida's *sexual pluralism* and Hélène Cixous's *the other bisexuality* and advocating her own *trans-sexual politics*.

In *Pinter's Female Portraits*, however, though Sakellaridou wishes "not to impose yet another superstructure upon Pinter's already heavily systematised and classified work," presenting her "use of Psychoanalysis, Sociology and Feminism" as "illustrative rather than theoretical" (15), her promotion of the "ideal" of androgyny still limits her descriptions of Pinter's achievements. Yet she deploys careful allusions to sociological and psychological studies and to other Pinter criticism to build and to support her feminist position. Her "free-wheeling, though selective, textual analysis of those aspects of the plays which reflect subconscious writing processes" is, moreover, unprecedented in its sensitivity to subtle variations in Pinter's characterization of women and to changes in Pinter's characterization of men too. Her references to specific performances, to other aspects of theatrical productions, films, and radio and television broadcasts, and to her own and other audience responses effectively contextualize her analysis.

I myself may question Sakellaridou's allocation of Pinter's shifting "sympathies" (e.g., regarding *A Night Out*, *Night School*, and *Betrayal*), her idea that in *A Slight Ache* Flora transcends "social stereotype" by expressing remembered (and/or fantasized?) enjoyment of being raped (76), her confidence in the male characters' "self-confidence" in *The Collection* (91), her adamant attempt to "prove" who "takes the initiative" in *The Lover* (101), her avoidance of the racial factor in *Monologue*, and her underestimating a film audience's ability to discern the irony of "Marian's self-deception" at the end of *The Go-Between* (177). Yet often otherwise (and "genderwise") I am impressed by much else of what she says about Pinter's plays. From a fresh perspective she views Ruth in *The Homecoming* as Pinter's "breakthrough to an unprejudiced objective portrayal of the woman" (119). Despite some characteristic overemphasis ("undoubtedly true"), she becomes eloquent in speculating about Pinter's identification with Beth (*Landscape*) and Sarah (*The French Lieutenant's Woman*) as artists (149–52). Whereas her privileging of objectivity itself betrays the degree to which patriarchal binary linguistic codes still control feminist reading/writing, her understanding of Deborah in *A Kind of Alaska* (Pinter's "very sensitive and delicate study of a female adolescent consciousness entrapped by nature's accident in an ageing female body") as one who "fabricates her own fictional reality" (206–7) offsets this trend.

Critical disagreements and consensus spring from various individual interpretive divergences and convergences: personal, social, and cultural difference and similarity. If Sakellaridou conflates the playwright's attitude and the dramatized behavior of his characters too often for my taste, blurring the sharpness of his comic satire, and if she occasionally states her case too absolutely (vestiges of the 1984 dissertation here revised?), perhaps these tendencies mark her own unique situation as a Greek woman who has studied the work of Pinter in England, as kind of an "odd man out" herself.

Pinter's own tacit knowledge of more recent, widespread *exploding* of "unilateral sexual myths" informing the "archetypal patterns in his plays" (24) may further explain changes in his dramaturgy. His "progress" toward achieving in his later work what Sakellaridou calls "the marvellous insights of androgyny" (175) is contingent not only on Pinter's own personal, social, cultural, and artistic background and experience but on the history and expectations of the critics making such assessments. Such factors influenced Sakellaridou's own choices of topic and perspective and some details of her interpretations.

A native of Thessaloniki, Greece, Sakellaridou earned a B.A. in English Language and Literature from Aristotle University of Thessaloniki in 1972. Though her parents had sent her to the university as educational preparation for marriage, after her marriage Sakellaridou began to develop her career, and it had become "as important" to her as her marriage, "perhaps more important." While still using her married name, Elizabeth Hadzispyrou, she went to London to begin her postgraduate study of English literature, earning a General M.A. in English Literature from the University of Leeds (1979–80). But she still felt unfulfilled as a wife and mother and wanted to develop her professional life further. She returned in October 1981 to begin doctoral studies in English at the University of London, Royal Holloway College, living in London for most of the year, while her husband cared for their child in Greece, and returning frequently in the course of earning her Ph.D. in English Drama (1984). Since 1975 she has taught at the University of Thessaloniki, where she has been senior lecturer in English and Drama since 1988.[37]

While her choice of Pinter for a dissertation topic grew out of a keenness for his work, Sakellaridou's choice of a feminist approach appears to have been related more directly to the critical point that she was experiencing in her life as a woman. She was confronting a fairly typical female crisis, one that has often been resolved, in the case of academic women, through a turn toward feminist criticism, toward (in the phrase that she attaches to Pinter's later female creations) "a clearly defined feminine ideology and discourse."

Although she has remained married, Sakellaridou has changed her last name from Hadzispyrou to Sakellaridou-Hadzispyrou to Sakellaridou, a development possibly indicative of her growing assertiveness about her own individual identity as a woman. In a 1985 Christmas letter to me (20 December) Sakellaridou shared two pieces of news suggesting a resolution to both her own female crisis and her work on Pinter: "after eleven years," she had "decided to become a mother once again"; and her thesis had been accepted for publication by the Macmillan Press (in England). Two years later she wrote me that her second daughter was a year old and "has given a new dimension to family life" and that she expected her book to be in print later in the year. In a move common to those who take a feminist critical perspective on male writers, Sakellaridou expected to "work on a woman dramatist next—probably Louise Page," whom she first met and interviewed in Salonika in November 1986 (letter to author, 14 January 1987) and again in September 1988.[38] Her main scholarly research has become British socialist theater and feminist theory; her current project examines "how contemporary British women dramatists . . . recreate myth and history" (letter to author, 7 November 1988). "Your research into the background of critics," she also writes in this letter, "reflects my own preoccupation with my personal development as a feminist academic and critic with growing power and responsibility trying to keep up family at the same time."

Unlike the dissertations of the other Pinter scholars whom I have interviewed for this book (and my own dissertation too), which were all directed by men, Sakellaridou's doctoral research was directed by a woman, Professor Katharine Worth. While Worth supervised Sakellaridou's work "with real interest and enthusiasm" (v/viii), Sakellaridou views the connection of another woman with her project as "mere chance," observing that her "first interest for Pinter originated in" work with her male M.A. thesis supervisor. Nevertheless, the feminine direction may have left a significant mark on both the dissertation and the published book and on Sakellaridou's subsequent feminist criticism of drama.

In a letter responding to my query about this relationship, Professor Worth says that "it is rather difficult for me to know how—if at all—my approach would differ from that of a male supervisor. . . . [A] good critic (or supervisor) is a good critic, no matter what the sex. Any good critic would be bound to be interested in Pinter's portrayal of women in his plays and in the striking changes in his authorial attitudes to his women characters. She/he would surely have an open mind about possible reasons for this and about their dramatic effectiveness." "Given that criticism at a certain level is difficult to characterise from the sex of the writer—and that the advice I would give to a postgraduate could well be much the same as that to be expected from any other experienced critic, male or female," Worth adds:

> I was especially interested in Elizabeth's approach because she started from a strongly feminist position and I was curious to see how this would affect her critical assessments. I think she would agree that what she needed especially from her stay in London, while working under my supervision, was a fuller experience and understanding of the plays in performance—and of theatrical values generally. Her approach was strongly theoretical and, to make it hold, it was important to test it continually in relation to the subtle ambiguities and shifting tones of the plays as living theatre. This necessarily involved continual re-appraisal of the feminist criticism which provided Elizabeth with stimulating but sometimes over-theoretical viewpoints.

Clearly, then, more at issue for Worth was the relation between theory and practice in the study of dramatic literature/theater than the specifically feminist aspect of the theoretical approach itself. Thus, as she characterizes it, their mutual "aim was to create a convincing tension between theory (especially feminist) and direct response to the plays (as experienced by audiences, directors, Pinter himself, reviewers, and so on)." Worth concludes: "In this I believe Elizabeth succeeded admirably. She effectively adjusted the proportion of theory she included in her final assessments and revalued it interestingly." This judgment contrasts somewhat with my previous discussion of the emphasis on "androgyny" in *Pinter's Female Portraits*. Still, Worth feels, it may have been "helpful to her to have as supervisor someone who was sympathetic to the feminist approach but resistant to theorising (whether feminist or not) of the kind which makes large claims with little reference to minute particularities."

"Another key issue," Worth adds, and one that I have already discussed, "was the handling of biographical material as a factor in Pinter's changing treatment of his women characters." She confirms my impression that Sakellaridou "took great pains to maintain a sensitive distance between references to the author's life and to developments in the plays which seemed connected with them," going on to report: "My advice here was in tune with her own feelings," but she adds: "Whether a male supervisor's would have been any different, who can say?" While recognizing that Worth's direction was "rather gender neutral (intentionally at least)," Sakellaridou wishes she could "rewrite the book using my present knowledge of feminist theory (textual and cinematic) and making stronger statements without necessarily damaging the mise-en-scène aspect of the plays" (letter to author, 9 October 1989).[39]

### Relations of Gender and Personal Concerns in Criticism

Just as Sakellaridou expressed reluctance to discuss connections between Pinter's personal life and his work as cited above, though generously sharing some other significant details about how her personal experience relates to her research interests in our private correspondence, she has asked me not to divulge them in print. While honoring her request for such privacy, I do cite with permission her statement about the *cathartic* nature of her experience of writing her thesis on Pinter, and I feel within the bounds of "decency" (her word) generalizing about the strong connections that I perceive between her personal experience and her interpretations of Pinter's women characters as "castaways." Since I myself have documented similar connections between my own feelings in response to *the same aspect* of Pinter's characters (both male and female) in "Fantasy behind Play," I understand firsthand both her reticence and the strength of such connections. Other female Pinter scholars whose work I discussed earlier (Gordon and Gabbard, and, to a lesser degree, Burkman) have expressed comparable discomfort in discussing their own private experience as it relates to Pinter's work or in speculating about connections between Pinter's work and private life or his "motives"; often these women scholars went "off the record" when such matters entered our taped conversations. Martin Esslin does not want me to use our interview (taped in London on 1 July 1982). The other male Pinter scholars whom I interviewed (Gale, Quigley, and Mengel) showed less interest in and/or reticence about how their own personal lives related to their work and how Pinter's life related to his than the women did.

If the academic women were generally more concerned than the men about their own privacy, this would reverse the tacit expectation that women are more readily "personal" than men. Such an apparent reversal seems less strange if we recognize that the women may have thought differently about the personal connections between their own lives and their responses to Pinter's plays, becoming more fully aware of the embarrassment that they might feel *as professional scholars* (positions achieved through much personal hardship) if I were to reveal such connections. Even the men most established professionally, having revealed less personal material in our interviews both on and off the record than most of the women, may have (for various reasons) felt too much at stake if I were to publish what they told me. Whereas some of the men did communicate more concern than some of the women about possible off-the-record material in our interviews, their concerns also seemed to deal more with their status in the professional community. But, generally, they simply did not give as *much* attention to personal matters as the women did.

Sexual-role orientation is not a distinct factor in my study, since all the men and women scholars whom I interviewed seemed to be heterosexual in orientation. Were some of these scholars homosexual, my generalizations might be different. For example, homosexual men might be more sensitive to the issue of "castaways" and "outcasts" that Sakellaridou and I raised in our dissertations than the heterosexual men in this study appeared to be. Though I am not at liberty to disclose any specifics about this matter, two Pinter scholars were particularly concerned that I *not* publish details about the homosexuality of others connected with their projects and/or their lives, I believe to protect these others' privacy.

The issue of homosexuality is relevant to several of Pinter's plays (*The Dwarfs, The Collection, No Man's Land, Betrayal*, and even, for some critics, *The Caretaker*), and the putative lesbianism of Kate and Anna in *Old Times* has been heatedly debated in criticism and in the staging of the play.[40] For example, in "Death and the Double" Burkman takes issue with Gabbard's interpretation of the relationship between these two female characters. Kate's "symbolic annihilation of her double" does not "rid herself of a repressed 'earthly, sensual self'" as Gabbard says. "On the contrary," Kate "rids herself of a possessive, homosexual self (Anna's and Kate's relationship has taken on lesbian tones, suggested by Anna's exploits in Kate's underwear which she tells Deeley she shared with her room-mate in the dark . . .) who is actually very like her husband for whom . . . Anna is also a double."[41] But it is possible to see Anna as a repressed wishful side of Kate (the "earthly" and "sensual" side), and vice versa (Kate as the ethereal and cerebral side of Anna), understanding a source of their perhaps once mutual attraction, without insisting on their lesbianism or homosexuality as to a degree Burkman does. For a young woman to borrow the underwear of a close woman friend does not necessarily signify that they are lovers or even would-be lovers. It may reveal an actual or wished-for intimacy (or even identity [Sakellaridou, 164]) that is not sexual. Whatever way critics read Pinter's "creative ambiguities" (Cave, 15) depends on both the text and them.

Pinter's angry objections to Visconti's production of *Old Times* in Rome would suggest that, in his own view, Kate's and Anna's relationship cannot be accurately portrayed as *overtly* sexual. Because of such controversy over implications of lesbianism perceived in *Old Times*, directors of the play take care to decide how obvious they want to make suggestions of a past lesbian liaison between Anna and Kate (Scales et al., interview with author).[42] If close friendship between women is threatening to men (as Kate's and Anna's past friendship was/is to Deeley in the play), to present it on stage as overtly sexual or to label it in criticism as lesbian may be a way to deny its legitimacy by denying its normalcy. Though I do not apply this point to any particular critic, since I do not know his or her motivations—homophobia/gynephobia may motivate criticism written by women as well as by men. As Sakellaridou observes further, "Pinter's totally amoral stance, which may seem extreme and revolting to many critics, at least serves, in this particular case, to prove, on a more abstract level, the collapse of all feminine taboos and the complete sexual freedom of women—a privilege that the dramatist had up to [*Old Times*] granted only to men" (169): that is, to buttress a feminist ideology sympathetic to androgyny.

The influence on my study of my own femaleness, heterosexuality, and particular critical orientations must also be taken into account in trying to understand the variety of responses to me as an interviewer, "fellow" scholar, and, at times, confidante. While I cannot expect to offer any conclusive findings about the relation between gender and a reluctance to speak and write personally about literary and critical matters, I do think that this is an important subject, one that merits further study. While any connection between gender and personal revelation may be far too idiosyncratic to generalize, the history of criticism as a male-dominated institution with pretensions to the objectivity of science conventionally has constrained widespread acknowledgment of the subjective or personal features of literary and critical response. The desire of feminist critics to address formerly taboo subjects like gender-biases in the characterizations of women by men writers may bind such critics in a paradox. The desire to move toward a balance of power is part of a feminist urge born of a power politics within patriarchal institutions such as literary studies.

That cultural issues affecting personal and social identity play a strong role in education has been widely established. But it is less generally acknowledged that prejudices and preferences repress critical discovery as "high up" as doctoral and postdoctoral studies and that they may operate in unexpected directions (I generalize from "off-the-record" remarks about dissertation committee supervision). Restrictions on acknowledging homosexual relations relating to Pinter's characters would severely undermine appreciation of *The Collection*: how could one enjoy the comic ironies when Stella claims to have slept with Bill, if one were not "allowed" to assume homosexuality in his relationship with Harry; or the "outcast" status of Stella toward the end of the play, if one could not recognize similar ironies when James attempts to make her jealous of his attraction to Bill? With regard to *The Dwarfs* and *No Man's Land*, too much would be lost to mention only briefly here. In the case of *Betrayal*: how could one savor the ironic comic effects when, speaking of his best friend and her lover, Robert tells his wife, Emma: "I've always liked Jerry. To be honest, I've always liked him rather more than I've liked you. Maybe I should have had an affair with him myself" (4:225)? How could one articulate the subtleties of the "brutally honest" way that Robert retaliates against Emma by saying that the men don't want "a woman around" before, during, or after their "battle" on the squash court (209–10)? The producer of the film version of *Betrayal*, Sam Spiegel, cautiously avoided casting "homosexual actors" to play Jerry and Robert because, he said, "[i]f there is the slightest suspicion that these two men had a homosexual relationship, the whole story falls to pieces" (Farson, "Sam Spiegel's 'Betrayal' "). Though perhaps merely cognizant of the delicacy of the play's comic innuendos, such caution unfortunately suggests that a homosexual actor cannot play a heterosexual role without betraying his own sexual orientations, licensing unwarranted discrimination against homosexuals in casting decisions and maybe even heightening homophobia in general.

I doubt that Pinter would oppose a critical interpretation that remains sensitive to sexual issues raised by his plays or his characters' possible sexual orientations. Rather, he seems to oppose directorial heavy-handedness that emphasizes certain aspects of his text over other aspects and to welcome instead a more *balanced* repesentation: one that does not make possible implications *too obvious*. Likewise, it seems to me, Pinter's celebrated "ambiguity" is in part a sign that he prefers an *equilibrium*—a coexistence (even if not a "peaceful" one)—not only between "the sexes" in his plays, but among other ambivalent cultural forces. No matter what his own preferences, however, Pinter seems to remain quite aware that potentially destructive imbalances exist. His plays dramatize the personal, social, and cultural politics energizing such imbalances.

Whether or not it is possible for any politics to move toward a balance of power, echoing Pinter (cited in the first part of this chapter) I would urge that we continue "to try to think and see things as clearly as possible." We must try to understand as best we can how our own personal, social, and political tendencies—our own quests for power and dominance—affect our critical and cultural biases and orientations. If these tendencies impede the development of personal and communal knowledge beneficial to ourselves, our students, our colleagues, and a larger community outside academe, then we must attempt to confront them squarely, to come to terms with them, and to overcome their perniciousness. Only then can we—a group of sometimes disparate people with heterogeneous backgrounds and perspectives—move "toward a balance of power," that is, move beyond the more insidious effects of competition to develop cultures based on cooperation and collaboration, "ethical cultures" that all of us can share selectively according to our own interests and tastes and without hurting others.

In "The Personal Is Political" Michelene Wandor observes: "The resurgence of feminism has introduced new questions about the relationship between the individual and his/her society and the nature of political change, and it is from this source that we might see a new definition of political subject matter for theatre" (58). This resurgence of feminism, as part of current interest in cultural studies, has been reconstituting political subject matter for criticism as well. As several essays in *Changing the Subject* (Henriques et al.) indicate, there is a strong need for balance in articulating the intricate relations affecting the behavior of "the individual" subject in "society" and our concepts of how these "entities" operate. Many would agree with Sakellaridou that "the good writer and the good critic must aim at transcending the limitations and biases of gender (as seen as sexual and cultural difference)" (letter to author, 7 November 1988). Whether or not any such transcendence is possible is still being vigorously debated, however (see Fish, *DWCN*, 246–67). Critical judgments of literary (and critical) taste and value are contingent on the changing personalities, cultural backgrounds, and contextual situations of the people making them. Sociopolitical and sexual orientations and gender influence these judgments, as do many other related "contingencies of value."

# III

## Social Relations of Critical and

## Cultural Change

# 9

# Contingencies of Value Judgments

## of Pinter's Plays

This category business is the most facile of things. My only categories are plays that I like and plays that I don't. . . . The critic is afraid to either sink or swim when he sees a play; he must grasp the lifebelt of a category.—Harold Pinter

"[T]he more difficult and consequential questions of judgment posed by genuine evaluative diversity and conflict" point to "fundamental and perhaps irreconcilable diversity of interest . . . exhibited in currently charged political contexts" (Smith, "Contingencies," 8, 9). Such conflicts of opinion as those already discussed, many of which seem to arise from fundamentally irreconcilable interests, also dramatize the degree to which interpretation and evaluation interact. "[O]ur interpretation of a text and our experience of its value are to some extent mutually dependent: *both* depend upon the particular assumptions, expectations, and interests with which we approach the work" ("Value/Evaluation," 454). Critical evaluation of Pinter's plays substantiates this assumption: "[l]ike all other utterances, value judgments are context-dependent and shaped by the relation of the speaker to his or her audience and by the structure of interests that sustains the verbal transaction between them" ("Contingencies," 21).[1]

Though the "political contexts" affecting recent interpretive and evaluative conflicts over Pinter's plays differ from those Smith mentions (involving African and feminist authors), these conflicts have also been "highly charged." In their past status as what Smith terms "noncanonical" works, Pinter's plays were perceived as "highly innovative" texts raising difficult kinds of evaluative problems (cf. Marowitz, *Confessions*, 47). For some audiences and readers, especially those not native to England, or unfamiliar otherwise with London's seedier districts and out-of-the-way English seaside resorts, Pinter's first several plays still can seem (in Smith's phrase) "culturally exotic." At the start, however, value judgments made about Pinter's plays were not made "by or on behalf of" so-called noncanonical or culturally exotic audiences; many members of

Pinter's audience *were* "students, critics, or professors of literature." Even so, a larger, more diverse audience (6,380,000 viewers) was established by the television broadcast of his short play *A Night Out* on ABC-TV's "Armchair Theatre" in 1960 (Brandt, 1). Most who saw that production, or heard an earlier version broadcast on BBC Radio throughout Britain and Ireland (in Smith's words) "perhaps never were and never will be within the academy or on its outskirts." For some of those who later became scholars and theater journalists, these programs were their own first experience of a Pinter play too.[2]

In "Theatre in the Sixties," written in 1961, Robert Bolt evaluates the plays of a new "school" of playwriting including Samuel Beckett, Eugene Ionesco, N. F. Simpson, and Harold Pinter. He points to a "danger" arising "when you break totally away from a tradition, particularly from a naturalistic or realistic one, and have something that is so totally abstract as action painting or as a Beckett, Ionesco, Simpson or Pinter play" (10). In such cases, Bolt observes, "it is frightfully difficult to tell the authentic from the spurious. Here, I think, our critics have a serious duty to be tough with us [playwrights], and honest and humble with themselves, because they are on a tight rope. On the one hand they may be throwing out a masterpiece, and on the other they may be selling us something totally worthless. We do need education in this matter." Bolt ends the essay citing his "latent suspicions regarding this school": "I do not think it is in the main tradition of our writing and I doubt whether it will be more than rather short-lived. However, when I think of the courage and honesty of Beckett, of the profoundly iconoclastic humour of Ionesco, and of the humility and sensitivity of Pinter in accepting what he sees, and when I consider that this looseness of form cannot but be relevant to the rather confused situation we are in, then I cannot believe that these writers will not in some way be incorporated into the mainstream of our literature" (10).

In his speech to the Student Union of Drama at Bristol University in 1962, Pinter quoted Bolt's concluding clause, commenting: "In some way. The odds are still pretty long, I gather. Still, it's nice to have that little bit of encouragement to take home to bed." Pinter mocks Bolt's attitude toward literary canonization:

> Certainly Mr. Bolt seems very worried about who's going to get into the main stream of our literature and who isn't. I think he is acting here as some kind of Customs Officer, to whom you are required to

declare your allegiances and your loyalties, before whom you must lay bare your obsessions and your preoccupations (including the rather sexual ones [of Ionesco, as described by Bolt]), before he will allow you to merge cleansed into the main hall of our literature.

The assumption here seems to be that one writes plays with one eye cocked to the prospect of a gold or silver medal at some hypothetical prizegiving. I would rather doubt whether this was in fact the case. ("Between the Lines")[3]

Even though in the Bristol speech Pinter supposes an indifference to "prizes" among writers, he may be alluding to competition for a specific literary award. A year earlier, in 1960, Pinter's *Caretaker* had won the London *Evening Standard* Drama Award for "Best Play," beating Bolt's *Man for All Seasons* and occasioning a spate of interviews with Pinter.[4] In the period from 1960 to 1962 there were clearly economic as well as personal, social, and professional benefits at stake for each writer in their articles, speeches, and interviews, and this context informs their evaluative dispute.

In the Bristol speech Pinter rejects Bolt's demand that contemporary playwrights disclose their "engagement" clearly and sensibly in their plays, unmasking what he calls "prophecy" in playwriting, rejecting what he calls "our empty preferences," and warning against playwrights wearing a "pulsating" heart on their sleeve and against moralistic writing as "a prison of empty definition and cliché." He extends what he told John Sherwood in 1960: "I don't think the theatre is a place to sermonise, and if anyone wants to give an explicit point of view they can always go to a political meeting or church, or stand on a soap-box instead, or write an essay in a magazine. The theatre should be a living moment, something that's happening then, and is self-explanatory in what it means, in what it says, and what the characters say" (Pinter, "Playwright").

In the intervening two decades both the "economics" and the "politics" of world theater have changed, and Pinter and Bolt have, as it were, traded places. In 1962 Bolt was probably invited to comment on Pinter's (and others') work, and Pinter criticized him at Bristol for betraying his "fellow playwrights" when he engaged in "critical judgment" on their work. In 1980, as a celebrated and financially successful writer becoming more political and perhaps even more moralistic in his plays, Pinter defended Bolt's play *State of Revolution* as "[a] much underrated piece of work" and "admirable, [the product of] a first-rate mind looking at the

Russian Revolution" (Barber, "Precise Words"). Time, and all the changes in fortunes and perspectives that it entails, is a "much underrated" contingency of changing values and evaluations, compromising claims for their absolute "validity."[5]

The Bolt-Pinter debate can also be explained in terms of Jaussian "horizons of expectations" (as qualified in Mailloux, *Interpretive Conventions*, 174 n.41): though Jauss claims "that the 'aesthetic value' of a literary work resides in the extent it challenges the contemporary horizon of expectations . . . Jauss does not stress that a text can challenge expectations and still be considered worthless later. . . . The crucial point is not simply whether a work challenges contemporary expectations, but whether such a challenge is valued in *later* horizons of expectations." The horizon of expectations represented by Bolt's 1961 remarks was generally challenged by Pinter's early work, and that challenge *was* valued enough by later critics to render some of that same work the status of "classics."

Defining "the cultural re-production of value," Smith says: "Like all other objects, works of art and literature bear the marks of their own evaluational history, signs of value that acquire their force by virtue of various social and cultural practices and, in this case, certain highly specialized and elaborated institutions" ("Contingencies," 23). Such "institutions" constituting the "structure of power" of plays by Pinter (and Bolt, and others) would include: the worldwide theater; the publishing industry, including both university and trade presses; other media/communications industries—radio, television, and film; the so-called literary academy; and other schools, including acting schools, such as the Royal Academy of Dramatic Art (RADA), which Pinter attended briefly in the late 1940s, and the Central School of Speech and Drama, where he studied later. Editors in the publishing industry join forces with professors in the literary academy to ensure (and insure) what becomes recognized as literary and performance art.

Pinter wrote his first play, *The Room*, in an academic context. His friend Henry Woolf had asked him to write it for presentation in the Drama Department at Bristol University, where Woolf directed it, and a new production was later entered in the London *Sunday Times* competition at the 1957 National Union of Students Drama Festival, also at Bristol University, where Pinter would later be invited to speak about his work. In fewer than five months *The Birthday Party* premiered in Cambridge and went on to Oxford and the "provinces," where it was generally much better received than it was to be in London.[6]

The review of *The Room* by Harold Hobson, included in his annual festival report for the London *Sunday Times* ("Larger Than Life"), presages the enthusiasm of Hobson's later review of *The Birthday Party* written before its London closing at the end of its first week of performances ("Screw Turns Again"). Early supporters like Hobson and various personnel of BBC Radio helped to develop Pinter's career as a playwright. R. D. (Reggie) Smith, the BBC Radio producer who had served on the London Arts Council jury recommending Pinter for a scholarship to attend RADA, supported him for acting roles (even after Pinter dropped out). Donald McWhinnie was assistant head of radio drama from 1953 until 1960, when Martin Esslin replaced him, Esslin becoming head in 1963. As Gray and Bray point out, both McWhinnie and Esslin were powerful at the BBC: "They were thus concerned not only with individual plays but with the whole policy of broadcast drama, shaping the listening experience of several generations" (292).[7] Both men commissioned Pinter's radio plays for BBC programs throughout the 1960s, and Esslin also included Pinter's work in *The Theatre of the Absurd*, first released in 1961 (the same year as Bolt's article). Esslin's *Theatre of the Absurd* appeared in a revised edition in 1969 and his *Peopled Wound* in 1970. As Bolt predicted (however ambivalently), Pinter's work was being institutionalized within literary academe and world theater.

By 1970 also Pinter's plays were already the subject of postgraduate examinations (my Ph.D. qualifying examination in Drama at Indiana University, Bloomington, e.g.) and several dissertations; by the early seventies Pinter had entered the curricula of British, American, and West German postsecondary, secondary, and even elementary schools (fueled, in Germany, by the Esslins' translations). To extrapolate from the worldwide translations of Pinter's plays listed by Esslin and Gale, by 1978 they were being read and taught all over the world. Pinter had even entered American "popular culture" through references to "a Pinter play" and "Pinter heroines" in songs and other plays and movies (e.g., "The Ladies Who Lunch," from Stephen Sondheim's musical *Company* [1970], and Neil Simon's *California Suite* [1978] and a series of parodies, most recently Maximilian Bocek's *Very Nearly a Pinter* [pronounced with a long *i*]). As well as being anthologized and published and parodied, they are still produced often; they remain a staple in professional theaters around the world, and, at least in America, in regional, community, and academic theaters as well; throughout England they are produced less frequently. In London, New York, and Paris, however, some premiere productions of Pinter's recent work (e.g., *Betrayal, Other Places, Mountain Language*) and recent revivals (e.g., *The Birthday Party*) have sold out. In Ireland Pinter's plays have consistently been produced (Finegan and Nowlan). In West Germany, Paul Goetsch explained to me, by 1982 Pinter was generally "dead" in subsidized theater as he was being seen as a "commercial" playwright, though he still had limited academic appeal. In the last several years, with Pinter's dramatization of political issues, however, this perception has been changing in Germany, as elsewhere. Recent events in Germany and Eastern Europe would seem to be enhancing Pinter's "relevance."

Though in the sixties Pinter's popularity was attributed simply to "fashion," or to his fame or celebrity (as we saw in chapter 1), given Smith's perspective the phenomenon now appears a great deal more complex. "Every literary work . . . is thus the product of a complex evaluative feedback loop," involving not only "the ever-shifting economy of the artist's own interests and resources," but "all the other diverse forms of evaluation" that will mark, reproduce, and transmit its value, such as: "the innumerable implicit acts of evaluation performed by those who, as may happen, publish the work, purchase, preserve, display, quote, cite, translate, perform, allude to, and imitate it; the more explicit but casual judgments made, debated, and negotiated in informal contexts by readers and by all those others in whose personal economies the work, in some way, 'figures'; and the more highly specialized institutionalized forms of evaluation exhibited in the more or less professional activities of scholars, teachers, and academic or journalistic critics" ("Contingencies," 24–25). These professional activities include "not only their full-dress reviews and explicit rank-orderings, evaluations, and reevaluations, but also such activities as the awarding of literary prizes, the commissioning and publishing of articles about certain works, the compiling of anthologies, the writing of introductions, the construction of department curricula, and the drawing up of class reading lists"—all of which "figure significantly in the production of literary value" (25). Though they bring a work into "the orbit of attention of a population of potential readers; and, by making it more accessible to the interests of those readers . . . they make it more likely both that the work will be experienced at all and also that it will be experienced as valuable," such activities are "only a small part of the complex process of literary canonization."[8] In considering the "converse" of "this process" too, through which "those who occupy positions of some cultural power" (anthology editors, teachers) *exclude* some works, Smith defines all such acts as "not merely recommendations of value but . . . also determinants of value" (25–26).

From Smith's perspective the process through which Pinter's work has been canonized might seem so complex as to defy documentation. There may be so many "innumerable" factors and "variables" at play in the cultural institutionalization of any author's work that no one person could convincingly account for all of them in a lifetime of study. The empirical, collaborative research of Rosengren on the reception of nineteenth-century Swedish authors suggests an effective means of limiting the field of inquiry for my own more modest purposes: he concludes that contemporary "reviewers, essayists and academics" jointly exert the most powerful influence on future reviewers of literature (24).[9]

Such writers have functioned in Pinter's "canonization" and in his present position in the contemporary literary (in Rosengren's phrase) "hierarchy of fame." Performance reviews and book reviews of some of Pinter's published works, surveys and monographs of an introductory nature, and more general "handbooks" or "histories"—both nonacademic and academic kinds of writing evaluate Pinter and his plays for audiences often unfamiliar with them. Rosengren observes: "the variables based on volume exert a stronger influence than the ones based on mentions; academic critics exert a stronger influence than essayists, but probably not very much stronger than that exerted by the 19th century reviewers; [and] the influence from Swedish histories of literature is quite strong, while that from general histories is next to negligible" (20). The last conclusion would suggest that the power of general histories (or handbooks) upon later essayists and academic critics is relatively weak. They have a strong "pedagogical presence" in contemporary Anglo-American culture, however, because they are stocked routinely in academic and public libraries.

Though obviously not a factor applicable to Rosengren's study of nineteenth-century authors, the impact of Pinter's exposure through nonprint media like radio, television, and film on his critical reputation as a playwright has not been (and perhaps cannot be) measured exactly; yet it is an important contingency of his ongoing cultural value to consider. From this angle Taylor interprets the "fashion" controversy discussed in chapter 1: "[T]he difference between the general critical and commercial failure of *The Birthday Party* in [1958] and the critical and commercial triumph of *The Caretaker* in 1960 was almost entirely the work of television, which with *A Night Out* and a new production of *The*

*Birthday Party* familiarized a vast audience with Pinter's style and created the climate of opinion in which his later work could command instant acceptance" (*Anger and After*, 197–98; see also Hewison, 149). [10] Though it is common to say that Pinter does not give many interviews, he did participate in frequent interviews on radio and television during the sixties, and such media exposure also helped to develop potential audiences for his stage plays, as his films have done subsequently.

### Contextualizing Evaluations in Performance Reviews

In drama and theater studies, according to William Free, "understanding the evaluative judgment of playscript and performance" has lagged behind other theoretical concerns, becoming in the 1970s "a growing hostility to the idea of judgment, especially if applied to the performer." This hostility, Free speculates, derives from "a lack of understanding of what aesthetic judgment involves, especially when applied to the total dramatic/theatrical experience" ("Theory," 77). Free offers several premises to guide in formulating "any comprehensive theory of evaluating theatre art" and a "heuristic model that attempts to separate four levels of appreciation"—*sensory feeling*, *vital feeling*, *psychic feeling*, and *spiritual feeling*—"and the acts of judgment relevant to each" (78–79). Throughout Free stresses the plurality of levels of consciousness, structure, semiosis, and vocabularies implicated by judgments of play performances. [11]

Given these further complexities and the plethora of "signs" in "the field of drama"—transmission of a literary text; directorial interpretation; setting, lighting, sound effects, and music; acting methods; particular actors; audience receptivity; prior reviews; social and cultural conventions; critical and personal assumptions, expectations, and interests; natural human predilections; and so on—all potentially capable of affecting a critical reviewer's judgments, I do not aim to define exhaustively how and why specific evaluations of Pinter and his plays may have been made or may change, nor will I predict the causes and outcomes of future evaluations. Others may wish to examine their own and others' judgments of Pinter and his work as guided by Free. I will illustrate contextual forces at play in selected, often divergent, evaluations of some of Pinter's work.

Giles Gordon observes "an increasing tendency, in our non-elitist times, for theatre critics to be sucked into a vortex which has more than a little to do with the camaraderie of the theatrical, rather than literary or critical, fraternity" (4). Two prominent English reviewers, Sir Harold Hobson and Irving Wardle, who have reviewed Pinter's plays for the London *Times*, were kind enough to speak with me about Pinter and his work. Each man's particular relationship with Pinter pertains to his various assessments of Pinter's development as a playwright. Briefly considered also are judgments by a few Americans who have reviewed stage productions of Pinter's plays over an extended period of time: John Simon, drama critic for the *Hudson Review*, the *New Leader*, and *New York*; Henry Hewes, drama critic of the *Saturday Review*; and Walter Kerr, longtime drama critic of the *New York Times*. Lehman Engel's accounts of the work of Simon and Hewes and Roderick Bladel's study of Kerr have helped me establish contexts for their reviews of Pinter.

## Sir Harold Hobson:
### The Promptings of Personal Experience

By now Hobson's review of the first London production of *The Birthday Party* may seem overly familiar (G. Gordon, 3): "Deliberately, I am willing to risk whatever reputation I have as a judge of plays by saying that 'The Birthday Party' is not a Fourth, not even a Second, but a First; and that Mr. Pinter, on the evidence of this work, possesses the most original, disturbing, and arresting talent in theatrical London" ("Screw Turns Again"). Hobson explains his anxiety that the play will close prematurely (as it did, even before the review appeared) and thus subvert "the discovery and encouragement of new dramatists of quality . . . the present most important task of the British theatre."

Hobson's anxiety about the play closing prematurely and his championing of Pinter as a world-class playwright relate to a specific context. Michael Codron, the producer of *The Birthday Party*, had been thinking of keeping the play on after its Saturday night performance if Hobson would be able to give the production substantial space in that Sunday's edition of the London *Times*. When this appeared to be impossible, Codron went ahead with plans to withdraw the play after Saturday night. After a phone call from Margaret Ramsay, acting informally on Codron's behalf, however, Hobson decided to catch the Thursday matinee and then revised his original review, lengthening the portion devoted to

Pinter (Gussow, "Profiles," 45; Hobson, "Vagaries"). Alan Brien jokingly imagines another phone call involving Pinter, saying that though the Lyric Hammersmith production of *The Birthday Party* has already closed, "I think it worth worrying it a little in its grave if only in the hope that the author, Harold Pinter, will be galvanised into ringing me up and telling me what it was all about." Personal relationships (real and imagined) between Pinter and his critics (and producers and their agents) are both determinants and effects of his success as a playwright.

An initial basis of the relationship between Hobson and Pinter was Hobson's review of the first production of *The Birthday Party*, whose importance Pinter has acknowledged not only on his career as a playwright but on his personal ability to recover from an early failure; Pinter told Barber, for example: "That was a hell of a destruction, what happened in 1958. Hobson's notice did bolster me up at that point" ("Precise Words"). This relationship may have enhanced Hobson's "favor" of Pinter to some extent, but Hobson's reviews of productions of Pinter's plays have not all been raves. As with a review of *The Homecoming* that annoyed Pinter (see below), however, subsequent interpretive disagreements have not had significant negative effects on their friendship.[12] "[Hobson] didn't like every play I wrote at all . . . and I think that's a very important fact. People generally feel that if you are a playwright you insist on 'good notices.' Nonsense, of course. Every critic is perfectly entitled to test and find wanting any piece of work. What the hell, why not? Mind you, I have my views about certain critics and their predispositions and prejudices" (Barber, "Precise Words").

Yet any reviewer who is "friends" with a playwright must be somewhat conscious of the potential effects of subsequent reviews on their friendship. Though it is possible that judgments may not be altered by the circumstances of a friendship in any crucial way, such a relationship does differentiate reviewers' judgments regarding evaluations of a friend's work from their other decisions. The actual personal and social relationship between a reviewer and the author whose work is being reviewed (or otherwise commented on) may inhibit what the reviewer says about it. But such inhibitions are rarely acknowledged in literary criticism and theory. When mentioned, these problematic influences are most often skirted or otherwise repressed. The subject of such influences is generally regarded as taboo.[13]

The following passage appears in Hobson's 1979 review of the London premiere of Pinter's play *Betrayal*:

Whilst writing drama criticism was the principal activity of my professional life, I always found that the most influential reviews I wrote were those in which the emotion was prompted by some personal experience in my own life. In an attempt to find out what are the true motive forces of drama criticism I have tried to analyse in my autobiography, *Indirect Journey*, the influence upon art of personal experience. In one way this is contrary to modern theory, for it means that criticism, like drama itself (both being an interpretation of life), is almost entirely subjective. This is irreconcileable [*sic*] with the contemporary belief that art should be judged in relation to certain objective realities. (43)[14]

Then, a bit later on, Hobson remarks: "But for one fact it would be impertinent to speculate whether Mr. Pinter's view of adultery arises out of an intellectual conviction, or a subjective emotion arising from experience." That "one fact" is Pinter's "surely unprecedented breach of convention" in his program announcement "that he is living with a lady [Lady Antonia Fraser] to whom he is not married." Puzzled by this announcement, for which he can find "absolutely no reason at all," Hobson "brood[s]" fruitlessly about its possible relevance to the play, concluding: "Anyway, *Betrayal* is a very fine play, beautifully and originally constructed, and excellently played in a manner that suggests that, in adultery, it is the men who feel the jealousies and the pain" (44). But, instead of supporting these judgments and interpretations with details of the text or production, or of his own or Pinter's actual experience, he ends by discounting them entirely: "Of course, I may myself have completely misunderstood it." This review of *Betrayal* betrays Hobson's personal discomfort with both the play and reviewing it.

As quoted by Gussow ("I Started," D7), Pinter asserts that the breakup of his marriage to Vivien Merchant was "totally irrelevant" to his writing of *Betrayal*; the assumption that *Betrayal* is "about" his affair with Lady Antonia Fraser is "really nonsense": "Normally, in programs, they say he is 'married to so and so.' I simply decided to put the thing very clearly because that's what the situation was. All those rumors and gossip. I thought I might as well put the matter straight in a context, which was actually a tradition of program notes. But it has absolutely nothing to do with the play. The play is about a nine-year relationship between two men who are best friends." Yet Hobson's preoccupation with the autobiographical context of the program note may have motivated the passage in his review of *Betrayal* about the "subjective" nature of reviewing and the role of "personal experience" in his reviews as quoted above. Though it could seem that the passage serves merely to rationalize his concern with Pinter's personal life in this single instance, it provides some insight about how Hobson's own personal experience relates to his theater criticism in general and his criticism of some of Pinter's other plays in particular.[15]

When Hobson perceives a play to be either portraying or lacking what he regards as proper morality or respect for marital love, his interpretive judgments seem to reflect his approval or disapproval accordingly. In his review of the London premiere of *The Homecoming* ("Pinter minus the Moral"), Hobson's interpretation of Teddy as merely *pretending* to be Ruth's husband and a professor of philosophy enables him to rationalize the man's behavior toward his wife. Teddy is simply *not* Ruth's husband. Teddy is not really an American professor; he merely picks Ruth up, takes her home, and presents her as his wife. Though Hobson still describes *The Homecoming* as Pinter's "cleverest play," his judgment against the play's "moral vacuum," like his denial of Teddy and Ruth's marriage, suggests his personal distress at the play's portrayal of marriage and what Pinter has called the characters' misdirected "love."

In 1969, when *Landscape* was first produced on stage at the Aldwych Theatre, along with *Silence*, both Harold Hobson and Irving Wardle reviewed it. Wardle describes *Landscape* as "a short masterpiece" ("Pinter Theatrical Twins"). Though, like Wardle, he focuses on the theme of memory, Hobson was even more laudatory ("Paradise Lost"). The effect of personal context on Hobson's judgment of *Landscape* is more striking in his 1981 *Drama* review of its benefit revival at the Lyttelton, featuring the same cast as its premiere. As Wardle earlier praised "a beautiful pair of performances" from Dame Peggy Ashcroft and David Waller, "who convey the full weight of the unspoken beneath the glassily composed surface," Hobson describes this performance as "extraordinarily beautiful," expressing in general terms the depth of his own complex emotions: "This play is the landscape of two minds whose juxtaposition is infinitely lovely and infinitely pathetic, so that when Beth speaks the last line— 'My true love, I said'—one's heart turns over at the realisation of a world of love into which Duff will never be able to enter, and which indeed it has been given to few in any audience to experience with such joyous, sad intensity" (29; cf. Cave, 7).

Reviewing *Old Times* (1971 Royal Shakespeare Company, Aldwych),

Hobson writes: "Behind everything is the uncontrollable fear of being the odd man out, and the racing terror in which Deeley's brain conceives and plays out the awful, helpless male horror of lesbianism" ("Remembrance"; cf. Scales et al.). In Hobson's more recent "personal view," along with "an excessive preoccupation with homosexuality" and an increasing, "unjustified contempt for entertainment plays," contemporary British theater has "too much talk of sex and not enough of love" (*Theatre in Britain*, 235). To borrow Pinter's phrase, such "predispositions and prejudices" figuring in the judgments of influential drama critics signify the power that these contexts wield in critical practice.

### Irving Wardle: Local Social Contexts
### of Personal Associations

Though Irving Wardle and Pinter were friends in the late fifties, Wardle may have hurt Pinter in the course of writing reviews of his plays subsequently, and their friendship did not survive.[16] Like Hobson, Wardle wrote a "postmortem" review of the first production of *The Birthday Party* ("Birthday Party"); that "less well known positive review," as Scott notices too, "put[s] into perspective" Hobson's initial "comparisons between the play and Henry James's *The Turn of the Screw*" (10). "Comedy of Menace," which first applies this label to Pinter's work (see chap. 1), describes Pinter as one of "several playwrights who have been tentatively lumped together as the 'non-naturalists' or 'abstractionists'" (28). In addition to Pinter, Wardle includes Nigel Dennis, David Campton (who had actually first used "comedy of menace" as a subtitle for one of his plays, *The Lunatic View*), and N. F. Simpson. "Comedy of Menace" centers on *The Birthday Party* because it is the only play of Pinter's that Wardle had seen at the time, yet he speculates on the basis of "descriptions of [Pinter's] other plays, *The Room* and *The Dumb Waiter*, [that Pinter] is a writer dogged by one image—the womb" (33). Mentioning the acknowledged "literary influences" on Pinter's work—"Beckett, Kafka and American gangster films"—Wardle argues that "*The Birthday Party* exemplifies the type of comic menace which gave rise to this article." Pinter's comic handling of "destiny" is "an apt dramatic motif for an age of conditioned behaviour in which orthodox man is a willing collaborator in his own destruction."

Retracting "Comedy of Menace" in reviewing *The Caretaker* just two years later, Wardle writes: "On the strength of *The Birthday Party* and the pair of one-acters, I rashly applied the phrase 'comedy of menace' to Pinter's writing. I now take it back" ("There's Music," 130). This review generally commends Pinter for *The Caretaker* ("I see no point in invoking the name of Beckett or of any other supposed influence—the play is quintessentially the work of a very considerable artist"), yet Wardle is critical of Aston's long speech at the end of act 2, where "the sense of exploration breaks down," because "Pinter, one feels, knew too much about the speech before he began writing it, and its effect is inappropriately naïve" (131). Though more recently Pinter has denied that critics' negative judgments of his plays affect him personally (Farson, "Reviews," 1D), this early criticism of *The Caretaker* could have initiated Wardle's falling out with Pinter.

Wardle's special "competence" as an interpreter of Pinter in 1960 derived from certain local social contexts giving *The Caretaker* personal significance for him at that time, perhaps rendering the catch-all phrase *comedy of menace* less meaningful. After calling Pinter "the poet of London Transport" for delimiting the world of *The Caretaker* by "the London bus routes," Wardle goes on to describe this world impressionistically as one "beyond which lies unknown territory—an empty landscape in which a hospital, a monastery, or a transit camp exist in stark isolation like mythological beasts sprawling over unexplored continents in an old map" ("There's Music," 131). "Besides its other associations," for Wardle "this view of the world has a distinct smack of the Army. . . . From his way of speaking one knows, long before [Davies] informs the audience, that the tramp has done his spell abroad; and is it an accident, I wonder, that Sidcup, his unattainable El Dorado, happens to be the headquarters of the Army Pay Office?" (131–32). "I'm not offering this as a theory of any importance," Wardle stresses: "I happen to have done my two years and consequently the play carries those associations for me" (132). Wardle's leap from these more local associations to the play's "universality" anticipates much subsequent criticism of the play: "Equally valid readings, no doubt, could be made from many alternative fixed points of view. In other words the play has universality—attaining this without any reliance on the localized social framework currently regarded as indispensable."

More recently, to support the view that "specific 'subcultural conventions' . . . may derive from the finer points of social milieus or a knowledge of the connotations of the meaning of certain words," Martin Esslin refers to *The Caretaker*: "The mention by the tramp Davies . . . that his personal documents are being held for him in Sidcup evokes hilarity in a London audience, simply because the name of that particular suburb suggests certain associations of lower-middle class semi-detached houses that are the very antithesis of a repository of official documents" (*Field*, 142). Apparently, Esslin, a nonnative Englishman who was born in Hungary and educated in Austria before emigrating to England, is unaware of Wardle's claim that Sidcup actually did house the Army Pay Office and is guessing about other "subcultural" associations that may or may not be shared by individual members of "a London audience." Esslin's more unique interpretation qualifies literary claims of "universality" such as Wardle's and Esslin's own prior stress on Pinter's use of "universal archetypes." "What produces evaluative consensus, such as it is," Smith observes, "is not the healthy functioning of universal organs but the playing out of the *same* dynamics and variable contingencies that produce evaluative divergences" ("Contingencies," 16; cf. *Contingencies*, 39). Pinter's "universality" results from various contingencies at play in interactions of many people, from various cultural backgrounds, on both sides of the stage as well as on both sides of the Atlantic.

### John Simon: Writing for Myself

Perhaps the most consistently negative notices of Pinter's plays by an American critic are those written by John Simon. Simon has occasionally included a few begrudgingly positive remarks in otherwise negative reviews of Pinter's plays, but he has written predominantly positive evaluations of them only rarely.[17] A review of the 1976 New York production of *No Man's Land* for the *Hudson Review* is representative of Simon's writing on Pinter. Making a transition from his negative summary of another play, Simon begins this review by saying that *No Man's Land* "places its author even lower on my scale, on which he never rated very high" ("Theatre Chronicle," 101). A long paragraph minimizing the value of "Quigley's hermeneutics," despite (or perhaps because of) Simon's own previous admission that he cannot understand the meaning of *No Man's Land*, concludes (rather defensively, it seems to me): "I must say that *I* never found Pinter's plays tantalizingly enigmatic; I recognized them plainly for the three-dollar bills they were. Nor did I ever believe that truth, reality and communication [topics raised by Pinter] ought to conform to certain norms [defined by Quigley]; but I did and do believe that plays should conform to certain conceivable, even if not immediately recognizable, notions of truth, reality and communication. What I emphatically reject is that 'any other' concepts are mere moves in language games, though I am quite willing to grant that Pinter's concepts are, even if the game is hardly worth the candle" (102). After pointing out "some new elements of gamesmanship" introduced in *No Man's Land*, "to wit, a goodly amount of scatology and obscenity, which curiously combines with what smacks of misogyny," and some other of Pinter's "usual tricks," Simon wonders, "But what does it all amount to?" (102–3). "Not even a scorching contest of wills, as in *The Homecoming*"; for "here everyone is either too flabby or too shadowy to register strongly" (103). These last few sentences encapsulate Simon's overall view of Pinter: "The formula has frozen into place: menace here, menace there, menace between the lines in the pauses, and the whole thing interspersed with gaudy non sequiturs for cheap laughs. And behind all of it one hears the author's mean-spirited, misanthropic, smugly self-serving cackle" (103). Is Simon projecting a sense of himself on Pinter?[18] In reviewing the 1971 *Homecoming*, alluding to John Lahr's *Casebook*, Simon quips, "Instead of a casebook on *The Homecoming*, I'd like a case history on its author." Some might feel a similar desire for a case history on Simon.

"Reviewing is an accomplishment; criticism is a vocation," Wardle has written. "You may write for a public, but you do it for yourself" ("Criticism," 26). Similarly, in "confessing" that he is an "elitist," Simon admits that even if a lack of "compassion" and a desire to "serve the cause of theater by being as passionate, subjective and truthful as I can be" does make "me into an elitist, I do subscribe only to myself" (*Uneasy Stages*, xiv–xv). In an account of Simon's work, while granting him some positive traits as a critic (superb style and wit, some moral concern), Lehman Engel cites Simon's view that the "responsibility" of the "serious" critic is "first and last to himself," observes that "too frequently" Simon "sells his soul for a quip," and wishes that "as a critic [Simon] felt a greater responsibility to others and a bit less (as he has said) to himself" (185, 193–94). Engel questions how much of Simon's writing relates to "dramatic criticism," suggesting that some of the "opinions" cited are "purely personal and even psychopathic" (186–87). Contextualizing evaluations of Pinter's plays seems even more necessary when we are dealing with reviews by a critic who "is generally mistrusted by producers, directors, writers, actors, and his colleagues" (203).[19] Fortunately, Engel suggests, Simon's "power" is limited by "the necessary tardiness of his review and the comparatively small circulation which his periodical [*New York*] claims."

## Henry Hewes: The Power of Gentleness

The "influence" exerted by Henry Hewes, the reviewer for the *Saturday Review*, is also relatively "limited by both the circulation of his magazine [in 1976, 500,000 copies every other week, much of it outside New York City] and the time-lapse between a show's opening and the appearance of Hewes's opinion," and further reduced by the secondary interest of the *Saturday Review*'s audience in the arts (203–4). But, in contrast to Simon's, Hewes's reviews of Pinter's plays have been generally positive. While Engel points out a predilection in Hewes for Beckett and Albee, he also suggests a difference of temperament or personality between Hewes and Simon in the former's ability to criticize a play without destroying it. Citing Hewes on Albee's *All Over*, for example, Engel reveals "a critic's honest attempt to come to grips with an estimable playwright's work, his failure to agree with it altogether, and his respectful regret"; whereas, like Simon, "[t]oo many reviewers lack the ability to be negative after a sincere but fruitless search for meaning in an artist's work without a cruel, facetious or even angry kiss-off[,] Hewes . . . is interested in the play and the future of the playwright and not in attracting attention to his own desire to amuse" (213). In Engel's view Hewes is "observant, concerned about theater, and precise in conveying to his readers what he sees and how this affects him," and he exhibits "gentleness and tolerance" (216).

Engel's metacritical evaluations are, of course, themselves *contingent* on Engel's own temperament and various other factors; such evaluations suggest how we contextualize these writers' reviews of Pinter even as we read them. If we have the experience, we read such judgments of Pinter's plays as Hewes's 1961 recognition that *The Caretaker* is "probably a masterpiece" and "the truest and most universal piece of theatre Broadway has had in some time" and that Pinter is "clearly the best new English playwright since John Osborne" ("Nothing") or his 1967 judgments that "While *The Birthday Party* is less sure-handed than such subsequent plays as *The Caretaker* and *The Homecoming*, one can see in it the origins of Pinter's style" ("Like Birth") and that it is an "intriguing play" ("Disobedience," 47) in the context of our own past reading of Hewes's evaluations of other works by Pinter and of works by others.

## Walter Kerr: Eclectic Thoughts Embodying
## Sensitive Feelings

Walter Kerr, during his tenure as the chief drama critic for the *New York Times* through the 1970s, was perhaps the most powerful and influential of American theater reviewers. Roderick Bladel writes: "As a theater critic, Walter Kerr is an impressionist and a relativist. His reviews are impressionistic in that they attempt to describe an experience inspired in him by a given play. He is a relativist in that he tries to avoid rigid preconceptions as to what that experience should be. He believes a play establishes for itself the demands placed upon it. The only criterion which approaches an absolute is that the play must *involve* him either cerebrally or emotionally. If his reviews are more convincing than his theoretical writing, it may be because the reviews are based almost solely upon his own reactions" (174). In his "practical criticism" Kerr's eclectic theories are secondary: "[Kerr] first reacts subjectively, just as any other impressionistic critic. Then he makes a judgment in the review, describing specific, concrete elements in the play and production which have brought about his reaction."

Especially intrigued by Pinter's work, Kerr published a monograph on Pinter as an "existential" playwright in 1967. This extensive involvement with Pinter informs Kerr's subsequent evaluations of Pinter's plays on the New York stage, such as his 1971 review of *Old Times*. In this play, Kerr writes, "the irony is gone; the tangible has been reduced to an absolute minimum. In effect, Mr. Pinter has stripped away nearly all of those things that first seemed to guarantee us solidity and chosen to present his theme as nakedly as possible, in its barest, whitest bones" ("Is Mr. Pinter," 7). Though Kerr admits, "I do not admire this nakeder formula so much," comparing *Old Times* to *The Collection*, which he finds "lighter" and "more active," he acknowledges that the former "possesses the stage of the Billy Rose coolly. There it sits, serene, neutral, imperturbable, present. I responded in kind, with a cool neutrality. But I listened." In the course of this review Kerr gives a vividly detailed account of how the particular production stimulated his response. This passage in which Kerr describes the end of the play illustrates Kerr's sensitivity to his own impressions and his ability to find larger significance in them:

> [W]ithout warning, the stage lights suddenly blaze up full, harsh, blinding. The people on stage stay just as they were. After a few

moments the lights fade away again and the curtain condescends to fall. I had an erratic impulse at this point—an amused, not an angry one—to scribble on my notepaper, "Fake!" My first thought was that director Peter Hall, in conspiracy with the man running his lightboard, was indulging himself in trickery, adding to the customary mysteries of Pinter a merely showy and gratuitous stage trick. Then I thought twice. No, I thought, the trick with the lights is saying exactly what Harold Pinter is saying: that people, when fully illuminated, remain exactly as ambiguous as they were in the half-dark. (1)

Kerr reconceptualizes his initial evaluation of *Old Times* ("Fake!") and his other thoughts and feelings in this account from an existential viewpoint developed further in his essay "The Playwright as Existentialist."

A "thoughtful" critic is one who attempts to reconsider his or her initial responses from other perspectives, but in order to do this the critic must be sensitive to the responses themselves. The critic's readers must become similarly self-aware in appraising such judgments. We must consider that, no matter how "accurate" a critic's rendition of the details of a performance, ultimately evaluations depend on much more than "the play itself." Kerr could watch the end of *Old Times* in "cool neutrality," partly because he perceived Deeley's sobbing as "not quite convincingly" played by Robert Shaw. Nevertheless, I watched the end of the same production, breathless, on the edge of my seat.[20] Several years before Kerr worried that "more people are going to be put off than turned on" by the 1967 New York production of *The Birthday Party* ("Put Off," 1). Yet, whereas Kerr (an already "dedicated Pinterite") found the evening "by and large a bore" (5), I (a novice theatergoer then) had become so "turned on" that I began what has become by now over twenty years of continuing theatrical enjoyment and scholarly research.

### The "Intercontextuality" of Performance, Film, and Book Reviews

In a 1983 review of Pinter's volume *Other Places* (including *A Kind of Alaska*, *Victoria Station*, and *Family Voices*), the reviewer for *Booklist*, Denise P. Donavin, speculates: "Interest in these plays may be escalated with the popularity of the movie version of the playwright's recent work, *Betrayal*." Comparing evaluations of Pinter's film of *Betrayal* with judgments of the London and New York stage versions and subsequent book reviews of *Other Places* substantiates Donavin's prediction. The stage reception of *Other Places* also had an important impact on its book reviews. And since *One for the Road* replaced *Family Voices* in the New York production of *Other Places*, the stage production and reception of *One for the Road* may have influenced its subsequent book reviews too. Such influences constitute the "intercontextuality" of performance, film, and book reviews.

Susan Rusinko, a professor of English at Bloomsburg University, has written some book reviews of Pinter's plays for *World Literature Today*, as well as book reviews for the journal *Modern Drama* and other academic criticism of modern drama.[21] As David Bleich has observed of my account of my first response to *Old Times* on stage (*SC*, 126–28), and as I have noticed about Kerr's review of this play too, Rusinko's prior involvement with Pinter's work and Pinter criticism marks her book review evaluating the three plays in *Other Places*. Rusinko judges *A Kind of Alaska* as "[e]specially effective," citing Michael Billington's "instant" impression of it (on stage) as "a masterpiece." Acknowledging that *Family Voices* first aired on radio (Pinter actually wrote it for radio and only later adapted it for the stage), she describes the volume as "quintessentially Pinterese, without the theatricality that characterizes his major plays." Rusinko concludes: "Pinter's triptych is a refreshing and highly satisfying group of plays, particularly in the wake of *Betrayal* [1978], whose stage production received mixed (some negative) notices for its gimmicky structure and realistic style."[22] In contrast to this report, the anonymous reviewer for *Theatre Crafts* describes the play in its published version as "[a]n exquisitely simple play about infidelity—unraveled in reversed chronological time" ("Book Notes"). Lack of reference to the play's stage reception (regarding the play solely as a published text) changes the parameters of evaluation.

In 1978 several veteran theater critics reviewed the National Theatre premiere of *Betrayal* in major world publications: among them, Benedict Nightingale (the *New Statesman* and the *New York Times*), Jack Kroll (*Newsweek*), Harold Hobson and Anthony Curtis (*Drama*), and Martin Esslin (*Plays and Players*). Contrary to "[t]he only safe remark" tendered by Sakellaridou, much more than "the baffling nature of the play itself" has produced "all this [interpretive] controversy" (*PFP*, 180). This handful of reviews of the London premiere of *Betrayal* demonstrates the crucial importance of previous experiences of an author on reviewers' current interpretations and evaluations. Included in this previous experience are not only personal factors but exposure to prior reviews—"the individual's own personal 'intertextuality' " (Esslin, *Field*, 149)—and more social and cultural "intercontextuality."

These performance reviews also demonstrate how particular controversies animating criticism of this play relate to book reviews of Pinter's later plays (such as those by Donavin and Rusinko) and to reviews of the film version of *Betrayal*. Most hotly contested is the emotional "depth" conveyed by the play in its various incarnations, with arguments ranging from its being totally superficial and emotionally remote to its being deeply profound and emotionally intense. This controversy about the play's "banality"/"depth" marks much later academic criticism too.[23]

Benedict Nightingale begins his first review by responding to many of his London colleagues. "[C]ontrary" to previous opinion, Nightingale argues, *Betrayal* is "one of Pinter's more successful exercises in presenting the least and evoking the most. What looks flat commonly has fissures of feeling beneath it, and what sounds banal can be magnificently resonant." Overturning already prevalent attacks on *Betrayal*'s "anti-clockwise" scheme, he adds: "It substitutes the question 'how?' for the cruder 'what next?' in the minds of the audience. And in my view it deepens and darkens our perception of the play, infecting the most innocent encounters with irony, dread and a sense of doom." Finally, as he declares the play to contain no "idle word," Nightingale concludes that every line expresses "desire, hurt, regret, rage or some concatenation of the impulses that are pounding about the slippery brainboxes of these artful dodgers" ("Anti-Clockwise," 718).

Three days later Jack Kroll's review appeared in *Newsweek*, agreeing with Nightingale ("Each line, each word, is a drop distilled from the sloshing mess of ordinary emotion") and placing Pinter as among the "giants of world theater," along with Tom Stoppard and Peter Brook ("Oh, to Be in England," 65). Anticipating (or being echoed by) *Theatre Crafts* (as cited above), Kroll also describes *Betrayal* as "an exquisite play, brilliantly simple in form and courageous in its search for a poetry that turns banality into a melancholy beauty."

Just ten days after expressing his views in the *New Statesman*, Nightingale reported on *Betrayal* (and Stoppard's *Night and Day*) again in the *New York Times*, echoing Kroll as he escalated his enthusiasm for both Pinter and Stoppard: "No British playwright presently stands higher than either Harold Pinter or Tom Stoppard in the stockmarket of taste"

("Have Pinter and Stoppard"). Noting that "both plays have had mark-edly more reserved reviews than either author is accustomed to receiv-ing," Nightingale wonders here, in the voice of the dissenting critics: "why is Mr. Pinter squandering his talent for ambiguity on the kind of drab triangle-drama that went out of fashion two decades ago?" He reiterates his "passionate" disagreement with "the bleaker notices," re-stating most of his previous arguments and concluding that "only the mentally snoozy" will find *Betrayal* "flat or dull."

Anthony Curtis (whose review appeared in the same issue of *Drama* as Hobson's possibly to balance the latter's "subjectivity," as discussed earlier) agrees with Nightingale on the whole. Despite the apparent "banalities" in *Betrayal*—"Never can the speech of an educated elite have been so impoverished" (47)—Pinter nevertheless provides "an undercur-rent of highly charged emotion that is almost Racinian." Curtis doubts "if the theatre has ever seen a greater master of dramatic inference than Pinter."[24]

In contrast to Nightingale, Kroll, and Curtis, while still maintaining Pinter's excellence as a playwright, in *Plays and Players* Esslin takes the "totally arid" emotional quality of the characters' relationships (par-ticularly "between the men and the woman") as "the point the play is making . . . by no means a trivial point . . . [but rather] central to the sickness of our society" ("Betrayal," 15). Esslin even faults the casting of "the infinitely more attractive Daniel Massey" in the role of the husband as against the less considerable "physical charm" of Michael Gambon, playing the lover, because it detracts from "the point of the play . . . that these people's lives, lacking human values, have been reduced to the casual operation of mechanical physical impulses."[25]

By the time the production moved from London on to New York, the "sphere of influence" on reviewing (its "intercontextuality") had become even more vastly complex. While Esslin had opened his review of *Be-trayal* wondering "Is this a new Pinter? A Pinter free from ambiguities and dream-like uncertainties, elaborate speeches with oblique reference points, a wholly realistic Pinter," Eleanor Blau entitled her preview, including interviews with Blythe Danner, Raul Julia, and Roy Scheider, members of the New York cast, and Peter Hall, its director (as in London), "Does 'Betrayal' Reveal a New Pinter?" (Blau echoes Esslin though she cites the play's producers as her source; Esslin may have been *their* source or vice versa.) In response to the claim that *Betrayal* is more *"accessible"* than Pinter's earlier works, Blau relates, Hall "shrugged at the report," retorting (perhaps unconsciously echoing Jerry's line to Emma "I don't think we don't love each other" [4:197]): " 'I don't think Pinter's plays are *in*accessible.' " Hall commented further: "The only way 'Betrayal' is more accessible than the others is that at the heart of every other Pinter play is a strange enigma, a puzzle. This one does not have an enigma. It is about betrayal."[26] Echoing earlier critics (and Pinter) once again, Hall added, "It is not simply about adultery. There is as much betrayal between the two men as between Emma and Robert." How complicated and elusive these influences can become is further shown when Sheila Benson, the film critic for the *Los Angeles Times*, alluding indirectly to Bennetts, misattributes a source, crediting *Pinter* with a description of *Betrayal* actually made by the film's producer, Sam Spiegel (Bennetts, "On Film," 23, as quoted below; cf. Benson, 2).

In reviewing the New York production of *Betrayal*, Robert Brustein stresses the coldness of Pinter's characters (as Russell Davies and John Barber did too) and the coldness of the play's irony, but he attributes this frigidity to Pinter himself: "Left-wing critics have criticized this play because the people are of such microscopic importance, but one doesn't have to be a Marxist to agree that Pinter has lavished considerable gifts on a situation of crashing triviality. For a few moments, I thought this might even be the point of his play—that overcivilized people, having lost the vocabulary of feeling, respond to emotional provocations with banalities and strategems [*sic*]. But the sangfroid belongs to the author as well." Despite his "cold admiration" for Pinter, Brustein allows *Betrayal* "importance largely as a lesson in dramaturgy" and offers "equally qualified" admiration for the production. He misses "the relevance of the text itself, the occasion for all this expertise, some evidence that Pinter was using his miniaturist genius to some significant purpose."[27]

My own impressions of the Broadway production of *Betrayal* support some New York critics' disappointment, particularly with the casting and the acting. Kroll considers the New York production unfortunate in several respects, including the acting, though (unlike Brustein) he approves of John Bury's "brilliant" set, considers Peter Hall "the Toscanini of Pinter directors," Pinter's dialogue "exquisite chamber music," and *Betrayal* "one of the best plays by the most significant voice in the English theater" ("Pinter's Dance"; cf. Hughes, "Betrayals"). While Brustein's more negative review of *Betrayal* could seem to be just one among several more "mixed" reviews in New York, it had unique consequences. Though Pinter has said that he is "pretty indifferent" to reviews (Farson,

"Reviews"), he was not indifferent to Brustein's. When it came time to choose which theater company would present the American premiere of *The Hothouse*, angered by Brustein's review of *Betrayal*, Pinter refused to give *The Hothouse* to his American Repertory Theatre, affiliated with Harvard University. Ultimately, it was produced by Adrian Hall's Trinity Square Repertory Company, resulting not only in Pinter's visit to Providence, Rhode Island, to work with the cast, and in his coincidental honorary doctorate from Brown University, but also in Trinity Square Rep's successful transfer of the production to Broadway.[28]

While these debates about the first London and New York stage productions of *Betrayal* heightened interest in its publication, as Donavin speculated about *Other Places*, the reception of the film of *Betrayal* revived interest in the play too. On its first screening in New York in February 1983, the film was received with great enthusiasm. Leslie Bennetts claims that "[t]he differences between play and movie consist primarily of texture: a shift of emphasis here, a more fully realized dimension there" ("On Film," 23). Though she quotes Pinter's assertion "It's the same work. Essentially I don't think it differs at all," Bennetts observes that "the medium has permitted [Pinter] to add some delicate touches to enhance certain facets less fully explored in the play," especially "the introduction of both sets of children, in some cases suggested off-screen and in some cases shown," which humanize the film.[29] As Brustein criticized Pinter's so-called sangfroid, David Jones, the film's director, argues that "the two men" in the Broadway production, Roy Scheider and Raul Julia, "were corseted by their attempt to handle the British accent, and they made the cardinal error of assuming that emotions which are subterranean don't exist at all. I found both of their performances very remote emotionally." According to Bennetts, transforming *Betrayal* to film enabled the English actors "to refine the subtleties of their performances." The "generally more favorable" reception of the film of *Betrayal* Rusinko attributes to the "fluidity" of the film medium, which avoids the "awkward and, perhaps, even gimmicky" effects of the play's time sequence when performed on stage (*Tom Stoppard*, 106).

Perhaps the most telling testimony of contextual sources for major differences between the play on stage and on film comes from its producer, Sam Spiegel, "a close friend of Mr. Pinter," who had but "limited enthusiasm for the play." Whereas, like Brustein, Spiegel felt " 'kind of indifferent' " to the play, which he regards as " 'basically about the mortality of love,' " " 'rather immoral,' " and " 'dangerously cynical,' " he considers the film as (in Bennetts' words) "less cynical and more moral than the play": according to Spiegel, "No matter how you look at it, all the emotions connected with love are not really immortal; like all other passions in life, they are bound to fade at some point. The trick is to convert love into some lasting friendship that overcomes the fading of passion. But that requires effort and an honest attitude on all parts, and since this was based on dishonesty, everyone betrayed the very nature of what love is about. That's why I thought it was a rather immoral piece." These differences between the play and the film were intentional: "I felt we should try to put the center of gravity in the film on human feelings rather than philosophical attitudes. I've never believed you could have art without morality; dramatic art is by definition a morality play. So we show more anguish than the play does. You didn't see the pain on the stage. It was glib; we removed the glibness from it. Once you see the people suffer during the period of their dishonesty, you give it the texture of a Greek tragedy. We didn't want people to shed tears when they saw this film. We wanted them to see it and say, 'There but for the grace of God; this could have happened to me, my best friend, my wife' " (quoted in Bennetts, "On Film," 23). That some of the film's audience members feel spared the fate of Pinter's characters, as Spiegel suggests, may be an emotional basis for the film's popularity, along with the highly acclaimed performances of Ben Kingsley (Robert), Jeremy Irons (Jerry), and Patricia Hodge (Emma).[30]

Vincent Canby, chief film critic for the *New York Times*, did not see the Broadway stage production, but he claims that "[d]espite its antecedents, 'Betrayal' is no filmed play. . . . this 'Betrayal' is a riveting film." In sum, Canby says, "I can't think of another recent film that is simultaneously so funny, so moving and so rigorously unsentimental. The writing is superb, and so quintessentially Pinter that it sometimes comes close to sounding like parody, though, in the entire screenplay, there's not one predictable line or gesture, the sort of thing that would expose the fake or the merely hackneyed. This is pure Pinter well served by collaborators" ("Film"). In a later review Canby describes the film *Betrayal* as "moving" and "immaculate," as "nothing less than the best screen translation yet of a Pinter piece written originally for the theater" ("Film View," 17, 18). "Though 'Betrayal' has a handsome, vaguely chilly look that is in keeping with the spare beauty of the Pinter dialogue," Canby considers it "an immensely moving film," raising its potentiality for "Oscar consideration" in 1984 (18).[31]

Recalling John Simon on both *No Man's Land* and *Betrayal* and some other negative reviews of stage productions of *Betrayal*, David Denby reverses Canby: "For much of *Betrayal*, the dramatic issue at hand is not adultery or betrayal or love but simply Pinter's ability to sustain his famous mood, his style, his ambience. His plays are stunts, and even the presence of a great actor like Kingsley can't alter their special nature. Seeing him in *Betrayal* makes one hungry not for more Pinter but for Shakespeare." Likewise, Lawrence O'Toole finds the characters in *Betrayal* "a tongue-tied triad" of "emotional zombies . . . who mean what they say but never say what they really mean"; echoing Denby's title "The Pause That Refreshes" (though their reviews appeared on the same day), O'Toole declares it "time for [Pinter] to reverse the process and find pauses that refresh rather than stretch patience."

The *Newsweek* film critic David Ansen (also on the same day) disagrees with both Denby and O'Toole: "[Kingsley's] is not just Pinteresque threat. Under the supercilious innuendo you see the inner bleeding, the sheer anguish of the man"; for Ansen the "rewards" of paying "close attention to what passes between people in a room . . . the signals— hidden, declared, inadvertent—of love and withdrawal and complicity" were "intoxicating" (74, 75). Against Brustein's complaints of the play's "sangfroid," Ansen describes the film as "emotionally rich, wickedly funny and devastatingly acute in its depiction of a painful, very English game of romantic musical chairs" (74).

Stanley Kauffmann explains another context for the contradictory evaluations of *Betrayal*, both on stage and on film, when he observes: "The tonal change in *Betrayal* from stage to screen has much less to do with the 'breaking open' of a stage work than with intensification of [the] high-comic style in middle-class London life" (23). Given the dwindling of the upper classes in English life and the proportionate growth of "an educated, reasonably affluent middle class," along with those Kauffmann terms "lesser English writers such as Tom Stoppard and Simon Gray," Pinter delineates the "gamesmanship" of "English high comedy": "many of the English middle class now conduct their lives and conversations with a style as formal and smoothly cruel and reticently affectionate and articulately witty as they can make it, based on upper-class paradigms— perhaps impelled by a quite English imperative to maintain elegance, to keep the social backbone arched. Pinter, preeminently among his colleagues, has perceived this social shift and writes high comedy about these middle-class people who, as far as their dailiness will permit, try to live their lives with high-comedy panache."[32] If variance in "subcultural" responses to features constituting such "high comedy" is great even among "English" audiences (as was demonstrated by Esslin's and Wardle's associations to Sidcup cited earlier), we can understand how many Americans, who may be more accustomed to emotional "honesty" (or veritable outbursts), would find the reticence of Pinter's English characters foreign ("culturally exotic," in Smith's phrase) and hence unacceptable; it might leave some Americans (like Brustein) "cold."

Finally, in another interview with Sam Spiegel, conducted by David Sterritt, the producer suggests "the influence of television" on moviegoers and their own role in the demise of "literate and intelligent entertainment" in America, such as the film of *Betrayal*. What people— including theater and movie critics—are *used to* seeing may affect their subsequent responses. If audiences can no longer "listen to dialogue" because they are "benumbed by the sound of crashing cars and shooting guns," it is unlikely that they will appreciate the "lure of language, the beauty and nuance of language" in work such as Pinter's.[33]

Whether the film *Betrayal* is "Pinter at his wicked best, having us on with his verbal pyrotechnics until the emotional truth explodes in our faces" ("Picks and Pans") or "an elaborately trite, mind-numbing trio for nonentities" (Arnold) has to do at least as much with contexts as with texts. Such contexts (as all those that I have been discussing) help to explain why Pauline Kael can find herself unable to "sit through" the same film that Michael Seitz exclaims "is as perfectly realized a motion picture as I've ever seen—tensely vibrant and consistently engaging," and why John Simon can "feel compelled to try to speed [*Betrayal*] on its way with a swift kick to the side it so proudly presents to us" ("Surfaces," 951).

### "Academic" Evaluations: Surveys, Handbooks, Guides, and General Introductions

It is quite common to encounter evaluations of Pinter as "the best dramatist writing in the English language today" in separate academic monographs and journal articles devoted to Pinter's work.[34] Such judgments, undoubtedly sincere and widely shared, nevertheless serve to legitimize critics' own endeavors. Surveys and handbooks of a more introductory nature should be impervious to such "intercontextual" influences, some might say. But Smith's theory suggests the opposite. "Intercontextualizing" reviews of Pinter's individual works suggests the need to situate larger claims of Pinter's "intrinsic" value as a playwright. Value judgments of an author made in more academic writing, such as introductory surveys of drama and dramatists or even more general literary handbooks, are supposed to *strive* for objectivity and somehow to *transcend* contextual "roots." Yet such writing is also the product of *people*, whose judgments resymbolize their personal and social experience.

The *Current Biography Yearbook 1963* entry for Harold Pinter describes the wave of "young writers" following John Osborne: "many of them from the working class," these writers "swept away the polite tradition of the 'well-made' play and filled English theaters with passionate discussion of moral and political issues, and every kind of technical experiment" (326). "In the forefront of this revolt," it continues, "is Harold Pinter, a former actor who is still in his early thirties." As I mentioned in chapter 8, like some criticism of *Betrayal* just cited, more recent judgments of Pinter qualify his "revolt" against "middle-class entertainments by middle-class writers" and point out Pinter's own entrance into the middle class and his current upper-class associations. Such a shift in Pinter's social and economic status clearly affects not only his own writing but others' evaluations of it. (For further discussion, see chap. 10.)

But other contexts, perhaps relating more directly to the critics themselves, may become "determinant factors" of their evaluations. Our knowledge of these contexts, in turn, influences how we read evaluations of Pinter. For example, knowing that Irving Wardle is the "I.W." contributing the essay on Pinter to the 1969 edition of *The Reader's Encyclopedia of World Drama* and that Wardle wrote "Comedy of Menace" and subsequent essays retracting this description of Pinter's work informs our reading of passages like this one, written by Wardle for the *Encyclopedia*: "Early in his writing career Pinter admitted to three influences: Franz Kafka, American gangster films, and Samuel Beckett. . . . At that time his plays, more than those of any other playwright's [*sic*], were responsible for the newly coined term 'comedy of menace.' This phrase certainly makes sense when applied to *The Birthday Party* . . . or to *The Dumb Waiter*. . . . But 'menace' is hardly the word for *The Caretaker*, and still less for subsequent plays in which Pinter increasingly exchanged his derelict settings and down-and-out characters for environments of moneyed elegance" (657–58). Whereas a reader who knows Wardle's previous writing on Pinter can perceive these repetitions of points that Wardle has already made elsewhere, another might regard the passage as novel. But a reader able to authorize Wardle's encyclopedic remarks on Pinter's "comedy of menace" might still regard them as more valuable than Myron Matlaw's second-hand observation that "the most striking quality of Pinter's plays is their evocation of terror. . . . that quality—allied with farcical dialogue and 'business'—which led reviewers aptly to dub Pinter's drama the 'comedy of menace' " (*Modern World Drama*, 606). Even our own value judgments of others' value judgments are contingent on such prior knowledge.

Similarly, it helps to know that Michael Anderson, the author of the entry on Pinter in *Crowell's Handbook of Contemporary Drama* (1971), went on to publish *Anger and Detachment* (1976), which includes an entire chapter on Pinter.[35] While in the earlier essay, Anderson echoes Wardle's *Encyclopedia* entry (also published by Crowell) when he states "Pinter has built up an international reputation that places him at the forefront of contemporary English dramatists," even in the early seventies Anderson knew enough about both the popular and critical reception of Pinter's plays to add that Pinter "has stimulated, in critic and theatergoer alike, a major reassessment of the relationship between dramatist, play, and audience" ("Pinter," in *Crowell's*, 351), a point that Wardle does not make. More advanced academic study enables Anderson to recognize that though "Pinter's role as an innovator has been frequently stressed," critics have emphasized "less . . . the steady personal development in theme and style that can be traced in his work and which invests the later plays with a quality quite different from that of the earlier work upon which most discussion of Pinter's technique has been based" and to acknowledge the transmutation of *The Homecoming*'s "overt violence of sexual aggression and surrender . . . into a compassionate understanding of male and female psychology" (*Crowell's*, 351, 355; cf. *Anger and Detachment*, 116, 97–98, 104–5, & 107–11).

Our knowledge of Anderson's own perspective and achievement may give his handbook evaluation of Pinter more clout than that of (for example) Kevin Gough-Yates, who may be less familiar, asserting that Pinter's "work achieves the effect of being casually written, but it hides a considered style which creates a feeling of tension between the characters, unequalled by any other contemporary playwright" (490). Yet this description approximates Anderson's view of "the clash between the surreal, unfamiliar nature of the action and the instantly recognizable, exact realism of the dialogue that imparts a unique flavor to Pinter's work" (*Crowell's*, 352).

We may wonder why some encyclopedia of literature do not offer revised assessments of an author like Pinter, though given plenty of time. The 1984 edition of one handbook still describes Harold Pinter as "technically the most adroit and accomplished of the young playwrights" even though, by then, he was nearing his midfifties (*Major Modern Dramatists*, 194). A 1986 volume of another still names Pinter as "perhaps the most established of the new dramatists" (*Reader's Adviser*, 104). Entries for Pinter in the 1972 and 1984 editions of the *McGraw-Hill Encyclopedia of World Drama* are much the same; biographical information includes only a small change to acknowledge Pinter's separation from Vivien Merchant and his subsequent marriage to Lady Antonia Fraser. The editors do not update the history of Pinter's writing or the production history of his work. The most noticeable differences between the editions are additional sections on *Old Times*, *No Man's Land*, and *Betrayal* and the inclusion of different photographs of the stage productions. Yet the lists of "Editions" of Pinter's plays and "Criticism" are barely expanded, omitting both the Methuen and the Grove Press collected works and books on Pinter written after 1979. Limitations on funds, problems with permissions, delays in publication, or even lack of serious interest on the part of editors may have contributed to the paucity of revisions.

Our earlier discussion of Pinter and politics (in chap. 8) may help contextualize Martin Seymour-Smith's changing evaluations in two accounts of Pinter published twelve years apart, in *Funk and Wagnalls Guide to Modern World Literature* (1973) and in *The New Guide to Modern World Literature* (1985). The first account follows a discussion of Arden, describing Pinter as "Arden's one genuine rival . . . who continues to write brilliantly original plays" and as "[w]ith Arden, stand[ing] head and shoulders above his contemporaries in the theatre" (265, 266). The revised account of Pinter also follows the discussion of Arden (and his collaborator and wife, Margaretta D'Arcy), with much the same transition: "Few approach the level of seriousness sought for here, although there are many skilful dramatists who can put together effective theatre pieces." But now Seymour-Smith describes Pinter as having written "several original plays before losing his gifts in the tedious labyrinth of theatrical politics. With Arden . . . Pinter stood head and shoulders above his contemporaries in the theatre. But since *The Homecoming* he has nothing to add, and new plays are self-parodic." Pinter has written "a number of screenplays for pretentious novels" and is "eminently professional," but, in this account, he is now merely "also" working "in the theatre" and is "now a predictably 'establishment figure' " who has "just announced that he is now 'politically committed.' " The grounds of these shifting opinions of Pinter suggest ideological influences perhaps, or those based on taste. Seymour-Smith's original expectations of Pinter as an avant-garde playwright may not have been fulfilled, or there may be a whole host of other explanations for the change. While a librarian or a teacher may not need to know these contexts in recommending (or not) one or both of Seymour-Smith's accounts to students or other readers, he or she could make more informed recommendations if aware of the changes between them.

When there are different contributors to such introductory essays, the difference of author may make an important difference in what is written. If we compare the essay on Pinter written by Tish Dace for St. Martin's *Dramatists* (1979) with that written by Lois Gordon for St. Martin's *Contemporary Dramatists* (1982), we can see that changes in Pinter's writing over time are not so significant as the change in who is writing about it. Dace applies a greater interest in women's issues. The passage "Pinter's vision is archetypically male. He epitomizes the view of woman as the Other, a figure to be desired and feared, venerated, reviled and, often, lost" introduces a paragraph analyzing several of Pinter's women characters (469–70). Gordon reprises and updates her earlier viewpoint expressed in *Stratagems* and defines "a new direction" in Pinter's work, extending the viewpoint of "Harold Pinter—Past and Present" (634–35).

*The Reader's Adviser* points out that "almost every one of [Pinter's] plays [is still] in print" but adds that Pinter "has eluded final critical definition," speculating that perhaps "[t]his last is not entirely the fault of the critics" (104). But if critics continue to try to "contain" Pinter's plays (as this "layman's guide" suggests that they failed to do with *The Homecoming*), then criticism will continually be "left behind" (105). If criticism is as contingent on contexts as Smith theorizes and as I have tried to substantiate here, so is any literature that it interprets and evaluates. Aiming to "contain" or to "get ahead" of literature subverts some of the customary relations between critics and other writers. Not merely does institutional evaluation function to "keep up with" new writing, it can stimulate, encourage, and sustain it. When critics try to *get ahead* of literary authors, or to displace them, they *compete* with them, possibly stimulating, possibly thwarting, or possibly having no impact at all on their development as writers. As critics recognize and participate in more collaborative and cooperative features of their enterprise, the contexts of evaluation, while remaining just as contingent, change. Such changes can affect the cultural production and reception of literature and criticism.

# 10

## The Case of Pinter: Toward Theory as Practice

## in Critical and Cultural Change

GUARD. Tell her she can speak in her own language. New rules. Until further notice. — *Mountain Language*

Beginning with "progress" in Pinter studies (or a purported lack of it), chapter 1 cited Ralph Cohen's "Propaedeutic on Literary Change" and Stephen Jay Gould's various warnings against certain biases in our notions of natural evolution. Cohen suggests that "change can be seen only against continuity" (2), that "continuities and discontinuities" are systematically explained by critics who construct these explanations (or "fictions") from particularized viewpoints (4–5), and that, as "it is the nature of literary structures that change and persistence are present together . . . [t]he kinds of relations between them account for the kinds of changes critics identify" (6). Gould cautions against construing change in deterministic and gradualistic terms as occurring in "stately, logical stages" and as coherent adaptations with clearly definable causes, marching higher and higher up the "ladder" of "progress."

Presenting Pinter criticism as a case study in critical change and following Cohen and Gould, we have assumed that certain "systems" and "structures" of Pinter criticism form the stability against which we can perceive change in this field. We have been examining some particular strategies of Pinter critics, defining some stabilities and innovations. Various personal and social contexts of continuities and discontinuities in Pinter criticism suggest a framework for critical and cultural change.

### Change

"The pursuit of inquiries into literary change," Cohen also observes, "has an element of the unpredictable" ("Propaedeutic," 5). Some might have predicted that in an essay on "change" reprising some issues already discussed by Cohen (though not citing him), Stanley Fish would defend his own notion of "interpretive communities," originally offered to resolve the question of whether "the source of interpretive authority" lies in "the text or the reader" (423/141).[1] Temma Berg perceives a radical shift in Fish's work, concluding that in his more recent theoretical writing "[t]he interpretive community is . . . at once the mechanism of stability and the mechanism of change" (255–59, 258).

In "Change" Fish defines "the idea of an interpretive community" as "not so much a group of individuals who shared a point of view, but a point of view or way of organizing experience that shared individuals in the sense that its assumed distinctions, categories of understanding, and stipulations of relevance and irrelevance were the content of the consciousnesses of community members who were therefore no longer individuals, but, insofar as they were embedded in the community's enterprise, community property" (423–24/141). As Fish describes "the mind (and, by extension, the community)" as "an engine of change" (429/146) and various "parties now contending for control of the literary profession's machinery" as struggling to "turn the theory [of interpretive communities] to most advantage (440/156), he first obscures and then spotlights the human dimension of change.[2]

Chapter 2 discussed Fish's view that criticism as persuasion is superior to criticism as demonstration because the former produces changes in institutional practices, even in the institution of criticism itself. After taking Culler to task in "Demonstration vs. Persuasion" for what Fish calls Culler's failure to effect large institutional change, in "Change" Fish cites again Culler's claim that "theoretical inquiry leads to 'changes in assumptions, institutions, and practice'" as exemplifying "an article of faith held by theorists and antitheorists alike," but now he would dispute "[t]hese large claims" (437/154; see 444/567 nn. 10 and 11). He has changed his priorities: in "Change" Fish argues that "a *theory* of change, complete with criteria and a predictive formula" is "impossible." "It becomes increasingly obvious," he says now, "that there could be no such theory and that change is something that does or does not occur in particular institutional situations where this or that set of already-in-place concerns can (but not *must*) lead to the noticing and taking into account of an open-ended, although not infinite, range of phenomena" (437/153). He even claims further a bit later on that though "a theory does cause change since it will give rise to controversy and lead to the calling of symposia, and the founding of journals, and the funding of chairs" (all conditions pertaining to Fish's own recent professional experience), "these are the consequences of any practice that can be identified and imitated: they are not consequences that can be described as revolutionary or groundbreaking" (439/155).[3] He has already asserted: "The answer to the question 'what can cause change?' is 'anything,' although in a specific situation 'anything' will be qualified by the structure of relevancy the situation displays: everything cannot be noticed at every moment. It would seem that if change can be understood at all, it is only in the context of a historical reconstruction of its empirical conditions and not in the context of any (impossible) general account" (437/153).

But anything *and anyone* can cause change. In disavowing the "free" agency of individual members of interpretive communities in these communities' operation and effects, Fish overcompensates by obliterating the humanity and the original and imaginative contributions of these members to change. Working from particular examples, later we may be able to classify somewhat more precisely what and who cause change.

Just prior to interrogating "the relationship between the theory of interpretive communities and change," Fish observes (vaguely echoing Cohen): "Theory is a form of practice, as rooted in particular historical and cultural conditions as any other, and, as in the case of any other, the extent to which its introduction will or will not give rise to changes, small and large, cannot be determined in advance" (439/156). While Fish denies that his theory of interpretive communities has "political implications built into [it]," he does admit that there are "political consequences of having the theory as a resource": "It is undoubtedly the case that the practice of professing interpretive communities will, like any other practice, participate in the ongoing modification of the enterprise, but the shape and the extent of that participation are not predictable because the relationship between the emergence of a theory and change is not theoretical" (440/156–57). In presenting his nontheory of change, Fish refers to new historiographical assumptions that "forbid the discovery of a pattern too regular or too rational" so as to produce another "story" of change—what Berg calls the "uncanniness of the conversion process"—focusing on its abruptness as well as its discontinuousness (442/158; cf. Berg, 259). Yet, as Fish astutely points out, "In all of these cases, and in any others that can be imagined, a theory of change is inscribed in the self-description that at once directs and renders intelligible the characteristic labors of workers in the community."[4]

Setting aside for a moment the question of the "political implications" of this nontheory, however, we can well imagine the practical consequences of theoretical positions when those making them (like Fish himself) occupy positions of power and influence within social institutions like academe (see Fish's own example on 428–29/145–47, discussed below). It is currently fashionable to label one of these consequences "hegemony." In "Change" (and later writings) Fish himself reflects (as he reflects on) and recreates (as his argument is created by) "the level" of change that the current "hegemony of theory" has been having on literary studies. He disputes the claims of "those who either see [theory] as the means of salvation or fear it as the subverter of values" (439/155)—what he elsewhere calls "theory hope" and "theory fear" (see *DWCN*).

The rhetoric in "Change" recalls recent claims that we do not write texts so much as they write us. The personifications are strikingly innovative (and fashionable) metaphors that reverse the agency commonly granted to human beings so as to favor doing what critics enjoy doing most: textualizing all experience; they mark what I would term "textual hegemony" (a hegemony of the text). Fish's strategy renders both texts and readers "functions" of all-powerful (authoritative) communities. Of course, as Fish says, "everything cannot be noticed at every moment," but, in my view, this does not warrant theoretically obscuring and reifying (making a thing of) human beings as, in Fish, individuals become the "property" of some community (424/141) or "no more than sets of institutional practices" (436/153).

Attributing agreement to "the communal nature of the interpretive act" (as opposed to congruities among individual readers and "the self-identity of the text"), Fish abrogates the individual contributions of each member (each author, each reader; each text) to the achieved consensus. This "new vision" of how rival interpretive communities settle disputes about texts, Fish claims, resolves the question of whether the reader or the text is responsible for interpretive disagreements and agreements by revealing such disputes to be about "the interpretive 'angle'" from which texts are construed (and constructed) and not about texts or readers (424/142). "In this new vision," he says, "both texts and readers lose the independence that would be necessary for either of them to claim the honor of being the source of interpretive authority; both are absorbed by the interpretive community which, because it is responsible for all acts interpreters can possibly perform, is finally responsible for the texts those performances bring into the world." But this "resolution" of the problem of interpretive authority is another instance of theoretical engulfment, an intellectual version of the early computer game Pac Man; community agency and responsibility gobble up human agency and responsibility, virtually annulling them. To vary the metaphor, Fish lets each critic (including himself) off the hook. Fish's discussion of "responsibility" (439–40/156) does not address the question that I am raising here: To what degree are individuals (not simply conventions) responsible for their interpretations?

Recognizing that individual people empirically make up the theoretical "interpretive communities" readmits individual human agency and responsibility into theories of interpretation and evaluation and change. Such individuals change their minds in the context of their particular experiences within actual communities. Though it is tempting to generalize about "the" community of Pinter scholars and critics, even this dual reference to "scholars and critics" indicates the plurality of communities to which each of us belongs and in whose context we function. Our individual aims interact with our social responsibilities as critical readers and writers, because, even though we may be members of various interpretive communities and practitioners of a variety of conventions and practices, as people, we still act as individuals. *We* are responsible for what we choose to do and say; however forceful our shared interpretive assumptions, beliefs, and practices, we also have an important kind of behavioral control: we must choose among them. We are simultaneously both "free" and "constrained"; though free to act according to our beliefs, wishes, and fears, they operate as "internal" constraints on this freedom (cf. Fish, "Force," in *DWCN*, 517–22).

Though Fish says that an interpretive "angle" delimits an interpretive community, any writer's interpretive angle is substantially enough different from another's to merit making distinctions between their points of view. It is misleading, for example, to say that two critics (say, Gale and Burkman or Esslin and Gabbard) are "thematic," "ritual," or "psychoanalytic" critics, if any communal interpretive "angularity" suggests agreement belying disagreements in their interpretations of discrete elements of a text or a textual experience. Critics with the "same" angle of vision may not only perceive different themes and imagery but their aims and goals in analyzing what they see may differ markedly. Moreover, as these critics have demonstrated in their evaluations of *The Lover*, the "thematic," "ritual," or "psychoanalytic" angle may not explain much about their divergent evaluative judgments of the same play. Knowing the conventions of their interpretive practices cannot enable us to predict what their evaluations will be with any degree of probability. A predictive "theory of change" is "impossible" because *people* have "angles," and *they* "do things with/to texts" unpredictably.

Despite the consequences of an epistemological shift to a constructivist view that reality is not independent of our descriptions of it (Fish, "Change," 426/143–44), as Pinter has emphasized in talking about *One for the Road*, there is still "only one reality" to describe. We all live palpably in the world about which we "discourse," even if we would describe what we perceive from different angles or in terms of different metaphors. (Contrary to popular academic opinion, discourse is not all. Some of us merely make it seem so.) Though Fish must be aware that even members of an interpretive community adjudicate competing interpretations of "pieces of the world," he weighs the operation of that whole as more than the operations of its parts, since he accords greater priority to his notion of community than to the individual members of it (427–30/144–47).

Interpretive change does occur in the *context* of community (cf. Cohen, "Propaedeutic," 2). But beliefs do not change so much as, in a variety of contexts, people who "hold" beliefs change and change them—that is, people change their minds (how and what they think)—and allow their minds to be changed (or, at least say that they do). To vary Bleich's view that (in Holland's words) "Texts do not, after all, have fantasies—people do" (Holland, "Letter," 22): communities do not, after all, have beliefs—the people constituting them do. Contra Fish, beliefs do not share people, people share beliefs. Fish's "new" view reverses the direction of a dead metaphor; however striking this enlivening reversal, it is nonetheless still merely a novel manner of speaking; not a fact, but a (re)construction of a fact. Both active (agents) and passive (acted upon) in change (persuasion), individual people *make* change (whether acting "alone" or in groups). However we redraw or reconceptualize the "outside"/"inside" distinctions that Fish calls "misleading" (431/148), we must still consider the "site" of the change in critical beliefs and practices (and in discourse)—*people* (Holloway). Fish's account (or nonaccount) of change also devalues how people's *experiences* figure in such change. As in his earlier theory where affective (personal) experience became "affective stylistics" ("literature in the reader" as a construct, or *something* else), now Fish represses individual human psychology further, favoring "the new historiography" (442/158) and "New Historicism," perhaps even moving beyond "post-contemporary interventions" toward "post-history."

Even if Fish does negotiate the "impasse" created by his conception of "persons not as free agents, but as extensions of interpretive communities" (435/152)—the incapacity of such communal operations to allow for change—he does so at a great loss. If "the very notion of change" requires, as Fish quotes Robert Nisbet as saying, " 'some object[,] entity or being the identity of which persists through all the successive differences' " (436/152–53)—persistence, in Cohen's word—then critical change requires persistence and difference in the "beings" called critics. The change in every critical practice implies a change in some critical person(s).[5] Despite a conventional reluctance among writers to "retract" published viewpoints, people do announce a change of previous critical position—like Fish's "new" belief in the priority of interpretive communities. Were Fish someday to retract his theory of interpretive communities, he would have to find new terms in which to interpret this change as consistent with his newer "angle," whose angularity might (or might not) be the persisting feature (see Fish, "Force," in *DWCN*, 518–19).

If it "can be understood at all," Fish would understand change "only in the context of a historical reconstruction of its empirical conditions" ("Change," 437/153). Any such reconstruction involves the experiences, feelings, beliefs, aims, goals, and other contexts (assumptions, expectations, interests, affiliations, and so on) of the persons whose work constitutes the "objects" or "entities" through which both change and continuity or persistence are being substantiated and of the persons doing the reconstructing. Fish concludes that "the members of a community will always believe in the ends for which they work" (444/160). But, in arriving at this conclusion, he shows too little concern for an important question: What causes people to change or to persist in these beliefs and ends?

In part and in the context of competition for critical dominance, people often persist in or change their minds as a result of their responses to personal, social, and professional success and failure and the attendant rewards and penalties. The case of Pinter, of Pinter critics discussed here, demonstrates that such success and failure (rewards and penalties) enable both persistence and change. Some of the critics whom I have interviewed or whose work I have considered otherwise have persisted in their beliefs and practices when they have been rewarded (for their writings); others have shifted these when their writings have not been rewarded and in a variety of ways they have been penalized. More complexly, sometimes when a critic *perceives* some personal or professional rejection in response to his or her beliefs and practices, the critic has changed them; whereas, other times, despite (or because of) such a perception of failure, the critic has persisted. And some critics have changed their views and viewpoints despite former success. Persistence and change in these matters may depend at least as much on the personal temperamental proclivities and professional institutional contexts of particular individuals and on these individuals' reactions as on the "machinery" of some interpretive community as an "engine of change."

Like Fish I would not proceed from these generalizations to a formulaic or predictive "theory of change." I would emphasize the unpredictable features of human experience (both "individual" and "social") that resist such formulation. Though in "Change" Fish gives some privilege to unpredictability and uncertainty (" 'I don't know' " [440/156]), his rhetoric (*machinery, engine of change*) otherwise camouflages human sources of these conditions of our "knowledge." Ironically he even contradicts his claim of "unpredictability"—"I venture to predict" (443/159). "Critical Self-Consciousness" also equates change with persuasion (*DWCN*, 463), again refusing deliberately "to speak in the language of prediction or of (assured) cause and effect" (to resist the "temptation to conceive of persuasion [change] as either too regular or too rational") (461). At first Fish's rhetoric here seems to account for the human factor: "One simply cannot tell in advance what will work a change in someone's views; and the range of possible change-producing agencies extends far beyond formal argumentation to include family crises, altered financial circumstances, serious illness, professional disappointment, boredom, and so on, ad infinitum," but the final *ad infinitum* undercuts it.[6]

Elsewhere in "Change" Fish touches on a human factor relevant to my own experience (which I will recount shortly). Here Fish considers "the puzzle of individual change: how can someone whose perceptions and judgments are delimited by the norms, criteria, and definitions of an interpretive community take note of anything that would lead him to revise those norms, criteria, and definitions? How can a mind that cannot see anything outside its horizon change?" (427/144–45). To argue that "the mind is, in fact, able to take into account something not already presupposed by its assumptions" would result in "enfeebling (and indeed emptying) the notion of an interpretive community," but the idea that "the mind remains forever confined within the circle of community assumptions" would require "the (counterintuitive) conclusion that no one has ever changed his mind." To "escape" each alternative, though not acknowledging so, Fish must deal with *not community conventions but individual relationships*. He focuses particularly on one such relationship: his own role as an instructor as a "stimulus" to a graduate student's change to "conventionalist views" (428/145). (Fish does not define what the student changed his mind from.) While disclaiming that the student was stimulated to change his mind by "the mere fact of my position as instructor," Fish does consider various "circumstances" in which "change, in the form of the reconsideration of received opinion, would be prompted by a suggestion that came from a source assumed in advance to be, if not authoritative, at least weighty" (428–29/145–46). Though Fish moves on to make another argument about how beliefs are "nested" or in hierarchies, I want to stop here to present another perspective on Fish's account of the student's change.

Fish alludes to the student's own personal assessment of Fish's authority as fuel in this particular "engine of change." The student's feelings about Fish as an authoritative source of change signal how personal and professional relationships between individuals such as Fish and Fish's student structure substantive critical change, even within a larger "interpretive community," in this case Fish's class. Particularly, what are the effects of the student's position as a member of a graduate seminar—"a highly defined and hierarchical situation" (429/146)—whose performance would ultimately be evaluated by Fish? Changing students' minds (persuading them) operates within this context of reward/penalty (desire/fear). Again, such change often implies success and/or failure. Teachers cannot be certain whether or not students have actually changed their minds for the purpose and duration of a class or in some larger and more lasting way. The affective and intellectual dimensions of individual experience within social relationships crucially affect both this change and interpreting and evaluating it (just as such dimensions are at work/play in my discussion of Fish on change).

Though he may have been able to do so, apparently Fish did not return to the particular student after the class in question to *ask* him what *he* himself thinks has led to his change of mind (or how long the change lasted); on the basis of the in-class discussion and perhaps other information not specified, Fish, as the instructor (practitioner) turned theorist, suggests that he can tell us. Apparently, members of Fish's interpretive community talk to each other long enough to change their minds, but they do not continue talking to work out together an interpretation of what may have caused the change.

Did Fish subsequently contact the student to learn the latter's own point of view on such a change? Or did he simply guess on his own? The lack of reference to an ongoing dialogue suggests the dissolution of the interpretive community; it even suggests that this so-called community was not composed of *shared* assumptions, beliefs, and so on (as Fish has defined this concept) so much as it constituted a relationship of power in which one "source of interpretive authority" (the instructor, Fish) "enlightened" a less authoritative person (the unnamed graduate student-teacher). Perhaps in Fish's terms, until the student came to think as Fish did, they did not belong to the same interpretive community. Or perhaps Fish and the student never constituted an interpretive community at all; the student was merely a member of Fish's class, euphemistically termed a "community." A factor in the difference between Fish's and his student's relationships with their classes that Fish does not name is *self-confidence*. This attitude is personal, not simply conventional.

Throughout his recent writing Fish seems to regard *theory* as "[s]ystematically organized knowledge applicable in a relatively wide variety of circumstances; especially, a system of assumptions, accepted principles, and rules of procedure devised to analyze, predict, or otherwise explain the nature or behavior of a specified set of phenomena," and as "[s]uch knowledge or such a system distinguished from experiment or practice." I would place in the foreground *theory*'s less scientific, more humanistic senses: "Abstract reasoning; speculation" and "Broadly, hypothesis or supposition." More archaically, recalling the classical senses of *theōria*, *theōros*, *theasthai*, and *thea*—signifying (respectively) "contemplation, theory," "spectator," "to observe," and "a viewing" ("see *theater*")—my ideas about change derive from both observation and speculation: my observation of what Pinter and his critics have done so far and, in some cases with their help, my speculation about why they have persisted or changed how they have done it.[7]

### Dramatic Change: The Case of Pinter

Irving Wardle has recalled that when he first encountered Pinter's plays in the late fifties and early sixties, he had no idea that Pinter would become as "big, especially as big a commercial success" as he did.[8] At first, Wardle had thought Pinter to be a "second-string" playwright and had not expected the huge success that Pinter became, on television, when he developed not only an elitist audience but also a mass audience. In 1964

Wardle wrote, "it is one of the ironies of the theatrical boom that [Pinter] should have bypassed the period of dedicated obscurity of the minority writer and become a popular success" ("Revolt," 32). In the later sixties, Wardle reminisced, it became fashionable to laugh knowingly at Pinter's dialogue. Wardle also felt "personally" that Pinter's plays have gotten less important as his characters have gotten more monied.[9]

Academic discussions of Pinter's "thematic progression," if they notice changes in Pinter's own socioeconomic status at all, tend to glance away from their pertinence to Pinter's playwriting.[10] Yet as these changes have led to Pinter's increasing involvement in social and political issues, as discussed in chapter 8, they are significant contexts of changes in Pinter's plays from *The Room* through *Mountain Language*.[11] Such contexts illuminate the artistic choices that a writer like Pinter makes at different times in his life. As we noticed also in chapter 8, Elizabeth Sakellaridou cautiously speculates that Pinter's relationship with Lady Antonia Fraser stimulated a change in his perspective on his women characters and on their relationships with men. The Pinter-Fraser marriage and Pinter's assimilation to a wealthy, cosmopolitan society distance him even further from his own working-class, Jewish background, which seems to intervene less directly in his more recent plays than it did in earlier ones. Changing social relationships and changing socioeconomic and political circumstances affect both literary and critical writing. These factors deserve prominence in any theory or nontheory of change.

### Critical Change—My Own Case

When I say "the case of Pinter," I also mean "the case of Pinter criticism"; our critical interventions in "Pinter" have become our only road to knowing "him." Most particularly, I mean "my own case": my own experience as a student and critic of Pinter and Pinter criticism. How and why I started to become interested in Pinter's work, in Pinter the man, in responses to Pinter, in Pinter criticism, and in critical theory is a case of critical change that I know firsthand. In my own case my interest in Pinter began in 1967, after I had attended separate performances of two plays in New York, several months apart—*The Homecoming* and *The Birthday Party*. It is possible that I would have done nothing in response to these experiences—powerful as they had been—if I had not also been enrolled at the same time (1967–68) in a graduate seminar in Modern Drama at Indiana University, Bloomington. This institutional and professional context led me to propose to my professor, Harry Geduld, that I write the essay on Pinter's women characters cited in chapter 8. Though Pinter was not an author then included in the course, Geduld, like Pinter, is a Jew from the East End of London, and, aware of Pinter's growing importance, he welcomed my seminar project. (Geduld himself published a review of *The Birthday Party* and *Accident* for *Humanist* that spring.) I enjoyed Geduld's class; he was an authoritative teacher, and I felt that he appraised my work fairly. Though he ultimately became a member of my dissertation committee, he was not as decisive a factor in my "critical change" as David Bleich became.

I first encountered Bleich in 1966 (his first year as an assistant professor and my first year as a graduate student), when, along with several other instructors in the Indiana University English department, we had participated in an experiment in evaluating student essays without grades. In 1968 I experienced his developing "reader-response" teaching approach through his visit to a no-credit seminar on Swift in which several of my graduate-student colleagues and I participated. (He was one of a few junior faculty members invited as instructors.) For this class Bleich circulated our reading responses to some of Swift's "scatological poems," prepared in advance according to his "Guidelines for Respondents," as revised later in *Readings and Feelings* (11–15). (He analyzes the responses of one member of our seminar, "Mr. G.," in *SC*, 287–91.) This was the first time that I had been asked to present my "emotional" responses to what I read for a class, and although doing so induced great anxiety in me at the time, I came to appreciate this experience later, as it served as a basis for my subsequent discussions with Bleich about my dissertation, for my own reader-response teaching, and, to some degree, for this book. Eventually, I was persuaded—my mind changed—from the New Critical dogma to reader-oriented critical views.

Coincidentally, for a two-week summer term later in 1968, I was assigned to teach as an intern in a fairly conventional freshman literature course taught by Bleich. (He was not yet applying his reader-response approach in his courses in the English department.) Later, he asked me about my plans for my dissertation. As I had already told other professors who had offered to direct my dissertation, I told him that I was sure that I wanted to write on Pinter's plays but I had not yet chosen an approach. None of the New Critical "angles" with which I was familiar and from which I had accumulated pages of notes—my analyses of game motifs and other themes and images, such as "the grotesque"—satisfied me as an explanation of Pinter's plays.[12] Bleich had recently finished teaching a graduate seminar in the Comparative Literature department on "Responses to the Absurd," which included *The Caretaker* (see Bleich, "Emotional Origins"), and so he already regarded Pinter from a reader-response perspective. Eager to direct his first dissertation, he intervened more directly in my work than any of the others "courting" my dissertation: he asked to see my notes. I gave them to him, and we met for a couple of hours to discuss what he thought of them. He said that it was a simple matter: separating my notes into two parts (textual patterns and my ideas), he gestured to each—"This is the stimulus and this is the response."

Bleich patiently encouraged me to learn his "angle" at my own pace. I read Holland's *Dynamics of Literary Response* and debated its premises with Bleich over a long lunch. Stimulated by this discussion, I continued reading psychoanalytic literary criticism. In the fall of 1970 I formally proposed that Bleich direct my study of (as then entitled) "The Pinter Experience: Disguised Play in a Theater of Excessive Reality," later writing the prospectus for "Fantasy behind Play," my psychoanalytic investigation of my own and others' "emotional responses" to *The Birthday Party*, *The Caretaker*, and *The Homecoming*. After its approval I spent approximately three months reading Freud and other psychoanalytic literature and criticism before embarking on several more months of rereading Pinter's plays and recording my responses to them (an order of events that may explain psychoanalytic imagery in my free associations; cf. Gabbard, as cited in chap. 6).

In 1970–71, when I started accumulating and typing up these responses and retyping my interpretive essays on the three plays, Bleich was on leave from Indiana. At the end of the summer that he returned, I left Bloomington for the "real world." All of our subsequent consultations about the project were done via my lengthy letters and his pithy telephone calls. Nevertheless, he was very explicit about how I could "interpret" my own free associations and guided my "psychoanalysis" of these "response-texts" with a strong hand. When at first I could not "see" any pattern in my free associations to *The Birthday Party*, for example, he enabled me to identify "the reliving of a fantasy in which I discover that I am anatomically and emotionally a girl, the feminine version of 'castration fantasy'—the discovery that I have been 'castrated' " ("Fantasy behind Play," 238; cf. 506–7). This hermeneutically circular (I see now) psychoanalytic fantasy and my variety of intellectual defenses against it (see, e.g., my recurrent fear of having to *cut* the *length* of my dissertation [cf. 306, 321–22]) became the "key" to my responses to all of the plays (what I called the "odd man out" syndrome, playing on the allusion to the film of that title in *Old Times*), and to relations between my free associations and my interpretive essays on the plays and between these "meaning-statements" and published criticism by others.

During the same period of time that I was doing my dissertation (1969–73)—which ultimately did turn out to be exceptionally long (570 pages)—I was adjusting to my first marriage and my first full-time teaching position. The two men central to my life, my former husband and Harold Pinter, competed for my attention, with the latter often winning. My own recognition of this competition and its related phenomenon—"falling in love" with Pinter—appears in my dissertation acknowledgments, where I allude to "my involvement with 'that other man' in our life" (ii).

This account of "choosing" a dissertation topic, an approach, and a director illustrates a phenomenon whose importance is too often ignored: the influence of a "weighty" authority figure (such as Fish or Bleich or Pinter)—to persuade, to change minds, to teach something new—depends on far more personal and affective, more social and interactive factors than what Fish specifies in his notion of "interpretive community" in "Change." As I have suggested, Fish's own example of the student who changed to Fish's "conventionalist views" does not establish precisely enough what these other more human factors are. As Fish might agree, one cannot predict from any general formulation of a particular experience like mine which dissertation director would be "best" to choose or even how to choose well. One cannot predict what would have happened had I chosen differently. A lot depends on personal, professional, and other social circumstances. It happened as it did given the personalities and situations of everyone involved, our persistence, and the requirements of the graduate school, but not just given simply (as Fish says) "anything" or even (as I have modified him) "anything and anyone." There were specific kinds of things and people effecting my critical change to a new "interpretive community."

Another important influence on my own developing reader-response approach to Pinter was another text (i.e., in addition to Holland's *Dynamics*): Gordon's *Stratagems to Uncover Nakedness*. Even before I read *Stratagems*, one of my first impulses in formulating a topic for my dissertation was to analyze the games that Pinter's characters play. As

Gordon observes, "Pinter evokes a perplexing variety of emotional responses from his audience" (5). "Fantasy behind Play" extends Gordon's thesis that the "word games" or "patterned words" of Pinter's characters serve as their "habitual stratagems to cover nakedness," hiding their "primitive and repressed feelings" (3, 5), to Pinter's audiences and critics. Literary and critical theory as well as Pinter criticism read since 1973 informs the game metaphor that I apply, scrutinize, and put "under erasure" in this book. [13]

At the 1987 MLA Convention special session "How My Mind Has Changed," all three speakers (Elaine Showalter, Robert Scholes, and Richard Ohmann) named resistance to change as a powerful influence on their ongoing work. I first encountered significant resistance to my reader-response approach in 1972, in my first full-time teaching post, at the University of Hartford. My first department chairman role-played a "touchy-feely" student to test the limits of the methodology that I was presenting at a departmental faculty retreat, which functioned as a kind of initiation rite. Several years later the next chairman objected to an aspect of my teaching approach when I presented it to a departmental faculty forum; as I discussed relations between emotional responses to literature and interpretations of it, he interjected: "But emotions are not as important as ideas." My reply to this objection was that *both* are important and that we must understand their interrelations.

While I was encountering such professional resistance to change, I recalled David Bleich's warning that if I chose to pursue this approach, life would not be easy. Instead of being daunted (in retrospect, as far as professional expediency goes, perhaps foolishly), I felt challenged. I persisted in a reader-response approach, both in my teaching and in my scholarship, because I believed in its value. Despite various professional obstacles, I have continued to refine this approach in relation to more recent critical, rhetorical, and pedagogical theory.

In my last year at the University of Hartford (1978–79), after negative tenure decisions concerning me and the three others hired along with me in 1972 were faits accomplis, the chairman who had questioned the importance of "emotions" in literary experience stopped me in the hall to tell me that he had been talking about his and his students' emotional responses to their reading in one of his classes—and that he and they were enjoying doing this. Entirely how this "change" in attitude came about I do not know; I doubt that it resulted from *my* authority as directly as Fish's explanation would suggest. The psychic and social "mechanisms" through which such "reaction-formations" occur seem more complex than that: once the chairman no longer perceived me and my reader-orientation as threats (now that both I and it were being expunged), perhaps he could dispose of both me and it more fairly and humanely and even graciously from his position of "superior authority."[14]

Another crucial change in my work on Pinter and my critical perspective in general resulted from my participation in New Directions in Literary Study, a Summer Seminar sponsored by the National Endowment for the Humanities and taught by Ralph Cohen at the University of Virginia in 1978. Like Bleich, though in quite different ways, Cohen is a powerful presence in the classroom, and my experience in his seminar exerted a decisive influence not only on my understanding of critical methodologies but on me personally too. Relevant to Cohen's impression on me and my work was the timing of the seminar—the summer before my "terminal year" at the University of Hartford. I had plunged into this new work with great zest, in search of a meaningful alternative to my recent past rejection.

My dissertation proposal had not been approved unanimously by the departmental Graduate Study Committee. The one dissenter—a professor who had wanted to direct my dissertation on another topic and who was unsympathetic to Bleich's approach—questioned "[h]ow well trained" I was "in analyzing defense mechanisms in published analyses of drama critics." Later, while I was still writing the thesis, a conversation with Bernard Kaplan, a distinguished psychology professor at Clark University, led me to wonder whether I could indeed differentiate between emotional responses to fantasies and intellectual defenses against such responses—a crucial aspect of my approach adapted from Bleich's revision of Holland. As a result of my experience in Cohen's seminar, I became even more skeptical of my former speculations about what other critics thought and felt. With this greater skepticism I also began to view a "psychoanalytic methodology" as just one of any number of possible critical approaches and to achieve a broader perspective on it. Having studied Derrida, Lacan, Heidegger, Gadamer, Foucault, and Kosík (among several other theorists) with Cohen, I decided to try to place Pinter criticism in the context of current literary and critical theory. In 1980–81, while teaching at Assumption College, in Worcester, Massachusetts, I conceived the present project, applying for a fellowship from the NEH to support it.[15]

If personal and social circumstances and contexts have as much to do with critical choices and changes as Bleich, Cohen, Smith, and Fish (among many others) suggest they do, then the opportunity of a research grant was a special occasion for such change. The announcement that the NEH would support travel for research and consultation with other scholars led to a "brainstorm" (my own "Aha!" experience) that eventually became a core of this project: the consultations would be personal interviews with scholars and other critics (including several journalists and some actors and directors) to improve my understanding of why others interpreted Pinter's work as they did. The NEH travel funds presented the opportunity for a "new" methodology related to reader-response criticism and teaching but different from it. I had kept a response journal, written response essays and critical interpretations, and analyzed these texts of responses to literature by myself and others in doing the dissertation directed by Bleich and in eight years of teaching. Now I traveled to the critics themselves and directly asked them questions about their experiences of and writing on Pinter's plays. Through the interviews with the Pinter scholars I learned from them firsthand the contexts for their publications, finding out what *they* thought were the sources of their own critical choices and changes, much as a journalist, a biographer, or an ethnographer would do. Aside from this critical "angle," the conjunction of the NEH seminar with Cohen and the subsequent yearlong NEH fellowship opportunity (and the depressed market for college teachers throughout the eighties) led me to persevere: to relate what I already knew about Pinter criticism and other responses to his work to some of the theoretical questions on which Cohen had centered the seminar— what is literature? what is criticism? what are the social relations between literature and criticism?

Even the political situation of the NEH at the time that I applied in 1981 was a factor in my own critical change, for, unlike more recently, the agency was receptive to projects dealing with critical theory. Though Congress was threatening both National Endowments with severe cuts, announcing a possible rescission of awarded funds, these did not actually materialize, and my project was funded as well as approved. I began work in June 1982.

The fall of 1982 brought changes in my personal and professional situation—a marital separation leading to an eventual divorce (1984) and various new environments and affiliations (1983 to the present)—that furthered my interest in change. During academic year 1981–82 I had participated in a yearlong training program in academic management,

Project-HERS (Higher Education Resource Services) at Wellesley College, in which forty women academic administrators and professors consulted with one another and seminar leaders from a variety of academic and nonacademic disciplines on how to improve their careers. In Fall 1982 I attended "Change," a daylong workshop sponsored by the Massachusetts Association for Women Deans, Administrators, and Counselors in Boston. My personal experiences and the more professional and social ones of writing my dissertation, teaching, and organizing and attending other seminars and conference programs—all these factors significantly altered my attitudes toward change and my understanding of the sorts of risks and responsibilities involved in producing it. Insights about the risks and rewards involved in such change metaphorically informed my introduction to an issue of *Critical Exchange* that I guest edited, including Ralph Cohen's invited position paper "A Propaedeutic on Literary Change" and several responses—the papers for two linked special sessions on Literary and Critical Change that, as a member of the Society for Critical Exchange, I had initiated and coordinated for the 1982 MLA Convention.[16]

Multiplying my experience and all the contingencies suggested by it by the number of people interviewed for this book suggests the absurdity of extrapolating from one person's experience to explain anyone else's. But at least the *field* of personal and social experience that my own story delimits is also a field of these others' critical changes. My presentation of some of their stories in earlier chapters of this book demonstrates this conjunction. While my analysis of these other people's experiences may only roughly parallel this more detailed account of my own critical changes and persistences, after speaking with them I am confident that, despite differences in our institutional circumstances, analogous kinds of experiences have affected their professional and critical choices and changes.

"The case of Pinter" involves many individuals experiencing and responding to personal, professional, social, and cultural changes. To serve the purposes of my analysis, my "sample" has been relatively small, twenty-seven in all. Yet those interviewed have aided in the development of this project, demonstrating the positive effects of cooperation among individuals (its value, in Smith's sense) in both critical and cultural change. Without the cooperation of each Pinter scholar, journalist, director, actor, librarian, bookseller, and even box office agent who was willing to talk with me, I could not have envisioned the kind of changes in criticism and culture suggested at the end of this book.

### Critical Change: The Case of Some
### Other Pinter Critics

While this book recounts some changes in intellectual and professional interests of a group of people whom I have been calling "Pinter critics and scholars," each of them has contributed to much more than Pinter criticism. Steven H. Gale, a professor in the humanities at Kentucky State University, continues publishing articles and books on the work of Harold Pinter, though currently he also pursues broader ongoing interests in film, the American dramatist David Mamet, the American humorist S. J. Perelman, and other American and British humorists, the latter editorial encyclopedia projects. In April 1989 he returned to his former institution Missouri Southern State College to codirect a production of *The Collection* and *The Lover* with Jay Fields. With a second collection of critical essays on Pinter in press (G. K. Hall) and a third being planned, he is also working on a book about Pinter's films, to be published by Greenwood Press.

Katherine Burkman, a professor of English and comparative literature at Ohio State University, has persisted in and developed her "ritual approach" to Pinter, applying it to a larger group of playwrights in *The Arrival of Godot*, but has also gone "back to Beckett" (Ruby Cohn's phrase) in her recent collaborative editorial project, *Myth and Ritual in the Plays of Samuel Beckett*. That this collection contains essays on Beckett from ten women and only one man suggests her own feminist critical impulse. She has directed a feminist Ph.D. dissertation including Pinter by Ann C. Hall and a Master's thesis on Pinter by Kelly Belanger, both of whom have published essays (cited earlier) in the *Pinter Review*, on whose editorial board Burkman serves. She is currently writing a book on doubling in modern drama, in collaboration with a psychiatrist, tentatively entitled "The Torment of the Mirror: Myth, Murder, and Modern Drama."

A professor of English and comparative literature and former chairperson of the Department of English at Fairleigh Dickinson University, Teaneck, Lois Gordon has turned from psychoanalytical perspectives on Pinter's characters' "word games" to broader interests in language and the arts. Since publishing her books on Donald Barthelme and Robert Coover, she is finishing a new study of Beckett's plays and has begun work on a study of the foundations of modernism and postmodernism in art, taking time off from these projects to collaborate with her husband,

Alan, on *American Chronicle*, an "almanac" recording "all the news, radio, television, movie, popular and classical music, theater, art, dance, literary, science and technology, sports, and fashion highlights of every year from 1920 to 1980," recently updated for a new edition through 1990. Gordon spent an afternoon and evening with Harold Pinter when he gave a reading of *One for the Road* at Fairleigh Dickinson (October 1986), and she is still engaged in criticism of his work, as she will update her essay for St. Martin's *Contemporary Dramatists* series, has already written an essay on Pinter for another series, covered Pinter's October 1989 reading at the Poetry Center of the 92d Street Y for the third issue of the *Pinter Review*, and is editing a collection of critical essays on Pinter for Garland Press.

Since I interviewed her in 1982, Lucy Gabbard has retired from her tenured teaching post at Eastern Illinois University and taken up residence in Chicago, along with her husband, "Gabby." Together each of them has begun second careers in professional acting, with Lucy, using the name Lucina Paquet, performing in over a dozen stage plays and in several films and television productions, as well as in commercials and industrials. In the summer of 1989 she reprised her role as the grandmother in the Steppenwolf Theater adaptation of Steinbeck's *Grapes of Wrath*, a great hit in London at the National Theatre (that Pinter himself enjoyed) and scheduled to move to New York in March 1990.

Following the disciplinary signposts suggested earlier, despite their differences of focus, Martin Esslin has turned to semiotics in *The Field of Drama*, as has Austin Quigley in "Genêt and the Empire of Semiotics" and in his current book on relations between linguistic and literary theory. Both Esslin, a professor of drama at Stanford University, and Quigley, a professor and chairperson of English at the University of Virginia, are also members of the editorial board for the *Pinter Review*.

Ewald Mengel, an associate professor of English literature at the Otto-Friedrich University of Bamberg, West Germany, and Elizabeth Sakellaridou, a senior lecturer in English drama at the Aristotle University of Thessaloniki, Greece, have been extending their vantage points on culture. In addition to the publication of his postdoctoral thesis on English historical novels by Carl Winter in 1986 and a book on Dickens by Peter Lang in 1989, Mengel has been writing essays on contemporary English drama, including Pinter. Sakellaridou's feminist study of "Pinter's androgyny" has led to her current book on relations between myth and history in plays by contemporary British women playwrights, and she has helped to organize a theater group at the University of Thessaloniki, where she has directed some plays by Pinter.

In all these changes we can observe individual persistence amidst personal and institutional circumstances, a move toward the trendy, and a trend (mostly involving a few of the more mature scholars) toward more collaborative work (editing, theater). Further indicating the trend toward collaboration in Pinter criticism, following suggestions first made in the early 1980s, at the 1986 MLA Convention Gale established the Harold Pinter Society, was elected as its president for the first three years, and announced plans to establish a journal of the new society, the *Pinter Review*. Even the editorship of this journal is a collaboration, as Gale is "coeditor" with Francis Gillen, whose home university, the University of Tampa, has donated funds for its publication. At the 1987 MLA Convention, during the second meeting of the Harold Pinter Society, Gale announced that the *Pinter Review* would premiere within a few months, and the discussion otherwise concerned plans for the society to become an Allied Organization of the MLA. The 1988 MLA Convention hosted the special session "Thematic and Structural Concepts of Time in the Works of Harold Pinter," with Gale as discussion leader and papers by Burkman, Quigley, and Clausius; directly afterward, members of the society approved a constitution, one of the requirements for becoming an Allied Organization of the MLA. The burgeoning of such organizations in recent years (see *PMLA* 103:913–14) is strong evidence of a move toward greater collaboration in professional studies of languages and literatures. Though the MLA is restricting the number of convention sessions associated with such organizations and especially those devoted to "single authors," Gale writes that the society's "future" is "promising."[17]

These activities aim to facilitate the kind of critical inquiry for which I have been arguing throughout this book: they could encourage more collaboration among Pinter critics, scholars, and theater professionals and foster the cooperation necessary for salutary critical and cultural change. As Gale writes in his first president's column for the *Pinter Review*, "an important motivational force" of establishing a Pinter Society is to "enable those interested in Pinter to share information" (v). In their first editors' column, referring to "the broad range of approaches to Harold Pinter's work" that I discuss in my essay "Recent Developments in Pinter Criticism," Gale and Gillen say that they "hope to add to this critical spectrum essays and notes by those actively involved in the production of Pinter's plays." The second issue of the journal includes an essay by Carey Perloff, director of the 1988 CSC Repertory Theatre production of *The Birthday Party*, along with two divergent reviews of the production (Dukore and Merritt). Forthcoming in the third issue is the text of my taped interview with Perloff and some members of the cast of her 1989 CSC Repertory Theatre production of *Mountain Language* and *The Birthday Party*, as well as Gillen's review of this production and Gordon's account of Pinter's October 1989 reading at the 92d Street Y. There is also "A Master Class in Play Direction," by Jay Fields, based on the April 1989 Missouri Southern State College production, and a book review of Richard Allen Cave's *New British Drama in Performance on the London Stage*, by Ann C. Hall, along with other essays, notes, book reviews, and my annual bibliography.

At the 1987 meeting I suggested that the Harold Pinter Society plan an international conference on Pinter to commemorate Pinter's sixtieth birthday (10 October 1990) on the pattern of some recent conferences on Beckett; Katherine Burkman has arranged for this meeting to take place on 19–21 April 1991 at Ohio State University in Columbus. A volume on Pinter (e.g., *Pinter at Sixty*), paralleling festschriften on Beckett published recently, perhaps as a special issue of the *Pinter Review*, could emerge from such a conference. Ongoing "international interaction" is also being cultivated (*Pinter Rev.* 1:vi).

The first issue of the *Pinter Review* suggests some of the kinds of change that collaborative publishing endeavors produce. After many years of lending copies of the manuscript of his unpublished novel *The Dwarfs*, begun in the midfifties, to such interested scholars as Martin Esslin, Francis Gillen, Elizabeth Sakellaridou, and Daniel Salem, Pinter agreed to publish a portion (chaps. 19 and 10, respectively) in the first two issues of the *Pinter Review*. This publishing event may generate new perspectives on Pinter's work. [18] It has encouraged Pinter to consider publishing the whole novel. In this manner critical and literary change are cross-fertilizing: an advance in a critical community can produce literary change (the publication of an "old" manuscript in a "new" form), and such an event can in turn affect the criticism of an author's work. New productions of Beckett's radio plays, initiated by and accomplished through involvement of members of the Samuel Beckett Society, were broadcast in America on National Public Radio in 1989. I have suggested to Charles Potter (of Radio Arts), who produced parts of the Beckett programs, that he consider producing radio dramas by Pinter, and he is exploring the idea. Even amidst the competitions fostered by current academic practices, individuals can work together to produce new organs of criticism and collectively enrich work in the media of culture.

If its members maintain a cooperative spirit, the Harold Pinter Society could foster greater collegiality among Pinter critics, affording them opportunities to resolve the "conflicting possibilities" in critical interpretation to which Quigley alludes in "The Temporality of Structure in Pinter's Plays" (19) and to overcome limitations imposed on scholars of contemporary drama by the current publishing environment to which Gale alludes in his first president's column. Foundation of the society has already strengthened the relations between Pinter scholars and Pinter: in appreciation of this recognition of his work, after receiving the first issue of the *Pinter Review*, Pinter graciously sent a copy of his typescript of *Mountain Language* to Frank Gillen.[19] He maintains a correspondence with both Gale and Gillen and invited Gillen to his London home for several hours of conversation in the summer of 1989.

In the editors' column for the second issue, seeking a "distinctive character" for the *Pinter Review*, Gillen asserts, "It must not pretend to 'explain' Pinter's work":

dramatic criticism itself is a mode of continued participation in the play, a form of intersubjectivity. As the curtain closes on a compelling dramatic work, we recognize its aesthetic closure, but precisely, I think, because it has affected us, often in ways which we cannot yet articulate, we want to expand and continue the intersubjective process, the field of play. . . . Far from closing off the dialogic process by presenting "the" interpretation, criticism, considered as play itself, invites others to join in that intersubjective process . . . that spirit of playful attention that sees the work, the criticism and the response to that criticism as interpenetrating, participatory acts. Let us play. (vi)

Gillen "particularly" invites "essays on Pinter's influence on other dramatists, on his later plays, and on his film adaptations," topics suggested by members of the Harold Pinter Society at its 1988 meeting. In concluding he remarks that he and Gale have decided "to alternate writing this column" in order "to avoid any suggestion of a pontifical 'we'" (vii). I hope that topics invited for future issues result from ongoing dialogues with members of the Harold Pinter Society and others; that the essays published enable critics to "play" with Pinter in socially responsible ways befitting Pinter's own concerns in his recent work; and that the coeditors continue to avoid pontificating either together or separately, both to encourage "participation" from those wishing to be "involved" in "any and all of the Society's activities" (v) and to engage these others in planning future ones.

### Critical Collaboration as a Means of Cultural Change

Robert Markeley, editor of the journal *The Eighteenth Century: Theory and Interpretation*, has "argued that the publishing world does not simply further the spread of knowledge. The process whereby journals and presses choose what articles and books to print also maintains a system that elevates a relatively few individuals to positions of power within academe." On a more general level—the cultural production of knowledge within such social institutions—Markeley extends the kind of change in criticism that I have been advocating throughout this book even further: "We need far more attention focused on publishing as—potentially, at least—a collective enterprise." He proposes "publishing collectives—devoid of first author, second author, and research-slave hierarchies." Such "a restructuring of the politics of publishing" would have, Markeley claims, salutary consequences for other features of the academic profession, "lead[ing] to teaching and bargaining collectives and render[ing] the current system of tenure obsolete." If the utopia that Markeley envisions were to materialize, the "mainstream" and "marginal" might disappear; we would have to reconstitute, at least realign, our notions of fashion and progress and power within new paradigms—or replace them with new concepts of human success.

Although we cannot ignore the needs of individuals—their drive for (or avoidance of) individual success and its rewards, their fear of (or attraction to) failure and its penalties—we must also heed demands for an ethical and just society—one in which individuals work together to reduce and to eliminate inequities and attendant indignities and hardships for all human beings—not just those who succeed "on their own."

While I have spent many years working on this book as an "individual," as an "independent scholar," I have had support from the NEH and maintained crucial research affiliations with academic institutions (Clark University, Cornell University, and Oregon State University). I say "crucial" because without these library facilities and other resources for faculty, completing this project would have been even more difficult, if not impossible. The many people who have helped me all along have made my work a cooperative venture (and adventure). Though such remarks conventionally appear only in the preliminaries of a book, at this point I highlight them further because they indicate clearly a collaborative feature of any individual research effort.

Critical inquiry often depends on alliances among individuals and among groups modeled on "think tanks" and organizations of affiliated scholars—societies, allied organizations, centers, and institutes. Clearly, academic publishing, like criticism, already *is* a "collective enterprise." But we need to maximize the advantages of what we have institutionalized, while minimizing its disadvantages. As Graff's *Professing Literature* and some other recent works chronicle, the history of academic literary studies is marked by internecine conflicts and rivalries among factions from both within and without. By fostering productive relationships in which issues in conflict are discussed openly and at least regarded as resolvable if not "fully resolved" (Quigley, "Temporality," 19), we can promote a world of discourse in which we could thrive. Such relationships do not occur in any of Harold Pinter's plays until A *Kind of Alaska*, where even still Pinter shows us how difficult it is to get "the matter in proportion" (*Other Places*, 40).

If we want to improve cultural criticism, if we want to effect important changes in and through it, we must try to improve our own relationships. Critical and cultural change is produced by people who happen to be critics but who are also other people's wives, husbands, and lovers; mothers and fathers; sisters and brothers; daughters and sons; teachers and students; employers and employees—to mention just some of their other social roles. Lucy Gabbard, for example, is not only a scholar who produced a psychoanalytic study of Pinter's plays but also the mother of two sons (the psychiatrist Glen and the literary comparatist Krin) who have themselves together recently produced a book on psychoanalysis and film (*Psychiatry and the Cinema*), an influential teacher of John Malkovich—the actor and director of Steppenwolf Theater's revival of *The Caretaker* (among Malkovich's many recent achievements), and an actor in Steppenwolf and other productions. Unpredictably, human relations bring about critical and cultural change.

No one who has experienced it would say that change comes easily. Not only is there external resistance to any important change, but the internal resistance is daunting. To change ourselves and others takes courage, persistence, and imagination. Perhaps we avoid trying to make salutary changes happen because we are deficient in these qualities. Such "character flaws" produce weaknesses in our cultural institutions and practices; for our media of culture (McLuhan explained decades ago) are extensions of ourselves.

## The Point of Change

"[W]hat's the point?" Fish asks finally; "for many people, an intellectual enterprise—be it literary criticism or philosophy of science—is legitimized finally by its goal, and it is in relation to some goal that changes must be justified. Otherwise, it is often said, change would be 'mere' change or meaningless change or change for change's sake. The idea is that change is intolerable unless it is perceived as progress and that the sense of progress must be underwritten by a belief in the achievability of some desired end." Punning on *end*—"that time when a particular activity will cease, because, for example, all the world's goods will have been equitably distributed or all the world's texts correctly described"— Fish questions what "a practitioner in the field really wants": "Is it really the case that we do what we do so that there will come a day when we are not called upon any longer to do it? Should such a day ever seem to be approaching, in literary studies or any other, I venture to predict that there will suddenly be the discovery that the problem was more complicated than we had assumed, the discovery that the last word has not yet been explicated" ("Change," 443/159).

But what if the "problem" is more *simple*? We remain caught in this maelstrom only because we assume that the "end" (goal) of literary criticism *is* to describe, to explicate, to "explain" texts "correctly"; when, in Jonathan Culler's words, "interpretations" become "goals" rather than "data." "To take interpretation as data rather than goals does not mean an end to interpretation but rather a displacement of our present goal: the production of new interpretations of literary texts as the aim and test of literary study" ("Interpretations," 289).

Earlier, in differentiating literary studies from the interpretation of data in other humanistic disciplines (anthropology, history), Culler maintains: "one of the signal virtues of literary criticism is that it does not deem its texts to be simply data about something else. If we study literature, it is because literary works and their complexities are of interest in themselves" (278). Yet literary critics share with anthropologists and historians this understanding: human practices and events and their complexities (resulting in the production and reception of literary works) are of more than "simply" isolated interest. As we must resist extolling either exclusively intrinsic or exclusively extrinsic models of knowledge, given the cultural "stakes" of interpretation that Culler and others continue to profess, so must we advocate doing more than mere explication—"just play."

To resolve the apparent theoretical impasse between those granting privilege to the individual and those championing the "machinery" of the community (including the classroom), we need to recognize the importance of *both* individual *and* community—and their simultaneous interrelations. "Intertextuality is the academic 'game' that has come to overtake the purposes, intersubjectivity, and historicity of reading communities found in university classrooms. . . . The game idea is part of the ethical and psychosocial mentality of the academy . . . [which] neither wishes to deal with [the classroom] nor change its own style of functioning. . . . I will try to say, in my own language, how we can change the way we think about our subject, and through another simultaneous perspective, can change how we are the citizens of our various communities—in the classroom and in the academy" (Bleich, *DP*, 23, 25). Overcoming what Harold Bloom calls "the anxiety of influence," in *my* own language and the language of *other* Pinter critics, through our *multiple* perspectives, I have identified and situated particular constituents of "reading and writing groups," suggesting their potential as critically cooperative communities.

To continue to produce literary criticism for its own sake—to benefit only those who write it and not even the relatively few in this computerized age who might actually have time and inclination to read it—is no change at all. It would be better to do something else instead. If any important changes in criticism and culture are to occur, they require from each one of us greater self-scrutiny: of our critical and pedagogical aims and goals and our personal and social motives. If socially equitable goals prevail in criticism, perhaps the changes that future critics produce will enhance both cultures and the cultural condition of their interrelated, individual human subjects. Given the immense industry that literary and performance studies and other cultural criticism have become, we all have a mutual obligation to scrutinize our own reasons for this proliferation. If we contribute to it, we must do so responsibly. For we are accountable for

our acts of scholarship and criticism, just as we are for other things that
we do in our lives.

## Some Guidelines for Critical
## and Cultural Change

How do we function *beyond play* in more *socially responsible* ways? While it
might seem unrealistic and undesirable to propose that all work be
wholly collaborative, each of us needs to expand our participation in
cooperative critical networks to unfetter cultural work from the shackles
of competition.[20] Based on my own and others' experiences, the following ten suggestions, extended from and intended as customary guidelines
rather than ground rules, strive to avoid critical exclusiveness and elit-
ism. To "open" the questions that they raise, in the spirit of dialogic
inquiry, I offer them for debate.

(1) Propose to do only those projects that need to be done so as to avoid
unnecessary duplication of efforts. This requires knowing what has been
done or is being done already. But do not develop a project only because it
is different. It must serve some important societal needs. "Importance" is
itself a contested attribute, ideologically contingent; such contingencies
come into play in deciding what to do.

(2) In determining how valuable an enterprise is, among other contingencies, consider the sources of your own interest: examine your
motives, aims, and goals, and the potential benefits and risks to yourselves and others. While keeping in mind the possible unpredictability of
these consequences, in defining them, maintain concern for all disadvan-
taged individuals and groups, however peripherally involved. If the risks
to a group or individual outweigh the benefits to them, even if the
benefits to the whole are greater, either change the enterprise accordingly
or dissolve it. Otherwise, forge on, full speed ahead, mobilizing the
energies of all.

(3) Take advantage of opportunities to announce new projects and to
solicit help from peers in appropriate sections of professional journals like
"Professional Notes and Comments" in *PMLA*. Responses to your notice
will help determine whether your project is actually new and give you
needed assistance.

(4) Seek out collaborators and support from foundations and other
sponsors so that together you can incorporate a variety of perspectives in
your projects and enhance their chances of completion, ultimate publica-

tion or dissemination, and widest appeal. Involve competent students in this work, but only as full-fledged members of the collaborative with equal responsibilities, equal rights, and equal acknowledgment. Avoid establishing hierarchies of power unalterably concentrated in too few members (officers and editorial boards, for example, that never change).

(5) Affiliate yourselves and your work with any organizations already devoted to inquiry in the area of concern. Or, in the event that no such organization exists, establish one to further your research (observing the rest of these guidelines). Advertise this organization through journals and other appropriate promotional means so as to seek new members to strengthen both it and your affiliated projects.

(6) Publicize the projects through collaboratively authored writings. Not every member of the research collective needs to be involved in every publication, but ultimately everyone should be an author, and everyone should be credited by name for his or her actual role in the final products—whether publications or artifacts for media other than print.

(7) When encountering resistance—whether from inside or outside the collaborative—discuss the issues in conflict and try to resolve them to the satisfaction of everyone concerned. (This may involve inviting critics to address the group or going to other groups to address them.) If such communal resolution is impossible, try to understand and formulate the reasons why. Consider defections by individuals and secessions of factions from the whole only as a last resort. With greater efforts among committed members so-called irreconcilable differences can often be reconciled.

(8) Persist in the face of substantial resistance *only* if, as a group, you understand it to result from ignorance or unself-examined biases. Try to educate the resisters about these problems of perception.

(9) If the group finds the resistance reasonable and the objections legitimate, accommodate them by changing your aims. While your cocollaborators will help you to achieve the perspective you need to make such decisions, and while the decisions will be reached through consensus, you are each individually responsible and accountable for whatever role you play in formulating the critical and cultural strategies of the whole.

(10) If at some time projects seem no longer feasible or otherwise doomed, give them up to pursue more worthwhile endeavors. If this means abandoning an organization, consider such a course of action. The broader aims and the cooperative spirit of these guidelines take priority in making such decisions about any single project or group.

If codifying apparently common or standard practices like these seems too *simple* an explanation of how we can operate, my doing so nevertheless may remind us that these common "professional" practices are too rarely being practiced professionally and that our "discipline" suffers from our own lack of discipline in managing often petty squabbles. More attention to such practices might help us to focus less on our own sense of self and foster more a sense of other.

Conventions in fashion exert a hammerlock on the systems of critical peer review throughout all our professions. We all remain in the grip of dominant trends and strategies and models limiting critical judgments about what gets written and published and otherwise produced. To dramatize these forces, we might imagine what could happen if, instead of publishing *only* those essays and books that have achieved some degree of critical consensus (the customary agreement of two out of three editorial board readers), as an experiment, editors of every journal and press chose *arbitrarily* to publish in every issue/annual book list at least one of those writings that had been rejected by everyone. The otherwise silent would become heard—the banned and banished, citizens of the world of discourse.

What would happen if we were to hear ourselves in "Such a silence" as Ellen hears in Pinter's play *Silence* (3:211)? Would we too wonder: "Am I silent or speaking?" Would new languages come into being that would otherwise remain undiscovered and hence unknown? Could we learn some important things that we do not yet know? From what Barbara Herrnstein Smith terms "the margins of discourse," when the marginal gains centrality, does the concept of the marginal disappear—or does it, occupied but differently, still remain? Is "the double perspective" of which David Bleich speaks in his own language a "simultaneous" perspective, or is it an alternation between perspectives in the manner of some optical illusions?

What if, as William Cain observes most literary critics eventually counsel, there were to be "a 'moratorium' . . . on the production of criticism" to prevent "the imminent death of literature and culture" (*Crisis*, 86): a moratorium on writing and on speaking criticism? Can there ever be such a universal silence that will not become even a subtle form of censorship imposed by some who would rather speak over others? Both speech and silence do operate simultaneously: to speak is to silence others and to remain silent is to encourage and even to engage in a kind of speech.

If "communication" is, as Pinter has said, "too alarming," so avoidance of communication is also "too fearsome a possibility" (1:15). Not *trying* to communicate something is *not* among the "possible worlds" imagined by most literary critics. Does "the end" (in both senses—goal and finish) come when we have played ourselves out, when we are (however) out of play? Francis Fukuyama's "End of History?" posits "the end of the end" (post-history). Does endism proclaim the end of any new beginning, the end of human life? Is not any such end the next creative start? Can humanity ever be post-contemporary, post-history, post-theory, post-criticism—and still be alive? Is anything definite/definitive, anything certain, beyond the immutability of change and human attraction and resistance to it?

At the end of *Mountain Language* the Elderly Woman will not "speak in her own language" as directed. By not speaking in *any* language, through her silence (in effect if not by intention) she resists oppression by the Guard: "Silence is the final defiance" (Gillen, "From Chapter Ten," 4). Strategies become oppressive, overwhelming subjects of inquiry, but "the rules" of critical discourse seldom stipulate silence, however salutary a change it might produce. "When true silence falls we are still left with echo but are nearer nakedness": paradoxically, as the case of Pinter shows, when confined by the language of others, by their "free play"—however "better" it may be "to scream against injustice than to remain silent" (*London Theatre Record*, 1469)—at times the most concealing and revealing final word *is* silence.

# Notes

My citations of works generally use short titles. When quotations from Pinter's work are from the Grove Press edition of the *Complete Works*, for economy I have omitted the title, giving volume and page numbers only. Occurrences of *Harold Pinter* in titles are generally abbreviated *HP* or "HP." (Full bibliographical information appears in the list of works cited.)

## 1 "Progress" and "Fashion" in Pinter Studies

1 Carlson, *Theories* offers a comprehensive discussion of these tendencies in theater theory and criticism. (See also chaps. 4 & 8 below.)

2 Quoted from excerpts of Gould, lecture.

3 For a summary of the theory of literary change in Cohen, "Propaedeutic" and an introduction to several critiques of it, see Elliott, "Theoretical Writing."

4 On "the model of *punctuated equilibria*" proposed by Gould and Niles Eldredge as an alternative model to "gradualism," see chap. 17 in *Panda's Thumb*, 179–85: "The Episodic Nature of Evolutionary Change." Cf. *Time's Arrow*, 2–3, 133 n.6, & 179.

5 For a detailed study of such contingencies of contemporary scientific models of evolution, see Hull.

6 Attributing Pinter's assurance of "a public familiarity" to the "mass media" and to scholarly publications on his work and life, cf. Jennings, 156–57. See also King, "Pinter's Progress," 246–47; Klein; and various writings by Brater and Hudgins.

7 Cf. Esslin: "Each work comes to us surrounded and enveloped by the critical reactions it has evoked and which have adhered to it; . . . the work of art and the reaction it has evoked become fused, inextricably linked. We cannot see a work of the past independent of the critical reaction that surrounds it, and in reacting to the work itself we cannot but also react to its reputation, its previous critical interpretation" ("Search," 207). On what I call the "intercontextuality" of critical judgments, see chap. 9.

8 De Man's perspective has new resonance due to current debates about his writings for two Belgian newspapers in 1941–42.

9 Quigley, *MSOW* explicitly addresses the question of progress in criticism and issues of continuity and innovation that are among my concerns in this study of Pinter criticism, and I am indebted to his perspective.

10 See Newton, 48–49.

11 See Almansi and Henderson and Van Laan as discussed in chaps. 3 & 4.

12  See Barber, "Precise Words" (source of the epigraph for this chap.); Gussow, "I Started," 7; cf. Schroll, 38, 80.

13  But see Langley, 30; Ganz, 1; Nightingale, "Human Zoo," 74; and Kane, "Weasel," 30.

14  See, e.g., Gordon, 5; Hollis; and Rusinko, *British Drama*, 50–52. Chap. 4 in Esslin, *PW*: "Language and Silence" plays upon Pinter's "two silences." Langley, 30, even uses the "two silences" to describe Pinter's interview manner. (An excerpt from this speech serves as my epigraph for chap. 6.)

15  In this production, according to Pinter, Deeley "masturbat[es]" Kate, there was overt physical intimacy between Anna and Kate, and Deeley and Anna "powder the naked breasts [of Kate] on stage" (Nichols, "Mr. Pinter," 1). The setting in the round implied a boxing ring in that the sounding of a "gong" replaced Pinter's "silence" (see Murphy). But whereas Pinter protests, "I did not write a play about two lesbians who caress each other continually" (Nichols, 1), Murphy responds, "there is no more lesbianism on stage than is implied in the words of the play."

16  Pinter also worked with the cast of the 1984 Roundabout Theater production of *Old Times*. According to Anthony Hopkins, who played Deeley, as quoted in Bennetts, "Clockwork," when Hopkins asked Pinter " 'what does the end mean?' " Pinter said: " 'I don't know, just do it.' "

17  Cf. Pinter, letter to Francis Gillen, quoted in *Pinter Rev.* 1:vi: "I recognise and respect the seriousness of all concerned in this enterprise, including the names on your editorial board."

18  See Hobson, review of *Betrayal*, discussed in chap. 9.

19  See Cohen, "Joys and Sorrows," 122–23; cf. Bleich, *SC*, 9, and *DP*; and see also distinctions between "literary understanding" and "knowledge" in Steig, xiii. For related "reflections" on the role of the theater critic, see Marowitz; Kissel, "Wise Counselor"; and Rogoff.

20  See "Between the Lines" and "Writing for the Theatre," 80.

21  I am playing here upon a line in the cross-examination of Stanley by Goldberg and McCann in *Birthday Party* (1:62). The earlier part of this dialogue on whether "the number 846" is "possible or necessary" (60) relates too. For a unique explication of it, in terms of "Gematryia, the non-verbal Jewish preoccupation with the numerical value of words," see Kane, "Weasel," 22.

22  On "the dogma of [a fundamental] dichotomy" between the sciences and the humanities and "other fundamental dichotomies like reality vs. fiction, subject vs. object, individual vs. society, etc.," cf. Schmidt, "Foundations," 5.

23  Cf. C. Nelson, "Reading Criticism"; Ong; and Schmidt, "Fiction."

## 2  Aims, Kinds, and Contexts of Criticism

1  Sparshott does, however, define four practical uses of the word *criticism* connecting with "four quite different concepts," there being "no prospect of reducing them to one," though they can "converge" (6–8).

2  See esp. Booth, *Critical Understanding* and "Freedom of Interpretation," 54 n. 13; Booth's note provides a historical context for his arguments for pluralism.

3  Writing after Ellis, some critics have played upon *eccentric* by coining phrases like "Excentric Criticism"; see Jay and Miller.

4  In support of this view, Ellis cites Wellek, "The New Criticism." For a more recent version of this argument, see Alter. A related viewpoint on Ellis's argument appears in Cain, *Crisis*, 112–13.

5  In his later writing Fish revises his position against "cultural relativism"; see, e.g., *DWCN*, 29–30.

6  Fish attacks what Rawson terms the Establishment of theory throughout his own more recent writings: "theory's day is dying, the hour is late; and the only thing left for a theorist to do is to say so, which is what I have been saying here, and, I think, not a moment too soon" (*DWCN*, 341; cf. 14–15). Rhetoric's day, however, has come again and not yet gone, as we will see later in this chapter.

7  More recently, Fish has reiterated his emphasis on argumentative power, or *force*; see "Resistance and Independence," 127; cf. "Force," in *DWCN*, 503–24.

8  Fish's later argument against the authoritative function of "disciplining rules" extends this discussion; see "Fish v. Fiss," in *DWCN*, 120–40.

9  See Fanto, "Professionalization," in response to Fish's 1983 MLA Convention paper "Anti-Professionalism," later abridged in *New Literary History* and the *Cardozo Law Rev.* and reprinted in *DWCN*, 215–46. For a context for Fanto's criticism of Fish, regarding Fish's position as an unchanging dogmatic contextualism, see Fanto, "Contesting Authority." For Fish's more recent argument *against* proposing "a theory of change," cf. Fish, "Change," as discussed in chap. 10 below.

10  See also Fish's critique of Fanto, "Contesting Authority," a part of the MLA version of Fish, "Anti-Professionalism" omitted from the *New Literary History* article, but reprinted in *DWCN*, 237–39. Cf. the argument about "institutional position" in "Fish v. Fiss," in *DWCN*, 135–36.

11  Cf. C. Nelson, "On Whether"; for references to other work by Nelson, see 266 n. 1.

12  Now conditions of even initial employment demand "substantial publications," in the phrase of advertisements in recent *MLA Job Information Lists*. For discussion of some related issues, see Shumway, "Getting."

13  See Burgess; Lerner and Rogerson, 166; Graff, 14–15, 249; and Smith, "Contingencies," 2–7.

14  Perhaps Booth does "overdramatize" the situation, but, as Hernadi suggests in his introduction to *What Is Criticism?* (as cited earlier), the *feeling* that he depicts is very common. (Cf. Harari, as discussed in chap. 3.)

15  Cf. Hernadi, *Re-Viewing Reviews*, in which a group of academics, including Wayne Booth, Jonathan Culler, Martin Esslin, Edith Kern, Murray Krieger, Herbert Lindenberger, and Theodore Ziolkowski, discuss reviews of their own books. See esp. Lindenberger, "Re-Viewing," 43–46: "On Reviews and Reception in General." I cite this section of Lindenberger again and Esslin, "On Being Reviewed" in chap. 7.

16  For the proposal that "dramatic discourse" is rhetorical, see Eagleton, "Brecht and Rhetoric," 634. See also Mailloux, "Rhetorical Hermeneutics" and "Interpretation"; Fish, "Rhetoric," in *DWCN*, 471–502 & 525–54; and Hernadi, *Rhetoric*.

17  Cf. Mailloux, *Interpretive Conventions*, 202: "Most reader response critics simply do not see that 'the reader,' like 'the text,' is constituted by the descriptive discourse of which it is a part."

18  Cf. Siebers, 186–219, esp. 186–87, 197–98.

19  On the need for historical definition and confrontation of critical conflicts rather than

masking or submerging them, and for a "dialectical" analysis of "hyperpoliticized discourse" in recent critical debate as a response to "depoliticized discourse," see Graff, 11, 14–15, 177.

20 See Merritt, letter to the editor.

### 3 Criticism as Strategy

1 For a recent summary of Michel de Certeau's uses of *strategy* and *tactics* as borrowed from "game theory and military terminology," in "On the Oppositional Practices of Everyday Life," see Maclean, 40–41.

2 See, e.g., Culler, *OD*, 18, 116, 141, 146; "Jacques Derrida," 155; "Interpretations," 279, 280; and Fish's use of *at stake* and similar criticism-as-game metaphors discussed in chap. 2. Bleich complains that such uses of *at stake* lack both clarity about actual academic consequences and "concrete social purpose" (*DP*, 114 & 114 n.33).

3 For similarly contrasting definitions of the traditionalist and postmodernist stances in recent American criticism, cf. Mailloux, *Interpretive Conventions*, 140–49 & 152–54.

4 This viewpoint has become widespread in teaching writing in college; see, e.g., Dougherty; Ede; and Flower, *Problem-Solving Strategies*.

5 On the "cognitive basis" for such a distinction, see Flower, "Writer-Based Prose." See also Dougherty, 315–16. Cf. distinctions between "readerly" ("traditional") and "writerly" ("postmodern") texts in Barthes, *Pleasure of the Text* and *S/Z*; and Lentricchia, 142–44.

6 For limitations of Kinneavy's "more rigid distinctions among the [four] 'aims of discourse' "—expressive, referential, literary, persuasive—in contrast to James Britton's "three 'function categories'—transactional, expressive, and poetic"—which "represent a breakthrough in discourse theory," see Stull, 131–32.

7 See also Lindenberger, "Postlogue," 540, 541.

8 See "Writing for Myself," 173, as cited by D. Thompson, 1. On Pinter's acting career, see also L. Smith, "Pinter the Player."

9 Dukore mistakenly states that "[a]s head of radio drama," Martin Esslin "was responsible for commissioning Pinter to write *A Slight Ache*" (*HP*, 1st ed., 128; 2d ed., 148). Donald McWhinnie commissioned it and produced it from 1958 to 1959, when he was still assistant head and before Esslin replaced him in this position (see Pinter, letters).

10 Discussion with Pinter after the 1981 East Anglia talk; for background, see also Gussow, "Profiles," 57, and H. Hill.

11 For a discussion of Pinter's attitudes toward his playwriting, esp. his creation of characters, see Esposito, 168.

12 On the relations between reviewing ("one variety of criticism which survives in the realm of mass culture") and academic criticism (the variety commonly "juxtaposed" to it), see Pratt, as discussed in chap. 2.

13 Tompkins, "Me and My Shadow" demonstrates and discusses the implications of two such oscillating "voices" in conflict, particularly for feminist critics.

### 4 Pinter's "Semantic Uncertainty" and Critically "Inescapable" Certainties

1 See Gale's description of his recent collection: "Neither this volume nor any of the individual essays . . . is trying to give the answer to what Pinter and his works are all

about. Rather, as in the dramatist's plays, the attempt has been made to provide a wide range of possibilities" (*HPCA*, 20). Fuegi relates "the uncertainty principle" to Pinter's "modern drama" in the concluding essay. See reviews of Gale's collection by Frankel and Merritt.

2  For Jauss's source of the concept "open work," see Eco, 3–43. Cf. Culler's description of "the easy shift between freedom and constraint" in "stories of reading" so-called open works (*OD*, 70–71); and de Man, *Blindness*, 285–87.

3  See, e.g., Sosnoski; Peck; Cain, "English," 103 n. 10. For the retrospective admission that "Beyond Interpretation" was "optimistically entitled," see Culler, "Interpretations," 278n.

4  For other statements more critical of the tendency toward dogmatism in pluralism, see Mitchell, *Pluralism*.

5  On *Dumb Waiter* as a "parody play," ironically parodying "the styles and techniques of theater, film, and television," cf. Diamond, 93–109.

6  Carpenter cites Taylor, "Accident," 184. Cf. Cima, 44; Mortimer, 719; and Nightingale, "Human Zoo," 74.

7  See reversals of this anti-interpretive and anti-absurdist stance in Carpenter's more recent commentaries on *Birthday Party*, *Caretaker*, and *Homecoming*. The title within the title of Carpenter's article on *Birthday Party* alludes to Len's speech to Mark in *Dwarfs*, describing his uncertainty about who or what this other person is: "What have I seen, the scum or the essence?" (2:112). (The metaphor is drawn from ocean tides.) Cf. the revised version by Carpenter: though adding Derridean " 'counter-notes,' " he still *both* urges "[t]he symbol-hunter in Pinterland . . . to bear in mind that fallout of any type"—symbolic or otherwise—"is more akin to scum than to essence" *and* stresses his "major point . . . that a critical reading of a Pinter play must be *essentially* speculative and inconclusive" (in Bold, 109–10, 109–10 n.1; emphasis added).

8  See Culler, "Jacques Derrida," 167–68; Norris; and other works suggested by Jay and Miller, 189. For a summary of the "moves" involved in deconstructing an opposition, see Culler, *OD*, 150. Cain observes that such handbooks or guides to Derrida "inevitably domesticate his work, untangle the gnarled, tortuous prose, and give us access to new interpretive schemes" ("English," 90).

9  Among other examples, Quigley considers Ben's "explanation of the misbehavior of the lavatory"—"It's got a deficient ballcock, that's all" (1:133).

10  The last quoted phrase is from Felman's "poststructuralist" reading of Henry James's *Turn of the Screw*. Cf. the final paragraph in Schechner, 184.

11  Van Laan uses a kind of stimulus-response model for Pinter's "play" with his audience, aiming to redress what he considers inappropriate responses to Pinter's plays (499). Even if Pinter does "prompt" his audience, many still fail to respond as dutifully as he would like. For Van Laan they would be responding "improperly" to the play. Cf. Hudgins, "Intended," 115.

12  Diamond's view of *Dumb Waiter* as a parody of the "established conventions" of American gangster films and British detective stage plays regards the play as "about" these conventions (108–9). Thompson claims that the "ambivalent ending" of *Dumb Waiter* is necessitated by Pinter's mixing elements from circus, thrillers, and music hall (77).

13  See Culler, *OD*, 81–83; cf. de Man, *Blindness*, 107, and *Allegories*, 131. That Culler sees

deconstruction as able to explore "the problematic situation to which stories of reading have led us" and as "the culmination of recent work on reading" demonstrates the introjective/projective interplay at work in any reading theory, including de Man's.

14 See Rabkin, 142, 146, and Paul, 6.

15 Reviews of the first London production of *Dumb Waiter* were mixed; though some expressed frustration with "Pinter's" failure to provide a meaningful experience, at least one critic stressed how "extremely funny" it was (Alvarez, "Wanted," 150). The 1987 ABC-TV production of *Dumb Waiter* underscores its comic dimensions through several additional sequences.

16 Cf. Mortimer, 718, and D. Thompson, 118.

17 On the theme of "authority" in *Dumb Waiter*, cf. Pinter, "A Play," 7. See chap. 8.

18 My phrase alters "motive-mongering" in Almansi and Henderson, 17. Cf. Carpenter's description of the critic as a "profundity-monger" ("Absurdity," 281).

19 The Sumus Theatre production of *Dumb Waiter*, part of *No Holds Barred*, was based on a similar interpretation, according to director Keith Scales in a conversation with me after the performance on 28 August 1986.

20 Cf. Almansi and Henderson's view that Pinter plays "con-tricks" on his audience, and his characters on one another (11–23, 93). See also Kalson and Prentice.

21 Quigley bases his own philosophical pluralism on that of William James and on Nelson Goodman, who emphasizes "right versions" of "worlds." See esp. Quigley, *MSOW*, 41–43.

22 Regarding the *Modern Drama* articles on *Dumb Waiter* by himself and Van Laan, see Quigley, *MSOW*, 301 n.7; cf. Quigley's critique of Van Laan in "Design and Discovery": "The critic's task is to achieve the *appropriate* generic *balance* between inferential connection and functional discontinuity" (100 n.2; emphasis added). Quigley's own current book in preparation explores what he calls "the appropriate relationship" among various theories and practices regarding language, linguistics, and literary studies.

23 Cima defines effects of Pinter's use of "the Heisenberg principle of indeterminacy" on performance and interpretation (52); Deemer says that Pinter develops "a world on stage that mirrors the strange new world of the new physics [Quantum Mechanics]"; Fuegi regards Beckett's and Pinter's "world where the principle of uncertainty is maintained in the form, structure, and language of the aesthetic construct itself" and considers the "uncertain future" of "[t]he drama of uncertainty" (207); and Klein connects "the rudimentary tension and mechanism of Pinter's work" with Heisenberg's "radical revision of our conception of the universe and our epistemological relation to it" (192).

24 See Deemer; Hudgins, "Intended," 112; cf. Carpenter, "Victims."

25 Cf. de Man's view that reading is "an act of understanding that can never be observed, nor in any way prescribed or verified. . . . Criticism is a metaphor for the act of reading, and this act is itself inexhaustible" (*Blindness*, 107). On the concept of metaphor (*la métaphore vive*), see Ricoeur; cf. Lakoff and Johnson, 139–46: "New Meaning."

## 5  Thematic Tactics and Ritual Ruses: Searches for Meaning

1 See, e.g., pt. 1 of Lentricchia, 2–210: "A Critical Thematics, 1957–77."

2 For another perspective on Gale's attempts to recuperate Pinter's intended meanings, see

Mailloux, *Interpretive Conventions*, 152: "By communicative interpretation I mean the attempt by readers to recover the intention of the author."

3    On the importance of considering Pinter's plays in this context, see esp. King, "Pinter's Progress," and Klein. Cf. Gale: "One of the things that has always interested me is how stylistic changes parallel [Pinter's] changes in thematic focus. As I look at his films, I have become more involved in stylistic analysis—and I suppose my interest in Pinter's films may parallel his shifts in interest (thematic, technical, in choice of medium, etc.)" (commentary).

4    Cf. Gale, "Character and Motivation," originally entitled "*The Homecoming*: A Question of Need"; and "Life at a Standstill," 13–14.

5    More recently, Gale observes that contradictory critical statements about Pinter's plays are (as Pinter has described his characters' statements) "both true and false" and still "valid" (*HPCA*, 18).

6    Interview with author and commentary.

7    Repeating the thesis of *BGU* in *B*, Gale again quotes Pinter's explanation that Pinter's *Caretaker* is "about love," adding that love is "the clue to understanding those dramas which follow" (introduction, xiv).

8    See Dukore, *HP*, 1–2. On my account of my own first responses to *Old Times*, in Elliott, "Fantasy behind Play," 542–43, see also Bleich, *SC*, 127.

9    Cf. Gale: "A common criticism of most of the recent studies of Pinter's canon . . . is that they tend to play scholarly games with the works. . . . [T]hese attempts at deeper meaning all too frequently take us away from an enjoyment of the plays themselves and ignore the dramas' effectiveness as *theatre*" (review of Esslin, *PW*, 177). See also Scott: "We should not ask what [Pinter's] plays 'mean' but rather see them as theatrical experiences engaging and provoking an emotional and intellectual response from his audience" (9).

10    Gros Louis and Kimball King were readers for Duke University Press, and these comments are excerpts from their reports on *BGU* printed both on the dust jacket and in the catalog.

11    According to Pinter's first wife, Vivien Merchant, as quoted in "Pinter's Wife Names Antonia," Pinter's affair with Fraser began some time in January 1975. See also P. Hall, 154.

12    Gale, 153, n. 23, cites Hewes, "Probing" as "helpful" to him in understanding not only this play but Pinter's work overall. Cf. *BGU*, 148 n.30, and throughout.

13    In the discussion period after his October 1989 reading at the 92d Street Y, at first Pinter stated, "I can no longer write a play about a family and what happens to it"; then he realized that *One for the Road* is "in a rather odd way . . . about what happens to a family, and I think it [destruction by those in power] really does happen to a lot of families now, and there seems to be no stopping it, unless one really draws attention to it." Cf. "Radical," 4.

14    Cf. Gale, *BGU*, 22; *B*, xiv; "HP: Modern Dramatist," 81; and "Variable Nature," 17.

15    Cf. Gale, *BGU*, 174; "Significance"; and "Nature," 196.

16    Interview with author. Unless indicated otherwise, biographical information pertaining to Gale and statements attributed to him are from this source, as elaborated in subsequent commentary.

17    For a different perspective on a production of *Old Times*, in which Pinter himself played Deeley, see Gale, "Observations." Gale adds: "Besides *Old Times*, I find *The Lover*

moving; *The Collection*, *The Caretaker*, *Landscape*, *Night*, not so moving, but very funny" (commentary).

18  On intellectual distance in response to Pinter's *The Homecoming*, see Hudgins, "Intended." See also Gordon, "Pigeonholing Pinter."

19  Gale comments: "[My family] also *help* me—in discussions, in indexing, etc." In *BGU* Gale acknowledges his wife Kathy's "time-consuming aid and advice."

20  See also Bercovitch, 631, 635.

21  See Musser on implications of the metaphorical usages of *seminal*. Hinchliffe also writes in his 1981 revised edition of *HP*: "On this base of line by line examination other critics have been able to build their critical approaches" (28).

22  See thematic topics indexed in Gale, *B*. More recently published topics include identity and the self (Berkowitz; Ganz, *Realms*); time and memory (Braunmuller); friendship and betrayal (Knowles); play (Whitaker). The list could go on for pages. There are plans to update such a list in a revised edition of Gale's *Bibliography*, expected from G. K. Hall in a few years. On thematic and technical continuity and change in Pinter's later plays, see Hinchliffe, "After *No Man's Land*"; King, "Pinter's Progress"; L. Smith; and Stevenson. See also my annual bibliographies in the *Pinter Rev.* and "Supplement: Latterday Strategies," in Merritt, "Major Critics."

23  Cf. Burkman, "Harold Pinter's *Betrayal*," 505, and *Arrival*, 18–19.

24  See Burkman, letter to author: "the recreation of Stanley by Monty and Co. is a parody of seasonal ritual and . . . he is not 'reborn as the new spirit of spring and life' as Edward is." Cf. Burkman, *DWHP*, 35.

25  Cf. Gale, *B*, 56. See Burkman's epilogue: "Gone is the sacrifice of a scapegoat at the center of so many of Pinter's dramas. No exchange of power, no outer conflict or exterior confrontation shapes the drama"; however, she adds: "The dramas retain . . . not only a concern with the same themes and kinds of relationships but also the rhythms of ritual . . . [and] a ritualistic treatment of time" (141–42).

26  Cf. Gale, *BGU*, 35.

27  *Slight Ache* also serves as an extended example in Auburn and Burkman, 709–40. See also Burkman, "Death and the Double." Cf. Gale, *BGU*, 79.

28  Cf. Styan, "Drama as Ritual," 325.

29  Interview with author and letter to author. Unless indicated otherwise, biographical information pertaining to Burkman and statements attributed to her are from these sources.

30  For an anthropological and literary examination of myth and ritual in human society, providing a more up-to-date perspective on Frazer and Freud apropos of ritual sacrifice, see Girard, esp. 96, 193–222, & 316–18.

31  See also Burkman, "Earth and Water"; "*Family Voices*," 169–73; "Multiple Levels"; and "Pinter's *Turtle Diary*," 34–37.

32  See also Burkman, "Hirst as Godot." Flannery finds Burkman's "reading of Ionesco's *The Killer* and Pinter's *The Homecoming* in the light of their ritualistic substructure" to be "particularly insightful" and cites in detail "the archetypal level [of Ruth's transfer] uncovered by Burkman" (543).

33  In addition to those mentioned in my text below, see Cardullo, 10; Dutton, 53; Fischer-Seidel; Hornby, 171; and J. A. Nelson.

### 6  Psychoanalytic Maneuvers: Smoke Screens against Recognition

1   For a more recent philosophical viewpoint on the "verification" issue that Pinter presents in "primarily emotional terms," see Dobrez, 368, 314. On *Betrayal* as a "drama of inquiry," cf. Quigley, *MSOW*, 221–52 (see chap. 4).

2   Pinter says that he wrote *Birthday Party* "more or less at the same time" as *Dumb Waiter*, in 1957 ("A Play," 8). Esslin explains that "Pinter submitted the two further plays he had written after *The Room*: *The Party* (later *The Birthday Party*) and *The Dumb Waiter*" to Michael Codron, who produced "the former" (*PTP*, 19–20). *Dumb Waiter* was first performed on stage in 1959 (in German), a year after the first London performance of *Birthday Party*. *Room* and *Birthday Party* and *Dumb Waiter* and *Caretaker* appeared together in separate early editions by Grove Press. Vol. 1 of Pinter, *Complete Works*, collects the first three plays together with *Slight Ache* and other works.

3   Cf. contrasting judgments in Burkman, *DWHP*, 104–7; Gale, *BGU*, 135. See also A. C. Hall, "Beat," 54.

4   See also Köhler, "Establishment"; Mengel, *HPD*; and Sakellaridou, *PFP*, as discussed in chap. 8.

5   Interview with author and subsequent conversations and correspondence. Unless indicated otherwise, biographical information relating to Gordon and other statements attributed to her are from these sources.

6   In contrast, see Sinyard, 27–28. Gordon also notices that Pinter emphasizes "[t]he Oedipal situation in which Leo is involved" ("*Go-Between*," 88–90).

7   Introduction to the 1st edition, in Esslin, *PTP*, 10. Unless indicated otherwise, subsequent references in my text are from the 1984 edition.

8   On *Caretaker* and *Homecoming*, cf. Esslin, 114–15 & 154, 159–60.

9   On *Betrayal* as only somewhat of a "departure" for Pinter, cf. Hornby: despite the "conspicuous . . . absence" of "the ambiguity that characterize's his usual work," it is "not a complete departure" epistemologically; rather, it is a deconstruction of "dramatic realism" (172–73, 177).

10  Barranger observes that *PW* is "in one way superior to other recent books on Pinter because [Esslin] has been given access to manuscripts and drafts that appear to be unavailable to other critics" (475). Cf. Gale, review of *PW*, 177.

11  Cf. Gale, review of *PW*, esp. 180 and *B*, 80. See also Hughes, "Playwright," 49; Luddy, review of *PW*, 34–35; Mortimer, 719; Peter, "Two Views," 70.

12  Some disagreement occurs even in two judgments of the chronology: cf. Luddy: Esslin "gets at the quality of Pinter's life rather than merely enumerating facts"; and Gale: "Though it reads somewhat like a series of notecards, it is the most complete gathering of facts about the artist's life yet" (177).

13  Cf. Hughes, "Playwright," 49.

14  See also Gale, review of *PW*, 177; Peter, "Two Views," 70; and Warner, 748–49.

15  See this excerpt from Bly's headnote: "Martin Esslin was trained as a director at the Reinhardt Seminar in Vienna, and studied English and philosophy at the University of Vienna. After the occupation of Austria by Hitler in 1938, Esslin went to England and joined the BBC in 1940. He worked for the BBC for 37 years, the last 17 as head of the Radio Drama Department. Mr. Esslin retired from the BBC in 1977 and has been

Professor of Drama at Stanford University since that time. He has also served since 1977 as Dramaturg at the Magic Theater in San Francisco" (19). Bly and Esslin also discuss Esslin's work as a production dramaturge at the Eugene O'Neill Center in Waterford, Connecticut, since 1969.

16  Chap. 4 is still the most critically appreciated portion of his monograph on Pinter. Gale evaluates it as "excellent" (*B*, 80). Even Gilman, whose review of *PW* is one of the most negative that I have examined, concludes: "At his best . . . Esslin is able to offer some very helpful illustrations of how Pinter's dialogue achieves its effects" (36). (For further discussion of Esslin's work on Pinter's language, see chap. 7.)

17  The other questions that Esslin lists are as follows: "What do you think of this picture (poem, novel, book, symphony)? How does it affect you? Why do you like (or dislike) it? Do you advise me to see (read, hear) it? What should I look for in it to derive pleasure or profit from it? How does it relate to other works in its field? What can I learn from it to help me excel in the same art form?"

18  Cf. Dennis, 22; Rusinko, review, 115; Peter, "Two Views," 70; Warner, 748.

19  See chap. 6 in Wright, 79–104: "Object-Relations Theory: Self and Other."

20  For opposing views, see Dearlove, 127 and Jiji, review, 115.

21  Letter to author, 31 March 1982, and interview with author. Unless indicated otherwise, biographical information about Gabbard and statements attributed to her are from these sources.

22  Gabbard ruled out Beckett because so much had already been written on him and Albee because a member of her dissertation committee did not like him. After publishing her dissertation on Pinter, Gabbard also published some criticism on Albee, as well as a book on Stoppard.

23  An early working title for my own dissertation, "The Child in Pinter's Audience," reflects a similar viewpoint. Cf. Schiff and others cited in the first paragraph of this chapter.

24  Burkman used similar terms in describing her sense of the "basis" of Pinter's plays in Frazerian ritual (interview with author).

25  On Pinter's characters' "defense mechanisms" of projection and denial in *Room*, *Slight Ache*, and *Caretaker*, cf. Gabbard, "Roots."

26  Moi suggests that patriarchal customs produce this emphasis in criticism on "the Realm of the Proper" (110–13). For further discussion of gender related issues concerning Pinter criticism, see chap. 8.

27  Cf. Jiji: "[Gabbard] specifically excludes Pinter as subject. . . . And yet, the plays are literally taken as dreams, even characterized as to their dream function. . . . Yet, we must ask, if we are not to see them as Pinter's dreams, whose dreams are they?" (review, 115–16). See also Dearlove: "[W]hose dream structures Pinter's plays? Although an archetypal dreamer is suggested, the progression [in the dream series] implies that the dream is Pinter's. On the other hand, the specific plays are treated as if the dreams are those of one or more characters" (126).

28  Cf. Brooks, 334.

29  For a similar presentation of audience response to *Dumb Waiter*, cf. Gabbard, "Pinter Surprise," 184–85.

30  This desire to protect Pinter as well as themselves was perhaps most noticeable in my interviews with Gordon, Gabbard, and Sakellaridou. For further discussion, see chap. 8.

31  Cf. Kane, "Weasel," as cited in chap. 5. On Pinter's rejection of his own Jewish background and identity, see also Woodroffe, "Taking Care." David Bleich has suggested to me in conversation (October 1986) that failure to "understand" Pinter may derive in an important way from intervention of the author's Jewishness in certain facets of his work, making it unrecognizable and unfathomable for many (non-Jewish) members of his audience. This factor may contribute to the peculiar "alienation effect" of Pinter's dramaturgy.

32  While also providing a biographical account of Pinter, focusing especially on his Jewish background, Baker and Tabachnick, 4, point out the difficulties of this approach to him. See also Tabachnick and Baker. Cf. D. Thompson, viii, 61.

33  Salem, "L'Implicite déchiffrable," on the psychic symbolism of *The Room*, further extends Paul Diel's theories to "deciphering" Pinter. For a more recent summary of Salem's point of view in English, see "Impact." See also articles by Back and Suter; Dobrez, 317–23; and Spitz.

34  Burkman, "Harold Pinter's *Betrayal*" alludes to Lacan, René Girard, Mircea Eliade, and others, updating her references to Freud and Frazer. See also work by A. C. Hall; Savran; and Woodroffe.

35  Cf. Esslin, "Search," 202, 206–7, as cited above.

### 7  Some Other Language Games: Linguistic Parlays and Parleys

1  Cf. *Philosophical Investigations*, 5e, which develops this point, and 80e, where Wittgenstein refers again to "the analogy between language and games."

2  As in my previous chapter, all references to Esslin's monograph on Pinter are to the 1984 edition, unless indicated otherwise. "Language and Silence" (chap. 4) is substantially the same in the 1st and 4th editions. Aside from relatively few minor alterations in typography, grammar, and style, the most substantive change extends a generalization about "the highly compressed stage poetry of recollected experience in *Landscape* and *Silence*" (*PW*, 208) to include *Old Times*, *Betrayal*, and *A Kind of Alaska* (*PTP*, 235).

3  Cf. Winston, 397–98.

4  Cf. Quigley, *PP*, 141.

5  For a more recent exploration of the functions of Pinter's linguistic "duality," see Stevenson, 35–36. See also Meltzer, "Unconscious."

6  The quotations within my quotations are from Wittgenstein, *Philosophical Investigations*, 11e, as quoted by Quigley, *PP*, 39.

7  Quigley is citing *Philosophical Investigations*, 126e; cf. *PP*, 40.

8  Culler defines *intertextuality* as "the interaction within a text of various modes of discourse or of languages drawn from other literary texts and from discourse about the world" ("Structuralism," 984).

9  For a historical account of relationships between Stanislavski's notions of creativity in acting (animating "subtext") and pre-Freudian psychological notions of the unconscious ("subconscious") and consequences for actors' portrayals of Pinter's characters, see Schmitt, 349, 350. See also Durbach.

10  Quigley quotes Pinter's account to Bensky: "I went to a Jewish club, by an old railway arch, and there were quite a lot of people often waiting with broken milk bottles in a particular alley we used to walk through. *There were one or two ways of getting out of it—one*

*was a purely physical way*, of course, but you couldn't do anything about the milk bottles—we didn't have any milk bottles. *The best way was to talk to them*, you know, sort of 'Are you all right?', 'Yes, I'm all right.' 'Well, that's all right then, isn't it?' And all the time keep walking toward the lights of the main road" (*PP*, 47–48; Bensky, 31; emphasis added by Quigley).

11 Cf. Quigley, *"The Dwarfs,"* esp. 417, 421–22.

12 The other two functions are the "ideational" and the "textual." Quigley, *PP*, 44–45, summarizes two of the three functions but omits explicit reference to the "textual."

13 Quigley, review of Diamond, 514.

14 The first usage of the word *context* in *Webster's New World Dictionary* (2d college ed.) is just as problematic as the definitions of *subtext* already cited: "the parts of a sentence, paragraph, discourse, etc. immediately next to or surrounding a specified word or passage and determining its exact meaning [to quote a remark out of *context*]." This definition of *context* uses spatial concepts consonant with the referential theory of meaning. Here context is *beside* or *around* text, just as subtext is said to be "underlying" (*beneath*, *behind*, or *underneath*) it. A second definition is somewhat more to my point: "the whole situation, background, or environment relevant to a particular event, personality, creation, etc."

15 For a definition of *resymbolization*, see Bleich: "Symbolization occurs in the perception and identification of experiences; resymbolization, when the first acts of perception and identification produce in us a need, desire, or demand for explanation" (*SC*, 39).

16 Cf. Esslin on "ill-written criticism . . . contain[ing] its own corrective, eliminat[ing] itself": "It is, after all, precisely the fusion of form and content, the fact that *how* something is said deeply affects and determines the nature of *what* is said, which distinguishes literature [and criticism] from other forms of verbal communication" ("Search," 210).

17 Cf. Harold Bloom: "In the finest critics . . . 'one hears the full cry of the human. They tell one why it matters to read. They do not give one mere linguistic problematics. I have never believed that the critic is the rival of the poet, but I do believe that criticism is a genre of literature or it does not exist' " (quoted in Lehman, 57).

18 Interview with author. Unless indicated otherwise, biographical information relating to Quigley and subsequent statements attributed to him are from this interview, as clarified by later correspondence.

19 See Buck; Gale; Hammond; Imhof; and the reviewer for *Choice*.

20 See Esslin: "One of the pitfalls of reviewing in the more serious general literary journals [e.g., the *Times Literary Supplement*; the *New York Review of Books*] is also the need to be amusing and witty at all costs," paralleling "a strand in the educational tradition of the older English universities, notably Oxford" that at times privileges wit "above the judiciousness or even truth of the judgement" ("On Being Reviewed," 23). Reviews of *PP* cited above might be reread from this perspective (as might be reviews of other books cited in earlier chaps.).

21 For acknowledgment of "gratitude" to John McH. Sinclair, see Quigley, *PP*, xiii. Quigley also mentions the importance of M. A. K. Halliday's work as "an important and influential factor" in his developing "interest in linguistics." See also Quigley, *"Dwarfs"* and "Stylistic Analysis."

22   See also Quigley, *PP*, 45 n. 30. (See chap. 2 above for discussion of some of Ellis's critical views.)

23   Ellis, "What Does Deconstruction Contribute" and "Playing Games with Wittgenstein"—a commentary on Staten, "Wittgenstein and the Intricate Evasions"—provide further examples of what Quigley calls the "rigorous . . . challenge" of Ellis's manner of "thinking things through" (*PP*, xiii). Replying to Ellis, however, Staten observes the same "exclusionary move" in Ellis's "Playing Games" and *Theory of Literary Criticism* that I have already noticed in chap. 2 ("Wittgenstein's Boundaries," 316). Here too Staten disputes Ellis's assumptions about relations between Staten's readings of Wittgenstein and Derrida by recounting his own experience. See also Ellis, *Against Deconstruction*.

24   In chap. 4 above I mentioned the prominence of this theme in Quigley's exegesis of *Betrayal*; see chap. 11 in *MSOW*, 221–52, esp. 226–27. As Quigley demonstrates, the so-called *subjective/objective* distinction is still useful in defining playwrights' complex philosophical attitudes toward themes: "For Pinter, we live somewhere between the poles of objectivity and subjectivity, and we repeatedly find ourselves in worlds that threaten to slide towards one or the other" (224).

25   Cf. the position on definitions of *literature* (and, by implication, *nonliterature* or *criticism*) in Cohen, "Propaedeutic." Quigley, "Wittgenstein's Philosophizing," 229–30, also cites Cohen's work on generic change ("History and Genre").

26   Cf. Quigley, "Taking the Measure," 7–11, and "Wittgenstein's Philosophizing," 213, 226, 232–33.

27   The women critics whom I have in mind include Burton; Cooper; George; Kane, *Language of Silence*; Korpimies; and Melrose.

28   For a more recent study of Pinter's "mannerism," see Strunk. Knowles does not cite Quigley but examines "the principal categories of names and naming, including such issues as social and existential identity, and the instrumentality of naming in the exercise of power" ("Names," 113). Cf. Lecca, who uses the theories of H. P. Grice to explain "conversational implicature" in Pinter's plays, for example, *No Man's Land*. French linguistic studies include Deurbergue; Lavédrine; Susinki; and Yvard. See also Santucci and Varley.

29   Applying Labov's and others' revisions of H. P. Grice's concept of "shared knowledge" to *Betrayal*, cf. Cooper: Pinter introduces commonplace "multiple imbalances in shared knowledge . . . lead[ing] his characters and his audience onto the quicksand where each belief they form is betrayed by the next thing they learn" ("Shared Knowledge," 116). Following George Steiner, see Kane: "In the play, as in life, silence is a moment in language" (*Language of Silence*, 17). See also Lahr and Lutterbie.

30   On the *non*cooperative aspects of conversation and on "indirect language games" through which Pinter's characters avoid confrontation in *The Room* and *Landscape*, see Cooper, "Continual Cross Talk" and "Mutual Ruthless Nonconfrontations," respectively. On the comic effects of communication failures (" 'infelicities' caused by the non-securing of uptake") resulting in "a form of 'talking at cross-purposes,' " cf. Elam, 164.

31   For analysis of the "discourse structures" and the "cohesive devices" of *Birthday Party* in terms of its "three mainstreams . . . mystery, menace and humour," building on the main research in discourse analysis and incorporating a generally sympathetic critique of Burton, see Korpimies, 260, 24–29, and esp. 71ff.

32 See also the articles on *No Man's Land* by Byczkowska and Napiórkowska.

33 For a definition of "semiotics" particularly pertinent to the semiotics of drama and theater, see Elam, 1; cf. Pavis, *Languages*. A definition of "four pitfalls that await the novice semiotician of the drama and the theatre" appears in Styan, "Quince's Questions," 4–6. For summary and evaluation of recent developments in this field, see Carlson, "Contemporary Concerns," esp. 281–82, 287; and see also Esslin, *Field*.

34 For a more recent account of developments in theater semiotics, see the three-part series by Shevtsova.

35 See also Santucci, 15–16, and throughout.

36 On the "hermeneutic or interpretative importance" of such "paralinguistic features" of drama and theater as Melrose discusses, cf. Elam, 78–83. For a very technical account of an excerpt from Pinter's *No Man's Land* from the perspective of "functional stylistics," with special emphasis on features of the actor's vocal tone and body, see Melrose and Melrose.

37 See also Barber, "Precise Words"; Gross; Ooi; and Pinter, *One for the Road*, 26. For further discussion, see chaps. 8–10.

38 Cf., e.g., articles by Brater; Knapp; and dissertations by Tucker and Kendzora. Gale is preparing a filmography of Pinter. See also "Supplement: Latterday Strategies," in Merritt, "Major Critics."

39 For further discussion of some relations between Pinter's plays and comic theory, see Clausius.

40 Cf. reviews by Esslin and Mercurio. See contrasting reviews by D. H. R.; Hinchliffe; and Pallen.

41 For a useful introduction to game and play theory and practical applications of the concept of game-playing in drama in education, therapy, and social conditioning, see Barker.

## 8 Cultural Politics

1 For an account of "leading critical trends in Brechtian criticism today," see Case. For a reassessment of the claim that Pinter is an absurdist, see Sakellaridou, "How Absurd?"

2 See, e.g., Taylor, *Anger and After*, 313–14; Esslin, *Theatre of the Absurd*, 238, 256, and *PTP*, 41; cf. Quigley, *MSOW*; and Diamond. On Pinter as a "new realist," see Sakellaridou, "How Absurd?" 103. For the view that true realism does not exist and that critics' dependence on "the binary opposition" of *realistic/unrealistic* limits them, see chap. 1 in Hornby, 13–28; Hornby argues that "Pinter deconstructs dramatic realism" (177).

3 For a context for some of Pinter's current activities, see Atlas.

4 See Henkle, 189 n.12; cf. Santucci, 5–17; and Sakellaridou, *PFP*, 3.

5 My discussions with Hans-Joachim Schaefer, Chief Dramaturg of the State Theater in Kässel, West Germany, and his colleague Hans-Jörg Grell establish this early perspective on Pinter's work in Germany.

6 Chap. 4 in Anderson, *Anger and Detachment*, extends Taylor's perspective. For a repudiation of the contemporary view of Osborne as a social revolutionary, see Hobson, "Political Slant."

7 For details of Pinter's attitude toward violence and his personal experiences engendering it, see Bensky, 30–31; and Gross, 25. Excerpts from Bensky's interview with Pinter

published in the *New York Times* article entitled "Pinter: 'Violence Is Natural' " have the continuing headline "HP: The World *Is* a Pretty Violent Place." On Pinter's views of the violence at the 1968 American Democratic National Convention in Chicago, see Bosworth. For a more recent discussion of violence in Pinter's work, especially *Hothouse*, see Mengel, "Closed Society," cited further below. See also "Radical," 5, 6.

8    See Pinter, "Author's Note," in *Hothouse*; cf. Bensky, 28–29. See also Gillen, "Nowhere," 86–87 & 96 n.5; cf. Knowles, "Hothouse," 134.

9    Adrian Hall told me (interview with author) that Pinter was "intrigued" when further remarks that he made about political prisoners, El Salvador, and other regimes interning people were omitted from W. Gale's published interview, wondering "whether he was being censored."

10   *One for the Road* lists productions in eight countries in addition to England, including the United States, Holland, Japan, Hungary, Canada, New Zealand, Australia, and South Africa; "Further productions were planned in West Germany, Denmark, Portugal, France, Bulgaria, Iceland, Norway, Poland, Italy and Sweden" (26). For a detailed comparison of the London stage productions, see Cave, 51–55.

11   For an account of improvements in Václav Havel's situation, both politically and financially, as a result of such efforts on his behalf, see Winn. Though Havel was released after the benefit in which the Pinters were involved, early in 1989 he was incarcerated again, becoming the focus of intense worldwide protests for his release, which finally occurred on 17 May. As a result of the remarkable national uprising in December 1989 ("the Velvet Revolution"), Havel became president of Czechoslovakia and was nominated for the Nobel Peace Prize (for the second time) on 28 January 1990. In February "[t]he Pinters visit Havel to share his triumph" (Angelo, 66).

12   Concerning the premiere of *Dumb Waiter* on American television in 1987, cf. Pinter's telephone remarks to Farber about the play's "topical relevance": "I think it also has a serious subject. I always considered it a political play, though it's not overt. But it is a play about dissidence. It's a play about questioning and criticizing powers that remain complaisant and sure of themselves and somewhere upstairs. I think that's still a timely subject."

13   Cf. Dukore, *HP*, 143–46. Pinter describes *Mountain Language* as a play "about suppression of language and the loss of freedom of expression" (quoted in Nichols, "Even the Language Is Taken Away"). See also "Radical," 4, 6.

14   For other reviews of the London premiere, see Ratcliffe and other reviews in the *London Theatre Record*. See also Gussow, "Pinter's Plays."

15   James regards "alternative theatre" as "political theatre" (in Craig's sense, as quoted above). Cf. Anderson, "This," 450, 456 n.11.

16   See "Pinter on the Screen," *Picture Parade* 53, BBC Transcription Service: "I'm talking about two people living socially, and if what takes place between them is a meaningful and accurate examination of them, then it's going to be relevant to you and to society. This relationship will be an image of other relationships, of social living, of living together" (quoted in Sykes, 101; cited by Köhler, "Establishment," 329 n.69).

17   On the "notion of the critic as social strategist," as exemplified by Terry Eagleton, see King, "Rewriting Richardson," 60–61.

18   Cf. Gillen, "From Chapter Ten," 4.

19   Williams finds it "impossible to believe [Pinter's] assurances [on *Saturday Review*

(BBC-2TV)] that 'I'm no longer much interested in myself as a playwright.' There was something willed, media-ridden, even schizoid about [Pinter's] assessment that, 'I've got an awful lot under my belt. It's no great loss.'" Cf. Pinter to Gussow: "I understand your interest in me as a playwright. But I'm more interested in myself as a citizen. We still say we live in free countries, but we damn well better be able to speak freely" ("Pinter's Plays," C17). Pinter has also been prominently involved in securing protection for and championing the cause of Salman Rushdie, the author of *Satanic Verses*, against whom the Ayatollah Khomeini issued a death threat on 14 February 1989. Almost a year later, Pinter delivered Rushdie's lecture "Is Nothing Sacred?" for Rushdie *in absentia* and joined other writers in signing an international petition of protest against the renewal of the death threat. Knowles discusses Pinter's role as a "citizen" in an article forthcoming in the *Pinter Review*. See also Pinter's comments in "Radical."

20  Cf. Pinter, "Language and Lies," and the refutation by Nyholm.

21  The parenthetical descriptions are all quotations from "HP: Growth of an Angry Playwright." See also Canby, "Critic's Notebook"; and Gussow, "Pinter's Plays," C17. Pinter has also adapted Joseph Conrad's antiwar novel *Victory* for the screen.

22  Santucci draws on some of the same sources but claims that Pinter's plays are not relevant to cultural matters and focuses strictly on their language.

23  On dramatic irony—"discrepancy of awareness"—in *Betrayal*, see Mengel, "Unterschiedliche Formen"; for a sociopsychological perspective on Pinter's characters, on "self-monitoring as a key to the understanding of Harold Pinter's plays," see "Das sozialpsychologische Konzept"; on relations between Pinter's *Other Places* and Sacks's *Awakenings*, see Mengel, "Yes!"

24  See Köhler, "Establishment," 328 nn.44–46, and his review of Mengel.

25  For the explanation that in *Homecoming* Pinter may be dramatizing "one of the root causes for late nineteenth and twentieth century anti-Semitism in Britain, namely Jewish involvement in prostitution rackets," see Kane, "Weasel," 24–26.

26  This pertains to literary sociology just as it does to any other field of inquiry. For an account of the problems besetting this field, consult Sammons.

27  Mengel, interview with author and letters to author. Unless indicated otherwise, biographical information about Mengel and statements attributed to him are from these sources.

28  Mengel defines two "historical reasons" for "the radical character of the English drama of the present": "in England the consciousness that there are different classes in society has always been much stronger than on the continent," and, more importantly, there was "the disappointment of all hopes for social change in the wake of the student rebellion of 1968" ("Closed Society," 21). For related historical context, see also Sammons, 5–6.

29  Since expressing these opinions about *Hothouse*, Mengel has changed his mind about it; see Mengel, "Closed Society," 17–19; this essay also goes beyond his earlier concern with "face-to-face" encounters to deal with the alienating "political dimension" of "the relation between the individual and society."

30  See the index in Gale, *B*: the listings for "love and lack of love" and "sex" indicate the prominence of these themes in commentaries about Pinter's work up to 1978.

31  This is a very common description of most of Pinter's plays in the period from *Room* (1957) through *Basement* (1967). Cf. Jiji, "Pinter's Four Dimensional House." On relationships between Pinter's men and women characters in his more recent plays, see

Adler, "Notes" and "Pinter's *Night*." Kathleen Tynan links "a new interest in sex" with "the change of background" to the upper-middle-class apartments and offices of the kind in which Pinter set *Collection, Lover,* and *Tea Party*.

32  This phrase is from *Birthday Party* (1:92). See Adler, "Notes," 382–83.

33  Cf. Köhler: "Actually, Teddy comes very close to a caricature of what he feigns to be when, in an unctuous tirade, he defends his image against his next-of-kin. . . . His is the mentality of a pretentious highbrow whose 'intellectual equilibrium' rests on opportunism. That is essentially why he does not object to his wife being enticed away from him by Lenny and Max who propose that she take up prostitution in their service; desirous to avoid any trouble he even encourages the project" ("Establishment," 320).

34  Cf. Sakellaridou, *PFP*, 160–61, as discussed in my next section. Cf. Ganz, *Realms*, 202.

35  See *Gender and Reading*, esp. Flynn, 284–86, and Bleich, "Gender Interests," 266. See also Culler, "Reading as a Woman," in *OD*, 43–64; Jacobus, "Reading Woman (Reading)," in *Reading Woman*, 3–24; and Siebers, 186–219. For useful recent surveys of feminist criticism, see Allen; Messer-Davidow; Moi; and Treichler. For critiques of Moi and Schweickart, see Schilb. See also Savona and Wilson for several pertinent book reviews.

36  I cite Sakellaridou-Hadzispyrou, "Masks of Women," and Sakellaridou, *PFP*, respectively; my subsequent references to these works in this section follow this format. The dual references substantiate some of the basic similarities and differences between the two versions on several key points. Where there are minor revisions of style, typography, or punctuation, my quotations follow the published version. Unless indicated otherwise, single page references are to *PFP*.

37  Hadzispyrou, interviews with author, 5 June 1982 and 1 July 1982; Hadzispyrou and Sakellaridou, letters to author. Unless indicated otherwise, biographical information about Sakellaridou and statements attributed to her are from these sources.

38  The later interview and a checklist appear in *New Theatre Quart*. 6 (1990): 174–87.

39  For reviews of Sakellaridou, *PFP*, see Merritt (an earlier version of material in this chapter); and Lee: "Highly recommended for all collections." A review by Leslie Kane in the *Pinter Rev.* 3 (1989) is in press.

40  See Sakellaridou, *PFP*, 168–69.

41  Burkman, "Death and the Double," 140; cf. Gabbard, *DS*, 250.

42  On Pinter's response to Visconti's production, see chap. 1 above; on Peter Hall's Aldwych Theatre production as well as Visconti's, see Sakellaridou, *PFP*, 168. On the Aldwych production, see also Cave, 8–19.

## 9  Contingencies of Value Judgments of Pinter's Plays

1  Passages that I cite from Smith, "Contingencies," 20–23, do not appear in the revised version in Smith, *Contingencies*, 42–43. Subsequent references in my text are also to the essay.

2  Sean Page, a professor of Spanish at University College, Dublin, and also a theater critic, recalled that the 1960 BBC Radio broadcast of *Night Out* was his own first encounter with Pinter's work (Elliott, telephone conversation). On Quigley's experience, see chap. 7 above.

3  This passage does not appear in exactly the same form in the revised version of the Bristol

University speech, published in "Writing for the Theatre," which removes all specific references to Bolt and some other passages.

4  For reports on the discussion of the *Evening Standard* Drama Awards Panel in judging "the Best Play of 1960," see Wintour et al., 16–17, 109. Unpublished correspondence between Pinter and BBC officials during this period indicates that Pinter was paid for his interview appearances; see Pinter, letters.

5  See Smith, "Contingencies," 22; cf. Esslin, "Search," 203, as cited in chap. 6.

6  See the *Wolverhampton Express and Star*; the Birmingham *Express and Star*; the *Oxford Times*; the Cambridge *Daily News*; the Oxford *Mail*; *Varsity*; and *Isis*—all cited in Hobson, "Life outside London."

7  See also Esslin, "HP's Work," and chap. 6 above.

8  Cf. Smith: "literary evaluation is no longer thought of as confined to the discrete verbal statements of journalistic and academic 'critics.' The evaluation of a work must be seen, rather, as a continuous process, operating through a wide variety of individual activities and social and institutional practices" ("Value/Evaluation," 449); see also 450–51.

9  Cf. Smith: "Although . . . literary evaluation is by no means confined to academic criticism, nevertheless the normative practices of scholastic institutions form a central part of the transmission and indeed *definition* of literary value within any community or culture" ("Value/Evaluation," 451).

10  Cf. an audience member: "Can you use television to 'go to the people' but in order to bring them eventually to the theatre? I'm thinking of how Pinter's *Birthday Party* . . . was shown on television before it became a great success in the theatre" (quoted in "After *Fanschen*: A Discussion," in *Performance and Politics*, 311). Both Taylor and this speaker refer to the Rediffusion-TV broadcast on 22 March 1960, directed by Joan Kemp-Welch (see Esslin, *PTP*, 25).

11  For another viewpoint on "the problem of subjectivity in value judgment," see Rod.

12  See Hobson, *Indirect Journey*, 215, and "Pinter minus the Moral."

13  Hartman, 105, seems cognizant of such a problem in commenting on an essay by collaborator Messer-Davidow. For a complex illustration of the conundrum of personal relationship and critical judgment, see Derrida, "Like the Sound." See also Pool, and previous discussion of "Reviewmanship" in chapters 2 and 7.

14  For a statement of this "belief," see paragraph two of Free, "Theory," 77.

15  For the importance of Hobson's early training as a historian and his personal attitudes toward religion and marital love to his dramatic criticism, see Hobson, *Indirect Journey*.

16  Wardle, interview with author. Unless indicated otherwise, biographical information about Wardle and statements attributed to him are from this interview.

17  E.g., Simon does refer to "the rare privileged moments of Pinter," who "mold[s] language into a mask under which the unspoken is the truth" (*Singularities*, 88); he also writes: "After Brecht there is virtually nothing till Beckett and the absurdists; after that, except for Pinter, there are no more playwrights" (99). Cf. Simon's favorable reviews of *Collection* and *Lover*, reprinted in *Uneasy Stages*, 6 & 38. His negative review of the 1971 New York revival of *Homecoming* recalls the 1967 production as "brilliant" staging while judging the play one of Pinter's "meager, stunted inventions" (347).

18  Cf. Simon: "In a theater full of phonies, there is, I believe, none bigger, none more pervasive, none phonier than Harold Pinter"; "There is wit sporadically in Pinter, but

much more sheer nastiness, and still more vagueness and deliberately self-contradictory mystification" ("Past Dismembered," 54, 55).

19 Nightingale reports that "the producer Alex Cohen has toilet paper bearing the distinguished visage of my fellow critic John Simon, with whom he's long been feuding" (*Fifth-Row Center*, 232).

20 Describing a more recent production of *Old Times* (Roundabout Theater), cf. Gale: "I have never seen a scene affect an audience as strongly as those silent final three minutes did. The audience sat breathless and stunned throughout the scene" ("Observations," 40); contrasting a production in which Pinter himself played Deeley (American Theatre, St. Louis, Missouri, in October 1985), Gale also observes: "there was more posturing among the characters as they created the dumb-show scene . . . and this may have lessened the impact of the moment a bit" (42).

21 See also Rusinko, *Tom Stoppard*, 6–11: "Stoppard and Pinter," and Rusinko, *British Drama*, 45–65: "HP: Minimalist."

22 Rusinko's generalization applies mainly to the premieres of *Betrayal* in London and New York; the reception of the long-lived Parisian production (*Trahisons*) was generally enthusiastic. (Excerpts from reviews are reprinted in the program for *Trahisons*, in "*Trahisons* et la critique parisienne.")

23 See, e.g., Ben-Zvi, who argues that *Betrayal* may be Pinter's "most powerful play" because "sufficiently confident in the handling of surface detail . . . he does not need to imply that the banal is merely a cover or pretext for some far more menacing—and more interesting—reality. The banal becomes, as in Chekhov's plays, the menace" (227).

24 Cf. Sakellaridou, *PFP*, 181: "The sparse and cryptic language of the play is full of hidden feeling. One has to follow clues, to listen hard and watch intensely to spot what is actually happening beneath an often glacial surface." Quoting Barber, who believes that the characters are "rigid with guilt" ("Three Pinter People"), Sakellaridou writes: "One reviewer characteristically suggested that despite their icy demeanour the characters 'underneath are screaming.'" (On "the unspoken beneath the glassily composed surface" of *Landscape*, cf. Wardle, as cited in my text above.)

25 Cf. Davies: Pinter's "new professional-class characters, so much more recognizable in their smugness than the old, are in the same degree more abstract too" (24); Barber describes *Betrayal* as "not a play but an intricate and unimportant machine" ("Three Pinter People").

26 In contrast, Hatch describes aspects of the film of *Betrayal* as "a puzzle that sets one to pondering how people build and dismantle their characters, and that, no doubt, is what Pinter intended" (316); cf. Sakellaridou, *PFP*, 181, as quoted above.

27 Kroll also notices the victimization of *Betrayal* by "a current critical infatuation with leftist clichés" but argues that "Pinter's theme of betrayal cuts through the class structure which still obsesses most younger playwrights" ("Pinter's Dance"). For other perspectives opposing Brustein, see Kerr, "Riveting Counterpoint," and Kakutani.

28 See Elliott, "Stalking Harold Pinter." The information about Pinter's refusing Brustein is from Adrian Hall, interview with author.

29 According to Pinter, "The whole idea of the children is not heavy, but it exists, and I was very glad we were able to do that. Most married couples who commit adultery also have children who are a major factor" (quoted in Bennetts, "On Film," 23).

30 "There but for the grace of God go I" was a response to the film of *Betrayal* and most of Pinter's other plays expressed by some academic Pinter critics in interviews with me, but more direct identification was characteristic of some others' experience, including my own.

31 *Betrayal* was nominated for "Best Screenplay" by the Academy of Motion Picture Arts and Sciences, though it did not win the award.

32 Cf. Nightingale: "these are sophisticated meritocrats, whose hostilities are obliquely expressed even by Pinter's standards of obliquity" ("Anti-Clockwise," 718).

33 Cf. Spiegel: "Our young audiences don't read any more. They don't listen to the music of beautifully spoken language. They listen to noises. TV producers dull the sensitivity with crashing planes and cars and God knows what. They're impervious to the joy of listening" (quoted in Farson, "Sam Spiegel's 'Betrayal' ").

34 See Gale's description of Pinter as "the best and most important dramatist of his generation" ("Observations," 43); Esslin describes Pinter as "one of the best screenwriters (and radio dramatists) in the world" (*Field*, 34). Dukore still ends his 1988 revised edition of *HP* with the same "critical commonplace" cited in the 1982 edition as "uncommon critical sense: Pinter *is* among the most important dramatists now living" (149).

35 Or that Gale wrote Simon and Schuster's Monarch Notes on *Birthday Party* and *Homecoming*. Graff observes that such "study guides" are "a phenomenon that cries out for attention from sociologists of criticism" (231).

## 10  The Case of Pinter: Toward Theory as Practice in Critical and Cultural Change

1 My references are to Fish, "Change," as published originally in *South Atlantic Quart.*, reprinted as chap. 7 in *DWCN*, 141–60. For the convenience of my readers, the page numbers from *DWCN* follow a slash in parenthetical references in the text.

2 For a critique of several reader-response theories (Bleich, Holland, Iser, Culler, and Fish), and exposition of a theory of "interpretive conventions," see Mailloux, *Interpretive Conventions*, esp. 22, 36, 57, 138, 150, & 151. In a review of Mailloux, while proposing "schemata" as a "more powerful heuristic [than interpretive conventions] by which to investigate questions about the nature of literature and the reception of literary works," Beers acknowledges "drawbacks to machine metaphors of human understanding" (92). See also Berg; and Steig, 3–16: "Theories of Reading."

3 Cf. the "no consequences" argument against theory in Fish, *Is There a Text*, and throughout writings collected in *DWCN*, esp. 336–41.

4 Mailloux observes that "the social reading models of Fish, Iser, and Culler have been specifically criticized for neglecting economic and political factors in their accounts" (*Interpretive Conventions*, 41). He concludes, however, that "the institutional conventions governing reading may be grossly determined by economic, political, and larger social structures; but once the conventions are in place, those extrainstitutional forces do not affect the specific dynamics of interpretation in reading. Therefore, Fish, Iser, and Culler can safely focus on the intersubjective categories and shared conventions of reading literature while bracketing more general sociological considerations." My argument in this book challenges this conclusion.

5 Cohen, "Propaedeutic," 1, also cites Nisbet.

6   For a brief analysis of the relations between "intra- and extraliterary horizons of
    expectations" proposed by Jauss's theory of reception and the power of literature to
    change society "by changing readers' social expectations," see Mailloux, *Interpretive
    Conventions*, 168–69. De Man suggests some limitations of both the concept *horizons of
    expectations* and "the horizon of Jauss's methodology," though he compares "an element of
    not-knowing . . . built within the model of the horizon" with "an element of indeter-
    minacy and arbitrariness" implied by "the concept of literary sign" (introduction to
    Jauss, *Aesthetics*, xii–xviii).

7   The quotations in this paragraph are from *American Heritage Dictionary of the English
    Language*, 3d ed., s.v. "theory." Cf. Beers: "[A]ny theory, even a theory of literary
    criticism, need only explain phenomena and predict events; it need not (though it may)
    proscribe particular methodologies" (84).

8   Interview with author. Unless cited otherwise, statements attributed to Wardle are from
    this interview.

9   Cf. Wardle, "Pinter, Harold," 657; "Holding," 36.

10  See, e.g., King, "Pinter's Progress"; Dukore, "My, How We've Changed"; Hinchliffe,
    "After *No Man's Land*"; and L. Smith, "Pinter's Later Plays." In contrast, reviewing the
    National Theatre production of *Betrayal*, Davies speculates that "recent changes in
    [Pinter's] domestic circumstances . . . may have helped to insulate Pinter for the time
    being against the threat of the engulfing Kullus" (24).

11  On changes in Pinter's plays through *Betrayal*, see also Gussow, "I Started."

12  Pertinent problems of the assumptions and practices of the New Criticism are succinctly
    described by Graff, 173–79.

13  The dissertation proposal outline lists all of Pinter's plays with game-related quotations
    from each one as epigraphs for each chapter (two of which I have reused with intended
    irony in the epigraphs beginning this book and in chap. 7). I later limited the body of
    the project to *Birthday Party*, *Caretaker*, and *Homecoming*, eliminating the epigraphs but
    not the game motif (which I have also reconstructed here). The proposal also describes the
    focus of Gordon and Esslin on "the 'unconscious life' of Pinter's characters as more risky
    and ultimately less rewarding than the analysis of the audience's unconscious responses"
    that I intended to do.

14  On Holland's "radical shift" to Bleich's viewpoint as the product of "some irrational
    leap" rather than a negotiated "consensus," cf. Berg, 271. On inconsistencies in
    Holland's change in "point of view," see Bleich, *SC*, 115–16 n.35. See also Elliott, "A
    *New* Critical Epistemology."

15  At this time I also encountered work in progress by Earl Miner, Richard Ohmann,
    Michael Riffaterre, Barbara Herrnstein Smith, and others for the 1981 MLA Convention
    special session that I organized on "The Cultural Institutionalization and Validation of
    Literature." For first bringing some of this work to my attention, I thank Ralph Cohen.

16  See Elliott, "Theoretical Writing as a Kind of Change."

17  "The journal invites articles, notes, production reviews, queries, bibliographical, and
    other information which furthers appreciation of work of Harold Pinter" (*Pinter Rev.*
    1:ii). In addition to those already mentioned and myself as bibliographical editor, the
    editorial board includes Thomas P. Adler (Purdue University); Linda Ben-Zvi (Colorado
    State University); Elin Diamond (Rutgers University); Bernard F. Dukore (Virginia
    Tech); Mark Estrin (Rhode Island College); Christopher C. Hudgins (University of

Nevada); Kimball King (University of North Carolina); Thomas R. Whitaker (Yale University); and Hersh Zeifman (York University). For the MLA's directives on new Allied Organizations, see *MLA Newsletter* 21 (Summer 1989): 5–6. My final quotations are from the *Pinter Rev.* 2:v. For reviews of the inaugural issue of the *Pinter Rev.*, see Centing; Katz; and McLintock.

18  See Gillen, "Introduction" and "From Chapter Ten."

19  I am grateful to Gillen for sharing a copy of *Mountain Language* with me before its publication in the *Times Literary Supplement*.

20  For a "radical critique" of competition, presenting cooperation as an alternative for social change, see Kohn.

# Works Cited

Adler, Thomas P. "Notes toward the Archetypal Pinter Woman." *Theatre Jour.* 33 (1981): 377–85.
———. "Pinter's *Night*: A Stroll Down Memory Lane." *Modern Drama* 17 (1974): 461–65.
Allen, Carolyn J. "Feminist Criticism and Postmodernism." In Natoli, 278–305.
Almansi, Guido, and Simon Henderson. *Harold Pinter.* Contemporary Writers, ed. Malcolm Bradbury and Christopher Bigsby. London and New York: Methuen, 1983.
Alter, Robert. *The Pleasures of Reading: In an Ideological Age.* New York: Simon and Schuster, 1989.
Alvarez, A. "Death in the Morning." *New Statesman,* 12 Dec. 1959, 836.
———. "Wanted—A Language." *New Statesman,* 30 Jan. 1960, 149–50.
Anderson, Michael. "Harold Pinter: Journey to the Interior." Chap. 4 in *Anger and Detachment: A Study of Arden, Osborne and Pinter.* London: Pitman, 1976.
———. "This, That and the Other: The Critic and the Alternative Theatre." *Modern Drama* 24 (1981): 445–57.
Angelo, Bonnie. "Profile: Not Quite Your Usual Historian." *Time,* 15 Jan. 1990, 66–68.
Ansen, David. "Movies: Love in a Cold Climate." *Newsweek,* 28 Feb. 1983, 74–75.
Arnold, Gary. " 'Betrayal': Stuck in Reverse." *Washington Post,* 31 Mar. 1983, E10.
Atlas, James. "Thatcher Puts a Lid On: Censorship in Britain." *New York Times Mag.,* 5 Mar. 1989.
Auburn, Mark S., and Katherine H. Burkman, eds. *Drama through Performance.* Boston: Houghton Mifflin, 1977.
Back, Lillian. "The Double in Harold Pinter's *A Slight Ache." Michigan Academician* 15 (1983): 383–90.
———. "Elements of the Uncanny in Harold Pinter's *The Room." Michigan Academician* 14 (1981): 5–12.
Baker, William, and Stephen Ely Tabachnick. *Harold Pinter.* Modern Writers Series. New York: Barnes, 1973.
Barber, John. "Precise Words of Pinter." London *Daily Telegraph,* 30 June 1980, 11.
———. "Three Pinter People in Emotional Agony." London *Daily Telegraph,* 16 Nov. 1978, 13.
Barker, Clive. "Games in Education and Theatre." *New Theatre Quart.* 5 (1989): 227–35.
Barnet, Sylvan, Morton Berman, and William Burto. *A Dictionary of Literary, Dramatic, and Cinematic Terms.* 2d ed. Boston: Little, Brown, 1971.
Barranger, M. S. Rev. of *PW,* by Martin Esslin. *Quart. Jour. of Speech* 57 (1971): 475–76.

Barthes, Roland. *A Lover's Discourse: Fragments*. Trans. Richard Howard. New York: Hill and Wang, 1978.

———. *The Pleasure of the Text*. Trans. Richard Miller. New York: Hill and Wang, 1975.

———. *S/Z*. Trans. Richard Miller. New York: Hill and Wang, 1974.

Bassnett, Susan. "Structuralism and After: Trends and Tendencies in Theatre Analysis, Part One." *New Theatre Quart.* 1 (1985): 79–82.

Batsleer, Janet, Tony Davies, Rebecca O'Rourke, and Chris Weedon. *Rewriting English: Cultural Politics of Gender and Class*. London and New York: Methuen, 1985.

Beale, Walter H. "Modes and Strategies of Discourse." Chap. 2 in *A Pragmatic Theory of Rhetoric*. Carbondale: Southern Illinois Univ. Press, 1987.

Beers, Terry. "Reading Reading Constraints: Conventions, Schemata, and Literary Interpretation." *Diacritics* 18, no. 4 (1988): 82–93.

Belanger, Kelly. "The Medieval Roots of Pinter's *A Slight Ache*: The Matchseller as Fool." *Pinter Rev.* 2 (1988): 39–53.

Bennetts, Leslie. "The Clockwork of 'Old Times': Three Actors Keep Balance in Pinter Play." *New York Times*, 9 Feb. 1984, C19.

———. "On Film, Pinter's 'Betrayal' Displays New Subtleties." *New York Times*, 27 Feb. 1983, sec. 2: 1, 23.

Bensky, Lawrence M. "The Art of the Theater III: Harold Pinter: An Interview." *Paris Rev.* 10 (Fall 1966): 12–37. (Excerpted in "Pinter: 'Violence Is Natural.'" *New York Times*, 1 Jan. 1967, sec. 2: 1, 3.)

Benson, Sheila. "'Betrayal': Affairs, Passion and Friendship." *Los Angeles Times*, 9 Mar. 1983, sec. 6: 1–2.

Ben-Zvi, Linda. "Harold Pinter's *Betrayal*: The Patterns of Banality." *Modern Drama* 23 (1980): 227–37.

Bercovitch, Sacvan. "The Problem of Ideology in American Literary History." *Critical Inquiry* 12 (1986): 631–53.

Berg, Temma F. "Psychologies of Reading." In Natoli, 248–77.

Berkowitz, Gerald M. "The Destruction of Identity in Pinter's Early Plays." *Ariel* 9, no. 2 (1978): 83–92.

Berne, Eric. *Games People Play*. New York: Grove, 1964.

*Betrayal*, by Harold Pinter. Stage production directed by Peter Hall. With Artro Morris, Daniel Massey, Glenn Williams, Michael Gambon, and Penelope Wilton. Lyttelton Theatre, National Theatre, London. Opened 15 Nov. 1978.

*Betrayal*, by Harold Pinter. Stage production directed by Peter Hall. With Blythe Danner, Ernesto Gasco, Ian Thomson, Raul Julia, and Roy Scheider. Trafalgar Theatre, New York. Opened 14 Jan. 1980.

*Betrayal*. Screenplay by Harold Pinter. Film directed by David Jones and produced by Sam Spiegel. With Ben Kingsley, Jeremy Irons, and Patricia Hodge. 95 mins. Distributed by Twentieth-Century Fox International Classics, 1983.

Bigsby, C. W. E. "The Politics of Anxiety: Contemporary Socialist Theatre in England." In *Modern British Dramatists: New Perspectives*, ed. and introd. John Russell Brown, 161–76. Englewood Cliffs, N.J.: Prentice-Hall, 1984.

Billington, Michael. "Pinter's Sleeping Beauty." London *Guardian*, 15 Oct. 1982, 10.

*The Birthday Party*, by Harold Pinter. Stage production directed by Alan Schneider. With

Alexandra Berlin, Ed Flanders, Edward White, Henderson Forsythe, James Patterson, and Ruth White. Booth Theatre, New York. Opened 3 Oct. 1967.

*The Birthday Party*, by Harold Pinter. Stage production directed by Carey Perloff. With Georgine Hall, David Strathairn, Peter Riegert, Richard Riehle, Robert Gerringer, and Wendy Makkena. The Classic Stage Company, CSC Repertory Theatre, New York, 17 Apr. 1988. Previewed 12 Apr. 1988.

*The Birthday Party*, by Harold Pinter. Stage production directed by Peter Wood. With Beatrix Lehmann, John Slater, John Stratton, Richard Pearson, Wendy Hutchinson, and Willoughby Gray. Arts Theatre, Cambridge, Eng. Opened 28 Apr. 1958. Lyric Opera House, Hammersmith. Opened 19 May 1958.

Bladel, Roderick. *Walter Kerr: An Analysis of His Criticism*. Metuchen, N.J.: Scarecrow, 1976.

Blau, Eleanor. "Does 'Betrayal' Reveal a New Pinter?" *New York Times*, 4 Dec. 1979, C7.

Bleich, David. *The Double Perspective: Language, Literacy, and Social Relations*. New York and Oxford: Oxford Univ. Press, 1988.

———. "Emotional Origins of Literary Meaning." *College English* 31 (1969): 30–40.

———. "Gender Interests in Reading and Language." In *Gender and Reading*, 234–66.

———. "Intersubjective Reading." *New Literary History* 17 (1986): 401–21.

———. *Readings and Feelings: An Introduction to Subjective Criticism*. Urbana: NCTE, 1975.

———. *Subjective Criticism*. Baltimore and London: Johns Hopkins Univ. Press, 1978.

Bly, Mark. "Dramaturgy at the Magic and the O'Neill: An Interview with Martin Esslin by Mark Bly." *Theater* (Summer/Fall 1986): 19–24.

Bold, Alan, ed. and introd. *Harold Pinter: You Never Heard Such Silence*. Critical Studies Series. London: Vision, 1984. Repr. Totowa, N.J.: Barnes, 1985.

Bolt, Robert. "Theatre in the Sixties." *New Theatre Mag.* 2 (July 1961): 8–10.

"Book Notes." *Theatre Crafts*, Nov. 1980, 8.

Booth, Wayne C. *Critical Understanding: The Powers and Limits of Pluralism*. Chicago: Univ. of Chicago Press, 1979.

———. "Freedom of Interpretation: Bakhtin and the Challenge of Feminist Criticism." *Critical Inquiry* 9 (1982): 45–76.

Bosworth, Patricia. "Why Doesn't He Write More?" *New York Times*, 27 Oct. 1968, sec. 2: 3.

Brandt, George W., ed. and introd. *British Television Drama*. Cambridge: Cambridge Univ. Press, 1981.

Brater, Enoch. "Cinematic Fidelity and the Forms of Pinter's *Betrayal*." *Modern Drama* 24 (1981): 503–13.

———. "*The French Lieutenant's Woman*: Screenplay and Adaptation." In Gale, *HPCA*, 139–52.

———. "Time and Memory in Pinter's Proust Screenplay." *Comparative Drama* 13 (Summer 1979): 121–26.

———. "Pinter's *Homecoming* on Celluloid." *Modern Drama* 17 (1974): 443–48.

Braunmuller, Albert R. "Harold Pinter: The Metamorphosis of Memory." In *Essays on Contemporary British Drama*, ed. Hedwig Bock and Albert Wertheim, 155–70. Munich: Hueber, 1981.

Brien, Alan. "Communications." *Spectator*, 30 May 1958, 687.

Brooks, Peter. "The Idea of a Psychoanalytic Literary Criticism." In Meltzer, *Trial(s)*, 334–48.

Brown, Bernard. Rev. of *BGU*, by Steven H. Gale. *World Literature Today* 53 (Winter 1979): 118.

Brown, J. R. Rev. of *BGU*, by Steven H. Gale. *Modern Language Rev.* 75 (Oct. 1980): 877.

Brustein, Robert. "Robert Brustein on Theater: Journeys to the End of the World." *New Republic*, 9 Feb. 1980, 26.

Buck, Richard M. Rev. of *PP*, by Austin E. Quigley. *Library Jour.*, 15 Jan. 1976, 341.

Burgess, Anthony. "Academic Criticism." *Literary Half-Yearly* 28, no. 1 (1987): 62–68.

Burkman, Katherine H. *The Arrival of Godot: Ritual Patterns in Modern Drama*. Rutherford, N.J.: Fairleigh Dickinson Univ. Press, 1986.

———. "Death and the Double in Three Plays by Harold Pinter." In Bold, 131–45.

———. "Displacement in Time and Space: Harold Pinter's *Other Places*." Paper presented at the annual meeting of the Modern Language Association, New Orleans, 29 Dec. 1988. Photocopy. Forthcoming in Gordon, *Harold Pinter*.

———. *The Dramatic World of Harold Pinter: Its Basis in Ritual*. Columbus: Ohio State Univ. Press, 1971.

———. "Earth and Water: The Question of Renewal in Harold Pinter's *Old Times* and *No Man's Land*." *West Virginia Univ. Philological Papers* 25 (1979): 101–7.

———. "*Family Voices* and the Voice of the Family in Pinter's Plays." In Gale, *HPCA*, 164–74.

———. "Harold Pinter's *Betrayal*: Life Before Death—and After." *Theatre Jour.* 34 (1982): 505–18.

———. "Hirst as Godot: Pinter in Beckett's Land." *Arizona Quart.* 39 (1983): 5–14.

———. Interview with author. Columbus, Ohio, 29 Oct. 1982.

———. Letter to author, 26 July 1988.

———. "The Multiple Levels of Action in Harold Pinter's *Victoria Station*." *Pinter Rev.* 1 (1987): 22–30.

———. "Pinter's *A Slight Ache* as Ritual." *Modern Drama* 11 (1968): 326–35.

———. "Pinter's *Turtle Diary*: Text into Subtext." *Pinter Rev.* 2 (1988): 33–38.

———, ed. and introd. *Myth and Ritual in the Plays of Samuel Beckett*. Rutherford, N.J.: Fairleigh Dickinson Univ. Press, 1987.

Burton, Deirdre. "Conversation Pieces." In *Literary Text and Language Study*. Explorations in Language Study, ed. Ronald Carter and Deirdre Burton, 86–115. London: Arnold, 1982.

———. *Dialogue and Discourse: A Sociolinguistic Approach to Modern Drama Dialogue and Naturally Occurring Conversation*. London: Routledge and Kegan Paul, 1980.

———. "Making Conversation: On Conversational Analysis, Stylistics, and Pinter." *Language and Style* 12 (1979): 188–200.

Byczkowska, Ewa. "Discourse and the Pattern of Personal Relationships in Pinter's *No Man's Land*." Anglica Wratislaviensia 7. *Acta Universitatis Wratislaviensis*, no. 454 (1979): 73–87.

Cain, William E. *The Crisis in Criticism: Theory, Literature, and Reform in English Studies*. Baltimore and London: Johns Hopkins Univ. Press, 1984.

———. "English in America Reconsidered: Theory, Criticism, Marxism, and Social Change." In *Criticism in the University*, ed. Gerald Graff and Reginald Gibbons, 85–104. Evanston, Ill.: Northwestern Univ. Press, 1985.

Canby, Vincent. "Critic's Notebook: Old Favorites Are No More at Cannes." *New York Times*, 18 May 1989, C23, 29.

————. "Film: Pinter's 'Betrayal,' Directed by David Jones." *New York Times*, 20 Feb. 1983, 78.

————. "Film View: Vitality and Variety Buoy New Movies from Britain." *New York Times*, 6 Mar. 1983, sec. 2: 17–18.

Cardullo, Bert. "Comedy and Meaning in the Work of Harold Pinter." *Notes on Contemporary Literature* 16 (May 1986): 9–12.

Carlson, Marvin. "Contemporary Concerns in the Semiotics of Theatre." *Semiotica* 48 (1984): 281–91.

————. "Theatrical Performance: Illustration, Translation, Fulfillment, or Supplement?" *Theatre Jour.* 37 (1985): 5–11.

————. *Theories of the Theatre: A Historical and Critical Survey, from the Greeks to the Present.* Ithaca and London: Cornell Univ. Press, 1984.

Carne, Rosalind. "Theatre: Space Probe." *New Statesman*, 23 Mar. 1984, 31.

Carpenter, Charles A. "The Absurdity of Dread: Pinter's *The Dumb Waiter*." *Modern Drama* 16 (1973): 279–85.

————. "Quicksand in Pinterland: *The Caretaker*." *Arizona Quart.* 33 (1976): 65–75.

————. " 'Victims of Duty'? The Critics, Absurdity, and *The Homecoming*." *Modern Drama* 25 (1982): 489–95.

————. " 'What Have I Seen, the Scum or the Essence?' Symbolic Fallout in Pinter's *Birthday Party*." *Modern Drama* 17 (1974): 389–402. Rev. and updated version in Bold, 93–112.

Case, Sue-Ellen, ed. *Distancing Brecht.* Special issue of *Theatre Jour.* 39, no. 4 (Dec. 1987): 425–553.

Cast of Trinity Square Repertory Company stage production of *The Hothouse.* Interview with author. Providence, R.I., 25 Mar. 1982.

Cave, Richard Allen. "Harold Pinter." Chap. 1 in *New British Drama in Performance on the London Stage: 1970 to 1985.* Gerrards Cross: Smythe, 1987. New York: St. Martin's, 1988.

Centing, Richard R. "Continuations . . . : A Column of Periodical Reviews." *Small Press,* Dec. 1988, 29.

Cima, Gay Gibson. "Acting on the Cutting Edge: Pinter and the Syntax of Cinema." *Theatre Jour.* 36 (1984): 43–56.

Clausius, Claudia. "Different Times in the Dramas of Harold Pinter." Paper presented at the annual meeting of the Modern Language Association, New Orleans, 29 Dec. 1988.

Cohen, Ralph. "History and Genre." *New Literary History* 17 (1986): 203–18.

————. "The Joys and Sorrows of Literary Theory." In *Innovations/Renovations: New Perspectives on the Humanities.* Theories of Contemporary Culture, ed. Ihab Hassan and Sally Hassan, 113–30. Madison: Univ. of Wisconsin Press, 1983.

————. "A Propaedeutic for Literary Change." *Critical Exchange* 13 (Spring 1983): 1–17.

————. "The Statements Literary Texts Do Not Make." *New Literary History* 13 (1982): 379–91.

————, ed. *Wittgenstein and Literary Theory.* Special issue of *New Literary History* 19, no. 2 (Winter 1988): 209–451.

Cooper, Marilyn M. "Continual Cross Talk: Indirect Language Games in Pinter's Plays." In preparation. Photocopy of table of contents.

————. "Mutual Ruthless Nonconfrontations: Harold Pinter and Language." Paper presented at the annual meeting of the Modern Language Association, Washington, D.C., 27 Dec. 1984. Photocopy.

————. "Shared Knowledge and *Betrayal*." *Semiotica* 64 (1987): 99–117.

Craig, Sandy. "Unmasking the Lie: Political Theatre." In *Dreams and Deconstructions*, 30–48.

Culler, Jonathan. "Beyond Interpretation: The Prospects of Contemporary Criticism." *Comparative Literature* 28 (1976): 244–56. Repr. in *Pursuit*, 3–17.

————. "Interpretations: Data or Goals?" In Hernadi, *Rhetoric*, 275–90.

————. "Jacques Derrida." In *Structuralism and Since: From Lévi-Strauss to Derrida*, ed. John Sturrock, 154–80. Oxford: Oxford Univ. Press, 1979.

————. *On Deconstruction: Theory and Criticism after Structuralism*. Ithaca: Cornell Univ. Press, 1982.

————. *The Pursuit of Signs: Semiotics, Literature, Deconstruction*. Ithaca: Cornell Univ. Press, 1981.

————. "Structuralism." In *Princeton Encyclopedia*, 983–86.

————. *Structuralist Poetics: Structuralism, Linguistics, and the Study of Literature*. Ithaca: Cornell Univ. Press, 1975.

Curcio, Vincent. Rev. of *Pinter: The Player's Playwright*, by David T. Thompson. *Los Angeles Times*, 8 Dec. 1985.

Curtis, Anthony. "London." *Drama*, no. 131 (Winter 1979): 47–49.

Dace, Tish. "Pinter, Harold." In *Dramatists*. Great Writers of the English Language, ed. James Vinson, 465–70. New York: St. Martin's, 1979.

Davies, Russell. "Pinter Land." *New York Rev. of Books*, 25 Jan. 1979, 22–24.

Dearlove, J. E. Rev. of *DS*, by Lucina Paquet Gabbard. *South Atlantic Quart.* 77 (1978): 126.

Deemer, Charles. "Pinter's Way of Looking at the World." In program for *The Homecoming*, n. pag. Stage production directed by Gary O'Brien. New Rose Theatre, Portland, Oreg. 4 June to 12 July 1986.

de Man, Paul. *Allegories of Reading: Figural Language in Rousseau, Nietzsche, Rilke, and Proust*. New Haven: Yale Univ. Press, 1979.

————. *Blindness and Insight: Essays in the Rhetoric of Contemporary Criticism*. 2d ed., rev. Theory and History of Literature, vol. 7. Minneapolis: Univ. of Minnesota Press, 1983.

Denby, David. "Movies: The Pause That Refreshes." *New York*, 28 Feb. 1983, 84.

Dennis, Nigel. "Pintermania." *New York Rev. of Books*, 17 Dec. 1970, 21–22.

Derrida, Jacques. "Like the Sound of the Sea Deep within a Shell: Paul de Man's War." *Critical Inquiry* 14 (1988): 590–652.

————. *Positions*. Trans. and annotated by Alan Bass. Chicago: Univ. of Chicago Press, 1981.

Deurbergue, Jean. "Sujet, personnage, parole dans *The Caretaker* de Harold Pinter" [Theme, Character, Speech in *The Caretaker* by Harold Pinter]. *Recherches Anglaises et Américaines* (Strasbourg) 5 (1972): 47–62.

D. H. R. Rev. of *Pinter: The Player's Playwright*, by David T. Thompson. *West Coast Rev. of Books*, July 1986, 37.

Diamond, Elin. *Pinter's Comic Play*. Lewisburg, Pa.: Bucknell Univ. Press, 1985.

Dobrez, L[ivio] A. C. *The Existential and Its Exits: Literary and Philosophical Perspectives on the Work of Beckett, Ionesco, Genet and Pinter*. London: Athlone; New York: St. Martin's, 1986.

D[onavin], D[enise] P. Rev. of *Other Places*, by Harold Pinter. *Booklist*, 1 Sept. 1983, 21.

Dougherty, Barbey Nyce. *Composing Choices for Writers: A Cross-Disciplinary Rhetoric*. New York: McGraw-Hill, 1985.

Drake, Sylvie. "Acting Is Just like 'Old Times' for Pinter." *Los Angeles Times*, 29 Oct. 1985, sec. 6: 1, 6.

*Dreams and Deconstructions: Alternative Theatre in Britain*. Ed. Sandy Craig. Ambergate, Derbyshire, Eng.: Amber Lane, 1980.

Dreitzel, Hans Peter. *Die Gesellschaftlichen Leiden und das Leiden an der Gesellschaft: Vorstudien zu einer Pathologie des Rollenverhaltens* [Social Suffering and Suffering from Society: Preliminary Studies toward a Pathology of Role Behaviors]. Göttinger Abhandlungen zur Soziologie und ihrer Grenzgebiete, vol. 14. Stuttgart: Ferdinand Enke, 1968.

Dukore, Bernard F. *Harold Pinter*. Grove Press Modern Dramatists. New York: Grove, 1982. 2d ed. Macmillan Modern Dramatists. London: Macmillan, 1988.

————. "'My, How We've Changed.'" In Gale, *HPCA*, 25–29.

————. Rev. of CSC Repertory Theatre production of *The Birthday Party*. *Pinter Rev.* 2 (1988): 71–73.

————. *Where Laughter Stops: Pinter's Tragicomedy*. Columbia: Univ. of Missouri Press, 1976.

*The Dumb Waiter*, by Harold Pinter. Stage production directed by Mark Scrimshaw. With Graham Fawcett and Nicholas Lumley. The Finborough Arms, London, July 1982.

*The Dumb Waiter*, by Harold Pinter. Television production directed by Robert Altman. With John Travolta and Tom Conti. ABC. KEZI, Eugene, Oreg., 12 May 1987.

Durbach, Errol. "'The Caretaker': Text and Subtext." *English Studies in Africa* (Johannesburg) 18, no. 1 (1975): 23–29.

Dutton, Richard. *Modern Tragicomedy and the British Tradition: Beckett, Pinter, Stoppard, Albee and Storey*. Brighton, Sussex, Eng.: Harvester; Tulsa: Univ. of Oklahoma Press, 1986.

Eagleton, Terry. "Brecht and Rhetoric." *New Literary History* 16 (1985): 633–38.

————. *Literary Theory: An Introduction*. Minneapolis: Univ. of Minnesota Press, 1983.

Eco, Umberto. *The Role of the Reader: Explorations in the Semiotics of Texts*. Advances in Semiotics. Bloomington: Indiana Univ. Press, 1979.

Ede, Lisa. *Work in Progress: A Guide to Writing and Revising*. New York: St. Martin's, 1989.

Elam, Keir. *The Semiotics of Theatre and Drama*. New Accents. London and New York: Methuen, 1980.

Elliott, Susan Merritt. "Fantasy behind Play: A Study of Emotional Responses to Harold Pinter's *The Birthday Party*, *The Caretaker* and *The Homecoming*." Ph.D. diss., Indiana Univ., 1973.

————. "A *New* Critical Epistemology." *Hartford Studies in Literature* 7 (1975): 170–89.

————. "New Solutions to Pinter's Puzzles." *Univ. of Hartford Studies in Literature* 9 (1977): 237–43.

————. "Stalking Harold Pinter." *Worcester (Mass.) Sunday Telegram*, 4 Apr. 1982, sec. F: 3, 14.

————. Telephone conversation with C. W. E. Bigsby. July 1982.

————. Telephone conversation with Sean Page. July 1982.

————. "Theoretical Writing as a Kind of Change." *Critical Exchange* 13 (Spring 1983): ii–ix.

Ellis, John M. *Against Deconstruction*. Princeton: Princeton Univ. Press, 1988.

————. "Commentary: Playing Games with Wittgenstein." In Cohen, *Wittgenstein and Literary Theory*, 301–8.

————. "The Logic of the Question 'What Is Criticism?'" In Hernadi, *What Is Criticism?* 15–29.

————. *The Theory of Literary Criticism: A Logical Analysis.* Berkeley: Univ. of California Press, 1974.

————. "What Does Deconstruction Contribute to Theory of Criticism?" In Cohen, *Wittgenstein and Literary Theory,* 259–79.

*The* Encore *Reader: A Chronicle of the New Drama.* Ed. Charles Marowitz, Tom Milne, and Owen Hale. London: Methuen, 1965. Reissued as *New Theatre Voices of the Fifties and Sixties.* London: Eyre Methuen, 1981.

Engel, Lehman. *The Critics.* New York: Macmillan, 1976.

Esposito, Marisa D'Orazio. "Creative Possibilities: Harold Pinter and His Characters." Ph.D. diss., Kent State Univ., 1982.

Esslin, Martin. "Betrayal." *Plays and Players* 26 (Jan. 1979): 14–15.

————. *The Field of Drama: How the Signs of Drama Create Meaning on Stage and Screen.* London and New York: Methuen, 1987.

————. "Harold Pinter's Work for Radio." In Gale, *HPCA,* 47–63.

————. "Mountain Language Opens in London." Rev. of National Theatre (Lyttelton) production of *Mountain Language. Pinter Rev.* 2 (1988): 76–78.

————. "On Being Reviewed." In Hernadi, *Re-Viewing Reviews,* 19–24.

————. *The Peopled Wound: The Work of Harold Pinter.* Garden City, N.Y.: Doubleday, 1970. *The Peopled Wound: The Plays of Harold Pinter.* London: Methuen, 1970. 2d ed. Repr. as *Pinter: A Study of His Plays.* London: Eyre Methuen, 1973. Expanded (3d) ed. New York: Norton, 1976. 4th ed. Repr. as *Pinter: The Playwright.* London and New York: Methuen, 1982. Corrected repr. 1984.

————. Rev. of *Pinter: The Player's Playwright,* by David T. Thompson. *Pinter Rev.* 1 (1987): 54–57.

————. Rev. of *PP,* by Austin E. Quigley. *Jour. of Beckett Studies,* no. 2 (Summer 1977): 102–5.

————. "A Search for Subjective Truth." In Hernadi, *What Is Criticism?* 199–211.

————. *The Theatre of the Absurd.* Garden City, N.Y.: Doubleday, 1961. Repr. London: Eyre and Spottiswoode, 1965. Rev. ed. London: Pelican, 1968. Repr. Garden City, N.Y.: Doubleday, Anchor Books, 1969.

Fanto, James. "Contesting Authority: The Marginal." In "The GRIP Report: Second Draft," vol. 1 (July 1983). (Unpublished research in progress; available from the GRIP Project, Department of English, Carnegie Mellon Univ.)

————. "The Professionalization of Stanley Fish." *Critical Exchange* 15 (Winter 1984): 31–51.

F[arber], S[tephen]. "Topical Relevance." Telephone interview with Harold Pinter. *New York Times,* 10 May 1987, sec. 2: 25.

Farson, Sibyl. "Reviews Good? Bad? He's 'Indifferent,' He Says with a 'Pinteresque' Pause." *Worcester (Mass.) Sunday Telegram,* 10 Apr. 1983, 1D, 4D.

————. "Sam Spiegel's 'Betrayal': Labor of Love." *Worcester (Mass.) Sunday Telegram,* 13 Mar. 1983, 31A.

Felman, Shoshana. "Turning the Screw of Interpretation." *Yale French Studies,* no. 55/56 (1977): 94–207.

Fetterley, Judith. *The Resisting Reader: A Feminist Approach to American Fiction.* Bloomington and London: Indiana Univ. Press, 1978.

Finegan, John. Interview with author. Dublin, 13 July 1982.

Fischer-Seidel, Therese. *Mythenparodie im modern englischen und amerikanischen Drama: Tradition und Kommunikation bei Tennessee Williams, Edward Albee, Samuel Beckett und Harold Pinter* [Parody of Myth in Modern English and American Drama: Tradition and Communication in the Work of . . . ]. Anglistische Forschungen, no. 174. Heidelberg: Carl Winter, Universitätsverlag, 1986.

Fish, Stanley. "Anti-Professionalism." Paper presented at the annual meeting of the Modern Language Association, New York, 27 Dec. 1983. Excerpted in Shumway, introd. Abr. version in *New Literary History* 17 (1985): 89–108.

———. "Change." *South Atlantic Quart.* 86 (1987): 423–44.

———. "Demonstration vs. Persuasion: Two Models of Critical Activity." In Hernadi, *What Is Criticism?* 30–37.

———. *Doing What Comes Naturally: Change, Rhetoric, and the Practice of Theory in Literary and Legal Studies.* Post-Contemporary Interventions, ed. Stanley Fish and Fredric Jameson. Durham and London: Duke Univ. Press, 1989.

———. *Is There a Text in This Class? The Authority of Interpretive Communities.* 1980. Repr. Cambridge, Mass. and London: Harvard Univ. Press, 1982.

———. "Literature in the Reader: Affective Stylistics." *New Literary History* 2 (1970): 123–62.

———. "Resistance and Independence: A Reply to Gerald Graff." *New Literary History* 17 (1985): 119–27.

Flannery, James W. Rev. of *The Arrival of Godot*, by Katherine H. Burkman. *Theatre Jour.* 39 (1987): 542–44.

Flower, Linda. *Problem-Solving Strategies for Writers.* New York: Harcourt Brace Jovanovich, 1981.

———. "Writer-Based Prose: A Cognitive Basis for Problems in Writing." *College English* 41 (1979): 19–37.

Flynn, Elizabeth A. "Gender and Reading." In *Gender and Reading*, 267–88.

Foucault, Michel. "The Subject and Power." *Critical Inquiry* 8 (1982): 777–95.

———. "What Is an Author?" In Harari, 141–60.

Frankel, C. David. Rev. of *HPCA*, ed. Steven H. Gale. *Pinter Rev.* 2 (1988): 81–82.

Frazer, Sir James George. *The Golden Bough.* Abr. ed. in 1 vol. New York: Macmillan, 1951.

Free, William J. "A Theory of Evaluating Drama and Theatre." *Jour. of Dramatic Theory and Criticism* 1 (Fall 1986): 77–85.

———. "Treatment of Character in Harold Pinter's 'The Homecoming.'" *South Atlantic Bulletin* 34 (Nov. 1969): 1–5.

Freud, Sigmund. *The Future of an Illusion.* Trans. W. D. Robson-Scott. Rev. and ed. James Strachey. 1927. Rev. ed. 1961. Repr. Garden City, N.Y.: Doubleday, 1964.

———. "The Relation of the Poet to Day-Dreaming." 1908. In vol. 4 of *The Collected Papers of Sigmund Freud*, trans. Joan Rivière and ed. Ernest Jones, 173–83. 5 vols. The International Psychoanalytical Library, vols. 7, 8, 9, 10, 37. New York: Basic Books, 1959.

———. *Totem and Taboo: Some Points of Agreement between the Mental Lives of Savages and Neurotics.* Trans. James Strachey. 1913. Repr. New York: Norton, 1950.

Fuegi, John. "The Uncertainty Principle and Pinter's Modern Drama." In Gale, *HPCA*, 202–7.

Fukuyama, Francis. "The End of History?" and "Responses to Fukuyama," by Allan Bloom, Pierre Hassner, Gertrude Himmelfarb, Irving Kristol, Daniel Patrick Moynihan, and Stephen Sestanovich. *National Interest*, no. 16 (Summer 1989): 3–18, 19–35.

Gabbard, Krin, and Glen O. Gabbard. *Psychiatry and the Cinema*. Chicago: Univ. of Chicago Press, 1987.

Gabbard, Lucina P[aquet]. "The Depths of *Betrayal*." *Jour. of Evolutionary Psychology* 4, no. 3–4 (1983): 228–37.

————. *The Dream Structure of Pinter's Plays: A Psychoanalytic Approach*. Rutherford, N.J.: Fairleigh Dickinson Univ. Press, 1976.

————. "Edward Albee's Triptych on Abandonment." *Twentieth Century Literature* 28 (1982): 14–33.

————. Interview with author. Charleston, Ill., 24 Oct. 1982.

————. Letters to author, 6 and 31 Mar. 1982 and 9 Oct. 1988.

————. "The Pinter Surprise." In Gale, *HPCA*, 175–86.

————. "The Roots of Uncertainty in Pinter and Stoppard." *Univ. of Houston Forum* 16, no. 3 (1978): 53–60.

————. *The Stoppard Plays*. New York: Whitston, 1982.

Gale, Steven H. *Butter's Going Up: A Critical Analysis of Harold Pinter's Work*. Durham: Duke Univ. Press, 1977.

————. "Character and Motivation in Harold Pinter's *The Homecoming*." *Jour. of Evolutionary Psychology* 8, no. 3–4 (1987): 278–88.

————. Commentary enclosed with letter to author. 21 Aug. 1989.

————. "The Films of Harold Pinter." Westport, Conn.: Greenwood Press, in preparation.

————. *Harold Pinter: An Annotated Bibliography*. Boston: G. K. Hall, 1978.

————. "Harold Pinter: Modern Dramatist." *Science/Technology and the Humanities* 2, no. 1 (1979): 73–81.

————. *Harold Pinter's* The Birthday Party *and Other Works*. Monarch Notes. New York: Simon and Schuster, 1972.

————. "Harold Pinter's *Family Voices* and the Concept of Family." In Bold, 146–65.

————. *Harold Pinter's* The Homecoming *and Other Works*. Monarch Notes. New York: Simon and Schuster, 1971.

————. Interview with author. Joplin, Mo., 25–27 Oct. 1982.

————. Letter to author, 21 Mar. 1988.

————. "Life at a Standstill: Harold Pinter's 'No-Man's [*sic*] Land.'" *Jewish Quart.* 24, no. 4 (1976/77): 13–18, 20.

————. "Nature Half Created, Half Perceived: Time and Reality in Harold Pinter's Later Plays." *Jour. of Evolutionary Psychology* 5, no. 3–4 (1984): 196–204.

————. "Observations on Two Productions of Harold Pinter's *Old Times*." *Pinter Rev.* 1 (1987): 40–43.

————. "President's Column: The Founding of the Harold Pinter Society." *Pinter Rev.* 1 (1987): v–vi.

————. "President's Column." *Pinter Rev.* 2 (1988): v.

————. Rev. of *Harold Pinter*, by Alrene Sykes, and *DWHP*, by Katherine H. Burkman. *Jour. of Modern Literature* 3 (1974): 746–47.

————. Rev. of *Harold Pinter*, by Guido Almansi and Simon Henderson. *Modern Drama* 29 (1986): 143–44.

————. Rev. of *PW*, by Martin Esslin. *Chicago Rev.* 25, no. 1 (Fall 1972): 177–80.

————. Rev. of *PP*, by Austin E. Quigley. *Jour. of Modern Literature* 5 (1977): 784–86.

————. "The Significance of Orson Welles in Harold Pinter's *Old Times*." *Notes on Contemporary Literature* 13, no. 2 (1983): 11–12.

————. "Thematic Change in the Stage Plays of Harold Pinter, 1957–1967." Ph.D. diss., Univ. of Southern California, 1970.

————. "The Variable Nature of Reality: Harold Pinter's Plays in the 1970s." *Kansas Quart.* 12, no. 4 (Fall 1980): 17–24.

————. "The Writing of Harold Pinter: An Overview." *Literary Half-Yearly* 22, no. 2 (1979): 79–89.

————, ed. *Critical Essays on Harold Pinter*. Essays on British Authors. Forthcoming Boston: G. K. Hall, 1990.

————. *Harold Pinter: Critical Approaches*. Rutherford, N.J.: Fairleigh Dickinson Univ. Press, 1986.

Gale, William K. "Pinter Believes Trinity Rep Will Do 'Damn Well' in Staging His 'Hothouse.'" *Providence Jour.*, 12 Feb. 1982, A1, 16.

Gallagher, Kent G. Rev. of *DWHP*, by Katherine H. Burkman. *Quart. Jour. of Speech* 58 (1972): 250.

Ganz, Arthur F. "Harold Pinter: The Retreat from Power." In *Realms of the Self: Variations on a Theme in Modern Drama*. The Gotham Library. New York and London: New York Univ. Press, 1980.

————. "Introduction." In *Pinter: A Collection of Critical Essays*, ed. Arthur F. Ganz, 1–18. Twentieth-Century Views. Englewood Cliffs, N.J.: Prentice-Hall, 1972.

Garner, Stanton. "Bodied Spaces: Performance Field in Contemporary Drama." In preparation.

Geduld, Harry M. "The Trapped Heroes of Harold Pinter." *Humanist* 28 (Mar./Apr. 1968): 24, 31.

*Gender and Reading: Essays on Readers, Texts, and Contexts*. Ed. Elizabeth A. Flynn and Patrocinio P. Schweickart. Baltimore and London: Johns Hopkins Univ. Press, 1986.

George, Kathleen. *Rhythm in Drama*. Pittsburgh: Pittsburgh Univ. Press, 1980.

Gillen, Francis. "Editors' Column." *Pinter Rev.* 2 (1988): vi–vii.

————. "From Chapter Ten of *The Dwarfs* to *Mountain Language*: The Continuity of Harold Pinter." *Pinter Rev.* 2 (1988): 1–4.

————. "Introduction to Harold Pinter's Unpublished Novel: *The Dwarfs*." *Pinter Rev.* 1 (1987): 1–3.

————. "'Nowhere to Go': Society and the Individual in Harold Pinter's *The Hothouse*." *Twentieth Century Literature* 29, no. 1 (1983): 86–96.

Gillen, Francis, and Steven H. Gale. "Editors' Column." *Pinter Rev.* 1 (1987): vii.

————, eds. *The Pinter Review* 1 (1987): i–85; 2 (1988): ii–95; 3 (1989): in press.

Gilman, Richard. "A Study of a Playwright and His Plays." *New York Times Book Rev.*, 13 Sept. 1970, 34, 36.

Girard, René. *Violence and the Sacred*. Trans. Patrick Gregory. Baltimore and London: Johns Hopkins Univ. Press, 1977.

Goetsch, Paul. Interview with author. Freiburg, W. Ger., 13 June 1982.

Goffman, Erving. *Interaction Ritual: Essays on Face to Face Behaviour*. New York: Penguin, 1967.

————. *Strategic Interaction*. Philadelphia: Univ. of Pennsylvania Press, 1969.

Goodman, Nelson. *Ways of Worldmaking*. Indianapolis: Hackett, 1978.

Gordon, Giles. "A Subjective View of Reviewers and Critics." *Drama*, no. 144 (Summer 1982): 3–5.

Gordon, Lois G. *Donald Barthelme*. Twayne's United States Authors Series, no. 416. Boston: G. K. Hall, 1981.

————. "*The Go-Between*—Hartley by Pinter." *Kansas Quart.* 4 (Spring 1972): 81–92.

————. "Harold Pinter—Past and Present." *Kansas Quart.* 3 (Spring 1971): 89–99.

————. Interview with author. New York, 14 May 1983.

————. "Pigeonholing Pinter: A Bibliography." *Theatre Documentation* 1 (Fall 1968): 3–20.

————. "Pinter, Harold." In *Contemporary Dramatists*. Contemporary Writers of the English Language, ed. James Vinson, 631–36. 3d ed. New York: St. Martin's, 1982.

————. *Robert Coover: The Universal Fictionmaking Process*. Carbondale: Southern Illinois Univ. Press, 1983.

————. *Stratagems to Uncover Nakedness: The Dramas of Harold Pinter*. Missouri Literary Frontiers Series, no. 6. Columbia: Univ. of Missouri Press, 1969.

————. Telephone conversation with author. 8 Feb. 1988.

————, ed. *Harold Pinter: A Casebook*. New York: Garland Press, 1990.

Gordon, Lois, and Alan Gordon. *American Chronicle: Six Decades in American Life: 1920–1980*. New York: Atheneum, 1987. Retitled as *American Chronicle: Seven Decades in American Life: 1920–1990*. Rev. and expanded ed. Forthcoming New York: Crown, 1990.

Gough-Yates, Kevin. "Pinter, Harold." In *Twentieth Century Writing: A Reader's Guide to Contemporary Literature*, ed. Kenneth Richardson, 490–91. London: Newnes, 1969.

Gould, Stephen Jay. Lecture presented at Harvard Univ. Televised on "Nova: Adventures in Science." PBS. WGBH-TV, Boston, 1984.

————. *The Panda's Thumb: More Reflections in Natural History*. New York and London: Norton, 1982.

————. *Time's Arrow, Time's Cycle: Myth and Metaphor in the Discovery of Geological Time*. Cambridge, Mass. and London: Harvard Univ. Press, 1987.

Graff, Gerald. *Professing Literature: An Institutional History*. Chicago and London: Univ. of Chicago Press, 1987.

Gray, Frances, and Janet Bray. "The Mind as a Theatre: Radio Drama since 1971." *New Theatre Quart.* 1 (1985): 292–300.

Gross, Miriam. "Pinter on Pinter." London *Observer Rev.*, 5 Oct. 1980, 25, 27.

Gursel, Mustafa. "Turkey Censors Blast on Rights by Two Authors: Miller, Pinter Say Torture a Fact in Turkey." *Washington Post*, 24 Mar. 1985, A27.

Gussow, Mel. "A Conversation [Pause] with Harold Pinter." *New York Times Mag.*, 5 Dec. 1971.

————. "Harold Pinter: 'I Started with Two People in a Pub.'" *New York Times*, 30 Dec. 1979, sec. 2: 5, 7.

————. "Pinter's Plays Following Him out of Enigma and into Politics." *New York Times*, 6 Dec. 1988, C17, 22.

————. "Profiles: Play Agent." *New Yorker*, 23 May 1988, 35–60.

————. "Review/Theater: In 'The Birthday Party,' Pinter's Daily Terrors: The Motif of Betrayal." *New York Times*, 18 Apr. 1988, C16.

Hadzispyrou, Elizabeth. Interviews with author. London, 5 June and 1 July 1982.

————. Letter to author, 5 Jan. 1981.

Hall, Adrian. Interview with author. Providence, R.I., 4 Mar. 1982.

Hall, Ann C. "The Beat Goes On: Sexual Politics in Harold Pinter's *The Lover*." *Pinter Rev.* 2 (1988): 54–59.

————. *A Kind of Alaska*: Harold Pinter's Metaphor for the Politics of Femininity." Abstract.

————. "*A Kind of Alaska*: Women in the Plays of Eugene O'Neill, Harold Pinter, and Sam Shepard." Ph.D. diss., Ohio State Univ., 1988.

Hall, Peter. *Peter Hall's Diaries: The Story of a Dramatic Battle*. Ed. John Goodwin. New York: Harper, 1984. Repr. New York: Limelight Editions, 1985.

Halliday, M. A. K. "Linguistic Function and Literary Style: An Inquiry into the Language of William Golding's *The Inheritors*." In *Literary Style: A Symposium*, ed. Seymour Chatman, 330–68. New York: Oxford Univ. Press, 1971.

Hammond, Geraldine. "Something for the 'Nothings' of Beckett and Pinter." *CEA Critic* 39, no. 2 (1976): 40–47.

Harari, Josué V., ed. and introd. *Textual Strategies: Perspectives in Post-Structuralist Criticism*. Ithaca: Cornell Univ. Press, 1979.

"Harold Pinter: Growth of an Angry Playwright." London *Observer*, 16 Oct. 1988, 13.

"Harold Pinter (1930–)." In *McGraw-Hill Encyclopedia of World Drama*, 3:425–29. New York: McGraw-Hill, 1972.

"Harold Pinter's *The Caretaker*: A Comedy of Menace." Advertisement for *The Caretaker*. *New York Times*, 26 Jan. 1986, sec. 2: 7.

"Harold Pinter Talks to Michael Dean." *Listener*, 6 Mar. 1969, 312.

Hartman, Joan E. "Reflections on 'The Philosophical Bases of Feminist Literary Criticisms.'" *New Literary History* 19 (1987): 105–16.

Hatch, Robert. "Films: *Betrayal*." *Nation*, 12 Mar. 1983, 315–16.

Heilbrun, Carolyn G. "Androgyny and the Psychology of Sex Differences." In *The Future of Difference*, ed. Hester Eisenstein and Alice Jardine, 258–66. Boston: G. K. Hall, 1980.

————. *Toward a Recognition of Androgyny: Aspects of Male and Female in Literature*. London: Victor Gollancz; New York: Knopf, 1973.

Henkle, Roger B. "From Pooter to Pinter: Domestic Comedy and Vulnerability." *Critical Quart.* 16 (Summer 1974): 174–89.

Henriques, Julian, Couze Venn, Valerie Walkerdine, Wendy Holloway, and Cathy Urwin. *Changing the Subject: Psychology, Social Regulation and Subjectivity*. London and New York: Methuen, 1984.

Hernadi, Paul, ed. and introd. *Re-Viewing Reviews*. Special issue of the *Bulletin of the Midwest Modern Language Association* 11, no. 1 (Spring 1978): 1–64.

————. *The Rhetoric of Interpretation and the Interpretation of Rhetoric*. Special issue of *Poetics Today* 9, no. 2 (1988): 251–472.

————. *What Is Criticism?* Bloomington: Indiana Univ. Press, 1981.

Hewes, Henry. "Disobedience, Civil and Uncivil." *Saturday Rev.*, 28 Oct. 1967, 46–47.

————. "Like Birth Warmed Over." *Saturday Rev.*, 21 Oct. 1967, 50.

————. "Nothing up the Sleeve." *Saturday Rev.*, 21 Oct. 1961, 34.

————. "Probing Pinter's Play." *Saturday Rev.*, 8 Apr. 1967, 57–58, 96–97.

Hewison, Robert. *In Anger: British Culture in the Cold War 1945–60*. New York: Oxford Univ. Press, 1981.

H[ill], F[rances]. "Pinteresque." *Times Educational Supplement*, 10 Dec. 1982, 22.

Hill, Holly. "How Do Playwrights Make a Living?" *Theatre Jour.* 33 (1981): 517–26.

Hinchliffe, Arnold P. "After *No Man's Land*: A Progress Report." In Gale, *HPCA*, 153–63.

———. *Harold Pinter.* Twayne English Authors Series, no. 51. New York: Twayne, 1967. Rev. ed. Boston: G. K. Hall, Twayne, 1981.

———. "Mr. Pinter's Belinda." *Modern Drama* 11 (1968): 173–79.

———. Rev. of *Pinter: The Player's Playwright*, by David T. Thompson. *British Book News*, July 1985, 436.

———. Rev. of *PP*, by Austin E. Quigley. *Modern Language Rev.* 72 (Oct. 1977): 933–35.

———. Rev. of *S*, by Lois G. Gordon. *Modern Drama* 13 (1971): 449–50.

Hobson, Harold. *Indirect Journey: An Autobiography.* London: Weidenfeld and Nicolson, 1978.

———. "Larger Than Life at the Festival." London *Sunday Times*, 5 Jan. 1958, 19.

———. "Life outside London." London *Sunday Times*, 15 June 1958, 11.

———. "Paradise Lost." London *Sunday Times*, 6 July 1969, 52.

———. "Pinter minus the Moral." London *Sunday Times*, 6 June 1965, 39.

———. "Plays in Performance: Hobson's Choice." Rev. of *Betrayal*. *Drama*, no. 131 (Winter 1979): 42–44.

———. "Plays in Performance: Hobson's Choice." Rev. of *The Homecoming*. *Drama*, no. 129 (Summer 1979): 46.

———. "Plays in Performance: Hobson's Choice." Rev. of *Landscape*. *Drama*, no. 139 (Winter 1981): 28–29.

———. "Political Slant." *Drama*, no. 165 (Autumn 1987): 17–18.

———. "Remembrance of Things Past." London *Sunday Times*, 6 June 1971, 29.

———. "The Screw Turns Again." London *Sunday Times*, 25 May 1958, 11.

———. *Theatre in Britain: A Personal View.* Oxford: Phaidon Press, 1984.

———. "Vagaries of the West End." London *Sunday Times Mag.*, 31 Jan. 1960, 23.

Holland, Norman N. *The Dynamics of Literary Response.* New York: Oxford Univ. Press, 1968. Repr. New York: Norton, 1975.

———. "A Letter to Leonard." *Hartford Studies in Literature* 5 (1973): 9–30.

———. *Psychoanalysis and Shakespeare.* New York: McGraw-Hill, 1966.

Hollis, James R. *Harold Pinter: The Poetics of Silence.* Crosscurrents/Modern Critiques. Carbondale: Southern Illinois Univ. Press, 1970.

Holloway, Wendy. "Gender Difference and the Production of Subjectivity." In Henriques et al., 228–60.

Holmberg, Arthur. "Stage View: From Lectern to Stage, New Views of Shakespeare." *New York Times*, 4 Nov. 1984, sec. 2: 5, 12.

*The Homecoming*, by Harold Pinter. Stage production directed by Peter Hall. With Ian Holm, John Normington, Michael Craig, Paul Rogers, Terence Rigby, and Vivien Merchant. The Royal Shakespeare Company, the Music Box, New York. Opened 5 Jan. 1967.

Hornby, Richard. *Drama, Metadrama, and Perception.* Lewisburg, Pa.: Bucknell Univ. Press, 1986.

*The Hothouse*, by Harold Pinter. Stage production directed by Adrian Hall. With Amy Van Nostrand, Dan Butler, David C. Jones, George Martin, Howard London, Peter Gerety, and Richard Kavanaugh. Trinity Square Repertory Company, Providence, R.I., 26 Feb. to 4 Apr. 1982. Playhouse Theatre, New York. Previewed 30 Apr. to 5 May 1982. Opened 6 May 1982.

"How My Mind Has Changed." Special session at the annual meeting of the Modern Language Association, San Francisco, 28 Dec. 1987.

Hudgins, Christopher C[hapman]. "*The Basement*: Harold Pinter on BBC-TV." *Modern Drama* 28 (1985): 71–82.

———. "Dance to a Cut-Throat Temper: Audience Response, Identity, and the Mass-Media Influence in the Absurdist Work of Harold Pinter." Ph.D. diss., Emory Univ., 1976.

———. "Intended Audience Response, *The Homecoming*, and the 'Ironic Mode of Identification.'" In Gale, *HPCA*, 102–17.

Hudson, Liam. "Intimate War Games." *Times Literary Supplement*, 9 Apr. 1976, 415.

Hughes, Catharine. "Betrayals." *America*, 9 Feb. 1980, 104.

———. *Plays, Politics, and Polemics*. New York: Drama Book Specialists, 1973.

———. "Playwright of Polymorphous Perception." *Catholic World* 213 (Apr. 1971): 48–49.

Hull, David L. *Science as a Process: An Evolutionary Account of the Social and Conceptual Development of Science*. Chicago: Univ. of Chicago Press, 1988.

Hunter, Paul. "'that we have divided/In three our kingdom': The Communication Triangle and *A Theory of Discourse*." *College English* 48 (1986): 279–87.

Hurt, James. Rev. of *DWHP*, by Katherine H. Burkman. *Jour. of English and Germanic Philology* 71 (Apr. 1972): 284–87.

Imhof, Rüdiger. "Radioactive Pinter." In *Papers of the Radio Literature Conference, 1977*, ed. Peter Elfred Lewis, 199–217. Durham, Eng.: Dept. of English, Univ. of Durham, 1978.

———. *Pinter, a Bibliography: His Works and Occasional Writings with a Comprehensive Checklist of Criticism and Reviews of the London Productions*. London and Los Angeles: *TQ* Publications, 1975.

———. Rev. of *PP*, by Austin E. Quigley. *Modern Drama* 19 (1976): 426–30.

Iser, Wolfgang. "Indeterminacy and the Reader's Response in Prose Fiction." In *Aspects of Narrative*, ed. J. Hillis Miller, 1–45. English Institute Essays. New York: Columbia Univ. Press, 1971.

Jacobus, Mary. *Reading Woman: Essays in Feminist Criticism*. New York: Columbia Univ. Press, 1986.

James, Alby. "Alternative versus Mainstream." *Gambit* 9, no. 36 (1980): 7–9.

Jauss, Hans Robert. "Literature and Hermeneutics." In Hernadi, *What Is Criticism?* 134–47.

———. *Toward an Aesthetic of Reception*. Trans. Timothy Bahti. Introd. Paul de Man. Theory and History of Literature, vol. 2. Minneapolis: Univ. of Minnesota Press, 1982.

Jay, Gregory S., and David L. Miller, eds. *After Strange Texts: The Role of Theory in the Study of Literature*. University: Univ. of Alabama Press, 1985.

Jennings, Ann S. "The Reactions of London's Drama Critics to Certain Plays by Henrik Ibsen, Harold Pinter, and Edward Bond." Ph.D. diss., Florida State Univ., 1973.

Jiji, Vera M. "Pinter's Four Dimensional House: *The Homecoming*." *Modern Drama* 17 (1974): 433–42.

———. Rev. of *DS*, by Lucina Paquet Gabbard. *Thought* 53 (Mar. 1978): 115–16.

Kael, Pauline. "The Current Cinema: Time-Warp Movies." *New Yorker*, 11 July 1983, 95.

Kakutani, Michiko. "The Pauses in Pinter Give Three Actors Pause." *New York Times*, 16 Jan. 1980, C19.

Kalem, T. E. "The Roomer." Rev. of *PW*, by Martin Esslin. *Time*, 12 Oct. 1970, 60–61.

Kalson, Albert E. "The Artist as Con Man in *No Man's Land*." *Modern Drama* 22 (1979): 339–48.

Kamm, Henry. "Two Playwrights Deplore Turkish Rights Record." *New York Times*, 28 Mar. 1985, A17 (late ed.).

Kane, Leslie. *The Language of Silence: On the Unspoken and the Unspeakable in Modern Drama*. Rutherford, N.J.: Fairleigh Dickinson Univ. Press, 1984.

———. "The Weasel under the Cocktail Cabinet: Rite and Ritual in Pinter's Plays." *Pinter Rev.* 2 (1988): 19–32.

Katz, Bill. "Magazines." *Library Jour.*, 15 Nov. 1988, 54.

Kauffmann, Stanley. "Books and the Arts: Stanley Kauffmann on Films: Unbetrayed." *New Republic*, 28 Feb. 1983, 22–23.

Kendzora, Kathryn Louise. "Going between Novel and Film: Harold Pinter's Adaptation of *The Go-Between*." Ph.D. diss., Univ. of California, Irvine, 1986.

Kennedy, Andrew [K.]. "Natural, Mannered, and Parodic Dialogue." *Yearbook of English Studies* 9 (1979): 28–54.

———. *Six Dramatists in Search of a Language: Studies in Dramatic Language*. London and New York: Cambridge Univ. Press, 1975.

Kermode, Frank. *The Sense of an Ending*. New York: Oxford Univ. Press, 1967.

Kerr, Walter. *Harold Pinter*. Columbia Essays on Modern Writers, no. 27. New York: Columbia Univ. Press, 1967.

———. "Is Mr. Pinter Telling Us Less Than He Knows?" *New York Times*, 28 Nov. 1971, sec. 2: 1, 7.

———. "The Playwright as Existentialist." In *God on the Gymnasium Floor, and Other Adventures*. New York: Simon and Schuster, 1972.

———. "Put Off—Or Turned On—by Pinter?" *New York Times*, 15 Oct. 1967, sec. 2: 1, 5.

———. "The Riveting Counterpoint of Pinter's 'Betrayal.'" *New York Times*, 20 Jan. 1980, sec. 2: 5, 7.

King, Noel. "Pinter's Progress." *Modern Drama* 23 (1980): 246–57.

———. "Rewriting Richardson." *Jour. of the Midwest Modern Language Association* 18 (Fall 1985): 42–63.

Kinneavy, James L. *A Theory of Discourse: The Aims of Discourse*. 1971. Repr. New York and London: Norton, 1980.

Kissel, Howard. "Harold Pinter: The Man in the Ironic Mask." *Women's Wear Daily*, 25 Mar.– 1 Apr. 1983, 18.

——— "The Wise Counselor? The Critic's Role in Contemporary Theatre." *Theatre Studies* 31–32 (1984–85/1985–86): 41–48.

Klein, Joanne. *Making Pictures: The Pinter Screenplays*. Columbus: Ohio State Univ. Press, 1985.

Klotz, Günther. "Internationalism and Present British Drama." *Zeitschrift für Anglistik und Amerikanistik* 27 (1979): 35–42.

Knapp, Shoshana. "The Transformation of a Pinter Screenplay: Freedom and Calculators in *The French Lieutenant's Woman*." *Modern Drama* 28 (1985): 55–70.

Knowles, Ronald. "Friendship and Betrayal in the Plays of Harold Pinter." *Long Room*, no. 28 & 29 (Spring–Autumn 1984): 33–44.

———. "Harold Pinter, Citizen." *Pinter Rev.* 3 (1989): in press.

———. "'The Hothouse' and the Epiphany of Harold Pinter." *Jour. of Beckett Studies* 10 (1985): 134–44.

———. "Names and Naming in the Plays of Harold Pinter." In Bold, 113–30.

Köhler, Klaus. "The Establishment and the Absurd: Trends, Ideologies and Techniques in Non-Realistic Drama from Beckett to Pinter (Part II)." *Zeitschrift für Anglistik und Amerikanistik* (Leipzig, E. Ger.) 32, no. 4 (1984): 315–29.

———. Rev. of *Harold Pinters Dramen technik*, by Rüdiger Imhof, and *Harold Pinters Dramen im Spiegel der soziologischen Rollentheorie*, by Ewald Mengel, and *Der Dialog in Harold Pinters Dramen*, by Ingrid Müller-Zannoth. *Zeitschrift für Anglistik und Amerikanistik* (Leipzig, E. Ger.) 28, no. 4 (1980): 369–72.

Kohn, Alfie. *No Contest: The Case against Competition*. Boston: Houghton Mifflin, 1986.

Korpimies, Liisa. *A Linguistic Approach to the Analysis of a Dramatic Text: A Study in Discourse Analysis and Cohesion with Special Reference to* The Birthday Party *by Harold Pinter*. Studia Philologica Jyväskyläensia, no. 17. Jyräskylä: Univ. of Jyräskylä, 1983.

Kosík, Karel. *Dialectics of the Concrete: A Study on Problems of Man and World*. Boston Studies in the Philosophy of Science, vol. 52. Dordrecht-Holland and Boston: D. Reidel Publishing, 1976.

Kroll, Jack. "Theater: Oh, to Be in England." *Newsweek*, 27 Nov. 1978, 65–66.

———. "Theater: Pinter's Dance of Deception." *Newsweek*, 21 Jan. 1980, 86.

Kuhn, Thomas. *The Structure of Scientific Revolutions*. 1962. 2d ed., enlarged. Foundations of the Unity of Science. *International Encyclopedia of Unified Science*, vol. 2, no. 2. Chicago and London: Univ. of Chicago Press, 1970.

Lahr, John. "The Language of Silence." *Evergreen Rev.* 13 (Mar. 1969): 53–55, 82–90.

Lakoff, George, and Mark Johnson. *Metaphors We Live By*. Chicago and London: Univ. of Chicago Press, 1980.

*Landscape*, by Harold Pinter. Stage production directed by Peter Hall. With David Waller and Peggy Ashcroft. Aldwych Theatre, London. Opened 2 July 1969. Benefit performance for Václav Havel at the Lyttelton Theatre, National Theatre, London, 10 Oct. 1980.

Langley, Lee. "Genius—A Change in Direction." London *Daily Telegraph Mag.*, 23 Nov. 1973, 30–36.

Lavédrine, Jean. "La fonction textuelle du progressif dans le théâtre d'Harold Pinter" [The Textual Function of the Present Tense in the Theater of Harold Pinter]. In *Rhétorique et communication: Actes du Congrès de Rouen*. Études Anglaises, no. 75. Societé des Anglicistes de L'Enseignement Supérieur. Paris: Didier, 1979.

Lecca, Doina. "Conversational Implicature in H. Pinter's Plays." *Analele Universitataţii Bucureşti-Limbă şi Literatură Străine* 1, no. 28 (1979): 77–85.

Lee, R. J. Rev. of *PFP*, by Elizabeth Sakellaridou. *Choice*, Sept. 1988, 122.

Lehman, David. "Books: Yale's Insomniac Genius." *Newsweek*, 18 Aug. 1986, 56–57.

Lentricchia, Frank. *After the New Criticism*. Chicago: Univ. of Chicago Press; London: Athlone, 1980.

Lerner, Laurence D., and Brewster Rogerson. "Criticism." In *Princeton Encyclopedia*, 158–74.

Lindenberger, Herbert. "Postlogue, Postlude, Postscript." *New Literary History* 13 (1982): 533–42.

———. "Re-Viewing the Reviews of *Historical Drama*." In Hernadi, *Re-Viewing Reviews*, 43–52.

Lingeman, Richard. "Reviewmanship." *Nation*, 22 Dec. 1984, 683–84.

*London Theatre Record*, 7–20 Oct. 1988, 1467–71.

Luddy, Thomas E. Rev. of *DS*, by Lucina Paquet Gabbard. *Library Jour.* 102 (1977): 1188.

———. Rev. of *PW*, by Martin Esslin. *Library Jour.* 95 (1970): 2680.

Lutterbie, John. "Subjects of Silence." *Theatre Jour.* 40 (1988): 468–81.

Maclean, Marie. "Oppositional Practices in Women's Traditional Narrative." *New Literary History* 19 (1987): 37–50.

McCormick, Kathleen, ed. and introd. *The New Rhetoric and the New Literary Theory.* Special issue of *Reader*, no. 14 (Fall 1985): 1–67.

McDowell, Edwin. "PEN Talks on Freedom of the Word." *New York Times*, 16 Jan. 1986, C17.

McLintock, K. Rev. of *The Pinter Review. Choice*, Jan. 1989, 884.

Mailloux, Steven. "Interpretation." Paper presented at the annual meeting of the Modern Language Association, San Francisco, 29 Dec. 1987.

———. *Interpretive Conventions: The Reader in the Study of American Fiction.* Ithaca and London: Cornell Univ. Press, 1982.

———. "Rhetorical Hermeneutics." *Critical Inquiry* 11 (1985): 620–41.

Markeley, Robert. "Discipline and Publish: The Politics of Ethical Power." Paper presented at the annual meeting of the Modern Language Association, San Francisco, 28 Dec. 1987. Cited in "Footnotes," *Chronicle of Higher Education*, 13 Jan. 1988, A4.

Marowitz, Charles. *Confessions of a Counterfeit Critic: A London Theatre Notebook.* London: Eyre Methuen, 1973.

———. "Reflections of a Lost Soul." In *Confessions*, 22–41.

Matlaw, Myron. "Pinter, Harold (1930–)." In *Modern World Drama*, 606–7. New York: Dutton, 1972.

Matthiessen, F. O. *American Renaissance: Art and Expression in the Age of Emerson and Whitman.* New York: Oxford Univ. Press, 1941.

Mayberry, Bob. *Theatre of Discord: Dissonance in Beckett, Albee, and Pinter.* Rutherford, N.J.: Fairleigh Dickinson Univ. Press, 1989.

Melmoth, John. "Theatre: Subversives and Hooligans." *Times Literary Supplement*, 30 Aug. 1985, 953–54.

Melrose, Susan. "Theatre, Linguistics, and Two Productions of 'No Man's Land.'" *New Theatre Quart.* 1 (1985): 213–24.

Melrose, Susan F., and Robin Melrose. "Drama, 'Style', Stage." In *Functions of Style*, ed. David Birch and Michael O'Toole, 98–110. Open Linguistics Series, ed. Robin P. Fawcett. London and New York: Pinter Publications, 1988.

Meltzer, Françoise, ed. *The Trial(s) of Psychoanalysis.* Special issue of *Critical Inquiry* 13, no. 2 (Winter 1987): 215–414.

———. "Unconscious." Paper presented at the annual meeting of the Modern Language Association, San Francisco, 29 Dec. 1987.

Mengel, Ewald. "The 'Closed Society': Structural Violence in the English Drama of the Present." Photocopy. Forthcoming in *Forum Modernes Theater.*

———. *Harold Pinters Dramen im Spiegel der soziologischen Rollentheorie* [Harold Pinter's Plays in the Light of Sociological Role Theory]. Ph.D. diss., Univ. of Freiburg, W. Ger., 1977. Neue Studien zur Anglistik und Amerikanistik, ed. Willi Erzgräber und Paul Goetsch, vol. 11. Frankfurt am Main, Bern, Las Vegas: Peter Lang, 1978.

———. Interview with author. Bamberg, W. Ger., 10 June 1982.

———. Letters to author. 7 Mar., 8 Apr., and 20 May 1989.

———. "Das sozialpsychologische Konzept des Self-Monitoring als Schlüssel zum Verständnis von Harold Pinters Dramen" [The Socio-Psychological Concept of Self-Monitoring as a Key to the Understanding of Harold Pinter's Plays]. *Poetica* 17, no. 1–2 (1985): 131–48. (Abstract by M[ichael] J. R[obertson], *Abstracts of English Studies* 30, no. 1 [1987]: 66.)

———. "Unterschiedliche Formen der Bewusstzeinsdiskrepanz und ihre dramatische Funktion in Harold Pinters 'Betrayal'" [Distinct Forms of Discrepancy of Awareness and Their Dramatic Function in Harold Pinter's "Betrayal"]. *Germanische-Romanische Monatsschrift* 32, no. 3 (1982): 333–44.

———. "'Yes! in the sea of life enisled': Harold Pinters *Other Places*" ['Yes! in the sea of life enisled': Harold Pinter's *Other Places*]. Forthcoming in "Harold Pinter," ed. Gerhard Stratmann. Photocopy. English translation forthcoming in Gordon, *Harold Pinter*.

Mercurio, Gregory. Rev. of *Pinter: The Player's Playwright*, by David T. Thompson. *Best Sellers*, Nov. 1985, 316.

Merritt, Susan Hollis. Letter to the editor. "Forum: Dialogic Discourse." *PMLA* 102 (1987): 830–31.

———. "Major Critics, Strategies, and Trends in Pinter Criticism." Forthcoming in Gale, *Critical Essays on HP*.

———. "The Power of Pinter's Women." 1968.

———. "Recent Developments in Pinter Criticism." *Pinter Rev.* 1 (1987): 68–76.

———. Rev. of CSC Repertory Theatre production of *The Birthday Party*. *Pinter Rev.* 2 (1988): 66–70.

———. Rev. of *HPCA*, ed. by Steven H. Gale, and *HP*, ed. by Michael Scott. *Modern Drama* 32 (1989): 459–62.

———. Rev. of *PFP*, by Elizabeth Sakellaridou. *Modern Drama* 32 (1989): 171–73.

———, comp. "Harold Pinter Bibliography, 1988–1989." *Pinter Rev.* 3 (1989): in press.

———. "Harold Pinter Bibliography, 1987–1988." *Pinter Rev.* 2 (1988): 83–92.

———. "Harold Pinter Bibliography, 1986–1987." *Pinter Rev.* 1 (1987): 77–82.

Messer-Davidow, Ellen. "The Philosophical Bases of Feminist Literary Criticisms." *New Literary History* 19 (1987): 65–103.

"Mr. Harold Pinter—Avant-Garde Playwright and Intimate Revue." London *Times*, 16 Nov. 1959, 4.

Mitchell, W. J. T., ed. and introd. *Pluralism and Its Discontents*. Special issue of *Critical Inquiry* 12, no. 3 (Spring 1986): 467–630. Chicago: Univ. of Chicago Press, 1986.

Moi, Toril. *Sexual/Textual Politics: Feminist Literary Theory*. London and New York: Methuen, 1985.

Moleski, Joseph J. Rev. of *DS*, by Lucina Paquet Gabbard. *Comparative Drama* 14 (Fall 1980): 289–92.

Mortimer, John. "Ben and Gus." *New Statesman*, 27 Nov. 1970, 718–20.

*Mountain Language*, by Harold Pinter. Stage production directed by Harold Pinter. With Alex Hardy, Charlotte Seago, Douglas McFerran, Eileen Atkins, George Harris, Irene Mac-Dougall, Jennifer Hill, Julian Wadham, Kika Mirylees, Michael Gambon, Miranda Richardson, and Tony Haygarth. Lyttelton Theatre, National Theatre, London. Opened 20 Oct. 1988.

*Mountain Language* and *The Birthday Party*. Both by Harold Pinter. Stage production directed by Carey Perloff. With Bill Moor, David Strathairn, Jean Stapleton, Miguel Perez, Peter Riegert, Richard Riehle, and Wendy Makkena. The Classic Stage Company, CSC

Repertory Theatre, New York, 12 Nov. 1989. Previewed 31 Oct. 1989. Opened 8 Nov. 1989 (benefit performance).

Murphy, Marese. "Pinter and Visconti." *Drama*, no. 109 (Summer 1973): 45.

Musser, Joseph F. "The Perils of Relying on Thomas Kuhn." *Eighteenth-Century Studies* 18 (Winter 1984–85): 215–26.

Napiórkowska, Krystyna. "Language as an Aspect of the Search for Identity in Harold Pinter's *The Homecoming*." *Studia Anglica Posnaniensia: An International Rev. of English Studies* 8 (1976): 151–56.

Natoli, Joseph, ed. *Tracing Literary Theory*. Urbana and Chicago: Univ. of Illinois Press, 1987.

Nelson, Cary. "On Whether Criticism Is Literature." In Hernadi, *What Is Criticism?* 253–67.

———. "Reading Criticism." *PMLA* 91 (1976): 801–15.

———, ed. *Theory in the Classroom*. Urbana and Chicago: Univ. of Illinois Press, 1986.

Nelson, Gerald. "Harold Pinter Goes to the Movies." *Chicago Rev.* 19 (Summer 1966): 33–43.

Nelson, Jeanne Andrée. "De la fête au sacrifice dans le théâtre de Pinter" [From Celebration to Sacrifice in Pinter's Theater]. *Revue d'Histoire du Théâtre* 36 (1984): 408–18.

Newton, Kenneth M. "Interpreting Pinter." Chap. 2 in *In Defense of Literary Interpretation: Theory and Practice*. London: Macmillan, 1986.

Nichols, Peter. "Even the Language Is Taken Away." *New York Times*, 5 Nov. 1989, sec. 2: 5.

———. "Mr. Pinter Accuses Signor Visconti of Staging 'Fiasco.'" London *Times*, 11 May 1973, 1, 6.

Nightingale, Benedict. "Anti-Clockwise." *New Statesman*, 24 Nov. 1978, 717–18.

———. *Fifth Row Center: A Critic's Year On and Off Broadway*. New York: Random, Times Books, 1986.

———. "Have Pinter and Stoppard Turned to Naturalism?" *New York Times*, 3 Dec. 1978, sec. 2: 4.

———. "The Human Zoo: On Harold Pinter." *Encounter* 48 (Feb. 1977): 71–74.

*A Night Out*, by Harold Pinter. Produced on radio by Donald McWhinnie. With Barry Foster, Harold Pinter, Vivien Merchant, and others. BBC Radio. Third Programme. 1 Mar. 1960. Produced on television by Philip Saville. With Harold Pinter, Tom Bell, Vivien Merchant, and others. ABC "Armchair Theatre." 24 Apr. 1960.

*No Holds Barred. Precisely*, by Harold Pinter. Stage production directed by Robin Stone. With Douglas Mace and Megan Taylor. *The Dumb Waiter*, by Harold Pinter. Stage production directed by Keith Scales. With Gary Brickner-Schulz and Ken Colburn. *One for the Road*, by Harold Pinter. Stage production directed by Gary O'Brien. With Daniel Kalapsa, Douglas Mace, Keith Scales, and Megan Taylor. MetroNorthwest Productions, Sumus Theatre, Portland, Oreg., 16 and 28 Aug. 1986. Benefit performance for Amnesty International of *One for the Road* on 28 Aug.

Norris, Christopher. *Deconstruction: Theory and Practice*. New Accents. London and New York: Methuen, 1982.

Nowlan, David. Interview with author. Dublin, 12 July 1982.

Nyholm, Per. "Language and Nicaragua." Letter to the editor. *Index on Censorship* 17, no. 7 (1988): 6.

Ohmann, Richard. "The Social Relations of Criticism." In Hernadi, *What Is Criticism?* 189–98.

*Old Times*, by Harold Pinter. Stage production directed by Keith Scales. With Laurie Holland, Luisa Sermol, and Peter Fornara. Portland Civic Theatre, Portland, Oreg., 6 Feb. 1987. Opened 9 Jan. 1987.

*Old Times*, by Harold Pinter. Stage production directed by Kenneth Frankel. With Anthony Hopkins, Jane Alexander, and Marsha Mason. Roundabout Theater, New York. Opened 12 Dec. 1984.

*Old Times*, by Harold Pinter. Stage production directed by Peter Hall. With Mary Ure, Robert Shaw, and Rosemary Harris. Billy Rose Theatre, New York, 26 Nov. 1971. Opened 16 Nov. 1971.

Ong, Walter J., S.J. "The Writer's Audience Is Always a Fiction." *PMLA* 90 (1975): 9–21.

Ooi, Vicki Cheng Har. "Pinter in Cantonese: Language, Stage and Meaning." *Sydney Studies in English* 2 (1976–77): 64–71.

*Other Places*. Three plays by Harold Pinter. Stage production directed by Peter Hall. *Family Voices*. With Anna Massey, Niger Havers, and Paul Rogers. *Victoria Station*. With Martin Jarvis and Paul Rogers. *A Kind of Alaska*. With Anna Massey, Judi Dench, and Paul Rogers. Cottesloe Theatre, National Theatre, London. Opened 14 Oct. 1982.

*Other Places*. Three plays by Harold Pinter. Stage production directed by Alan Schneider. *Victoria Station*. With Henderson Forsythe and Kevin Conway. *One for the Road*. With Caroline Lagerfelt, David George Polyak, George Hosmer, and Kevin Conway. *A Kind of Alaska*. With Caroline Lagerfelt, Dianne Wiest, and Henderson Forsythe. Manhattan Theatre Club, New York, 18 May 1984. (From 3 Apr. to 20 May 1984.)

O'Toole, Lawrence. "Films: A Tongue-tied Triad." *Maclean's*, 28 Feb. 1983, 50.

Owen, Michael. "Harold Pinter and His Lady and a Great Erotic Experience." London *Standard*, 11 Sept. 1981, 24–25.

Packard, William. "An Interview with Harold Pinter." *First Stage* 6 (Summer 1967): 82.

Pallen, T. A. Rev. of *Pinter: The Player's Playwright*, by David T. Thompson. *Choice*, May 1986, 1394.

Paul, Angus. "The Script's the Thing: Shakespeare in Performance Is New Area of Study." *Chronicle of Higher Education*, 30 Apr. 1986, 4–6.

Pavis, Patrice. *Languages of the Stage: Essays in the Semiology of the Theatre*. New York: PAJ Publications, 1982.

Peck, Jeffrey. "Advanced Literary Study as Cultural Study: A Redefinition of the Discipline." In *Profession 85: Selected Articles from the Bulletins of the Association of Departments of English and the Association of Departments of Foreign Languages*, ed. Phyllis Franklin, 49–54. New York: Modern Language Association, 1985.

Peckham, Morse. "Three Notions about Criticism." In Hernadi, *What Is Criticism?* 38–51.

*Performance and Politics in Popular Drama*. Ed. David Bradby, Louis James, and Bernard Sharratt. Cambridge and New York: Cambridge Univ. Press, 1980.

Perloff, Carey. "Keeping Up the Mask: Some Observations on Directing Pinter." *Pinter Rev.* 2 (1988): 60–65.

Perloff, Carey, Bill Moor, Peter Riegert, Jean Stapleton, and David Strathairn. Interview with author. New York, 12 Nov. 1989. Forthcoming in *Pinter Rev.* 3 (1989): in press.

Peter, John. "Beckett and Friends." *Drama*, no. 108 (Spring 1974): 78–79.

———. "Two Views of Pinter." *Drama*, no. 96 (Spring 1971): 70–71.

"Picks and Pans: Screen." *People*, 21 Mar. 1983, 12–13.

Pinter, Harold. "Between the Lines." London *Sunday Times*, 4 Mar. 1962, 25.

————. *Complete Works.* 4 vols. New York: Grove, 1977–81.

————. *The Hothouse.* Incl. "Author's Note." New York: Grove, 1980.

————. "Language and Lies." *Index on Censorship* 17, no. 6 (1988): 2.

————. Letter to author. 4 Mar. 1982.

————. Letter to the editor. London *Times*, 22 Mar. 1974, 17.

————. "Letter to Peter Wood." Pref. Martin Esslin. *Kenyon Rev.*, n.s., 3 (Summer 1981): 1–5. (Repr. in *Drama*, no. 142 [Winter 1981]: 4–5.)

————. Letters to various officials of BBC Radio, 1949–1964. BBC Written Archives Centre, Reading, Eng.

————. " 'Mountain Language.' " Letter to the editor. *Times Literary Supplement*, 7–13 Oct. 1988, 1109.

————. *Mountain Language. Times Literary Supplement*, 7–13 Oct. 1988, 1110–11. New York: Grove, 1989.

————. *One for the Road.* New York: Grove, 1986.

————. *Other Places: Three Plays. A Kind of Alaska, Victoria Station,* and *Family Voices.* New York: Grove, 1983.

————. "A Play and Its Politics: A Conversation between Harold Pinter and Nicholas Hern" and "Postscript." In *One for the Road*, 5–24.

————. "A Playwright—Harold Pinter." Interview with Harold Sherwood on "The Rising Generation." BBC Radio. European Division. 3 Mar. 1960. Photocopy of transcript from BBC Written Archives Centre, Reading, Eng.

————. *Precisely. Harper's*, May 1985, 37.

————. Readings of an excerpt from *The Hothouse* and of *One for the Road* and discussion with Mel Gussow, reading selected questions from the audience. The Poetry Center of the 92d Street Y, New York, 3 Oct. 1989.

————. "Speech: Hamburg 1970." *Theatre Quart.* 1 (July–Sept. 1971): 3–4. (Repr. in Pinter, *Complete Works* 4:ix–xiii.)

————. Talk presented at the Univ. of East Anglia, East Anglia, Eng., 29 Oct. 1981.

————. "Writing for Myself." Comp. Richard Findlater. *Twentieth Century* 169 (Feb. 1961): 172–75. (Repr. in Pinter, *Complete Works* 2:9–12.)

————. "Writing for the Theatre." *Evergreen Rev.* 8 (Aug.–Sept. 1964): 80–82. Rev. and expanded version of "Between the Lines." (Repr. in *English Dramatic Theories.* Vol. 4, *20th Century*, ed. Paul Goetsch, 118–24. Tübingen, 1972; and in Pinter, *Complete Works* 1:9–16.)

"Pinter, Harold." In *Crowell's Handbook of Contemporary Drama*, ed. Michael Anderson, Jacques Guicharnaud, Kristin Morrison, Jack D. Zipes, et al., 351–57. New York: Crowell, 1971.

"Pinter, Harold." *Current Biography* 24 (Nov. 1963): 41–44. Repr. in *Current Biography Yearbook 1963*, ed. Charles Marowitz, 326–29. Bronx, N.Y.: H. W. Wilson, 1964.

"Pinter, Harold (1930–)." In *McGraw-Hill Encyclopedia of World Drama*, ed. Stanley Hochman, 4:100–105. New York: McGraw-Hill, 1984.

"Pinter, Harold (1930–)." In *Major Modern Dramatists*, comp. and ed. Rita Stein and Friedhelm Rickert, 1:194–212. A Library of Literary Criticism. New York: Ungar, 1984.

"Pinter, Harold. 1930–." In *The Reader's Adviser: A Layman's Guide to Literature.* 13th ed. Vol. 2, *The Best in American and British Drama and World Literature in English Translation.* New

York: R. R. Bowker, 1986.

"Pinter's Wife Names Antonia." London *Guardian*, 30 July 1975, 7.

"Pinter Unperturbed." London *Daily Mail*, 28 Nov. 1967, 4.

Pittel, Christine. "How One Tiny Theater Snared Harold Pinter." *New York Times*, 8 Jan. 1989, sec. 2: 5, 40.

Pool, Gail. "Point of View: Too Many Reviews of Scholarly Books Are Puffy, Nasty, or Poorly Written." *Chronicle of Higher Education*, 20 July 1988, A36.

Pratt, Mary. "Art without Critics and Critics without Readers *or* Pantagruel versus The Incredible Hulk." In Hernadi, *What Is Criticism?* 177–88.

Prentice, Penelope. "The Ironic Con Game in *The Dumb Waiter*." In *Drama and Discussion*, ed. Stanley A. Clayes, 590–94. 2d ed. Englewood Cliffs, N.J.: Prentice-Hall, 1978.

*Princeton Encyclopedia of Poetry and Poetics*. Ed. Alex Preminger, Frank J. Warnke, and O. B. Hardison, Jr. Enlarged ed. Princeton: Princeton Univ. Press, 1974.

"Professional Notes and Comment." *PMLA* 101 (1986): 704.

Quigley, Austin E. "Design and Discovery in Pinter's *The Lover*." In Gale, *HPCA*, 82–101.

———. "*The Dumb Waiter*: Undermining the Tacit Dimension." *Modern Drama* 21 (1978): 1–11.

———. "*The Dwarfs*: A Study in Linguistic Dwarfism." *Modern Drama* 17 (1974): 413–22.

———. "The Dynamics of Dialogue: The Plays of Harold Pinter." Ph.D. diss., Univ. of California, Santa Cruz, 1971.

———. "Genêt and the Empire of Semiotics." Paper presented at the annual meeting of the Modern Language Association, San Francisco, 30 Dec. 1987.

———. Interview with author. Charlottesville, Va., 26, 27, & 30 May 1983.

———. Letter to author. 29 Aug. 1989.

———. *The Modern Stage and Other Worlds*. New York and London: Methuen, 1985.

———. *The Pinter Problem*. Princeton: Princeton Univ. Press, 1975.

———. Rev. of *Pinter's Comic Play*, by Elin Diamond. *Theatre Jour.* 38 (1986): 513–14.

———. "A Stylistic Analysis of Harold Pinter's *The Dwarfs*." Master's thesis, Univ. of Birmingham, Eng., 1969.

———. "Taking the Measure of Theoretical Models." *Univ. of Hartford Studies in Literature* 17, no. 2 (1985): 1–12.

———. "The Temporality of Structure in Pinter's Plays." *Pinter Rev.* 1 (1987): 7–21.

———. "Time for Change in Pinter's Early Plays." Paper presented at the annual meeting of the Modern Language Association, New Orleans, 29 Dec. 1988. Rev. as "Time for Change in *No Man's Land*" and forthcoming in Gordon, *Harold Pinter*.

———. "Wittgenstein's Philosophizing and Literary Theorizing." In Cohen, *Wittgenstein and Literary Theory*, 209–37.

Raben, Estelle Manette. *Major Strategies in Twentieth Century Drama: Apocalyptic Vision, Allegory, and Open Form*. American University Studies. Series 4, English Language and Literature, vol. 67. New York: Peter Lang, 1989. (Rev. version of Thaler.)

Rabey, David Ian. *British and Irish Political Drama in the Twentieth Century: Implicating the Audience*. New York: St. Martin's, 1986.

Rabkin, Gerald. "Is There a Text on This Stage? *Theatre/Authorship/Interpretation*." *Performing Arts Jour.* 26/27 9, no. 2&3 (1985): 142–59.

"Radical Departures: [Harold Pinter Talks to Anna Ford]." *Listener*, 27 Oct. 1988, 4–6.

Rank, Otto. "The Double as Immortal Self." In *Beyond Psychology*. New York: Dover, 1958.

————. *The Double: A Psychoanalytic Study.* Trans. and ed. Harry Tucker, Jr. Chapel Hill: Univ. of North Carolina Press, 1971.

Rao, N. M. "The Self-Commenting Drama of Our Times." *Aligarh Jour. of English Studies* 9, no. 2 (1984): 215–26.

Ratcliffe, Michael. "Theatre: Over the Peak." London *Observer,* 23 Oct. 1988, 40.

Rawson, Claude. "Before the Professors Took Over." Rev. of *A History of Modern Criticism: 1750–1950,* vol. 5, *English Criticism, 1900–1950,* and vol. 6, *American Criticism, 1900–1950,* by René Wellek. *New York Times Book Rev.,* 30 Mar. 1986, 8–9.

Rev. of *BGU,* by Steven H. Gale. *Choice,* Nov. 1977, 1212.

Rev. of *DS,* by Lucina Paquet Gabbard. *Choice,* July/Aug. 1977, 680.

Rev. of *PW,* by Martin Esslin. *Booklist,* 1 Dec. 1970, 284.

Rev. of *PP,* by Austin E. Quigley. *Choice,* Mar. 1976, 73.

Rev. of *S,* by Lois G. Gordon. *Choice,* Feb. 1970, 1768.

Rickert, Alfred E. "Perceiving Pinter." *English Record* 22, no. 2 (1971): 30–35.

Ricoeur, Paul. *The Rule of Metaphor: Multi-disciplinary Studies of the Creation of Meaning in Language.* Trans. Robert Czerny et al. Toronto: Univ. of Toronto Press, 1977. Originally published as *La métaphore vive* (Paris: Éditions du Seuil, 1975).

Rimmon-Kenan, Shlomith, ed. and introd. *Discourse in Psychoanalysis and Literature.* London and New York: Methuen, 1987.

Rod, David K. "The Problem of Subjectivity in Value Judgment." *Jour. of Dramatic Theory and Criticism* 2 (Spring 1988): 95–103.

Rogoff, Gordon. "Theatre Criticism: The Elusive Object, the Fading Craft." *Performing Arts Jour.* 26/27 9, no. 2&3 (1985): 133–41.

Roof, Judith. "Staging the Ideology behind the Power: Pinter's *One for the Road* and Beckett's *Catastrophe.*" *Pinter Rev.* 2 (1988): 8–18.

*The Room,* by Harold Pinter. Stage production directed by Duncan Rose. With Neville Galia, Susan Engel, and others. Old Vic Theatre School and Bristol Univ. Dept. of Drama, Bristol, Eng., 20 Dec. 1957.

Rosen, Carol. *Plays of Impasse: Contemporary Drama Set in Confining Institutions.* Princeton: Princeton Univ. Press, 1983.

Rosengren, Karl Erik. "Literary Criticism: Future Invented." Paper presented at a conference on Empiricism and Hermeneutics: The Invention of Facts in Literary Study, Indiana Univ. and the Society for Critical Exchange, Bloomington, Ind., 2–5 Oct. 1986. Photocopy.

Rusinko, Susan. *British Drama: 1950 to the Present: A Critical History.* Twayne's Critical History of British Drama. Boston: G. K. Hall, 1989.

————. Rev. of *PW,* by Martin Esslin. *Modern Drama* 14 (1971): 114–15.

————. "Theatre." Book rev. of *Other Places,* by Harold Pinter. *World Literature Today* 58 (Spring 1984): 269.

————. *Tom Stoppard.* Twayne English Authors Series, no. 419. Boston: G. K. Hall, 1986.

Ryan, Marie-Laure. "Criticism, Pleasure, and Truth: A Typology of Critical Statements." In Hernadi, *What Is Criticism?* 52–64.

Sacks, Oliver W. *Awakenings.* London: Duckworth, 1973. Repr. Garden City, N.Y.: Doubleday, 1974. Rev. ed. Harmondsworth: Penguin, 1976. New rev. ed. New York: Vintage, 1976. 1st ed., rev. New York: Dutton, 1983. New rev. ed. New York: Summit Books, 1987.

Sahai, Surendra. "Pinter's 'The Caretaker': A Treatise on Urbanization." *Indian Jour. of English Studies* 19 (1979): 69–79.

Sakellaridou, Elizabeth. "Harold Pinter: Transcending the Gender Boundaries." Lecture read at the British Council, London, 18 Mar. 1988. Photocopy.

———. "How Absurd? Some Reflections on Pinter's Position in the Contemporary Theatre." *Yearbook of the School of English, Univ. of Thessaloniki* (1987): 94–104. Offprint.

———. Letters to author. 20 Dec. 1985, 14 Jan. 1987, 7 Nov. 1988, 9 Oct. 1989.

———. *Pinter's Female Portraits: A Study of Female Characters in the Plays of Harold Pinter.* London: Macmillan; Totowa, N.J.: Barnes, 1988.

Sakellaridou-Hadzispyrou, Elizabeth. "Masks of Women: A Study of Female Characters in the Dramatic Work of Harold Pinter." Ph.D. diss., Univ. of London, Royal Holloway College, 1984. Photocopy.

Salem, Daniel. *Harold Pinter: Dramaturge de l'ambiguité* [Harold Pinter: Dramatist of Ambiguity]. Paris: Denoël, 1968.

———. "The Impact of Pinter's Work." *Ariel* 17, no. 1 (1986): 71–83.

———. "L'Implicite déchiffrable dans *La Chambre* d'Harold Pinter" [Decipherable Implicity in Harold Pinter's *The Room*]. In *L'Implicite dans la littérature et la pensée anglaises.* Centre Aixois de Recherches Anglaises 5. Aix-en-Provence: Presses Universitaires de Provence, 1984.

———. *Pinter ou le masque de la vérité* [Pinter or the Mask of Truth]. Lille: Presses Universitaires de Lille, 1983.

Salmon, Eric. "Harold Pinter's Ear." *Modern Drama* 17 (1974): 363–75.

Sammons, Jeffrey L. *Literary Sociology and Practical Criticism: An Inquiry.* Bloomington and London: Indiana Univ. Press, 1977.

Santucci, Lino Falzon. *Harold Pinter: Explorations in Verbal and Nonverbal Interaction.* Messina: Peloritana, 1981.

Savona, Jeannette Laillou, and Ann Wilson, ed. and introd. *Women in the Theatre.* Special issue of *Modern Drama* 32, no. 1 (Mar. 1989): 1–176.

Savran, David. "The Girardian Economy of Desire: *Old Times* Recaptured." *Theatre Jour.* 34 (1982): 40–54.

Scales, Keith, Laurie Holland, and Luisa Sermol. Interview with author. Portland, Oreg., 6 Feb. 1987. (About Portland Civic Theatre production of *Old Times.*)

Schaefer, Hans Joachim, and Hans-Jörg Grell. Interview with author. Kässel, W. Ger., 9 June 1982.

Schechner, Richard. "Puzzling Pinter." *Tulane Drama Rev.* 11 (Winter 1966): 176–84.

Schiff, Ellen F. "Pancakes and Soap Suds: A Study of Childishness in Pinter's Plays." *Modern Drama* 16 (1973): 91–101.

Schilb, John. "The Politics of the 'Author-Function' in Contemporary Feminist Criticism." *Critical Exchange*, no. 25 (Spring 1988): 96–107.

Schmidt, Siegfried J. "The Fiction Is That Reality Exists: A Constructivist Model of Reality, Fiction and Literature." *Poetics Today* 5, no. 2 (1984): 253–74.

———. "Foundations of a Constructivist Empirical Study of Literature." In McCormick, 5–22.

Schmitt, Natalie Crohn. "Stanislavski, Creativity, and the Unconscious." *New Theatre Quart.* 2 (1986): 345–51.

Schroll, Herman T. *Harold Pinter: A Study of His Reputation, 1958–1969.* Metuchen, N.J.: Scarecrow, 1971.

Schweickart, Patrocinio P. "Reading Ourselves: Toward a Feminist Theory of Reading." In *Gender and Reading*, 31–62.

Scott, Michael, ed. and introd. *Harold Pinter: The Birthday Party, The Caretaker, The Homecoming: A Casebook*. London: Macmillan, 1986.

Seitz, Michael H. "Britannia Waives the Rules." *Progressive*, May 1983, 51.

Seymour-Smith, Martin. Entry on Harold Pinter. In *Funk and Wagnalls Guide to Modern World Literature*. New York: Funk and Wagnalls, 1973.

———. Entry on Harold Pinter. In *The New Guide to Modern World Literature*. New York: Peter Bedrick; London: Macmillan, 1985.

Shevtsova, Maria. "The Sociology of the Theatre." Parts 1–3: "Problems and Perspectives"; "Theoretical Achievements"; "Performance." *New Theatre Quart*. 5 (1989): 23–35, 180–94, 282–300.

Shewey, Don. "Will the Sparks Fly When Steppenwolf Takes on Pinter?" *New York Times*, 26 Jan. 1986, sec. 2: 1, 6.

Shulman, Milton. "The Party, Mr. Pinter, Is Beginning to Bore. . . ." London *Evening Standard*, 19 June 1964, 4.

———. "Sorry, Mr. Pinter, You're Just Not Funny Enough." London *Evening Standard*, 20 May 1958, 6.

Shumway, David R. "Getting a Grip on Fish." *Critical Exchange*, no. 15 (Winter 1984): 57–67.

———. "A Unified-Field Theory for English." In McCormick, 54–67.

———, ed. and introd. Special issue of *Critical Exchange*, no. 15 (Winter 1984): 1–70.

Siebers, Tobin. *The Ethics of Criticism*. Ithaca: Cornell Univ. Press, 1988.

Simon, John. "Film: Surfaces, Mostly." *National Rev.*, 5 Aug. 1983, 951–52.

———. "The Past Dismembered." *New York*, 23 Jan. 1984: 54–56.

———. *Singularities: Essays on the Theater, 1964–1973*. New York: Random, 1975.

———. "Square Triangle." Rev. of *Betrayal*. *New York*, 21 Jan. 1980, 61–62.

———. "Theatre Chronicle." *Hudson Rev.* 30 (Spring 1977): 100–103.

———. *Uneasy Stages: A Chronicle of the New York Theater, 1963–1973*. New York: Random House, 1975.

Sinyard, Neil. "Pinter's Go-Between." *Critical Quart.* 22, no. 3 (1980): 21–33.

Smith, Barbara Herrnstein. *Contingencies of Value: Alternative Perspectives for Critical Theory*. Cambridge: Harvard Univ. Press, 1988.

———. "Contingencies of Value." *Critical Inquiry* 10 (1983): 1–35.

———. "Value/Evaluation." *South Atlantic Quart.* 86 (1987): 445–55.

Smith, Leslie. "Harold Pinter's Later Plays." *Adam* 41, no. 406 (1978): 49–64.

———. "Pinter the Player." *Modern Drama* 22 (1979): 349–63.

Sontag, Susan. *Against Interpretation and Other Essays*. New York: Farrar, 1966.

———, ed. *The Barthes Reader*. New York: Hill and Wang, 1982.

Sosnoski, Patricia Harkin, ed. "*Beyond Interpretation*." Special issue of *SCE Reports*, no. 6 (Fall 1979): 1–101. *Supplement: Annotated Checklist*, by Richard A. Barney: 1–27.

Sparshott, Francis E. "The Problem of the Problem of Criticism." In Hernadi, *What Is Criticism?* 3–14.

Spitz, Ellen Handler. "On Interpretation of Film as Dream: *The French Lieutenant's Woman*." *Post Script* 2 (Fall 1982): 13–29.

Staten, Henry. "Reply: Wittgenstein's Boundaries." In Cohen, *Wittgenstein and Literary Theory*, 309–18.

———. "Wittgenstein and the Intricate Evasions of 'Is.' " In Cohen, *Wittgenstein and Literary Theory*, 281–300.

Steig, Michael. *Stories of Reading: Subjectivity and Literary Understanding*. Baltimore and London: Johns Hopkins Univ. Press, 1989.

Steiner, George. "A Conversation with George Steiner." Televised on "Bill Moyers' Journal." PBS. WGBH-TV, Boston. May 1981.

Sterritt, David. "A Pinter Tale Told Backward, with Laughs and Insights." *Christian Science Monitor*, 17 Mar. 1983, 18.

Stevenson, Randall. "Harold Pinter—Innovator?" In Bold, 29–60.

Storch, R. F. "Harold Pinter's Happy Families." *Massachusetts Rev.* 8 (1967): 703–12.

Strunk, Volker. *Harold Pinter: Towards a Poetics of His Plays*. American University Studies. Series 4, English Language and Literature, vol. 44. New York: Peter Lang, 1989.

Stull, William L. "Literature, Literary Theory, and the Teaching of Composition." In *Research in Composition and Rhetoric: A Bibliographic Sourcebook*, ed. Michael G. Moran and Ronald I. Lunsford, 125–51. Westport, Conn.: Greenwood Press, 1984.

Styan, J. L. "Drama as Ritual." *Modern Language Quart.* 27 (1966): 323–31.

———. "Psychology in the Study of Drama: The Negative and the Positive." *College Literature* 10 (1983): 251–67.

———. "Quince's Questions and the Mystery of the Play Experience." *Jour. of Dramatic Theory and Criticism* 1 (Fall 1986): 3–16.

———. Rev. of *BGU*, by Steven H. Gale. *Jour. of English and Germanic Philology* 77 (Apr. 1978): 302–4.

Susini, C. "Le lieu et la parole dans le théâtre de Harold Pinter" [Place and Speech in the Theater of Harold Pinter]. *Recherches Anglaises et Américaines* 5 (1972): 3–34.

Suter, Anthony. "The Dual Character and the Image of the Artist in Pinter's 'No Man's Land.' " *Durham Univ. Jour.* 75 (June 1983): 89–94.

———. "A Psycho-Aesthetic Approach to the Plays of Pinter." *Études Anglaises* 32 (1979): 414–24.

Sykes, Alrene. *Harold Pinter*. New York: Humanities Press, 1970.

Tabachnick, Stephen E., and William Baker. "Reflections on Ethnicity in Anglo-Jewish Writing." *Jewish Quart.* 21, no. 1/2 (1973): 94–97.

Taubman, Howard. "Shared Quicksand: Our Reality Is Infirm, Says Pinter, As His Plays Probe Silence." *New York Times*, 9 Dec. 1962, sec. 2: 5.

Taylor, John Russell. "Accident." *Sight and Sound* 103 (Autumn 1966): 179–84.

———. *Anger and After: A Guide to the New British Drama*. London: Methuen, 1962. Rev. ed. Baltimore: Penguin, Pelican Books, 1963. (3d ed. London: Methuen, 1969.)

Tener, Robert L. "Uncertainty as a Dramatic Formula." *Humanities Association Bulletin* 24, no. 3 (1973): 175–82.

Thaler, Estelle Manette. "Major Strategies in Twentieth-Century Drama: Apocalyptic Vision, Allegory and Open Form." Ph.D. diss., St. John's University, 1983. (Rev. and published as Raben.) *Dissertations Abstracts International* 44 (1983): 163-A.

"Thematic and Structural Concepts of Time in the Works of Harold Pinter." Special session at the annual meeting of the Modern Language Association, New Orleans, 29 Dec. 1988.

Thompson, David T. *Pinter: The Player's Playwright.* London: Macmillan; New York: Schocken, 1985.

Thompson, Harry. "Harold Pinter Replies." *New Theatre Mag.* 2 (Jan. 1961): 8–10.

Tompkins, Jane. "Me and My Shadow." *New Literary History* 19 (1987): 170–78.

———. *Sensational Designs: The Cultural Work of American Fiction 1790–1860.* New York and Oxford: Oxford Univ. Press, 1986.

*Trahisons* [Betrayals], by Harold Pinter. Adaptation by Eric Kahane. Stage production directed by Raymond Gérôme. With André Dussollier, Caroline Cellier, Salvino di Pietra, and Sami Frey. Théâtre Montparnasse, Paris, 20 June 1982. Opened 11 Jan. 1982.

Treichler, Paula A. "Teaching Feminist Theory." In Nelson, *Theory in the Classroom*, 57–128.

Trussler, Simon. *The Plays of Harold Pinter: An Assessment.* London: Victor Gollancz, 1974.

Tucker, Stephanie. "To Mean So Much: Harold Pinter's Stratagems of Resonance." Ph.D. diss., Univ. of California, Davis, 1984.

Tynan, Kathleen. "In Search of Harold Pinter: Is He the Mystery His Critics Allege?" London *Evening Standard*, 26 Apr. 1968, 8. Pt. 2 of a ser. begun on 25 Apr. 1968.

Ulmer, Gregory L. "Of a Parodic Tone Recently Adopted in Criticism." *New Literary History* 13 (1982): 543–60.

Van Gelder, Lawrence. "At the Movies: Pinteresque Pinter." *New York Times*, 28 July 1989, B4.

———. "At the Movies: Togetherness." *New York Times*, 22 Jan. 1988, C6.

Van Laan, Thomas F. "*The Dumb Waiter*: Pinter's Play with the Audience." *Modern Drama* 24 (1981): 494–502.

Varley, Alan. "Actor, Author and Audience: Scene 7 of Harold Pinter's *Betrayal*." *Cycnos* (Nice Cedex, France) 3 (Winter 1986–87): 95–109.

Wandor, Michelene. "The Personal Is Political: Feminism and the Theatre." In *Dreams and Deconstructions*, 49–58.

Wardle, Irving. "The Birthday Party." *Encore* 5 (July–Aug. 1958): 39–40. Repr. in *The Encore Reader* and *New Theatre Voices*, 76–78. (Also repr. as "A Rare Pleasure," in Scott, 110–12.)

———. "Comedy of Menace." *Encore* 5 (Sept.–Oct. 1958): 28–33. (Repr. in *The Encore Reader* and *New Theatre Voices*, 86–91.)

———. "Criticism: A Hobson's Choice?" *New Theatre Mag.* 4 (Apr.–June 1963): 24–26.

———. "Holding Up the Mirror." *Twentieth Century* 173 (Autumn 1964): 34–43.

———. Interview with author. London, 7 July 1982.

———. "New Waves on the British Stage." *Twentieth Century* 172 (Summer 1963): 57–65.

———. "Pinter, Harold." In *The Reader's Encyclopedia of World Drama*, ed. John Gassner and Edward Quinn, 657–58. New York: Crowell, 1969.

———. "Pinter Theatrical Twins in Pools of Solitude." London *Times*, 3 July 1969, 13.

———. "Revolt against the West End." *Horizon* 5 (Jan. 1963): 26–33.

———. "There's Music in That Room." *Encore* 7 (July–Aug. 1960): 32–34. Repr. in *The Encore Reader* and *New Theatre Voices*, 129–32.

Warner, John M. "The Epistemological Quest in Pinter's *The Homecoming*." *Contemporary Literature* 11 (1970): 340–53.

———. Rev. of *PW*, by Martin Esslin; *HP*, by James R. Hollis; and *HP*, by Herman T. Schroll. *Jour. of Modern Literature* 3 (1974): 748–50.

Watkins, Evan. "Conflict and Consensus in the History of Recent Criticism." *New Literary History* 12 (1981): 345–65.

Wellek, René. "Appendix: A Historical Perspective: Literary Criticism." In Hernadi, *What Is Criticism?* 297–321.

———. "The New Criticism: Pro and Contra." *Critical Inquiry* 4 (1978): 611–24.

Wells, Linda S. "A Discourse on Failed Love: Harold Pinter's *Betrayal.*" *Modern Language Studies* 13 (Winter 1983): 22–30.

Whitaker, Thomas R. "Playing Hell." *Yearbook of English Studies* 9 (1979): 167–87.

White, Hayden. "Historical Pluralism." In Mitchell, *Pluralism*, 480–93.

Willeford, William. "Myth Criticism." In *Princeton Encyclopedia*, 955–58.

Williams, Hugo. "Mumbo Gumbo." Rev. of *Saturday Review* (BBC-2TV). *New Statesman*, 4 Oct. 1985, 36.

Winn, Marie. "The Czechs' Defiant Playwright." *New York Times Mag.*, 25 Oct. 1987.

Winston, Mathew. "The Incoherent Self in Contemporary Comedy." *Modern Drama* 29 (1986): 388–402.

Wintour, Charles, Sydney Edwards, Michael Billington, Michael Owen, Michael Coveney, Milton Shulman, Mary Clarke, and Clement Crisp. *Celebration: Twenty Five Years of British Theatre.* Foreword by Richard Burton. London: W. H. Allen, 1980.

Wittgenstein, Ludwig. *The Blue and Brown Books.* 1958. 2d ed. Oxford: Basil Blackwell, 1969.

———. *Philosophical Investigations.* 1958. Trans. G. E. M. Anscombe. 2d ed. Oxford: Basil Blackwell, 1967.

Woodroffe, Graham. "De *Kinsale Drive* à *Wessex Grove*: Une étude psychanalytique de *Betrayal* de Harold Pinter" [From *Kinsale Drive* to *Wessex Grove*: A Psychoanalytic Study of Harold Pinter's *Betrayal*]. *Cycnos* (Nice Cedex, France) 3 (Winter 1986–87): 111–27.

———. "'One says yes, the other says no': A Psychoanalytic Investigation of a Slip of the Tongue in Harold Pinter's *The Caretaker.*" *Literature and Psychology* 32, no. 2 (1986): 2–9.

———. "Taking Care of the 'Coloureds': The Political Metaphor of Harold Pinter's *The Caretaker.*" *Theatre Jour.* 40 (1988): 498–508.

Woods, Alan. "Emphasizing the Avant-Garde: An Exploration in Theatre Historiography." In *Interpreting the Theatrical Past*, ed. Thomas Postlewait and Bruce A. McConachie, 166–76. Iowa City: Univ. of Iowa Press, 1989.

Worth, Katharine. Letter to author. 10 Aug. 1989.

Wright, Elizabeth. *Psychoanalytic Criticism: Theory in Practice.* New Accents. London and New York: Methuen, 1984.

Yvard, P. "Texte, langage et communication dans *The Caretaker* de Harold Pinter" [Text, Language, and Communication in *The Caretaker* by Harold Pinter]. In *Échanges: Actes du Congrès de Strasbourg*. Paris: Didier, 1982.

# INDEX

Bias(es): in evolutionary theories, 5; Gale's
thematic, 54, 90
Bigsby, C. W. E., 16, 185
*Birthday Party, The,* 3, 9–10, 11, 13, 18,
19, 64, 110–11, 115–16, 123, 173,
175–76, 178, 179, 185, 187, 217–18,
219–20, 225–26, 231, 255, 257, 285
n.2; changing reception of, 5, 51; performance reviews of, 217, 221–22,
225–26, 229, 231, 232–36, 266; Pinter's strategy of "open form" in, 64. *Productions:* Lyric Opera House,
Hammersmith (1958), 3, 9, 10, 13,
217, 222, 225–26; Rediffusion-TV
(1960), 219–20; RSC, Aldwych Theatre
(1964), 18; Booth Theatre (1967), 231,
255; CSC Repertory Theatre (1988), 9–
10, 266; CSC Repertory Theatre (1989),
18, 19, 266
Bladel, Roderick, 221, 230
Blau, Eleanor, 234–35
Bleich, David, 47, 169, 232, 250, 260,
261, 271, 274, 287 n.31; account of au-
thor's critical work with, 256–58, 259.
*See also* Merritt, Susan Hollis
Bloom, Harold, 271
Bocek, Maximilian, 217
Bolt, Robert, 214–16, 217
Bond, Edward, 174
Booth, Wayne C., 49
Bowen, Elizabeth, 188
Bray, Barbara, 59
Bray, Janet. *See* Gray, Frances, and Janet
Bray
Brecht, Bertolt, 172, 180
Brien, Alan, 222
Bristol University, 214, 216
*British and Irish Political Drama in the Twen-
tieth Century* (Rabey), 179
Brooks, Peter, 135
Brustein, Robert, 235–36, 239
Bukovsky, Vladimir, 176
Burkman, Katherine H., xxv, 108, 109,
111, 115, 204, 205–6, 249; critical bi-
ography of, 103–6, 263; ritual and
myth analysis by, 100–107
Burton, Deirdre, 164–66

*Butter's Going Up* (Gale), 90–95, 96, 97,
98, 99, 155; reviews of, 93–95, 98

Cain, William E., 67, 274
*California Suite* (Simon), 217
Campaign for Nuclear Disarmament, 176
Campton, David, 225
Canby, Vincent, 237, 238
Canonization, literary, 42–43, 44, 214–
15, 216; of Pinter's work (*see* Pinter,
Harold: literary canonization of)
*Caretaker, The,* 9, 59, 79, 83, 111, 118–
19, 138, 173, 178, 184, 205, 219,
225–27, 229, 257; Esslin on subcultural
conventions in, 226–27; and 1960
London Evening Standard Drama Award,
215; performance reviews of, 225–26,
229; Pinter's description of audience's
laughter at, 52. *Productions:* Arts Theatre
Club (1960), 225–26; Steppenwolf
(1978, 1986), 128
Carlson, Marvin, 78, 172
Carpenter, Charles A., 3, 67, 69, 72, 76,
80, 83; on *The Dumb Waiter,* 70–71, 74,
77, 78
*Catastrophe* (Beckett), 186
Cave, Richard, 169
Certainty and certitude, 68, 85–86, 70
Change, 5–7, 24, 36, 245–75; critical (*see*
Critical and cultural change); unpredict-
ability of, 245, 250, 252, 269. *See also*
Cohen, Ralph; Fish, Stanley; Gould,
Stephen Jay
"Change" (Fish), 245–54. *See also* Fish,
Stanley
*Changing the Subject* (Henriques et al.),
208–9
Cixous, Hélène, 200
Class and class consciousness, xxii, 189–93
Codron, Michael, 221–22
Cohen, Ralph, 4–6, 21, 25, 37, 245–46;
account of author's critical work with,
260, 261, 262, 297 n.15. *See also*
Change; Critical and cultural change;
Merritt, Susan Hollis
Collaboration and cooperation: as alterna-

Susan Hollis Merritt is a Visiting Fellow in the
Institute for European Studies at Cornell University.
She is also Bibliographical Editor of *The Pinter Review*.

Library of Congress Cataloging-in-Publication Data
Merritt, Susan Hollis.
Pinter in play : critical strategies and the plays
of Harold Pinter / Susan Hollis Merritt.
Includes bibliographical references (p.   ).
ISBN 0-8223-1040-6 (cl.)
ISBN 0-8223-1674-9 (pa.)
1. Pinter, Harold, 1930–    —Criticism and
interpretation—History. I. Title.
PR6066.I53Z718    1990
822'.914—dc20      90-31163 CIP